WENDY

and the

LOST BOYS

ALSO BY JULIE SALAMON

Hospital

Rambam's Ladder

The Christmas Tree

Facing the Wind

The Net of Dreams

The Devil's Candy

White Lies

WENDY and the

LOST BOYS

The Uncommon Life

of Wendy Wasserstein

Julie Salamon

The Penguin Press
New York
2011

THE PENGUIN PRESS
Published by the Penguin Group
Penguin Group (USA) Inc., 375 Hudson Street,
New York, New York 10014, U.S.A. • Penguin Group (Canada),
90 Eglinton Avenue East, Suite 700, Toronto, Ontario, Canada M4P 2Y3
(a division of Pearson Penguin Canada Inc.) • Penguin Books Ltd, 80 Strand,
London WC2R 0RL, England • Penguin Ireland, 25 St. Stephen's Green, Dublin 2,
Ireland (a division of Penguin Books Ltd) • Penguin Books Australia Ltd,
250 Camberwell Road, Camberwell, Victoria 3124, Australia
(a division of Pearson Australia Group Pty Ltd) • Penguin Books India Pvt Ltd,
11 Community Centre, Panchsheel Park, New Delhi – 110 017, India •
Penguin Group (NZ), 67 Apollo Drive, Rosedale, Auckland 0632, New Zealand
(a division of Pearson New Zealand Ltd) • Penguin Books (South Africa) (Pty) Ltd,
24 Sturdee Avenue, Rosebank, Johannesburg 2196, South Africa

Penguin Books Ltd, Registered Offices: 80 Strand, London WC2R 0RL, England

First published in 2011 by The Penguin Press, a member of Penguin Group (USA) Inc.

Letters of Wendy Wasserstein reprinted by permission of
the Literary Estate of Wendy Wasserstein

Excerpt from "At the Ballet," music by Marvin Hamlisch, lyrics by Edward Kleban.
© 1975 Sony/ATV Harmony and Wren Music Co. Inc. All rights on behalf of Sony/ATV
Harmony administered by Sony/ATV Music Publishing LLC, 8 Music Square West,
Nashville, TN 37203. All rights reserved. Used by permission of Sony/ATV
Music Publishing and MPL Music Publishing.

Photograph credits appear on page 433.

Title page photo by Joanna Eldridge Morrissey

LIBRARY OF CONGRESS CATALOGING IN PUBLICATION DATA

Salamon, Julie.
Wendy and the lost boys : the uncommon life of Wendy Wasserstein / Julie Salamon.
p.   cm.
Includes bibliographical references and index.
ISBN 978-1-59420-298-8
1. Wasserstein, Wendy.   2. Dramatists, American—20th century—Biography.
I. Title.
PS3573.A798Z87   2011
812'.54—dc22
[B]
2011014581

Printed in the United States of America
1   3   5   7   9   10   8   6   4   2

DESIGNED BY MICHELLE MCMILLIAN

FOR PATTI LYNN GREGORY

CONTENTS

All children, except one, grow up. They soon know that they will grow up, and the way Wendy knew was this. One day when she was two years old she was playing in a garden, and she plucked another flower and ran with it to her mother. I suppose she must have looked rather delightful, for Mrs. Darling put her hand to her heart and cried, "Oh, why can't you remain like this for ever!" This was all that passed between them on the subject, but henceforth Wendy knew that she must grow up. You always know after you are two. Two is the beginning of the end.

—from PETER PAN, by J. M. Barrie

WENDY

and the

LOST BOYS

PROLOGUE

When Wendy Wasserstein died on January 30, 2006, at age fifty-five, hers was a rare obituary considered important enough to make the front page of the *New York Times*. Her memorial service, held in the 1,060-seat Vivian Beaumont Theatre at Lincoln Center, packed the house. The overflow was siphoned into a theater across the street at the Juilliard School, where an additional five hundred fans joined the other mourners via video monitors.

Strangers wept and columnists eulogized. She was remembered as a significant playwright, but also as a quintessential New Yorker, the toast of the tough and glamorous metropolis. She had an uncanny ability to know almost every major player in theater, publishing, and politics, right up to the White House. Because she wrote about women and the subjects that concerned them, she was designated a feminist. But with Wasserstein everything, including politics, tended to be personal.

Friends often mentioned her two voices: the high, girlish, giggly one she generally used and the deep, authoritative tone that said she meant business. Likewise her work ranged from the frivolous to the profound; her trademark was humor laced with poignancy.

Wasserstein was noticed as a playwright whose work became worthy of the Pulitzer Prize, and she was the first woman to win an unshared

Tony. But she became a celebrity by turning her life over to the public domain. In plays, autobiographical essays, and interviews, she opened her heart and her family album for the world to see. No personal detail seemed exempt from public consumption, including her decision to have a child at age forty-eight, as a single mother. In the *New Yorker,* in remarkable detail, she made the world privy to the difficult, miraculous birth of her daughter Lucy Jane, who weighed in at 790 grams, less than two pounds. The baby shower was recorded by a photographer and a reporter from the *New York Times.*

People she didn't know would stop her on the street and greet her, not with starstruck awe but with familiarity. Women identified with her dilemmas, petty and grand: What shoes to buy? Was it possible to lose weight without exercising or eating less? What was the most romantic spot in New York? Why couldn't she find a man who would want her? Was the problem her success? Could she create a family when she couldn't always cope with the one she'd been born into? What did it mean to be a good person? Where was fulfillment?

They believed they knew her well enough to ask about her daughter, her diets, her siblings, her boyfriends, her mother—and to tell her about theirs.

Yet after she was gone, what stunned those closest to her was how much they didn't know. What was the nature of her relationships with the numerous men, gay and straight, she called her "husbands" or "crushes"? Why had almost no one known she was pregnant, and who was Lucy Jane's father? If so many people were her best friends, why did none of them realize how gravely ill she was until the very end? Why did some of her obituaries say there were four Wasserstein siblings, while others said there were five?

Through drama she told many truths. In personal essays, drawn from her life, she freely reconfigured events, as though she were writing fiction. She was as covert as a spy, parceling out information to a host of confidants, allowing each of them to believe that he or she alone had access to the inner sanctum. Only later did they realize that Wasserstein had constructed her life as a giant game of Clue, full of hidden connections and compartmentalized players. She used humor as a dodge, intimacy as a smoke screen.

Such reinvention was the stuff of theater. But Wasserstein learned the tactic long before she began writing plays. Her parents, Lola and Morris Wasserstein, were immigrants who'd had the brains and ambition to become what they believed they should be (successful Americans), not what they had been (Jewish outcasts). They took their children to see the Broadway musicals that celebrated these notions far more often than they took them to synagogue. They displayed no nostalgia for the past, only intense hunger for the future.

Wendy Joy Wasserstein was born on October 18, 1950, in the thick of the Baby Boom, the postwar procreative binge that seemed like a collective impulse to replace what had been lost. Only five years had passed since the end of the twentieth century's second world war; 50 million lives had been extinguished. The Wassersteins were caught up in generational momentum, the postwar conviction that humankind's best chance was to look ahead, to shut the door on the past, to produce a new world—or at the very least to reproduce. They would defy death with life.

Wasserstein became the quintessential Baby Boomer, part of the generation captivated and characterized by Peter Pan, the brave, charming, petulant, and wistful boy (often played onstage by a woman) who would never grow up. She was one among the many babies named for Peter's beloved friend Wendy Darling, the girl who couldn't avoid her fate, that of becoming an adult. Peter's Wendy understood that her duties were to stay at home and tend to marriage and motherhood, while boys went out into the world to fight pirates and men became bankers. But Wendy Wasserstein came of age when women were supposed to do it all.

Her story tracks a period of momentous change in women's lives and personal relationships. The nuclear family, defined by the Census Bureau as a heterosexual married couple with children under eighteen, made up 45 percent of all U.S. households in 1960, when Wasserstein was ten years old. By 2000, when she was the fifty-year-old single mother of a toddler, that traditional configuration had fallen to 23.5 percent of all households.

Marriage was no longer a prerequisite for having children, and those children might even have parents who were gay.

Call it fate, demographic probability, or simply the kind of thing that would make Wasserstein laugh that famous high-pitched giggle, even as she spun the facts into another bittersweet, funny-serious story of a modern woman's search for her place in the world. She was part of an American generation convinced of its supremacy and an immigrant family whose children were expected to do it—whatever *it* was—better than anyone else. Her destiny was set the instant she emerged from Lola's womb.

A friend often told her, "You were born into great material."

Or, as Wasserstein herself would say, "Funny is a very complicated issue."

Part One

GROWING UP

1950–71

THE BROOKLYN YEARS:
LOLA, GEORGETTE, BRUCE, AND WENDY.

One

THE FAMILY WASSERSTEIN

Let other, weaker families dwell on their sorrows. That was the unspoken philosophy in the Wasserstein household.

Wendy would joke that when family members died, it was said, "They went to Europe." More intricate heartaches were ignored.

Secrecy pervaded the household, though the family would deny that anything was hidden. "It's not that there were secrets. Things were just not talked about, never mentioned," said Bruce Wasserstein, Wendy's brother. "It was what my parents wished."

The family produced überachievers. Wendy became the first woman playwright to win a Tony award *and* the Pulitzer Prize while also achieving commercial success on Broadway. Sandra Wasserstein Meyer, the eldest, became a high-ranking corporate executive at a time when the best job available to most women in Fortune 500 companies was boss's secretary. Their brother Bruce became a billionaire superstar of the investment-banking world.

Even Georgette Wasserstein Levis, the middle daughter who checked out of the race early—married young, had babies, moved to Vermont—ultimately became the successful owner of a large country inn, the Wilburton.

The Wasserstein children held Morris, their sweet father, in special regard as the source of comfort, quiet wisdom, and unconditional love. Morris and Lola were said to be the perfect couple, though it was also said their marital bliss was helped by the fact that Morris was practically deaf, his hearing damaged by illness when he was a boy. When he needed peace and quiet, he just turned down his hearing aid.

A decent, hardworking man, Morris Wasserstein had brains, foresight, and ambition, but not the fierce personality that produces titans or playwrights.

For the mythmaking ingredient, look to Lola.

She was of minuscule size but a powerhouse contender among legendary heavyweights, Jewish-mother division. Lola was the lightning rod, credited or blamed for her children's drive, their idiosyncrasies, their outsize successes and peculiar flaws.

Lola stories were legion. Perhaps most emblematic were those told after Wendy won the Pulitzer Prize. Lola was said to have responded in at least two ways:

"I'd be just as happy if she'd marry a lawyer."

"Did you hear? Wendy won the Nobel Prize?"

Either way, the clear message was that the Pulitzer wasn't quite good enough.

On the other hand, anything her children did was de facto the best. Lola decorated the walls of her apartment with lacquered collages of Wendy's press clippings and *Playbill*s, as well as articles about her other children. Their framed diplomas, school photos, and prizes were on display. Lola said her chest was so puffed out from pride that she needed a bigger bra.

That particular paradox—of being better than everyone else but not good enough—would become a recurrent theme in Wendy's life and in her work. In *The Heidi Chronicles*, the superior-inferior concurrence emerges when Heidi Holland, the heroine, is invited to speak at the all-girl prep school she'd attended. Heidi—by then a well-known art historian—has a meltdown as she enumerates the ways she feels that women of her generation have failed one another.

Discussing all the women she meets in her gym's locker room, she erupts into a fantasy about what she'd like to say to them. "I'm sorry I don't want you to find out I'm worthless," she says. "And superior."

The problem may have been that Lola never explained what would happen to the child who couldn't produce achievements that could be quantified and displayed. Would he—would she—still be worthy of love?

On January 4, 1993, *New York* magazine ran a lengthy article by Phoebe Hoban called "The Family Wasserstein" in conjunction with the opening of *The Sisters Rosensweig,* Wendy's homage to her two older sisters, Georgette and Sandra. Hoban interviewed Lola and Morris, Wendy's parents, at a hotel restaurant.

Lola offered the journalist her philosophy of life. "I've always taught my children that they have to be a person in their own right. I have this expression, 'I am.' This is to have the confidence in yourself, that what you are, nobody can take away. No matter what you do, just feel confident."

Their daughter Sandra reinforced the family's inflated version of its history.

"That Polish resort town in *The Sisters Rosensweig* is really where my grandparents had their villa with tennis courts and their own pastry chef," Sandra said. "They were very sophisticated and had a lot of money."

Sandra was fifty-five years old at the time, a senior officer for corporate affairs at Citibank. More than her younger siblings, she had always known that some truths were woven into her mother's confabulations and that others were hidden in stories that weren't told. In the spring of 1993, a few months after the *New York* magazine article was published, Citibank sponsored a concert tour of the New York Philharmonic. One of the stops was Warsaw. Sandra invited Wendy, then forty-two, to join her for what Wendy would call "a sisterly tour of our mother's Polish girlhood."

They set out to debunk the myths Lola had bequeathed them. Wendy recorded their findings. "Growing up, I always loved the stories about my mother's childhood," she wrote. "Lola's Poland was different from anybody else's mother's Poland. My schoolmates had grandfathers who were peddlers in Lodz, but my mother's family had a summer villa in a spa resort called Ciechocinek. My mother's family was the intelligentsia. At least according to my mother."

"Frankly, I always placed the truth of the summer villa right alongside my mother's sworn testimony to me in eighth grade that grown women would pay thousands of dollars for hair like mine, especially when it divided into thousands of damaged, frizzy split ends," Wendy wrote. "It might have been more than a slight exaggeration, but it was certainly comforting."

For their trip, Wendy and Sandra hired a driver in Warsaw to take them north along the Vistula River to Wloclawek, where Lola Schleifer was born on March 28, 1918. At least that's the date recorded on her New York State driver's license. Her contemporaries weren't convinced. "No one knows when she was born," said her first cousin, Jack Schleifer. Her marriage certificate to Morris says 1917. At family functions Morris quietly approached Lola's relatives and asked them, "Do you know how old Lola is?" He never got a definitive answer, because no one knew for sure. Lola enjoyed the game. At Georgette's sixtieth-birthday party, Lola asked a guest, "How can my daughter be sixty when I'm only thirty-eight?"

As it happens, her name wasn't even Lola. She was born Liska, a variation of Elizabeth, which is how she is listed on U.S. Census records from 1930—a fifteen-year-old girl, indicating that she was born in 1915 or 1916.

"Lola" came later, another invention.

In Wloclawek, Wendy and Sandra found a grim and polluted city of 120,000 people, an industrial center known for its hand-painted pottery. Their driver took them to Piekarska Street, where the Schleifers had lived, two blocks from a lovely park surrounding a fourteenth-century Gothic cathedral. For the Wasserstein sisters, the scene was alien but familiar. They recognized the white lace curtains hanging from Polish windows; they were the same kind of curtains that hung in their mother's bedroom back in New York. When their driver told them, "Poland is a country of churches," they smiled and nodded without response, struck silent by ancient fears. When he said, "Your mother must have been very well-to-do. Only the very well-to-do lived in corner houses," they smiled again. "My sister is a formidable banker, and I am a playwright," Wendy wrote. "But today we are two Jewish girls in Poland. It's not exactly comfortable to speak."

Wloclawek doesn't occupy much space in history texts. In the twelfth century, it was an outpost for the Roman Catholic Church, as the seat of the local provincial bishop. In the fifteenth century, Copernicus, the legendary Polish astronomer, studied there for a couple of years, giving the city a kind of "Lincoln slept here" academic cachet. In 1815 the kingdom of Poland came under Russian czarist rule, where it would remain until after World War I (which is how Lola managed to be born in Russia but raised in Poland without budging from Wloclawek). Eventually Wloclawek became the Akron of north-central Poland, a sturdy manufacturing center, home of the country's first paper mill and cellulose plant. The huge kilns that fired its signature pottery were built in the nineteenth century.

The population expanded accordingly. Simon and Helen Schleifer contributed four children to the growing community, which had reached 35,000 by 1909. Theirs was a relatively small brood; Simon had been one of ten children. Though Jews were prohibited from settling in Wloclawek until the eighteenth century, by the time Lola was born, one-fifth of the population was Jewish. In the city's all-Jewish enclave, Yiddish was far more likely to be spoken than Polish. Even modern Jews like the Schleifers obeyed the dietary laws, read Yiddish newspapers, and were educated in yeshivas. They lived with a lurking fear of anti-Semitism, a wariness that existed in memories of pogroms and the daily reality of restrictions on where they could work or go to school. They understood they were regarded as interlopers, temporary citizens—no matter how many generations back they could trace their ancestry in Poland. In turn they looked down on "Polacks," even as they trembled before them. A sign of Jewish prosperity was a Polish maid.

Superior-inferior.

For Wendy, Lola's declarative "I am" became an ongoing question: "Who am I?" Nurture versus nature, the connection between past and future; so many ephemeral unknowns determine a human being's sense of self: How was she to calibrate the significance of DNA, geographical displacement, societal pressure, birth order, gender, ethnicity, religion, the weight of history? Could Wendy extricate herself from the stories she'd never heard from the grandparents she'd never known?

Her grandfather Simon Hirsch Schleifer came of age in the late nine-teenth century. Simon—Shimon, as he was known then—was an intellec-tual, a *yeshiva bocher* and raconteur. He became a teacher in the yeshiva, not because he was religious but because there were few other options available to the Jewish intelligentsia, who were not permitted in the Polish civil service or, with few exceptions, to teach in public schools. (After Wendy won the Pulitzer Prize, "playwright" was added to Simon's résumé, but none of Lola's contemporaries remembered him writing plays.)

Wendy's grandmother Helen Schleifer was more conventional: She cooked, sewed, and took care of her children. She wore blowsy dresses and spoke Yiddish with Simon's mother, who didn't understand Polish. She dealt with the loss of a son, who'd died in childhood from illness. Helen was a beloved mother but never a role model for Lola, their baby, the most pampered of their children. Lola acquired her father's yearning, his desire for the larger world. Even as a young girl, she had style, a freckle-faced gamine dressed in knickers, aiming a provocative glance at a photogra-pher. When her family summered at the resort town of Ciechocinek, she most likely bathed in the mineral-rich waters. She would have strolled through the manicured gardens in Zdrojowy Park and eaten ice cream at the Bristol Cafe and danced at the band shell, which was then almost new.

Did they own a villa with tennis courts, as Lola had told her children? Or was the villa rented, or did the Schleifer family stay in a hotel? Did it matter?

Lola remembered what she remembered, in warm and gauzy re-collections.

"According to my mother, wherever she lived, wherever she danced, wherever she ate, was the best place to live, the best place to dance, and the best place to eat," wrote Wendy.

No meek shtetl humbleness for Lola. "I am," was already on her lips.

Nice bravado, but Lola and her fellow Jews were about to become part of the past tense—"they were"—footnotes in Polish history. Lola and her parents left the country more than a decade before the Nazi occupation in 1939. By the end of World War II, Poland's Jewish population was decimated. Fewer than 70,000 of the 3.3 million who lived there before the war survived.

Wendy noted the absence with sadness. "Today in Ciechocinek there are still the parks and even the famous spa water, but no one looks like my sister or me," she wrote after her 1993 trip with Sandy through the green Vistula River Valley. "No one even resembles the women from my mother's faded photo album. Fifty years ago the ethnic cleansing of Ciechocinek was so successful that there is no variety here. Everyone looks pretty much the same."

Most of Lola's immediate family escaped, part of the Great Migration, the karmic explosion of awakened consciousness that drew millions of desperate dreamers to the United States in the thirty years leading up to the First World War. The pattern was for the men to go ahead, try to get established, and then send for their wives and children.

Simon, Lola's father, had an abrupt and dramatic departure from Poland, according to family lore. In his exodus story, the Polish police suspected him of conspiring with Bolsheviks, sometime in the mid-1920s. Wendy had heard the legend. "He was at a café on the town square in Wloclawek with his intelligentsia friends, discussing all the latest isms— socialism, atheism, Zionism—when a pal arrived to say the police were on their way. It seems the Polish police were not as impressed with the ideologies of the twentieth century as Shimon Schleifer was. My grandfather never went home again."

He made his way to Greece, where he obtained a false passport identifying him as Greek. Passenger-boat records confirm that he arrived in New York on August 30, 1927, from Cherbourg, France, on a ship called the *Majestic*. His birth place is listed as Salonika, Greece, his age as forty-two, and his ethnicity as Hebrew.

His wife, Helen, followed in 1928, with Lola; her brother, Henry; and her sister, Gucci, who became Gertrude in the United States. Another sister, Hela, had recently married and stayed behind with her husband and children. They were doing well; they felt they could build a future in Poland. The illusion of prosperity would be their downfall.

In the United States, Simon would fall into a life not so different from the one he'd left behind. He became a Hebrew-school principal, at Paterson Talmud Torah in New Jersey—not a full-time occupation, but he'd never had one. He continued to hang out with his friends, smoking English Oval cigarettes while playing cards, debating, and discussing politics, philosophy, and history. He was as much of a bon vivant as a responsible greenhorn could be.

"He was a Hebrew-school principal, but that didn't keep him from visiting the racetrack occasionally," said Jack Schleifer, Lola's cousin. "I know one or two times he took me to Coney Island when Coney Island was something to visit. Simon had a lust for life, he had joie de vivre."

So did his daughter. Lola would transform the dislocation and loss into yet another spirited story.

"She had this reel of stories," said one granddaughter. "She didn't go to Ellis Island, she came over on the *Île de France,* they were wealthy, and she had a Polish maid. When she arrived in New York, they were picked up by her uncle's chauffeur, and he was the first black man she ever met, and she said, 'You must be dirty; wash your face.' She told this story over and over again. Why?"

Why?" was not a question Lola cared—or dared—to ask. Pondering why would be a luxury granted to future generations. She had no patience for introspection or angst. "My mother always presented her life as a very happy life. She was very loved, very admired by her father," said Georgette, the middle daughter.

Lola taught by example: she understood intuitively that power comes through control of the narrative. She had nothing to say about any insecurity she might have felt as an adolescent, newly arrived in a strange country whose language she didn't speak. (How did she tell that black chauffeur to wash his face, since she hadn't yet learned English?) Instead she told her children what she wore to high school in Paterson (a short, stylish camel-hair coat, saddle shoes), how she walked (with a seductive wiggle), and why she couldn't pronounce *l*'s (because of her Polish accent). Even this difficulty with language became a triumph, not an embarrassment. When she called a high-school friend "Wooie" instead of Louis, she only remembered that the mispronunciation had cracked Wooie up.

But Lola couldn't work her anecdotal sleight of hand on the next chapter of her life. She couldn't manufacture a plausible comic twist on the events that transpired in the years after she finished high school and that would shape the trajectory of Wasserstein family life. The scenario that began as a romantic comedy ended as tragedy, so she simply deposited those years into the file marked "Secrets That Aren't Secrets."

Her children would learn these secrets piecemeal. The older siblings knew more, but Wendy and Bruce had only vague awareness of a phantom brother, Abner, who was alive but was kept apart. They were adults before they understood that Abner and Sandra had a different father from theirs and Georgette's. The fact itself was far less disturbing than the cover-up, which deeply influenced Wendy and Bruce throughout their lives.

Georgette was caught in the no-man's-land of the middle child, not part of the experiences that formed the older children, yet more aware than the little ones. She had grown up knowing that she'd been named for her Uncle George. But she didn't discover until she was a teenager that her uncle was also her mother's first husband.

The secret was uncovered by accident, with Georgette rummaging through her mother's drawers, looking for a scarf to wear to school. A side panel loosened to reveal a hidden drawer. There she found a newspaper article about her uncle's death notice, listing his survivors. George, not Morris, was the father of her two older siblings. Lola had been his wife.

Shocked, Georgette stuffed the article back in the drawer and replaced the panel. "My parents had gone out for a walk, and when they came back, my mother asked me, 'Why are you so pale?'" Georgette said. "I didn't tell her I knew."

Eventually to Lola she confessed what she'd found, but they didn't discuss George until Georgette was fifty years old. One of her daughters, a young woman by then, had written a play, being performed at a theater in New York's East Village. Georgette and Lola took a bus downtown to see the show.

They got off the bus at Fourteenth Street, and Lola, somewhat mysteriously, told Georgette to come with her to Union Square.

When they arrived, Lola said, "This is where I met George."

It was a strange moment for Georgette. She was his namesake. But for most of her childhood, he'd been nothing more than that, a sentimental link to the past.

Lola offered a Broadway-musical version of how she'd met her first husband: George had gone to a political rally at Union Square; Lola was meeting her father at a coffee shop after a dance lesson. George was handing out leaflets; Lola threw hers in a trash can. Lola remembered being irresistible; George succumbed immediately. He trailed after her until she turned and asked, "Why are you following me?" As if she didn't know.

She continued toward her destination.

George joined her and her father, put his bundle of leaflets on the table, and began to talk to Simon. The match was made.

Or something like that.

Lola had street smarts and ambition. When she heard George's business plans, and that he wanted to have a family, she could see a promising future unfold. With her shrewd intuition, Lola wasn't likely to overlook George's unusual maturity. He wasn't much older than she was, maybe twenty when they met, but he was clearly a man. Like her, he was a Polish refugee. He had arrived in New York, however, under very different circumstances than the ones that had brought Lola there.

The Wassersteins were from Wizna, a village in northeastern Poland, around thirty miles from Bialystok. The landscape of their youth was bucolic; the children played near the banks of the Biebrza River, where they watched logs cut from the vast northern forests float by.

But, as old men would say over glasses of tea, you can't eat beauty. Like Simon Schleifer, George's father, Jacob, left for America, with vague plans for self-improvement and the promise he would send for his wife and five sons. Herman, the eldest, joined him in New York, and so did Jacob's only daughter. Herman worked for a while and then returned to Europe to bring the rest of the family to the United States.

In the spring of 1928, the five Wasserstein boys boarded the SS *Laconia* with their mother, Charlotte. Herman was followed by seventeen-year-old George. Morris was the baby, only six years old. In between came Joseph and Teddy, ages twelve and nine. The passenger list recorded them by their Hebrew names.

The crowded boat had limited facilities. Charlotte stood in a long line to reach the single water faucet, clutching the bottle she planned to fill for her children. From this small maternal act came disaster. The bottle broke and cut her hand. The wound became infected. By the time the boat docked in Liverpool, Charlotte was so ill she required hospitalization. Her two oldest sons, Herman and George, disembarked to take her to the hospital, where Charlotte remained, too sick to get back on the boat. Herman and George told their little brothers to continue on to New York. They would follow when their mother got better.

Herman and George's sojourn in Liverpool quickly became a death-watch. Charlotte died as her three youngest sons traveled toward America, to be greeted by a father they barely knew. Jacob Wasserstein took his sons to his apartment on the Lower East Side, where they would learn their first English sentence from children on a neighborhood playground, who snarled at the greenhorns, "Get outta here!"

The early details of this immigrant saga are sketchy, but family members generally agreed that Jacob Wasserstein didn't keep his end of the bargain. In America he had found another woman. Not long after the older brothers arrived, their father told them he had a girlfriend. Or, in Morris's unsentimental recollection, "Ma passed away. For a while we lived with *her husband*, and then he married again.

"Finally the older ones said, 'Let's move out.'"

The boys found a one-room apartment a few blocks away on Rivington Street. Theirs was a classic Depression-era story, filled with tales of grim scrounging and small triumphs. The older brothers found odd jobs; the younger ones went to school. The brothers sold newspapers in front of Ratner's, the famous dairy restaurant on Delancey Street, occasionally treating themselves to the luxury of a pickle sandwich. As the designated cook, Morris scavenged for supplies. He made the rounds of restaurants, using his ragamuffin charm to collect leftover bones to use for soup. When

he looked in the windows of those restaurants and saw people having a meal, putting food in their mouths without noticing what they were eating, he was left with a particular kind of hunger.

Morris told these stories with gratitude, not bitterness. He saw hopeful significance in the fact that the SS *Laconia* landed on July 3, the day before Independence Day. He took enormous pride in being accepted to Stuyvesant High School, the city's premier public high school. When he died in 2003, Wendy said at his memorial service, "My father and his brothers in many ways are the epitome of American optimism and opportunity in the twentieth century."

This was not an exaggeration. By the time George bumped into Lola near Union Square in the mid-1930s, the hardest days were behind him. He was already working his way toward the establishment of Wasserstein Brothers, a ribbon-manufacturing company. The Wasserstein boys survived their wrenching childhood by adapting, learning to figure things out. They would turn this skill to business, becoming inventors, managers, and investors.

Lola knew potential when she saw it. On January 16, 1937, she and George were married in Bayonne, New Jersey. Their wedding photograph shows a fairy-tale couple, a groom with fine, intelligent features and the

LOLA AND GEORGE,
THE FAIRY-TALE COUPLE.

bride a striking young woman with elegant cheekbones; she is wearing a traditional white gown.

They plunged into creating their future. Seven months after their marriage, on August 20, 1937, Sandra was born; three years later they had a son, Abner. Life was full. Besides their own children, the young couple took in George's younger brothers, Teddy and Morris. They, too, joined the family business. After graduating from Stuyvesant High in 1939, Morris took night courses in mechanical engineering at City College of New York. The brothers kept late hours, always refining better ways to make ribbons; frequently they slept at Wasserstein Brothers on cots.

The misery overwhelming Poland and Europe seemed distant at times, immediate at others, but the young immigrants were too busy to dwell. The Atlantic Ocean stood between them and the war. The business was growing, and so were the children. Lola and George found a more spacious apartment in Brooklyn when Sandra was small; Lola's parents moved to Brooklyn from New Jersey, to be close by Lola's family as well as to numerous other relatives. They had re-created a better version of Poland—still living among Jews, surrounded by family—but there was a crucial difference. In the United States they saw attainable opportunity, a chance to become part of the larger community.

Their dreams seemed on track to fulfillment until June 4, 1941, when George was taken to Harbor Hospital in Brooklyn with severe stomach pains. His appendix had ruptured, and the infection spread throughout his abdomen. George developed peritonitis, and he died on June 12, 1941, at the age of twenty-nine—four years before the first safe antibiotics were generally available, drugs that would transform appendicitis from a deadly disease to a dangerous but manageable occurrence.

Though Jacob Wasserstein, George's father, was still alive, Lola despised him as a ne'er-do-well. It was Simon Schleifer who took George to the hospital and who identified his son-in-law for the death certificate. Simon arranged the funeral service on the Lower East Side of Manhattan, just a few blocks from the apartment where, a dozen years earlier, George began the American chapter of his brief life.

Lola buried her husband and two years later, on June 26, 1943, married his brother.

Desire and expediency coincided with ancient tribal dictates. Deuteronomy 25:5–10 of the Torah, or Old Testament, mandates Jewish men to marry the widows of their deceased brothers. Referred to as the law of yibbum in Hebrew, the custom is followed in other clannish cultures and is generally known as levirate marriage, after the Latin levir, meaning "husband's brother." The custom grew from primal necessity, the urge to preserve the family and stake claim to immortality. The rule traditionally comes into play when the widow is left childless; the firstborn of her new marriage "belongs" to the husband who died, so his line can continue. The implication is profound: without children there is no hereafter.

Morris didn't have a chance.

He was twenty-one years old while Lola was at least twenty-five and possibly twenty-eight, either way a mature woman, the mother of two, who radiated the tough sex appeal of a movie siren. They tried to hide their courtship from the children, but it couldn't have been easy. Their sexual connection was palpable. Throughout their marriage they couldn't sit next to one another in the movies without kissing and squeezing each other's hand.

Sandra, Lola's older child, was six when their relationship shifted. She was away at camp when she found out Lola had married her Uncle Morris. When she received the telegram, she wondered whether she was supposed to call Morris "Dad" now. (The answer was yes.)

Within a year Morris and Lola had their first child. They named her Georgette, after George. Morris called his firstborn "Gorgeous." This would become a source of annoyance for Wendy. She thought it meant her sister was pretty and she wasn't, even though they shared similar, strong Wasserstein features.

Wendy didn't know how Gorgeous became Gorgeous:

After Lola delivered the baby girl, the doctor came to the waiting room to tell the young father. "Congratulations, you have a beautiful little girl" filtered through Morris's damaged hearing as "It's a boy." He telephoned the family, with the news and then went to see Lola and the baby. When he asked to see his son, she screamed, "It's a girl." Morris paused, adjusted, smiled at his baby, and said, "She's gorgeous." The name stuck.

They were on track to become yet another American-Jewish cliché, enmeshed in family, enjoying the abundance they'd earned through suffering and resilience. Both the business and the children were thriving. Sandra had a cute nickname, Sandy, and was enrolled at P.S. 206, the public elementary school right across the street from their apartment on East Twenty-second Street. Abner was developing as a bright, handsome little boy.

Almost every weekend, Lola and Morris took Sandy, Abner, and Georgette for Sunday dinner in Brighton Beach with Lola's family, including her parents and brother, Henry. They gathered at her sister Gucci's home, where she lived with her husband, Max Kaufman, a furrier, and their two sons.

Gucci helped their mother, Helen, prepare gigantic meals, beginning with chopped liver or gefilte fish, continuing with chicken soup loaded with kreplach or noodles, followed by vegetables doused in schmaltz, a

SANDRA AND ABNER
IN SIMPLER TIMES.

piece of chicken (meaning half a chicken per person), *and* a hunk of meat. The groaning feast was completed with Helen's special pistachio cake, every nut ground by hand.

Simon Schleifer grew so fat he wore a girdle.

Lola decided she was not going to be tied to the kitchen like her mother.

Still, she remained the baby of the family, dependent on her big brother for advice and on her mother and sister for comfort. Lola used her mother and sister as baby-sitters, often leaving Sandy alone with them in Brighton Beach. Sandy had warm memories of those afternoons, watching the women cook, basking in their uncomplicated affection, so different from Lola's thorny love. In this period of tranquillity, Lola may have been lulled into believing that fate had extracted a heavy enough toll. The war was pervasive, but it didn't take Morris away; he was exempt from the draft because of his poor hearing. The horror abroad was reaping benefits for Wasserstein Brothers. The company prospered as a supplier to Reynolds Metals, under contract with the government to manufacture decoys for U.S. aircraft. The ribbon makers produced streamers that contained a hairpin-width line of aluminum foil. These strips trailed several hundred feet behind the airplanes and tricked enemy radar, which detected the foil in the ribbon and directed anti-aircraft fire there, instead of at the planes.

For Lola, however, there were no exemptions from the fragility of existence.

No one could pinpoint when or exactly how the next round of trouble began. No one knew precisely how Abner got sick. Georgette heard he'd gone ice-skating and come down with a fever; maybe it was polio, something burned his brain. An uncle told a cousin that George's death was the cause; the shock had precipitated damage to Abner's immune system—an unlikely theory, since the child was only a year old when his father had died. Someone else said the fault lay with a cousin visiting from California; the cousin had meningitis and infected Abner. Scarlet fever was mentioned as the culprit. Wendy understood that her brother had contracted encephalitis.

Whatever the source, by the time Abner was about five years old, he began having violent seizures. Lola would scoop him up in her arms and place him in a baby carriage to subdue him. His speech stopped developing normally; he would become frustrated as words took longer to emerge. The family tried to adjust. "He would have fits," recalled Irving Redel, who worked for the Wasserstein brothers for many years. "Morris would bring him sometimes to the business. Everyone knew him. It wasn't something you would shout in the streets about, but it wasn't a secret."

As a child, Georgette grew impatient with her older brother's long silences, and she interpreted his impulsive bursts of speech as bossiness. His behavior became more disruptive.

Lola and Morris began looking for cures for Abner. They consulted specialists and began visiting schools and institutions, even traveling to California, a huge trip at the time, for experimental treatments.

Overwhelmed, they sent Sandy, age nine, to a boarding school in Florida, where she would stay for almost two years. For Sandy the exile to Florida became yet another loss to absorb. Unable to make friends in this strange place, she stayed alone in the library and read, developing the self-sufficiency she would exhibit for the rest of her life.

Then, news from Poland: Lola's sister Hela and her family were confirmed to be dead, shot by Nazis in their own yard.

Lola became pregnant again. On December 25, 1947, Bruce was born. Later, this would become a family joke: Bruce and Jesus Christ—the Messiahs, holy Jewish sons—shared a birthday. But in real time Bruce's birth meant that Morris and Lola were now raising four children—Sandy returned home that summer.

Abner became increasingly difficult to handle, but Lola never discussed her son's problems much with the family's growing network of cousins and in-laws. This was partly her nature and partly the times. It would be years before children with emotional or mental disabilities would not be regarded with shame.

By the time Wendy was born, Abner was gone. Lola and Morris had enrolled him in the Devereux School, a progressive institution for mentally disabled children. The school had been established in 1912 by a Philadelphia schoolteacher, Helena Devereux, who believed that "slow" children could be taught, not just to read and write but also the "skills of daily living." The family took monthly outings to Philadelphia so the children could visit their brother. The sight of his siblings, however, provoked Abner to have seizures. Georgette dreaded the trips. She was prone to carsickness, and the drive seemed endless. She and Bruce fought most of the way in the backseat, and then she would throw up.

Georgette believed that it was her fault he'd been sent away. "I think they did it for me," she said. "He was crushing my spirit."

Morris and Lola stopped taking the children to see their brother. For several years Abner came home for holidays, but these visits became awkward ordeals. His siblings saw him as a stranger.

Abner came home once or twice after Wendy was born, and then he disappeared from his siblings' lives, even from conversation.

Bruce, who was three years old the last time he saw his brother, chose to ignore his existence, even though numerous family photographs included Abner. "There was one picture with a boy there," he said, "but I didn't know who it was." Bruce developed an inability to deal with painful matters; as an adult he became known for his secrecy.

Lola and Morris continued to visit Abner on his birthday and a few other times during the year. They talked about him less and less. Abner ebbed from the family tableau; the children accepted the transformation of their brother into a ghost.

Before Wendy turned two, Lola became pregnant one more time. When she left for the hospital to deliver the baby, she promised the children she would be home soon, with a new brother or sister.

Instead she returned empty-handed.

"The baby lived for hours and just died," said Georgette. "That was the way my mother presented it. The baby had a hole in its heart. I remember being on the phone and saying, 'My mom had a baby, and the baby died.' She just came home and went on going."

Morris and Lola formed a tacit agreement to make things simple for the children left at home. From then on, there would be one set of parents, Morris and Lola, and four siblings: Sandra, Georgette, Bruce, and Wendy. The family Wasserstein was in place. The rest, so far as the children were concerned, was supposed to be history.

Like George, and the relatives left in Poland, Abner had disappeared. Yet unlike the others, he remained a distant presence, a hovering reminder that past and future have a way of converging, and that secrets are hard to keep.

Sandy, more motherly with her younger
siblings than Lola was, here with
baby Bruce in carriage.

Two

A BROOKLYN CHILDHOOD

1950–63

When siblings describe growing up, it often sounds as though they were raised in different households from one another. Sandy, the eldest Wasserstein child, grew up in a different universe. As a little girl, she listened to grandparents speaking Polish and Yiddish and watched her grandmother prepare homemade kreplach and grind her own meat. Sandy's early years were spent in the hardscrabble world of the new immigrant, during a catastrophic world war. These hardships were compounded and personalized by the family's losses.

During those difficult years, Sandy had to rely on a mother whose philosophy of "go-go" didn't allow time for tenderness, whose survival instincts didn't include empathy.

Her father was steadfast. True to obligation and inclination, Morris always treated Sandy as a daughter. She called him Dad and meant it. Still, she was well aware of the father who had died, and she resented having her early memories expunged from the record. Those memories included her brother, the one who was imperfect and had to be sent away.

Compare her experience with Wendy's. Sandy's baby sister was born into prosperity and a family structure that had stabilized. Their grandparents were out of the picture; the Old World and its travails were remote. Abner was a stranger in a photograph.

The summer after Wendy was born, Georgette and Sandy returned from camp to find yet another dramatic change in the Wasserstein household—only this one was pleasant. While the older girls were gone, the family had moved from a modest home to a three story, eighteen-room Dutch Colonial house on Avenue N—a palace compared with the apartment Sandy lived in as a baby. On the top floor there was a maid's room, though the Wassersteins didn't have a maid. Two bedrooms had terraces. The basement was outfitted with a billiards room, where the family put a Ping-Pong table. Downstairs there was another room with a bar and taps for beer, leading the children to fantasize that the former occupant had been a gangster during Prohibition.

For almost thirteen years, Wendy would live in this sprawling house, situated at the intersection of two tree-lined streets. In Brooklyn, as in Wloclawek, a corner house was a sign of prosperity.

Understandable that Wendy described growing up in Brooklyn as her Camelot, a time of innocence, while Sandy generally chose to pretend that her childhood had never happened.

"In retrospect, I realize that our eyes were always focused on Manhattan," Sandy told a reporter in 1984. "I used to go to the Art Students League in midtown Manhattan every weekend. I'd shop at Bendel's or Bloomingdale's, but I'd never even been to downtown Brooklyn."

Like her mother, she remembered what she needed to remember.

As firstborns often do, Sandy paved the way for the younger ones, a task that carried more weight when the eldest was also the first family member to be born in the United States. She became the pivot, the child with secret knowledge of the adult world, who acted as interpreter and protector for her siblings.

Lola had two ways of describing Sandy. One was *strazac,* the Polish word for "fireman," which Lola interpreted as a general in the Polish army. The other *shtarker,* was Yiddish for a strong person who takes charge.

When Wendy was born, Lola put her thirteen-year-old *shtarker* in charge of the infant. It was Sandy who decided the baby should be named after Wendy Darling, the character from J. M. Barrie's classic children's story, *Peter Pan.* Already exhibiting executive savvy, Sandy kept the responsibilities she liked and delegated tasks she didn't want, such as diaper detail. She paid Georgette a fee to change Wendy.

Apart from dirty diapers, Sandy enjoyed the baby, who was so much younger that their relationship was more like that of mother and daughter, without the tension. Sandy treated her sister like a doll, dressing her up in Bruce's clothing and taking her to high-school sorority meetings.

They avoided the sisterly squabbling that took place between Sandy and Georgette, who were closer in age. As oldest, Sandy had superior status, including the privilege of her own room, with a terrace, while Georgette had to share a room with Wendy.

Sandy was a perfect big sister, equipped with adult know-how but still one of the children. She was attractive and could be intimidating, having inherited Lola's hauteur as well as her high cheekbones. Georgette was shy and not always at ease around her confident older sister. But the little ones worshipped Sandy.

The younger children would always associate Sandy with a feeling of being protected from Lola's erratic behavior and with tenderness that wasn't Lola's to give. It was Sandy, not Lola, who put Bruce and Wendy to sleep with bedtime stories.

Their big sister seemed to know everything, including the words to every song ever written—at least those written for the Broadway stage. She loved to sing and taught her younger siblings everything from silly camp medleys like "Cannibal King" ("We'll build a bungalow, big enough for two, big enough for two my honey . . .") to the musicals that she loved. Name a show tune from the 1940s or 1950s, by Cole Porter, Irving Berlin, Rodgers & Hammerstein, Lerner & Lowe. Sandy could belt it out in a voice that was surprisingly sweet for such a strong-willed girl. She might miss a note, but she never forgot a lyric. She knew the scores from all the hits: *Oklahoma!, Guys and Dolls, Call Me Madam, Annie Get Your Gun, Kiss Me Kate, The King and I.*

The sing-alongs made a lasting impression, even on her brother Bruce, who would not be known for his sentimentality. Throughout his life his favorite song remained "Some Enchanted Evening" from *South Pacific*.

Sandy never lost her grip on her siblings, but they didn't share the same roof for long. The tough times for the Wasserstein family had drawn to a close just as Sandy was making her escape. Her education had been accelerated via the tracking system established in the 1920s by the New York public schools, to push children who were high achievers. The "Special Progress," or SP, system remained in place throughout the 1960s, as a way to manage the huge influx of Baby Boom kids into the system. It was common for students to skip one grade; the truly ambitious like Sandra Wasserstein skipped two. She was graduated from James Madison High School in 1953—in Brooklyn—and left for the University of Michigan that summer, just before her sixteenth birthday.

Situated in her expansive house, having survived heartache on heartache, and not one to fuss over housekeeping, Lola sought new outlets for her vast reserves of energy. While the Wasserstein brothers toiled in the ribbon factory and expanded into textiles and then real estate, their wives turned similar drive into their products: the children.

The competition among the sisters-in-law was fierce. Top performers in this hotly contested race were Lola and Florence, Jerry's wife. The goal was to see whose children provided the most bragging rights. No penalty for slight exaggerations. That was all part of the game.

Florence had the home-court advantage: She was native-born, raised in Manhattan's Yorkville section, the Upper East Side's predominantly German neighborhood, where Jewish families were rare. Like Lola, Florence had five children, but all of hers were home and accounted for.

Aunt Florence would provide marvelous material for the extended gag that Wendy would concoct from her Brooklyn childhood:

> On quiet afternoons at my family's house in Brooklyn, when my brother, Bruce, would be taking my sister [Georgette] for a mop ride and plotting openly to boil my blubber for oil like Moby Dick's, Aunt Florence would casually ring up to say hello and to inform us that "guess what," her son, our cousin Alan, had just finished reading and memorizing the *Encyclopaedia Britannica.*

"That's wonderful, Florence! Did he enjoy it?" My mother would always do her best to sound enthusiastic.

By this point my sister would have severed a few ligaments on the mop ride and I would be wailing that I didn't want my blubber boiled. My mother would approach us with the unchained wrath of Medea. 'You goddamned kids! Your cousin Alan just finished the *Encyclopaedia Britannica,* and what the hell are you doing?"

In a rare moment of sibling solidarity we would answer: "Mother, nobody reads the *Encyclopaedia Britannica!*"

So Aunt Florence loomed large as a standard-bearer for elementary education in the 1950s.

The madcap childhood Wendy wrote about wasn't far from the truth, though her version was consistently more amusing than real life. Lola's demands were relentless. Her children all remembered, one way or the other, bringing home a grade of 99 on a report card and being asked, "Where's the other point?"

As adults they portrayed themselves as a bevy of little geniuses. Actually, they brought home the report cards of smart but not exceptional students, with as many B's as A's, and even some C's.

They did have fun, as they created their New York Jewish version of the American dream. The children watched popular television shows like *Zorro, The Wonderful World of Disney, Bachelor Father,* and *The Millionaire,* a weekly drama that followed the consequences when a rich man gave a million dollars to a stranger. Morris and Lola joined a beach club, where the children swam. On weekends, when Wendy was small, Morris took Georgette and Bruce to the park to ice-skate, ride bikes, and have other adventures, while Lola stayed home with the baby. They learned to play tennis at camp. Lola enrolled the girls in dance class. Morris bought a movie camera, preserving a record, proof that his happy family existed.

They took drives into the country and cultural excursions into "the city," as outer-borough residents referred to Manhattan. They ate out at Cookys, a famous Brooklyn delicatessen.

In homage to *Lassie* and *Rin Tin Tin,* other television programs they watched as children, they tried to have pets, an alien concept for Eastern European Jews. The experiment was unsuccessful. Wendy would write:

I don't come from a long line of pet lovers. One of my earliest memories is of my mother, Lola, releasing our pet parakeet into a hurricane. She never explained how the bird flew out of her cage into the storm, but all we children knew it was involuntary. And then there was the time I came home from elementary school to find our newly acquired cocker spaniel on the roof. My mother swore that the dog had climbed up there for the view, but I certainly had never seen Lassie on the roof. The police arrived, and the dog survived and subsequently moved to live with relatives in the suburbs. The last straw was my father driving a cat from our house in Brooklyn over the bridge into Manhattan and dropping her off somewhere near Wall Street, apparently hoping that a generous stockbroker would take her in.

Morris avidly followed the news. He read the *New York Post,* the *Wall Street Journal,* the *New York Times,* and many business magazines. When he helped Georgette study for a seventh-grade history test about World War II, he seemed to know all the answers without looking in a book. When she asked him why, he answered, "For me that isn't history, it was the news of the day."

As the only son in residence, Bruce was anointed most brilliant by his parents, most obnoxious by his siblings. He was the know-it-all who beat everyone at chess, read history books for fun, and considered himself the supreme authority on everything—an attitude reinforced by Morris and Lola, who showered him with special attention. On Georgette's birthday both she and Bruce received Schwinn bicycles, which struck her as terribly unfair. Bruce may or may not have been six years old, as legend would have it, when he began following the stock market and reading *Business Week* and *Forbes.* However, he was young when Morris talked business with him—and listened to what his son had to say; at an early age, Bruce became accustomed to having his opinions treated as worthy of extra consideration. He declared himself King of Bruceania, a make-believe empire he created on family trips to the Catskills, when he and Wendy would pretend to be explorers like Hernando de Soto or Lewis and Clark.

Lola made it clear to her children that they were not to be part of any crowd. Waiting in line was for ordinary folks, not the Wassersteins. Every year, on the family's annual pilgrimage to Radio City Music Hall for the Christmas show, Lola would bypass the long queue and explain to the head usher that the family was visiting from Kansas and had just one day to tour the city. (She chose Kansas because the family had just watched *The Wizard of Oz* on television the night before.) Much to her children's chagrin, few people said no to Lola, despite her non-Midwestern, Polish accent.

She was a devout individualist. When other mothers teased their hair into bouffants, Lola chopped hers off into a severe helmet. While other prosperous 1950s housewives took care to keep their homes immaculate, Lola didn't mind a mess.

She was ahead of the times with her attitudes toward diet and exercise. There would be no platters of Old World dumplings and stuffed cabbage for her children, and no New World canned foods either. Frozen french fries were allowed; they could be baked. As other mothers filled out, Lola got slimmer. She and Morris walked miles, hand in hand.

Weight was a constant topic of discussion. Georgette was praised for being svelte, living up to her nickname of Gorgeous. Bruce and Wendy managed to grow chubby despite the fresh vegetables their mother had delivered to the house in crates. Lola had many theories about nutrition; her children couldn't bear to watch her eat—or rather, drink—breakfast, a mixture of soft-boiled eggs and orange juice. She insisted on feeding Bruce steak, as though he were a prizefighter being primed for the heavyweight championships. She didn't cook so much as roast and broil, chop and arrange, priding herself less on cuisine than on original presentation, like topping salads with kiwis and grapes. For Sunday brunch she served bagels, lox, and cream cheese, then criticized the children for being plump.

Lola emphasized wholesome foods and slender physiques, but the family dined regularly at Lüchow's, the German restaurant near Union Square known for its groaning platters of sauerbraten, Wiener schnitzel, and dumplings, accompanied by the music of an oompah band. Lola insisted on telling the musicians that it was one of her children's birthdays, even when it wasn't.

"I would have to sit there, head up, chest out, beaming with pride and confidence as they played 'Happy Birthday' on their accordions just for me," Wendy remembered. "Is it any wonder that to this day I have a terminal fear of men wearing lederhosen and tiny feathered caps?" Her embarrassment led Lola to designate Wendy the shy child.

Unlike the headstrong Bruce, who constantly rebelled, Wendy was conciliatory. After Lola mortified the children by showing up at school wearing a hat with cherries hanging from it, they cut off the cherries. Wendy felt so guilty she convinced Bruce to confess. They told their mother, "We just want you to be normal."

Perhaps in reaction to Lola's lack of sensitivity, Wendy became hyper-empathetic, even to inanimate objects. Every night before going to sleep, she said good night to each of the cadre of dolls and stuffed animals that slept with her. She rotated their positions on the bed so none of them would feel excluded.

Watching her little sister tend her make-believe flock, Georgette predicted she would grow up to be a happy housewife with "bologna arms" and many children. She promised Wendy—whom she called "Sweetsie-bud"—that she would be happy but warned her not to marry someone dull in the insurance business.

Lola pushed and prodded her brood. She heard Ethel Merman sing "There's No Business Like Show Business" in *Annie Get Your Gun* and changed the lyrics for home consumption. "There's no children like my children," she would say.

When it came to education, Aunt Florence might have set the standard, but Lola was not intimidated.

She didn't know better—and had no choice—with Sandy, who was educated in the New York City public-school system. Sandy's high school, James Madison, provided a solid education, but the Wassersteins had moved up in the world. They now lived in Midwood, the Brooklyn neigh-borhood on the affluent side of the Flatbush border. Lola owned a fur coat, and the family spent the Christmas vacation in Miami Beach. In keeping with their new status, they sent Georgette to private school.

She attended Brooklyn's Ethical Culture School, an offspring of the Ethical Culture movement founded by Felix Adler, son of a rabbi who became a humanistic reformer, whose motto was "Act so as to elicit the best in others and thereby in thyself." The school was a proponent of progressive education. The teachers there encouraged creativity and self-expression, at a time when these were radical ideas. The students planted seeds and wrote poetry. Art was considered as important as arithmetic.

This soft touch was fine for their daughter Georgette, but Lola felt that a boy needed something more rigorous. She also wanted Bruce to have a Jewish education, in deference to her late father. Simon might have scoffed at religion, but he'd spent most of his adult life as a Hebrew-school educa-tor. He avoided synagogues, except for holidays and special occasions, yet it wouldn't have occurred to him to eat pork—or to have a grandson who wasn't educated in Jewish teachings.

Morris and Lola enrolled Bruce at Yeshivah of Flatbush, even though Morris had unhappy memories of his religious education. His brothers had sent him to a Lower East Side yeshiva, but after a rabbi hit him, he switched to public school. Morris hadn't had a bar mitzvah, the ceremony that in-ducts Jewish boys into the requirements of their religion. As an adult, with his own family, he saw no reason to join a synagogue, though the Was-sersteins did celebrate Hanukkah with latkes and dreidl playing and trips to Ohrbach's department store to buy gifts. They gathered for seders at Passover. Lola sent Georgette to Hebrew school at the East Midwood Jew-ish Center; Simon had taught Sandy to read Hebrew. Lola's own religious education was questionable. At Bruce's bar mitzvah, she held the Hebrew prayer book upside down.

Given the family's ambivalent attitude toward religion, Yeshivah of Flatbush was not the obvious choice. The school had opened in 1927 in direct response to the immigration law enacted in 1924, which halted the huge influx of Jews from Eastern Europe. If Judaism were to survive in the

United States, the founders reasoned, it could no longer rely on a constant supply of newcomers. The goal at Yeshivah of Flatbush was to produce Jews who would be proud Americans but also true to their faith. This purpose became more determined with the rise of Nazism through the 1930s and was strengthened by the Zionist movement.

The school was kosher and called itself Orthodox, but it was revolutionary in its day. Unlike traditional yeshivas, this one placed equal emphasis on Jewish and secular studies, and stressed Hebrew not Yiddish, considered the language of Jewish exile. Even more radical: girls studied next to boys. The only division came with Torah studies, which were conducted separately.

One aspect of Yeshivah of Flatbush resonated with Lola. Its graduates, male and female, were expected to be superior in every way: they would be as well grounded in their own traditions and history as any traditional *yeshiva bocher,* yet also be trained to compete in the larger world. They were expected to march out of the ghetto into the mainstream, then climb straight to the top.

Graduates became Nobel laureates (among them Baruch Blumberg, director of NASA's Astrobiology Institute, and Dr. Eric Kandel, the Columbia University professor who won the Nobel Prize for his work in the molecular biology of memory). They also became rabbis, physicians, bankers, lawyers, professors, editors, and at least one jazz impresario (Art D'Lugoff, founder of the legendary Village Gate).

From kindergarten on, students were tracked according to their performance. "By high school there were six classes," said Gaya Aranoff, a Flatbush graduate who became a pediatric endocrinologist on the faculty at Columbia University Medical Center. "If someone was in the F class or E class, they were branded for life."

Competition was embedded into the culture. "There was this post-Holocaust desire for the kids to excel," Gaya said. "That was the message we got in school; that was the message we got at home. Expectations were very high."

In the Wasserstein home, the family made fun of the vegetable cheeseburgers the kosher school served at lunch. But when it was Wendy's turn to begin school, her parents sent her to Yeshivah of Flatbush with Bruce. The two of them walked to school together, Wendy trailing a few feet behind her big brother. He embarrassed her by knocking on the window of her first-grade classroom and sticking his tongue out at her. She adored him but also found him annoying—or "annoing," as she would write in her diary. Wendy was a smart little girl and a passably good student, but she couldn't spell and had difficulty reading. Later she said she was dyslexic.

"Words in books flew around the room when I tried to read them," she wrote. "I was convinced that the 'Fly to Europe' advertisements on the subway were actually offering tours to Ethiopia."

Lola took Wendy to reading specialists, and her comprehension improved. At the yeshiva, she made the A track, along with her classmate Gaya Aranoff, the future physician. "She was this plump, cherubic, curly-haired, sloppy kid who had a shy good nature," Gaya said. Her strongest memory of Wendy took place outside school, on the occasion of Gaya's ninth birthday. Wendy brought the most unusual gift to Gaya's party.

"She brought me a denim skirt of hers I had complimented her on," said Gaya. "After the party, when I was going through the gifts, my older sister said, 'What kind of a weird present is that? Why would she give you her old skirt?' I said, 'But I loved that skirt, and she knew I loved that skirt.' Wendy literally would give you the skirt off her back."

Wendy had a very different recollection of the party. Her father—unprepossessing Morris—had indulged himself by buying a Jaguar. The Jaguar had been Bruce's idea. At age twelve he advised his father to buy a car that would set the Wassersteins apart from the "Cadillac Jews" of Brooklyn. Morris refused to buy a Mercedes or any other German vehicle, so he chose a classy British car.

Unlike Lola and her brother, Wendy cringed at the thought of seeming flamboyant. She didn't want her Flatbush yeshiva friends to think she was a spoiled rich kid. On the way to Gaya's party, Wendy asked Morris to drop her off a few blocks from the Aranoff house, so no one would see her in the Jaguar.

Wendy's good-natured exterior covered a complicated mixture of insecurity and self-doubt. Being the youngest child in a large, competitive family would have been enough to contend with. The pressure was compounded by Lola's belief that survival lay in hiding the truth.

A playwriting teacher would tell Wendy, "There is order in art, not in life," to which Wendy replied, "Life can imitate art if the artists change the accepted variables."

Her ideas on this question were forming as early as second grade.

Wendy starred as Queen Esther in the Purim play at the yeshiva. Then she told Lola she was going to be in another play, costarring with a boy in her class named Eddie. For months Wendy talked about nothing else. She and Eddie had been cast as the romantic leads.

Lola bought Wendy a pink velvet dress and set her hair in ringlets the night before the opening. The next day Lola came to school and asked where the second-grade play was going to be performed.

"What play?" replied Wendy's teacher.

Without missing a beat, Lola said, "I must have the wrong room. It must be one of my other children." And she left.

Lola might have been demanding, but she was loyal. She could criticize her children, but just let an outsider dare. She waited until Wendy came home to yell at her for fibbing.

Recalling the incident in a letter to a friend, years later, Wendy wrote, "I remember feeling this total embarrassment and unwillingness to accept my own actions." She said the memory brought back a disturbing sensation, "the sense of running away from myself."

In the summer of 1956, just before Wendy started at Yeshivah of Flatbush, she was preoccupied with Sandy's wedding. Only nineteen years old, Sandy had fallen in love her second year of college and transferred from the University of Michigan to Syracuse, where her fiancé, Richard Meyer, was going to law school. The marriage was set to take place in the Wasserstein family's huge living room.

Wendy was five going on six during the planning phase. She was obsessed with her sister's upcoming nuptials, which seemed like part of a fairy tale. Lola bought Wendy a taffeta dress, with white gloves and pearls.

The little girl dreamed of how their house would look, decked out like a castle ballroom; she would be a princess, lady-in-waiting to her sister the bride.

Then, as Wendy saw it, tragedy struck. On the day of Sandy's wedding, Wendy was bedridden with tonsillitis and a temperature of 104. As the party rumbled downstairs, Bruce and Georgette raced upstairs to her sickroom to report on the excitement she was missing: "Cousin So-and-So had just fallen through the floor while freely interpreting the hora!"

(Later Wendy confessed, "I never saw the hole, I never heard of any broken limbs, but I still choose to believe the story.")

For the adults the scene must have been much more poignant. In the months before Sandy's wedding, both her beloved Aunt Gucci and Gucci's husband, Max, had died. The children weren't told that Gucci had suffered from breast cancer, though they were dimly aware that Max had had a heart attack. Lola's philosophy continued to be, "If you don't talk about it, it doesn't exist." So far as Wendy knew, Gucci and Max "went to Europe."

Two years later, after Sandy's marriage dissolved and she left the United States to live in London, Wendy broke into hysterical sobs when she heard of her sister's plans. For the little girl, "going to Europe" meant disappearing forever.

Gucci's son, Mitchell Kaufman, was eighteen years old, in his first year of college but living at home, when the second of his parents died. His brother Barry was fifteen, a sophomore at Abraham Lincoln High School. As Sandy's wedding was being planned, the orphaned boys moved in with Lola and Morris's family, into the maid's room on the third floor.

Though Lola did her duty by taking in her sister's orphaned children, she was still Lola. Dealing with an even busier household didn't inspire her to suddenly acquire empathy. As usual, she had submerged her own sadness over her sister's death and expected Gucci's sons to live by her rules.

Mitch, the older one, found life in his aunt's house intolerable. Lola's behavior only made him miss his own mother more. "She wasn't like my mother at all," he said. "My mother would cook and clean and take care of things. She was more of a mother." Lola's children didn't eat dinner with their parents but took their meals before Morris came home, in the kitchen.

Mitch couldn't relate to the girls and couldn't stand Bruce. "He wasn't a nice kid," he said. "Bruce believed that he knew it all and that he was king."

For Georgette, who was in junior high school, having the older boys in the house was exciting. She didn't reveal to her friends the fact that they were cousins, pretending that Barry was her boyfriend, a ruse she could pull off because they attended different schools.

Mitch lasted only a year. Already a college student, he felt he was old enough to stay out late. When he did, Lola locked the screen door so he couldn't get into the house. He simply took the door off the hinges, which infuriated her.

Mitch left abruptly, without telling Lola, and went to live with his father's cousins. He didn't speak to Lola and Morris again for six years.

For Wendy the cousins were just another addition to a lively collection of people who were older than she was. Her friend Gaya was impressed when she came to visit. "She lived in a big, beautiful corner house with cool older siblings," Gaya said. "There were a lot of cool people around."

None was cooler than Sandy, on the rare occasions she came home to visit. After separating from her husband at twenty-one and leaving for London, she returned to Brooklyn only twice during the five years she lived abroad. In England she began a career in advertising, reinventing herself along the way. When she came home, she was transformed into a thinner, crisper version of herself. She was more tailored, more elegant, more British.

Sandy was now neat and precise, in direct contradiction to Lola's chaotic housekeeping. Unlike her mother, who avoided the kitchen as much as she could, Sandy had become a gourmet cook. She knew how to make mysterious French dishes like cassoulet.

She told the family she was now to be referred to as Sandra, not Sandy. Wendy was dazzled.

On one of Sandra's visits home, when Wendy was in third grade, Lola told Sandra to pick her little sister up after her dance lessons in Manhattan.

She wanted the girls to reacquaint themselves with each other. Her suggestion: Howard Johnson's for grilled-cheese sandwiches followed by Radio City for the Rockettes and a Doris Day movie.

As an adult, Wendy wrote about that afternoon with great fondness:

My phantom neo-British sister in her gray flannel suit arrived at the dancing school, immediately warned me, "Don't tell Mother," and hustled me off to the House of Chan for spareribs and shrimp with lobster sauce. Neither dish was on the rabbi's recommended dietary list at the yeshiva. I was terrified that a burning bush or two stone tablets would come hurtling through the House of Chan's window. But I was with my glamorous big sister, who everyone told me was so brilliant, so I cleaned my plate.

After lunch, we skipped Radio City; Sandra had no interest in the Rockettes or Doris Day. We went to the Sutton Theatre on East Fifty-seventh Street, which seemed to me the ultimate in style: they served demitasse in the lobby. The feature film was *Expresso Bongo,* starring Laurence Harvey as Cliff Richard's tawdry musical agent. All I remember is a number in a strip joint with girls dancing in minikilts and no tops. I knew that in whatever Doris Day movie we were meant to be going to she would be wearing a top.

I never told my mother, but I loved everything about that afternoon.

The following summer Lola decided to take Bruce and Wendy out of Yeshivah of Flatbush. Wendy was contented there, but Bruce hated it. He said he felt uncomfortable because the other children came from families that were more religiously observant than his. More likely he was upset because he'd been demoted from the A track. "You were graded on your Hebrew, and we didn't know any of the prayers from home. We didn't know it from services because we never went," said Georgette. "We didn't know that Bruce had terrible eyesight and never saw the dots that indicate vowels. He went into the not-smart class, and his pride was very hurt."

Figuring he had learned enough to begin preparations for his bar mitzvah, Lola began to look at other schools, including Ethical Culture, where Georgette was about to begin her final year. Georgette had decided that for high school she wanted to go to Midwood, the local public school. She was already mapping a strategy to remove herself from the pressure to be extraordinary.

"I just wanted to blend in," she said. "I saw TV shows, and I wanted us to be all American." At fifteen she wrote in her diary, "Today was a very remorseful day. I have decided when I grow up I want to live in clean country air. I hate New York in the summer. It's hot and humid and takes all the pep out of me."

Wendy was never much of a journal keeper, but the summer after her third and last year at Yeshivah of Flatbush she was encouraged by Georgette to start a diary. Georgette gave her younger sister her own half-used diary, a vinyl-covered notebook decorated with the picture of a scantily dressed Indian maiden, hair done in a ponytail, a child peeping over her shoulder.

For several weeks, as she was about to turn nine years old, Wendy dutifully contributed entries, a brief but animated record of her concerns. The diary (which she often wrote as "Dairy") reveals intelligence, a developing theatrical sensibility, and the poor spelling that might have been related to her difficulties with reading.

Apart from recording her daily activities—going to camp, being annoyed by Bruce, shopping with Lola, swimming, taking dance lessons, playing tennis—she offered brief reviews of the many plays she saw with her family.

Blue Denim was "horrible," while *Once Upon a Mattress* was "very good." *Porgy and Bess,* on the other hand, "wasn't so good."

She was bent on self-improvement. "Dear Diary," she wrote one day. "Forgive me for all the days that I spell your name wrong. But I just can't spell."

She became convinced that her ballet teacher had a crush on her. "He always tells me to come up front and to be first on line," she wrote. "He always stares at me, too, after dancing."

The big news that summer came with the results of the IQ tests she and Bruce took. "I have a higher IQ than Bruce for the first time in my life," she noted.

The Yeshivah of Flatbush had done its work well. Both Wendy and Bruce were placed a grade ahead when they entered Ethical Culture that fall, he in eighth grade and she in fifth.

Wendy had been pleased by her interview there. "They said I'm the spitting image of Georgette," she wrote in her diary. "They will give me a foundation of a lot of languages. They have a T.V." Wendy went to bed the night before she started school at Ethical Culture excited but scared. She worried that her teacher would be an old grouch and she wouldn't have friends. But on arrival her fears about not making friends were dispelled. Almost immediately, she became "blood sisters" with Susan Gordis, who remained a lifelong friend.

At Yeshivah of Flatbush, students marched to the beat of intellectual advancement, bent on securing a spot in the A track. At Ethical Culture, students did creative dance in science class, had mandatory woodworking, and instead of report cards received lengthy written analyses of their progress, almost always encouraging. Most of the students were Jewish, and they had to endure weekly ethics instruction, but the school's religion was secular spirituality.

Children who lived far from the school were picked up in limousines.

On birthdays the children received red pencils inscribed, "Ethical Culture wishes you a happy birthday."

Wendy entered this cozy, cosseted world and was happy.

"Today was the first day of school." She wrote in her diary. "I made friends already. Blood sisters. I like Miss Lucky. The work wasn't hard. The car over is nice. Today we had shop. Love, Wendy."

Wendy's favorite class was interpretive dance with Adele Janovsky. She encouraged the children to dance the myth of Persephone with bright scarves in Prospect Park and used choreography to illustrate the difference between suspension bridges and swinging bridges. Mrs. Janovsky instructed her students, "Enunciate from the diaphragm" and "Dance to the colors," as they beat out "red" and "yellow" on a tambourine.

This gentle atmosphere was too rarefied for Bruce. He dismissed his one year at Ethical as a non-event. "It wasn't too rigorous an academic institution," he said.

He felt his education began when he entered the McBurney School, a college preparatory school for boys run by the YMCA, in Manhattan. Its graduates included J. D. Salinger, the celebrated author of *Catcher in the Rye* and *Franny and Zooey*. But another McBurney graduate would capture Bruce's imagination: Felix Rohatyn, the financier who became the legendary managing director of Lazard Frères, the most powerful and most secretive of the old Wall Street investment firms. One day Bruce would take Rohatyn's place there.

Wendy's warmest childhood memories were associated with the family's annual pilgrimages by train, and then plane, to Miami Beach during Christmas vacation. The Wassersteins were part of the annual southern migration of prosperous New York Jews, who stayed in marbled extravaganzas like the Fontainebleau or the Deauville, or lesser hotels, the Art Deco gems with pretentious airs, like the Sans Souci or the Casablanca.

Lola dragged her mink coat along—so what if it was seventy-five degrees outside? The family heard Harry Belafonte sing at the Eden Roc, they built sand castles on the beach, and they danced poolside to the music of Latin combos.

Every year, according to Wendy, her mother reenacted a comic routine that added a new dimension to Lola's pushiness. In this scenario her mother's unwillingness to be overlooked was acceptable, enlisted in the cause of social justice:

> In the 1950s Arthur Godfrey owned what was rumored to be an anti-Semitic hotel in Miami Beach—a glaring and odious anomaly, almost a contradiction in terms. The Kenilworth was billed as a retreat for those who preferred to be with people from "your own background and taste." Every year my mother would take my brother and me to the front desk at The Kenilworth and ask for directions to "the Cohen Bar Mitzvah." And every year she would be admonished, "Madame, there is no Cohen Bar Mitzvah here."

Twenty-five years later, when Wendy had begun to make her mark as a playwright, she tried to capture her feelings about her childhood years in a musical comedy called *Miami*. Significantly, she set the play in 1959, as John F. Kennedy, then a young senator from Massachusetts, was running for president of the United States. During the crucial penultimate scene, a campaign slogan appears in skywriting: KENNEDY FOR PRESIDENT, LEADERSHIP FOR THE FUTURE.

Just as that era represented, for the Baby Boom generation, the last convincing pretense of national innocence, *Miami* for Wendy evokes a memory of childhood pleasures and angst, when family togetherness meant everything.

The play reveals intense longing for a connection that was bound to change, if not disappear. Most striking is the bond between two main characters, a twelve-year-old named Cathy and Jonathan, the sixteen-year-old brother she worships. Cathy and Jonathan are stand-ins for Wendy and Bruce.

At the end of the play, Jonathan tells Cathy: "What really matters to Mom and Dad is bringing your family to Miami every year whether you had a good season or a bad season. But what matters to me is going to be very different from that. I know I won't grow up to be like Daddy. He's a very good man, but he's not going to change the world."

The sister responds, "I probably won't be like Mommy, either. I mean, I want to have babies and a husband like Mommy. But I'm funnier than Mommy. I want to be Lucille Ball, too."

While developing the character of Cathy, the playwright scribbled notes that offer insight into how she regarded herself at age twelve:

Massively uncomfortable with herself, especially physically," Wendy wrote. "She sees herself as grotesquely overweight but in reality she is plump. Not a cheerleader type, not unattractive. Very self-conscious. Her clothing conceals rather than reveals. She is not pathetic. She is liked, terrifically bright. She feels a need to please therefore she is funny, charming and overly sensitive to other people's need.

Despite this recollection of adolescent self-doubt, Wendy didn't intend to leave the impression that she'd had a miserable childhood. A poignant sentimentality suffuses *Miami,* particularly in the final scenes.

Toward the end, after the brother threatens to disrupt the family vacation but then reconciles, he tenderly asks his sister, "Did you enjoy your vacation?"

After acknowledging that the weather hadn't been great and that their hotel's nouveau riche pretensions were silly, she responds, "All in all, I had a lovely time."

Despite this warm gloss, Lola's children emerged from childhood carrying the indelible imprint of their mother's Darwinian ethos. "If you're smart, you take a leap and go first," the brother explains to his sister in *Miami.* "If you're stupid, you wait and look around and you're moving with a herd of cattle. And if you're slow, you get left behind."

WENDY WAS ONLY TWELVE WHEN SHE
STARTED HIGH SCHOOL.

Three

A GIRL'S EDUCATION

1963–67

In the fall of 1963, Wendy entered the all-female Calhoun School in Manhattan, a consequential change, not just of schools but of expectations and attitudes. The students at Calhoun seemed quite sophisticated to the sheltered girl, commuting from Brooklyn, beginning high school young, a month before her thirteenth birthday.

Her sweet, accommodating nature helped her to adapt. Just as she had at Ethical Culture and before that at Yeshivah of Flatbush, she easily made friends. Ilene Goldsmith was one of them, attracted to Wendy's warmth and sense of fun. Early into that first school year, Morris and Lola picked Ilene and Wendy up at Calhoun in the cinnamon-colored Jaguar. (The Jaguar was no longer an embarrassment, now that Wendy was enrolled in a fancy girls' school.) They drove home to Brooklyn, the trip to the outer borough an adventure for Ilene, raised on the Upper West Side of Manhattan. Even the car ride was festive; the backseat was filled with ribbons from Morris's factory. When they arrived at the big house on Avenue N, the girls went upstairs to Wendy's room, shut the door, put on dancing shoes, and spent the afternoon trying to work out the steps to Prokofiev's *Romeo and Juliet*. Ilene never topped five feet, two inches; Wendy had long, slender legs but was fleshy. Both girls took classes for years and—despite the physical improbability—dreamed of being ballerinas.

Lola periodically poked her head in to ask the girls if they wanted something to eat. She also advised them that if they wanted to be dancers, they would have to marry someone who could take care of them.

Getting married was something they thought about, even in ninth grade. Ilene and Wendy had long discussions about *Marjorie Morningstar* and whether the book's ending was positive or depressing. Marjorie Morgenstern, who gives herself the fanciful stage name "Morningstar," is the heroine of Herman Wouk's bestselling novel, a soap opera–worthy tale about a beautiful young Jewish woman torn between rejecting and respecting her parents' values. Published in 1955 and made into a movie starring Natalie Wood and Gene Kelly in 1958, the story of Marjorie's plight continued to capture an essential dilemma for ambitious girls, including high-school freshmen like Wendy and Ilene. They identified with Marjorie, the daughter of immigrant parents moving up the social scale, and her fantasies of becoming an actress. Wendy and Ilene wanted to be dancers, or *something* worthy of their talents. Like Marjorie, they were determined not to "grow up" and become "Shirleys," Wouk's designation for pampered princesses preordained to be suburban housewives.

Wendy and Ilene read and wept over Marjorie's fate—she wound up a Shirley after all. They were also torn. Would it be so bad to marry a doctor or a lawyer? But as they were asking the question, it was changing. Why shouldn't they *become* doctors or lawyers?

All the Wasserstein children felt pressure to succeed, but their mother made it clear her expectations were different for girls and boys. For Wendy's thirteenth birthday, Lola gave her daughter one-on-one personal training at the Helena Rubinstein Charm School, where Wendy learned that she must never carry a schoolbag on her shoulders as well as the proper way to enter and exit a taxi (slide the derriere in first, out last). What Wendy wanted, however, was the present that Bruce had received for his bar mitzvah, *Richard Halliburton's Complete Book of Marvels,* a travel guide to "the wonders of both the Orient and the Occident." She stole the book and studied the possibilities it contained, ranging from "New York, City Extraordinary," to "Blue Grotto, Cavern of Loveliness," to the Taj Mahal and Timbuktu.

In 1963, the year Wendy entered Calhoun, Betty Friedan published *The Feminine Mystique,* the manifesto that pronounced the exalted life of the American housewife a sham. Women made up about 33 percent of the workforce, but few held positions of power. There were two women senators in the U.S. Congress elected in 1960 and seventeen women in the 435-member House of Representatives.

Wendy looked to the exceptions, like her sister Sandra, already married and divorced and back in New York after her London escapade. Sandra now worked at General Foods, not in some lowly position as a secretary or a telephone operator but as an account executive for Maxwell House coffee. That seemed much better than serving a husband coffee!

Wendy also had another role model, this one larger than life and even more enchanting than Sandra: Doris Day, the pert blond actress adept at playing characters whose deceptive wholesomeness camouflaged ambition, brains, and a healthy sexual appetite. Doris Day movies were often fluffy romantic comedies, but the leading lady was portrayed as an interesting career woman—an interior decorator in *Pillow Talk,* an advertising executive in *Lover Come Back,* a journalism professor in *Teacher's Pet.* Doris was nice but firm, smart, *and* feminine.

As an adult, Wendy would reflect on how those movies influenced her. "Doris in her heyday was, despite her career-woman status, neither bitter nor desperate nor cold," she wrote. "She was not a spinster who raged against her biological clock or cried herself to sleep because she was still on the shelf at twenty-five. Doris was a gal on the town, a metropolitan *mensch* with a rich, full life."

But Doris also made Wendy realize something about herself. "I never thought of myself as undesirable or unattractive, frankly, until I turned twelve and began watching all these movies in which none of the men ever fell in love with anybody who looked remotely like me," she told an interviewer. "No one was ever Jewish, no one was hardly ever brunette."

At Calhoun, Wendy was just beginning her life as "gal on the town." The big move came after her freshman year. Georgette had already left for college, and Bruce was entering the University of Michigan. Home, for Wendy, became something else entirely. Morris and Lola packed up their rambling house, meant for a passel of children, and moved to an apartment on the Upper East Side of Manhattan, trading their backyard for Central Park, quiet tree-lined streets for nonstop urban buzz.

The Upper East Side carried the connotation of wealth and status; living there was a nice mark of achievement, but not nearly the end of the game for Lola and Morris. He was still a young man, in his early forties when they moved, not yet ready to clip coupons. Wasserstein Brothers continued to prosper. Wendy told her friends her father had invented velveteen; the actual product was more prosaic, crushed imitation velvet used for jeans. In 1968 Morris took out a patent on a better way to make ribbons, without the ends unraveling. The family's real-estate holdings began to rival the ribbon and textile business. Lola and Morris's travels expanded beyond Miami Beach to Europe and then the world.

The neighborhood was ritzy, the apartment less so; 150 East Seventy-seventh Street was a sixteen-story grayish white brick architectural nonentity. The building had been constructed just a few years earlier, and it provided the functional luxuries of a doorman and a lobby but little grace. They were right in the middle of the city hubbub, next to the Number 6 subway on the Lexington Avenue line. The three-bedroom apartment was spacious and airy, with French doors leading to a den, yet much smaller than the Brooklyn house. Wendy's bedroom contained twin beds, one for Georgette when she came home from college. There was one glamorous note, a terrace off the living room with views of "New York, City Extraordinary," as if taken from the pages of *Richard Halliburton's Complete Book of Marvels.*

Lola decorated the place with a mixture of domestic indifference and free-spirited impulse. She plunked down furniture they'd brought with them—a large sofa with huge tassels hanging over the edge, a footstool covered in a needlepoint canvas. One day, in a fit of artistic inspiration, she splatter-painted the kitchen floor, in homage to the abstract expressionist artist Jackson Pollock. On another occasion she strung lemons in the chandelier.

Food preparation stopped altogether. Lola's cupboards were noticeably bare. The deli downstairs provided morning coffee; takeout was readily available. But for special occasions, Morris and Lola returned to the "old country"—to Brooklyn. "They drove an hour to Cookys restaurant on Avenue M in Brooklyn to pick up Thanksgiving for 20 to go," Wendy remembered. "My parents were smuggling cranberry sauce and potato kugel over inter-borough lines."

Freed from the burden of managing a big house and doing the laundry of many children, Lola devoted more and more time to her passion. After sending her girls to dance classes all those years, she now sent herself, sometimes taking as many as four classes a day. She began wearing leotards as streetwear and pared down further, becoming not just slim but a muscled reed.

Wendy was now the only child at home, living in a vastly different location from where she grew up with her siblings. She and her parents had to adjust to a new family configuration while contending with "the city," with all its promise and excitement—and its tension. These changes were plenty for an adolescent girl to absorb, but there was more. All that was happening in Wendy's life was magnified by the gathering momentum of a dangerous, exhilarating decade.

The sixties were roaring through New York, calling everything into question, creating a fabulous din of provocation and creativity. Civil rights, pop art, the Beatles, feminism, pacifism, and protest—the world was changing fast. Two months after Wendy began high school, John F. Kennedy was assassinated. Nothing seemed safe.

For Wendy, as for so many of her contemporaries, the Kennedy assassination was etched in memory. "I was on an escalator in B. Altman's Department Store in New York City when I heard that President Kennedy had been shot," she recalled. "I was on my way to my high school bazaar, and I remember watching other people on the escalator burst into tears and hold each other."

It was a pivotal moment, the line of demarcation between conformity and rebellion, stability and chaos. In the spirit of the times, Wendy balked at rules about what girls could wear to school, cut classes to shop at Bergdorf's, and sneaked smokes in Riverside Park. She hung out with friends at Stark's restaurant on Ninetieth Street and Broadway, a short walk from school, drinking cherry sodas and eating candy. She was frequently marked tardy.

Still, Wendy was her parents' daughter. She rebelled enough to be noticed and conformed enough to succeed. At Calhoun she helped put on plays, became editor of the *Calhounder,* the high-school newspaper, and wrote earnest term papers. She aimed to be original, signing her name "Wendee Wasserstein," but sometimes she wanted to be part of the crowd, trying—with mixed success—to tame her unruly hair with rollers, hair spray, and headbands.

"Wendy would always write her papers on time and turn them in, but on the way to school she'd run it through the gutter to make it messy," said one of her teachers. "Part of her was quite traditional, and part of her was Wendy, her own person."

The burgeoning notion of female power was reinforced at Calhoun, where the girls encountered only the occasional male teacher. The school had been founded at the turn of the twentieth century as the Jacobi School, to educate the "Our Crowd" girls, the daughters of New York's wealthy, secular Jews. Few girls went to college, but Jacobi and then Calhoun graduates were expected to be "accomplished"; many of them did go on to have careers, in either professional or volunteer work.

The school's character changed significantly after World War II, when Elizabeth Parmelee and Beatrice Cosmey became headmistresses. These no-nonsense women were there when Wendy arrived, a Mutt-and-Jeff combination, one tall and skinny, the other a little fireplug, overseeing their young ladies in a time of revolution. Miss Parmelee and Miss Cosmey put college prep front and center. Some quaint customs continued, however, like the annual mother-daughter luncheon and fashion show, a fund-raiser for the school, held at elegant hotels like the Plaza, the Waldorf-Astoria, and the Pierre.

Miss Parmelee and Miss Cosmey became foils for exuberant young women and fine material for a comic writer looking back on those years. "You couldn't wear skirts that were an inch above your knees," Wendy recalled. "I can't tell you how many times Miss Parmelee and Miss Cosmey, our Headmistresses at the time, sent me home to change at eight-thirty in the morning. One time, I returned to the school wearing a longer skirt and bedroom slippers."

The *Calhounder* was a proper school newspaper, dutifully reporting the results of class elections, sports tournaments, and mixers with boys' schools ("a bevy of beauties welcomed the twenty-nine boys with great charm . . .").

By Wendy's senior year, however, the paper had begun to reflect the times, ever so gently. "Where the Protests Stop . . . and Peace Begins" was the headline on an article about the U.S. war in Vietnam, urging students to send aid to the Vietnamese people. In that same issue, a play was reviewed called *O the Times They Are A-Changing,* an allegorical spoof of the conflict between youth and the older generation. The play was directed by a Miss Lesser, and the cast included Wendy Wasserstein, as part of "The Ditty Bop Set."

Ann-Ellen Lesser was a secretary, assistant to the headmistress, not long out of college, who began teaching philosophy as an extracurricular subject, her credential being that she had majored in philosophy in college. When the head of drama left, Miss Lesser was asked to take that over, too. It was a small school with limited resources; Wendy's class had twenty-two girls in it.

The girls liked Miss Lesser. They thought she was hip, with appropriately "intellectual" looks—short pixie hair, dark-rimmed glasses. She encouraged them to experiment. It was the 1960s, after all. They did lots of theater of the absurd. "Existentialism was in," she recalled. They took scenes from short stories, put them to music, and performed an antiwar piece.

"This was an all-girls' school," she said. "You either did the one or two bad plays that were all women characters or you do other stuff and bother some boys from McBurney to help out and watch them get destroyed by our teenage girls."

As an adult, speaking at the dedication of a new performing-arts center at Calhoun in 2004, Wendy talked about Miss Lesser's productions:

One year, she had an idea to put on a play in our auditorium, which was at that time the Jewish Community Center on West Eighty-ninth

Street. The play she chose was Günter Grass's *The Wicked Cooks*. Günter Grass, for those of you who don't know, had two major claims to fame. The first was that he won the Nobel Prize for Literature in 1999. The second was that he had an all-girl high-school production of the absurdist play *The Wicked Cooks*.

My parents were in Europe during our rehearsal period, and my big sister Sandy, who was an executive at General Foods, came to stay with me. At night I would rehearse my lines with her, and she would make her Maxwell House account-executive buddies listen to it and ask them if it made any sense to them. There would be a stunned look on their faces, and they would ask me, "Why isn't your school doing *Annie*?"

The day of the performance arrived, and the proud parent body sat in the theater as we came out onstage with giant chefs' hats and aprons and began reciting lines in unison, like, "The moon is a potato / The star is a tomato / And everywhere are cooks / In all the halls and nooks." I distinctly remember seeing jaws dropping and a hushed silence, and at the end a burst of parental applause for the completely incomprehensible event.

Miss Lesser was amused by Wendy's account, which became part of the school's lore, eventually appearing on the Calhoun Web site, but Miss Lesser had a correction. After pointing out that the *Wicked Cooks* production was the handiwork of the previous drama adviser, she observed that Sandy's Maxwell House colleagues couldn't have asked why the students didn't do *Annie* instead of *Wicked Cooks*.

Annie didn't premiere until 1977, a decade after Wendy graduated from Calhoun.

"It's still a great story, but there is a bit of poetic license," said Miss Lesser.

Wendy had the most interesting mind of any student I ever had," said Ann-Ellen Lesser. "There's smart, which is what comes up on the IQ test. And then there's intelligence that has the element of imagination in it. Wendy had real intelligence, imagination, the ability to see beyond what was in front of her."

Yet during her years at Calhoun, no one was predicting a Pulitzer Prize for Wendy Wasserstein. Of more immediate concern: would her grades improve enough to get her into a good college?

School records report tardiness twelve times in a single semester one year. Her math grades hovered between C-plus and B-minus, and she consistently received C's in French and D's in gym.

The curriculum was rigorous and the teachers demanding. They were quick to point out weaknesses—a slapdash quality to her work—even in subjects where she excelled, like history and English. "Wendy's knowledge of history is extensive," wrote a teacher in her midterm report junior year. "The mechanics of her writing are poor—a fact which belies the intelligence of her thinking."

To escalate her prospects for college, she was encouraged to take summer courses at elite boarding schools. The programs were known to be exacting, and, Wendy understood, it wouldn't hurt to have names like Exeter and Andover on her application. She'd been learning the importance of name brands and always made sure to note that she took lessons at June Taylor's School of Dance, not just any studio. (Taylor's choreography featured Rockettes'-style high kicks; her dancers were regular performers on *The Jackie Gleason Show,* a popular TV variety program in the 1950s and '60s.)

After sophomore year she attended the summer program at the Phillips Academy, Andover, in Massachusetts, where she succumbed to the lure of the New England countryside and the school's exalted aura. That encounter began a lifelong infatuation with charming academic campuses situated in rarefied settings.

She returned from Andover to Calhoun a better student but not good enough for the headmistresses, Cosmey and Parmelee. Midway through her junior year, they offered this guarded evaluation: "Wendy has produced a good report. We are especially glad to note that she is passing physical education. Comments should be studied carefully, for Wendy needs now to take giant steps in academic growth, to begin to prepare for greater challenges next year and in college."

The following summer she returned to New England for another summer program, this time at the Phillips Exeter Academy in New Hampshire, where she was challenged by unsparing faculty. She took serious subjects—economics, philosophy, music appreciation—and wrote dull, lengthy papers in longhand. "Wendy, you have written over four thousand words when the assignment called for fifteen hundred," wrote a testy professor. "You have too much bulk here—repetitious passages, excessively long quotations, redundancies, and superfluous sections. A good rewriting of the entire essay could reduce it by half without losing any essential material. I appreciate your industry and sincerity in this enterprise, but I urge you to be more efficient by being precise and concise."

Regular grade—B-minus.

Grade due to penalty for lateness—C-plus.

Despite the grueling assessments and the repeated grade reductions for sloppiness and turning her papers in late, she produced remarkable work for a fifteen-year-old. Her papers demonstrate great effort and a complex intellect; she struggled to grasp conventional wisdom and then put her own stamp on it. In a paper analyzing the work of George Bernard Shaw, she wrote a snappy opening line that could be seen as a guidepost for a future writer of provocative plays: "The saint does not bring peace on earth and good will among men. The saint, rather, makes the world uncomfortable to live in."

When Wendy applied to college, she had begun to think that the University of Michigan, which both Sandy and Bruce attended, wasn't for her. She didn't want to follow Georgette's path either. Her middle sister had traveled in Europe after graduating from Hood College, then a small girls' school in Maryland, and was back in New York, taking classes at the New School. In the fall of Wendy's senior year, Georgette followed Marjorie Morningstar's example. Marjorie had succumbed to a Jewish lawyer; Georgette married a Jewish doctor. Albert Levis didn't exactly conform to the cliché; he was born in Greece, was studying clinical psychiatry at Yale, and exhibited an eccentric intelligence. Wendy didn't find him dull, just weird.

Georgette appeared rail thin and ethereal in her bridal gown. The wedding was a lavish affair at the Plaza Hotel, where Lola scandalized her more religious Schleifer relatives by serving shrimp. Wendy was reminded, looking at "Gorgeous," of her own failings in the get-slim department. She was also concerned, wondering if Georgette hadn't been cornered into making a wrong decision. Wendy discovered that the corollary to feeling superior and inferior was the unpleasant sensation of betraying a sister, whom she loved, by both mocking her choice yet in some ways envying her.

Her own ambitions had begun to take amorphous shape during her sojourn in the Manhattan private-school system. She turned her sights toward the Seven Sisters colleges, female counterparts of the Ivy League schools, which were then primarily all male, except for Cornell.

She applied to Michigan, but her heart was set on Mount Holyoke College, a world apart from Wendy's cloistered Jewish world in New York.

While her grades were a mixed bag, her recommendations were stellar. "Best student in five years," wrote her history teacher. "Quality of mind is exceptional. Thinking is imaginative and original. Is an intellectual rebel but does not as yet have the self-confidence to fight or argue for her conclusions."

The headmistresses chimed in: "An excellent, critical independent logical thinker," they wrote; "weaknesses stem from carelessness. Is gradually learning not to brush aside details. A born leader. Recommend enthusiastically."

Before completing the application process, in the fall of 1966 Wendy won an essay-writing contest sponsored by the World Youth Forum, a program created after World War II by the *New York Herald Tribune*. The idea was to promote international understanding by introducing young people from around the world to one another. Wendy saw an additional benefit in the program: "my secret weapon for gaining admittance to the college of my choice." The *Herald Tribune* folded in 1966, but WCBS-TV took over sponsorship of the program. The winners were scheduled to take a trip to Europe the following summer.

Wendy and other Youth Forum winners appeared on a local Saturday-afternoon television program called *The World We Want*, where students were asked questions like "How would you solve New York City's problems?"

When the program was broadcast, her mother provided a ratings boost. Lola went to the television department at Bloomingdale's and turned all the channels to *The World We Want*. That heady moment was quickly deflated: in April Wendy received a polite letter from the Mount Holyoke admissions office informing her that she was wait-listed.

The wait list was another stinging reminder that she might not be good enough. Calhoun hadn't been her first choice of the Manhattan private schools. She didn't get into Dalton, then a girls' school, favored by prosperous secular Jews. She was too intimidated to apply to the highly regarded Brearley School, which she imagined as a Wasp enclave, filled with thin, blond, beautiful girls, floating effortlessly through life.

Once again her merit was called into question.

Wendy would be such a good student, if only her work were neater, less convoluted, better.

Wendy would be such a pretty girl, if only she would lose weight.

Wendy would be perfect, if only she were someone else.

The blow from being wait-listed at Mount Holyoke was offset— somewhat—by romance.

James Kaplan lived a few blocks from Wendy, in the Imperial House, a slightly fancier version of the Wassersteins' white brick apartment building. Wendy's Calhoun classmate Kathy Roskind lived in Imperial House, too. The two girls became diet buddies, being the not-slender daughters of mothers who were annoyingly skinny. Mrs. Roskind, who was five feet, two inches and weighed ninety pounds, frequently reminded the girls of the upwardly mobile Jewish mother's motto: "You can never be too rich or too thin."

Mrs. Roskind was a chain smoker with emphysema, who often stayed home. She enjoyed Wendy, who used to amuse her friend's mother by singing the hit title song from the movie *Georgy Girl*. The lyrics—about a girl who appeared to be carefree but felt lonely inside—hit home.

Wendy wasn't the only teenage girl to be infatuated with *Georgy Girl*, about a large, awkward young woman who yearns for love and ends up taking care of her beautiful roommate's baby. The 1966 movie, though presented as a convoluted Cinderella story, tapped into feelings about deep issues: the nature of marriage, the lure of motherhood, the urge to be free, the desire to be loved for what you were.

Lynn Redgrave would become known in subsequent years as the spokesperson for the Weight Watchers diet plan. In 1966 she became, for girls like Wendy and Kathy, a rebuttal to Twiggy, the anorexic, doe-eyed teenage supermodel who made starvation a fashion statement. With Twiggy as the ideal, the pressure to lose weight was frequently disproportionate to the weight there was to lose. Photographs of Wendy and Kathy in the *Inkspot,* the Calhoun yearbook, show attractive girls who are not slim but certainly not fat. (Wendy's weight fluctuated, but in high school she often weighed around 130 pounds, on a five-foot-six-inch frame.) Wendy appears open yet guarded; she has a way of looking at the camera while seeming to look away.

Their mothers sent the girls to the same Fifth Avenue diet doctor, whose seven-dollars-a-visit charge included amphetamines for weight control. The rainbow-colored pills made Wendy nervous, so she threw hers away. She and Kathy went directly from the doctor's office to the drugstore, where they would buy (and consume) three candy bars each and vow to start their diets the next day.

Wendy pretended to be insouciant, but there was no way to feel good about Lola's constant pressure to lose weight. When they walked down the street together, Lola—wearing a dance leotard underneath her fur coat—would wave at the crowds passing by and say to Wendy, "They are all looking at you and thinking, 'Look at that fat girl.'"

Wendy noticed James Kaplan and asked Kathy to introduce her to him. Kathy was apprehensive. She was very aware of Jimmy Kaplan but was certain he was not at all aware of her existence. He was nice-looking, smart, Jewish, and extremely well credentialed: he went to Horace Mann, one of the city's most exclusive prep schools for boys. The fetching ribbon around this attractive package: Jimmy Kaplan had already been accepted to Yale.

Kathy worked up the courage to call him, to tell him she had a friend he should go out with. As Jimmy, who preferred James, remembered it, Kathy made certain to let him know that her friend had been dating someone and that *she* had broken up with him, not vice versa.

James agreed to meet Wendy. He wasn't quite smitten, but he liked her. Not a beauty, he thought, but she had a cute freckle face. He liked her intelligence and sensitivity and even her insecurity, which made him feel protective. They began to date.

The boys at Horace Mann were said to believe that the girls at Calhoun were "easy," but in 1967 it was unusual for high-school girls to "go all the way." Fear of unwanted pregnancy was a large concern; abortion wouldn't be legal in New York for another three years and nationwide until 1973. But that didn't stop sex and romance from being a primary extracurricular activity for teenagers—at the very least as a major topic of conversation.

Wendy pursued James, or so he felt. "She was making a play for me," he said. "She could be aggressive when she wanted things."

He liked her well enough to invite her to the Horace Mann senior prom, and to make out with her, but he didn't want to be exclusive. There was another girl he was dating at the time, whom he was more interested in, but that girl was less interested in him.

He was bothered by Wendy's tendency to put on weight, and he told her so. In subsequent decades he recalled his rude frankness ruefully; by then he was a middle-aged man, eighty pounds heavier than he'd been in high school. He regretted calling her a "fat Polack," a teenage boy's cruel term of endearment.

As he saw their relationship that spring, it was an enjoyable interlude before they both left home. They experimented with sex within the zone of safety, meaning no intercourse. They went to movies and had long talks but apparently didn't communicate as well as they might have.

"I saw her as someone I'd gone out with several times," said James. "The prom, I guess, to her indicated something of a commitment."

Both of them had plans to go abroad that summer. Wendy was leaving for the World Youth Forum trip, to represent American teenagers, an idea she took seriously but also found amusing.

James was heading for Turkey, to be part of the Experiment in International Living, another idealistic program meant "to foster peace through understanding, communication, and cooperation." Young people were dispersed to other countries, to immerse themselves in foreign cultures for a few weeks, a process that included living with local families.

In a later generation, participation in such programs would become more common. In 1967 not many teenagers, even from upper-middle-class families, traveled abroad on their own. For Wendy the fact that she and James had chosen similar ways to spend their summer demonstrated a commonality of spirit and purpose. Besides, he was the perfect specimen to bring home to Lola: a bright, Yale-bound Jewish boy with prospects— and she had caught him without being thin. They had similar backgrounds— fathers in the textile business, mothers with artistic urges (his mother was a sculptor). Wendy believed she wanted a family; Jimmy Kaplan was a viable candidate, if and when she decided to marry.

For James their summer plans simply provided a fortuitous opportunity to bring a casual relationship to an end.

They both managed to be wrong.

The summer of 1967 was hot and hateful. Dozens of American cities— including Cincinnati, Cleveland, Detroit, Newark—erupted in violence, called "riots" or "uprisings," depending on one's perspective. Three years earlier Congress had passed the Civil Rights Act of 1964; people living in inner-city slums failed to see racial progress. Martin Luther King Jr. preached nonviolence, but the street wanted action, not words. The system, springboard to success for the Wasserstein family, oppressed the black community, descendants of slaves, the immigrants who had made the journey against their will.

The American heartbreak spread around the world. America, slayer of Hitler, defender of freedom, had become the racist imperialist, mired in the Vietnam War.

White children whose families had prospered in the United States began reassessing. Was everything they'd been taught an illusion?

Summer of hate, "Summer of Love." Tens of thousands of young people converged on Haight-Ashbury, the "hippie" section of San Francisco, for a giant be-in. The counterculture rebellion was on, celebrating LSD, free love, universal harmony, tie-dye, and youth. The national media acted as public-relations operative, setting in place the mythology of a generation.

For Wendy, it was Summer Abroad with the World Youth Forum, whose participants were hardly rebels. If anything, this group of earnest, open-minded young Americans provided good public relations toward Europeans growing more and more disillusioned with U.S. foreign policy. The trip was grueling and exhilarating, densely scheduled with meetings and activities.

They toured factories and strolled through gardens in Germany, visited salt mines and got drunk at a folk festival in Austria. They ate Sabbath dinner with Jews in Nuremberg, after attending a service, not in a synagogue but a small room on the ground floor of an apartment house. Behind the Iron Curtain, in Yugoslavia, they met contemporaries in a youth work camp and interviewed the editor-in-chief of the *Vjesnik* newspaper agency in Zagreb. They missed a scheduled lecture at the Institute for the History of the Workers' Movement, but did meet with labor leaders at a factory that manufactured radios and televisions, to discuss the self-management of Yugoslavian workers. They saw *La Bohème* in Venice, where they also ate lunch with an Italian countess, who was an avid environmentalist. Their photograph appeared in a German newspaper. They were introduced to mayors and other politicians everywhere they went.

Wendy made an important connection on the trip. Abigail J. Stewart of Staten Island, another World Youth Forum winner, was attending Mount Holyoke College that fall. When Abby and Wendy discovered they were both going there—Wendy had been taken off the waiting list before graduation—they became fast friends.

"That trip was a very big experience for most of us," said Abby, speaking as the adult she became, a professor of psychology and women's studies. "None of us had experienced that kind of independence, in terms of being served wine and making decisions of where to go and what to do. There was the freedom, dealing with other languages and cultures and each other. . . . We saw ourselves as the intelligentsia. That was all our self-construction, but we were very involved in our self-construction."

Before they made their farewells, she and Wendy agreed to write to Mount Holyoke, to ask if they could be roommates. They got along well, and neither of them knew anyone else at Holyoke. The age of the computerized roommate match hadn't yet arrived. They wouldn't know if their request had been granted until they arrived on campus a few weeks later.

THE 1960S SEEMED TO HAVE BYPASSED MOUNT HOLYOKE, OR SO IT SEEMED
TO WENDY WHEN SHE ARRIVED IN THE FALL OF 1967.

Four
_____

GRACIOUS LIVING

1967–68

The four-year period that encompassed Wendy's years as a student at Mount Holyoke College, 1967 to 1971, would be remembered by a generation as a transformative period when attitudes seemed to change overnight.

From Wendy's vantage point—South Hadley, Massachusetts, autumn 1967—it seemed that overnight was taking forever.

She and Abby Stewart arrived at Mount Holyoke primed for experience, pumped by their summer adventures abroad, invigorated by the larger events that had turned the evening news into a nightly drama filled with war, riots, and sexual revolution.

It didn't take them long to realize they were in the wrong place at the wrong time. They didn't find the all-female intellectual citadel they had anticipated, and certainly not a campus fomenting radical thought. Instead they encountered a hothouse of girlieness, stuck in the 1950s, filled with bright women who seemed desperate to land a husband. In class it was sometimes hard to pay attention to the professor because of all the knitting needles clicking, as girls made sweaters for their boyfriends. Seniors didn't obsess about graduate school much; most were far more concerned about whether they would be leaving Holyoke with engagement rings on their fingers.

On their first day of school, the entering freshman heard this piece of advice when they gathered in the gymnasium: "This is where you can take sports, and you might want to think about golf and tennis, games you can play that would be good for your husband's business."

They were assigned Big Sisters to counsel them, as well as Elves, anonymous sprites who would leave the occasional gift for them, small tokens like candy.

Wendy and Abby were taken aback, though they shouldn't have been. The freshman handbook for the Class of 1971 offered incoming students a guide to the rules and customs that Mount Holyoke "girls" were meant to respect. Nothing epitomized the mind-set better than the section on "Gracious Living":

> On Wednesday evening and Sunday noon, the scene is set. . . . For these two meals, girls dress up more than usual and wear stockings and heels. "Gracious" provides a break in the everyday routine— gives you a chance to discard those Levi's and sweatshirts in favor of a paisley hostess skirt or a knit suit. Dinner is by candlelight, and coffee is served in the living room afterwards.

In addition, there were instructions on how much to eat, what to wear, how to behave, and whom to date.

> MEALS: . . . Some are so adept at this that they soon gain the proverbial "freshman ten" pounds and find that that new silver lamé mini-dress is a bit too skimpy after all.
>
> ATTIRE: Robes and curler caps may be worn to breakfast. Skirts are required for dinner with the exception of Sunday supper.
>
> DORM LIFE: . . . The Work Chairman . . . coordinates and assigns the "chores" each student is expected to do once a week. The jobs are small and easily performed: helping out with the dishwashing

at one meal, or sitting bells, which involves being on hand at the front desk to answer the telephone and receive callers. . . .

DATING: During the week the Mount Holyoke world is books and classes, coffee at the C.I., bridge when you should be studying, and staying up all night talking to the girl down the hall. It's a girl's world where no one really cares if you don't have time to set your hair. Come Friday, however, it's a different scene. The social whirl begins as suitcases are snapped shut and girls take off for Amherst, Williams, Wesleyan, Yale, Dartmouth, Princeton, Harvard, Brown, Trinity, Cornell and Colgate among others. At the same time boys begin arriving from these places for mixers and parties. From Friday to Sunday, it's a man's world.

Advance warning or not, Wendy and Abby felt gypped.

Wendy had been drawn to the school's pedigree as one of the Seven Sisters. Abby had succumbed to the romance of Emily Dickinson, who'd been a student there.

Both of them had been seduced by Mount Holyoke's picture-postcard New England campus, located in the tiny town of South Hadley, tucked in the hills of western Massachusetts, part of the lush Connecticut River Valley. They'd heard the history, of how the Mount Holyoke Female Seminary was started in 1837 by Mary Lyon, a remarkable schoolteacher who'd crusaded to make higher education available to women. It was crucial, she felt, that the curriculum be as rigorous as those in men's colleges, and available to women of all backgrounds.

The fantasies they had conjured didn't include Gracious Living and being handed cloth napkins with instructions to fold them at the end of each meal and tuck them into an assigned cubbyhole.

They lived in 1837 Hall, the dormitory named for the year of the college's founding. Despite its historic name, the dorm was another disappointment, a boxy modern rectangle, overlooking the Lower Lake. Soon everything that had lured them became suffocating. With its old-fashioned brick architecture, nestled in a landscape of lovely wooded paths and secluded ponds, the college was a portrait of rural civility that quickly felt too snug, too staid.

Wendy and Abby became closer than they might have, bonded by their feelings of being outsiders.

They understood that the Ivy League and the Seven Sisters emphasized academic excellence but hadn't quite grasped the way the schools perpetuated class preservation. There was an unstated expectation that students would form the old-boy and old-girl networks that would, after graduation, become advantageous connections in business, academia, politics, and high society. Mount Holyoke did have a long history of social responsibility—the school graduated its first African-American student in 1883. Yet diversity hadn't advanced past tokenism. In 1967 there were a handful of African Americans—eighteen "Negro" freshmen out of a class of 486—and not many Jews. The latter fact was unsettling to Wendy, who'd been surrounded by Jews throughout her education.

The college was more traditional than any school she had attended. Abby had already become politicized and was beginning to develop a strong feminist point of view. She found the idea of Gracious Living ridiculous.

The two girls, united by alienation, responded in very different ways. Abby, the future academic, took refuge in her studies. Wendy, the future playwright, entertained the other "misfits" who gathered in her room to listen to her vast record collection of Broadway show tunes and eat and talk. She seemed to live in her flannel nightgown and never to comb her hair. Everything became grist for a funny story, even her grades, which were the worst she'd ever had, C's and D's, even in the subjects she liked, English and history.

She made it all seem like a lark. When she and Abby took zoology together, they invented songs to help them memorize things. In the middle of the night, Abby watched Wendy tap-dance the sixteen functions of the liver (with a nod to Mrs. Janovsky, her dance teacher at Ethical Culture).

Abby was in awe of Wendy's sophistication. For Abby, a girl from Staten Island, Manhattan was the celestial city and Wendy lived there. She knew rare things. In her nimble way, she dropped references that were foreign to Abby: the music of Benjamin Britten, the medieval mystery *Play of Daniel.* Despite the frustrations she'd caused her teachers at Calhoun, Exeter, and Andover, Wendy had been paying attention.

It never occurred to Abby that her roommate was seriously struggling. Wendy joked about her bad grades, but she didn't seem that upset. Only once did Abby glimpse real distress, when Wendy got back a paper she'd labored over, an analysis of the William Faulkner short story "The Bear." After all her hard work, she received a D.

Abby also didn't notice they were drifting apart. In the spring they decided to room together again sophomore year. One day, without telling Abby why, Wendy said she'd changed her mind. She would be living in Pearson Annex, with a group of their friends from 1837. Abby was hurt and perplexed.

More than thirty years would pass before Abby learned the reason Wendy had reneged. The celebrated playwright had recently published a collection of essays, *Shiksa Goddess,* and sent the book to her former roommate, with whom she'd stayed in touch over the years. Abby had remained true to her academic interests. She earned her Ph.D. in psychology at Harvard and was a professor at the University of Michigan, in psychology and women's studies, as well as the director of the Institute for Research on Women and Gender.

Too busy to read Wendy's book when it arrived, she then forgot about it for several months.

One day she remembered *Shiksa Goddess.* She was about halfway through when she began to read the opening paragraph in an essay called "Women Beware Women."

"Women are the worst," Wendy wrote. "I will rot in hell for saying that. My toes will gnarl inward into tiny hooves, and I'll never dare to get another pedicure. All right. All right. Women are kind, decent, nurturing, the best friends women could ever have—until they're not. Then women can be the absolute worst."

Abby continued until she reached page 117 of the book, the middle of the essay. She stopped abruptly, feeling the years vanish. Once again she was a freshman at Mount Holyoke, wondering what she'd done to upset Wendy.

Two sentences explained everything.

"I moved out on my college roommate at a time when she thought we were the closest of friends," wrote Wendy. "She was too smart; I was flunking."

Then Abby realized how hard it must have been for Wendy to admit how bad she'd felt about her grades. Her nonchalance had been an act.

Abby called Wendy and apologized for taking so long to get to the book. She added, "Wendy, I didn't know you had something in there about us."

Wendy laughed and said, "I wondered if you'd ever notice."

Soon after they'd met, Abby had become aware of what she thought of as Wendy's "precocity worship." She often mentioned that Sandy and Bruce had entered Michigan when they were sixteen. *Franny and Zooey* came up in conversation more than once, Wendy consciously comparing her family to J. D. Salinger's fictional whiz kids. She told Abby how much she admired Bruce, who was a senior at Michigan, heading for Harvard Law School in the fall, and only twenty years old. He was the executive editor of the *Michigan Daily* and had his own column called "Publick Occurrences," after the independent newspaper published in Boston in 1690 and shut down by the British after one edition.

He and Sandy were the smart ones, Wendy said. She couldn't measure up to them.

Wendy depended on her sisters, frequently calling them to chat. Staying in touch required some effort in the era before cell phones and e-mail. In conversations with her roommate, Wendy was reverent toward Sandy, reciting her achievements as a woman executive, in awe of her independence, talent, toughness—the sum of which spelled success. Toward Georgette, Wendy was affectionate but critical of her conventional path. Sandy represented accomplishment, Georgette represented family happiness. Wendy said she felt pulled in both directions, but it was Sandy whom she idolized.

Abby had gotten a hint of the family's complexity during the World Youth Forum trip. There were those strange postcards from Lola—"Eating and thinking of you,"—which were funny and affectionate in one way, needling in another.

Wendy helped the long train and bus rides pass effortlessly, with her humorous tales of Lola and Morris and her siblings. She referred to another brother, Abner, who was sick and had been sent away. Wendy called him a "family secret." She said she didn't understand why he had essentially been obliterated by the family, who never referred to him. Abby saw that Wendy was troubled by this, but she didn't press for details, and none were offered.

When the girls returned from Europe, before college began, Abby visited Wendy at her apartment and met Lola and Morris. Abby felt she had stepped inside a vaudeville routine. There was no food in the house; Lola was always going off to dance class. Even their Thanksgiving meal was ordered in. The Wassersteins were different from Abby's parents, a lawyer father and a housewife mother.

Nothing about their behavior helped Abby understand Wendy's focus on her siblings' achievements—not at the time. "Morris was very, very sweet," said Abby. "It was very hard to get past sweet. He was a very lovely man who was very loving." Lola seemed more critical, Abby observed, but she found Wendy's mother "more strange than driven."

Camilla Peach, the head of hall for the 1837 dorm, was not amused by Wendy. In her evaluation she noted:

> Responsibility toward work in hall—poor
> Offices held in hall—none
> Qualities of leadership observed—none

"Wendy is a problem," Mrs. Peach wrote. "She is unkempt to say the least. Defiant when spoken to. I understand she's very bright. Her cooperation in the Hall is nil."

Mrs. Peach understood something about Wendy that other people missed. Wendy *was* defiant, though she usually couched her rebellion, as she did her unhappiness, in stories and jokes.

She also ate, ravenously, a simultaneous thumbing of the nose at Mrs. Peach and Lola. At Gracious Living, when other girls would eat daintily, mindful of squeezing into those silver lamé dresses, Wendy would wolf down two or three entire lemon meringue tarts, to the house mother's dismay.

Camilla Peach became a character in *Uncommon Women and Others,* Wendy's fictionalized account of her Mount Holyoke years. Mrs. Peach became Mrs. Plumm, the housemother at the unnamed girls' college where the play takes place.

Mrs. Plumm appears in an early scene. She introduces herself and welcomes the girls to tea.

> "Dear, take your feet off the table," she says, before continuing. "The tea fund was established by Lucy Valerie Bingsbee, class of 1906, after whom a Vermont orchid bog was recently dedicated by Governor Hoff at The Lucy Valerie Bingsbee Wildflower Sanctuary. I think you girls will find tea here very comfy. I knew Lucy. I never cared for her much."

Wendy came to appreciate both Mount Holyoke and Camilla Peach. She wrote to a friend, a few years after graduation, "Although I hated the reality of Mount Holyoke, recently I've become much more attached to the idea of it; the warmth, intelligence, and I guess (ha-ha) sincerity."

One of the people Wendy confided in during that troubling year was James Kaplan.

Before school started, the woman he was pursuing over the summer had made it clear she wasn't interested in him. He called Wendy and invited her to a football game at Yale, where he was a freshman. He was cautious; they kept things platonic. He was reserved, an understated young man, who tended to wear dark slacks and white shirts. Wendy gently mocked his reticence, referring to him as "Captain Charisma" when she discussed him with her girlfriends.

Wendy had an excuse to visit New Haven anyway; Georgette, Albert and their baby daughter, Tajlei, lived in Hamden, Connecticut, a short drive from Yale.

James was a safe confidant—close enough yet also distant. Wendy regaled him with stories of triumph and misery. She told him about scandalizing Mrs. Peach with her meringue-tart-eating escapades. She confessed that she was failing English and didn't know what she was doing at Mount Holyoke.

Her weight ballooned. Wendy told James she went to a therapist, who told her, unhelpfully, "You are what you eat."

James showed his affection for people by giving them nicknames. Wendy became "Dots," for her freckles, and then "Wemp" or "Wempell," his misreading of a letter Wendy showed him from Susan Gordis—an old friend from Ethical Culture. Susan called Wendy "Wendella," a mock Yiddishism. James became a sympathetic audience for Wendy's stories, mostly via the telephone, in conversations cut short by the lines that formed at the dorm pay phones.

By spring he'd become passionately involved elsewhere: Eugene McCarthy's campaign for the Democratic Party nomination against the incumbent, Lyndon B. Johnson. McCarthy had been gathering momentum since announcing his candidacy in November. He was running on a platform to end the war in Vietnam, a cause that struck a deep chord with young men facing the draft. His unofficial slogan became "Clean for Gene," referring to the college boys who shaved their beards and cut their hair to win votes for their progressive candidate from more conservative voters.

James was having his own freshman disillusionment at Yale. He felt trapped, unable to leave college or face induction into the army. He joined the campaign for McCarthy in New Hampshire, where the candidate's strong showing in March—42 percent of the vote to 49 percent for Johnson—indicated the divisiveness caused by the war. When Johnson pulled out of the race on March 31, the antiwar forces grew stronger and more determined to win. By then James was enrolled at Yale but was working almost full-time on the McCarthy campaign. He spent most of the spring in Wisconsin and, after that, Indiana, going door-to-door, working the phones, caught up in the exhilarating promise of changing the world.

He had no time to worry about Wendy and her revolt against Gracious Living. The concerns of campus life seemed meager compared with the weighty issues he was confronting on the campaign trail.

Midway through Wendy's freshman year, politics had finally begun percolating at Mount Holyoke. In February a new editorial board had taken over the *Mount Holyoke News* and changed the name to *Choragos.* In an impassioned announcement, the new editorial board explained:

> We are changing from passive reporters to active initiators of change with the goal of improvement. We no longer view our role solely as a mere commentator, a transmitter of information about what is already happening here. Rather we see ourselves in a leader's position, as an active force, an innovator. We will be talking about what could, and perhaps should, be happening here.
>
> Thus the name News, with its connotations of reporting only what is already being done by others, has become ill-fitted to our purposes. Choragos, the leader of the chorus in Greek drama, the one who asks questions and provokes discussion, is more in keeping with our new self image. . . .

At the end of April, for Fathers' Weekend, the Mount Holyoke College Dramatic Club staged a production of *Lysistrata,* the ancient Greek antiwar farce by Aristophanes, in which women refuse to have sex with their husbands until they end the Peloponnesian War with Sparta. Wendy was distraught because she'd been cast as a fat Corinthian woman. Instead of suffering the indignity, she dropped out of the play.

Visiting parents had their own problems with the Dramatic Club version of the play, performed in the amphitheater on a beautiful spring afternoon. Philippa Goold, a Latin and Greek professor who had been consulted for the production, suggested that the male actors brought in from Amherst wear balloon phalluses for comic effect. A recent arrival to the United States from Rhodesia (later to become Zimbabwe), she was surprised by the puritanical response to this bit of burlesque humor.

"The production was something of a disaster," she said. "It was 1968, and I thought anything would go. The parents were hideously upset. That's all I remember, is being dreadfully embarrassed afterward because everyone didn't take to it with the enthusiasm and joie de vivre I thought it would be greeted with."

This letter from an undergraduate student appeared in *Choragos*:

As I see it, the weekend was intended to please fathers and show them their annual $3,000 is going for a good purpose. I see no reason to prove our broadmindedness and freedom at the cost of shocking our fathers. My father has requested that I leave Mount Holyoke (and I am a junior).

On the other hand, Lorraine Garnett's father thought the play was hilarious. A working-class Italian American, he was unusual in the stuffy crowd of businessmen and professionals.

Lorraine, one of Wendy's dormmates, was hardly a radical, nor was she part of Wendy's crowd of misfits. Yet Wendy chose to live with Lorraine and her friends when her roommate Abby's good grades became too much of a burden for her to bear.

Their friendship developed a new dimension in May, when the Democratic National Committee offered free airplane tickets to students to campaign for McCarthy before the Indiana primary. Lorraine decided to go with some other girls from her dorm. Wendy went along.

Lorraine was struck by how innocent Wendy could seem, even though she was a savvy Manhattanite. Wendy *was* younger than most of them, thanks to Ethical Culture's having advanced her a grade. She turned seventeen the fall of freshman year and still seemed like a high-school kid. Lorraine felt protective toward her.

The Mount Holyoke "Clean for Gene" campaigners had a grand adventure. A Smith College alumna invited them to camp out in her house. They canvassed the area and attended a big rally where Robert Kennedy spoke. They felt themselves to be in the middle of enormous change, when anything could happen. Indiana was swarming with East Coast students. So it wasn't that unusual that Wendy saw James Kaplan there. The encounter was brief, just long enough to say hello.

By the end of freshman year, Wendy was eager for the familiar tumult of home.

Bruce was getting married on June 30, 1968, to his college sweetheart, Laura Lynne Killin, known as Lynne, who worked on the school newspaper with him. Bruce was overweight and slovenly, but Lynne was drawn to his personality and his power, already on exhibit at the *Michigan Daily*.

Her plan was to work for a while, save some money for a down payment on an apartment, and then start having children. "I wanted 2.5 kids, an English sheepdog, a vegetable and herb garden with a few roses," she said. It was 1968. Lynne was part of the transitional generation, when an educated woman's ambition didn't have to include conquering the world.

Neither family was happy, because they were young—Bruce was twenty—and because he was Jewish, she was Presbyterian.

Lynne had considered converting to Judaism in high school. On a church retreat, she'd had an epiphany: she didn't believe in the divinity of Jesus Christ. When she raised the matter with her parents, they objected, and she relented. When she and Bruce decided to marry, however, she became Jewish—not an easy process, requiring prolonged study with a rabbi.

A therapist would tell her that part of her attraction to Bruce was her desire to be married to his family. She adored Lola and loved Morris and Wendy. As an outsider she escaped Lola's criticism and felt only the warmth and engagement.

They married in her parents' living room, in Larchmont, an affluent suburb of New York. Bruce's family joined them on their honeymoon, at Lake Mohonk, just south of the Catskills, the same area where Bruce and Wendy used to play explorers in "Bruceania."

✦ ✦

That summer Wendy continued to think about James and what their future would be, if any. She'd been glad to see him in Indiana but didn't know if they had a relationship or not, or if that's what she wanted.

For him, politics had become everything. The stakes, he felt, were literally life and death. Exhausted and emotionally wrung out, he was devastated when Robert Kennedy won the important California primary in June, knocking McCarthy out of the race, only to immediately confront the shock of Kennedy's assassination, right after his acceptance speech. Martin Luther King Jr. had been shot two months earlier. Nothing about James's contained world on the Upper East Side or in New Haven made sense.

He felt immersed in madness. In August he and his college roommate traveled to Chicago for the melee called the Democratic National Convention. The city teemed with conventioneers, Yippies—the antiwar Youth International Party that specialized in street theater and public relations— and the Chicago police, who seemed intent on cracking as many heads as possible in the process of keeping the Yippies away from the convention.

James was at Grant Park when the Battle of Michigan Avenue erupted. The organizers of the rally at Grant Park had been issued a permit; the crowd was heavily weighted with youthful McCarthy supporters, like James, and middle-aged onlookers from the Conrad Hilton Hotel, where the conventioneers were staying. Mayor Richard Daley was hopped up on bluster and ego, driven to make it seem as though Chicago had things under control. He decided to crush the protesters, resulting in the spectacle of huge crowds of civilians being beaten by billy clubs and sprayed with tear gas.

When the political satirist Dick Gregory invited the demonstrators to come to his house on the South Side, James joined the vast, jostling parade until tanks blocked their way. He was stuck in Grant Park; his roommate had disappeared. When they found each other at McCarthy headquarters in the Hilton, his roommate told James that his mother had called, frantic, asking, "Is Jamey okay?"

Feeling defeated and worn, James returned to New York, not interested in joining his former McCarthy campaigners in their quixotic support for

Paul O'Dwyer. O'Dwyer, the Democratic nominee for U.S. senator from New York, was a lifelong pacifist who had opposed U.S. involvement in World War II. He was running against the liberal Republican, the venerable Senator Jacob K. Javits, ready to serve his third term. O'Dwyer didn't have a chance.

James was tired of lost causes. But he couldn't say no to the friend who asked him to hand out O'Dwyer campaign buttons over Labor Day weekend. Walking uptown along Fifth Avenue, he bumped into Wendy, going the other way.

He thought she looked great. She had lost weight since he'd last seen her, and her freckles had multiplied over the summer. Hearing her sweet, high voice came as a balm after the terror and disappointments of the past months. As they talked, he felt human again. She seemed to understand what he was saying in a way other people didn't. Her unrestrained giggle captured the absurdity of life, but without meanness.

He told her about his adventures on the McCarthy campaign and the horrors of the Democratic Convention. It had all taken place only a month earlier but now seemed vague, like a page out of history, far removed from the pleasant feeling he was having just talking to Wendy on a sun-drenched afternoon in New York. She listened sympathetically. Then, laughing, she told him about her flirtation with the New Majority for Rockefeller, a group of liberal students who supported the presidential candidacy of Nelson Rockefeller, the New York governor considered a moderate Republican, hoping he would fend off the darker forces represented by Richard Nixon, the candidate who won.

She'd flown down to Miami for the convention with a friend and returned disappointed but wearing an amusing souvenir: a dress with Nelson Rockefeller's picture on it. James envied her ability to find humor in the grave moment in which they were living.

She switched directions to walk with him. They continued up Fifth Avenue, talking and laughing their way into Central Park. How could he remain miserable, standing with a bright, engaging woman on Bethesda Terrace, overlooking the lake, a romantic prospect filled with ducks splashing and rowboats rocking. All of a sudden, it felt good to be home.

Wendy took James back to her parents' apartment. She became the first woman he slept with; he wasn't sure if the sexual initiation was reciprocal. (It doesn't seem to have been. Wendy alluded to at least one previous sexual encounter.) He no longer was put off by her intensity. Now he liked it.

Holyoke classmates Mary Jane Patrone and
Harriet Sachs came to represent the New Woman,
and remained Wendy's friends for life.

Five

GREAT EXPECTATIONS

1968–71

Mount Holyoke may have seemed like a finishing school when Wendy entered as a freshman, but the administration was not oblivious to the revolution taking place outside. In 1967 a report written by the admissions director expressed concern about the continued relevance of women's colleges. Applications had dropped at all the women's schools, except Radcliffe. The director cited two troubling magazine articles, published in the summer of 1967, one in *Mademoiselle* and the other in *Seventeen.* According to the author of the *Mademoiselle* article, the director observed, "the cream is thinning out, the life-style on these campuses is puritanical and drudgery pervades Mondays through Fridays; the colleges do not prepare graduates for today's world, students emerge exhausted and deflated, ambition is squelched."

The *Seventeen* article concluded that the isolated women's college "simply can't do its job as effectively today as it did when it was founded back in the nineteenth century." These articles were worrisome. "Both of these magazines are widely read by all teenage girls and they cannot help but have had some effect upon attitudes," the director concluded.

During Wendy's sophomore year, a new student handbook was drafted. When it was finished, in time for the freshman class entering in 1969,

Gracious Living would no longer be mandatory but rather decided by students in each residence hall. Two new categories were added:

> DRUGS: Mount Holyoke College cannot tolerate the use of narcotics or other drugs except under strict medical supervision. . . .
>
> PARIETALS: Male guests may be received in the dormitories at any time during the open hours of the dormitories. . . .

By the middle of Wendy's sophomore year, Mount Holyoke had become a different place. The smell of rebellion—and marijuana—was in the air. Undergraduate women took pains to say "fuck" whenever they could and to smoke weed as often as cigarettes. The Pill had opened the door to sexual freedom, but only for those over twenty-one; parental consent was required before a doctor could prescribe birth control to an unmarried "minor" woman. "Female matters" that had once been hidden became public and politicized. In 1969 a group of women in Boston began teaching a course that ultimately became *Our Bodies, Ourselves*, the landmark book that provided detailed information about birth control, venereal disease, lesbianism, childbirth, and menopause. Its calm, practical advice and graphic pictures became required reading. That same year Germaine Greer, the Australian academic and feminist writer, was working on the manuscript for *The Female Eunuch*, published in 1970, which argued that women were cut off from their own sexuality. Commentators often ignored Greer's serious points, preferring to highlight the ideas loaded with shock value— urging women to taste their own menstrual blood, for example.

Yet for Wendy the most significant event that year came outside the political realm. Wendy's friend Ruth Karl insisted that they take a drama class together at Smith College.

Ruth thought of Wendy as a complete original, unlike anyone else she'd met at Holyoke. One day when they were listening to the record album of the Cole Porter musical *Anything Goes*, Wendy figured out the choreography to a tap-dance number just from the sound of the taps. Most women on campus were stamped from the same fashion mold: long straight hair parted in the middle, jeans and a loose blouse or sweater. Wendy showed up wearing a black dress and black tights and a big shawl.

She was reluctant to take the drama course at first; she was a history major—how did this fit into the picture? It didn't seem serious. Ruth convinced her it would be worthwhile.

They were not an obvious match as friends. Ruth looked like a magazine cover girl, one of Wendy's "shiksa goddesses"—honey-blond hair, high cheekbones, and a heart-shaped face, with a demure expression that belied a gleefully foul mouth. She liked to provoke. Ruth was the one in their group who followed Germaine Greer's advice and tasted her own menstrual blood. She was a scholarship student who'd grown up in a Philadelphia suburb as part of a family she felt didn't have many worthwhile expectations of her.

Ruth found they could talk endlessly about everything, including and especially sex (Ruth's specialty, not Wendy's). Wendy was terrified of becoming pregnant. She was worried about James, who was freaking out about the war—about politics, about her, about everything. She was angry at him for dating other women, even though they hadn't exactly committed to each other.

Ruth recognized Wendy's affection for James but heard much more about her family. That bond seemed far deeper. Ruth had the sense that boyfriends weren't all that important to Wendy. "They were just something you were supposed to have," she said. "Family was important."

This was alien to Ruth. "I tended to throw my life away for a man," she said. "I was brought up to believe that was what you were supposed to do."

They enrolled in the course at Smith as part of the then-four-college consortium—Amherst, Mount Holyoke, Smith, and the University of Massachusetts Amherst that allowed students to take courses at one another's campuses, so long as the same course wasn't offered at a student's home base. A free bus connected the colleges, scattered in the Pioneer Valley region, but it was sporadic, so the students often hitchhiked.

Ruth and Wendy made up names for themselves when they thumbed rides, finding this game hilarious, too. Wendy always chose a blatantly non-Jewish name and pretended she was from the Midwest, saying things like, "We call soda 'pop' where I come from."

At Smith, Ruth and Wendy took playwriting with Leonard Berkman, a professor in his first year there, having arrived with a freshly minted doctoral degree from Yale School of Drama. Wendy found Berkman to be warm and familiar, a quirky Brooklyn Jew who showed up in class with a ponytail, a peace-symbol necklace, and high-top Converse sneakers in a variety of colors.

Although Wendy had performed and worked backstage on many school productions, it wasn't until Berkman's class that she began to grasp the mechanics involved in writing a play. For the first time, she was forced to think about how her words would translate into action. Wendy's debut effort for the class was called *Velveteen Goes to Taco Bell,* about a girl who goes to a Taco Bell drive-in restaurant in California, gets torpedoed by five hundred burritos, and then eats her way out.

The professor explained that no actor would be willing or able to do that every night.

He recognized an intriguing, unexpected impertinence beneath Wendy's shy exterior. For a playwriting exercise, she turned in a scene that involved women doing battle by throwing bloody Kotex at one another. "She shivered to share with the class," he said, "and finally I did encourage her to do it because it was so incredibly bold and wonderful and new."

Lightning didn't strike for either professor or pupil. Berkman didn't predict future stardom for Wendy, but he believed that something important happened for her in his class: "She found what she had to say could be said."

Wendy agreed. After years of academic stress, she reconnected with the pleasure in learning she'd had as a child at Ethical Culture. "This was the first time I realized that a person could get credit in life for what they liked to do," she said of Berkman's class. That realization would become more potent over time.

During Wendy's sophomore year, several of the all-male and all-female colleges decided to experiment with trial periods of coeducation. Wendy, eager for a change, was accepted into the program at all-male Amherst.

That spring, at a meeting for the women going there, she sat next to Mary Jane Patrone, a classmate she'd first met in 1837 Hall.

Mary Jane had gone to a Catholic girls' school for her entire education before Holyoke. Wendy's vaudevillian New York humor perplexed her. For example, Wendy always greeted her by saying, with a grin, "Your father is the dean of Northwestern Law School, right?"

Mary Jane's father wasn't an academic or a lawyer, though she was from Glenview, Illinois, a suburb of Chicago. "Who is this person who would say that?" Mary Jane wondered. She was too shy to correct Wendy, so she just giggled and kept quiet.

After thirteen years of nuns, irreverence didn't come naturally to Mary Jane. Through Wendy, she came to understand that you could be irreverent without being obnoxious.

They ended up together by default. Mary Jane's two best friends were taking a year abroad in Greece that year, and she didn't know any of the other women going to Amherst. Ruth Karl, Wendy's friend, couldn't do the program because she was on scholarship.

As the representative from Amherst went over various procedural matters, it dawned on Wendy and Mary Jane that all the women were going to be stuck in an old, funky freshman dorm.

"We're going to be juniors," she said to Mary Jane. "We're grown-ups. Why don't we say we don't think we should live there?"

They complained, and when they arrived at Amherst in the fall, they were assigned to Stone, a dorm much nicer than the one they'd originally been assigned to, divided into little suites, some all female and some all male. Mary Jane suspected that Wendy cared less about the integrated aspect and more about the improvement in living quarters. Wendy liked creature comforts.

The so-called Exchange Program was an odd, timid experiment. At Amherst twenty-three women were brought in for one semester to test the coeducational waters in a sea of 1,208 undergraduate men. The women felt like specimens in a jar. Mary Jane in particular attracted attention. She had long dark hair, intense eyes, and obvious sexual potential lurking beneath her blushing shyness—"an incredible hottie," a male classmate remembered.

Mary Jane felt under siege. Entering the dining hall, where the ratio of men to women was about 50 to 1, brought back the worst possible memories of high school, of being excluded from every clique. Only here it was worse. Instead of dealing with the snits of adolescent girls, something she knew how to do, she had to contend with legions of sex-starved college men accustomed to an all-male environment. She used to ask Wendy to make incursions into the cafeteria—enemy terrain—to grab peanut butter and jelly sandwiches and bring them back to their room for dinner, rather than face the leering crowd.

Male professors made rude jokes. Wendy's history professor bemoaned having to teach young women who would end up hanging their education on the clothesline. Mary Jane's psychology professor asked her repeatedly, "Which finishing school are you from? I can't remember."

When she received the highest grade on an exam, he gave her a backhanded apology in front of the class. "Mary Jane is a sterling example that intelligence might not in fact be sex-based," he said.

Mary Jane began dating one of the coolest guys on campus, a drummer from Montpelier, Vermont, who was aggressively eccentric in his dress and demeanor. He wore hot pink slacks. Wendy felt envious and acted disdainful, as though she wondered why this guy from the middle of nowhere was trying to be so hip. She dubbed the young man Montpelier Pa-zazz. He would have an offstage cameo role in *Uncommon Women,* where he would be referred to as Pink Pants.

Pink Pants also became the title character in *Montpelier Pa-zazz,* one of Wendy's earliest plays.

Mary Jane became Dottie, "the most popular girl in the class," who sits on her bed wearing a thin undershirt and bikini underpants. Her best friend, Bunny—the Wendy character—"enters in layers of clothing, work shirt, turtleneck sweater, kilt rolled around her waist because it is too tight."

Bunny says to Dottie, "With a girl like you around, Dottie, a girl like me doesn't stand a chance."

The line reflects Wendy's experience at Amherst. Men panted when they met Mary Jane; they liked to talk and have a laugh with Wendy.

⚘ ⚘

As turmoil became the operating mode on college campuses, Wendy was participant and observer, registering the details that would become part of a generation's collective memory. At Amherst strikes and upheaval became the unofficial curriculum. On December 2, 1969, the draft lottery ended exemptions for college students. The *Amherst Student,* the school newspaper, published a special report, "Drugs and the Campus." Students voted to abolish the student council. Black undergraduates from the Five Colleges—by then, Hampshire College had joined the consortium—occupied four buildings on the Amherst campus; a year later the university established a black-studies program.

The tinderbox exploded after President Richard Nixon announced, on April 30, 1970, that U.S. troops were invading Cambodia, an escalation of the Vietnam War. Student demonstrations erupted on campuses around the country. On May 4 the unthinkable happened. The Ohio National Guard opened fire on student demonstrators. A stunned generation witnessed the spectacle of military police murdering four unarmed civilian undergraduates. With the nightmare that became known as the Kent State massacre, college-age Boomers lost the last shred of their innocence. Amherst joined the nationwide call for strikes on campus.

Women decided to agitate for their rights as well. The female undergraduates at Amherst wanted to stay at Amherst past the one-year experiment. Other schools were going coed; Abby Stewart remained at Wesleyan, which had agreed to let its visiting women stay on.

At Amherst Wendy volunteered to help argue the cause before the Amherst faculty; she was one of a group of uninvited women who crashed a tense faculty meeting, adding to an already charged agenda, filled with demands for black representation, Marxist reform, budgetary overhaul, reassessment of grades.

Amherst didn't accept women for another five years, for the graduating class of 1975–76.

Carole Warshaw, one of those who stormed the faculty meeting with Wendy, considered herself a Marxist revolutionary. Wendy was a reluctant radical, but the two women became friends.

One day Carole was invited by Tillie Olsen, the feminist writer, to participate in a women's consciousness-raising session; Olsen was teaching at Amherst that year, her focus on poverty and oppression.

Carole brought Wendy along. Most of the other fifteen or twenty women who came to the lunch were faculty wives, women who had Ph.D.'s but not jobs.

Wendy didn't talk much, but she was listening, with startling acuity.

In *The Heidi Chronicles*, written almost twenty years later, she recapitulated the lunch. The play isn't a diary—Wendy always allowed herself much poetic license—but it captures the serious frustration of the women without overlooking the earnest foolishness that was part of the moment. In the play the women's meeting takes place in Ann Arbor, Michigan.

Heidi, the Wendy character, remains silent throughout the discussion. One of the women tells Becky and Heidi, the newcomers, that Fran, in addition to being a gifted physicist, is a lesbian and that the group supports her choice to sleep with women.

Fran turns to Heidi. "Do you support my choice, Heidi?"

Heidi responds, "I'm just visiting."

Heidi's waffling reflects Wendy's own confusion and self-doubt, her feeling of not being part of the group. Her need for self-protection could trip off inconsiderate, even cruel behavior when she felt threatened, as she was by Abby Stewart's superior grades. Rather than confront, she fled.

When she was overcome by ambivalence toward James Kaplan, she simply avoided him.

The summer before Wendy went to Amherst, she and James spent a great deal of time together, seeing movies and plays, enjoying the city they both loved. Wendy was on hiatus from academic and political concerns, working at a comfortable, dull job as a receptionist in a dentist's office on Central Park South. They were cautious, but they had romantic moments, most memorably on July 20, 1969. Walking across Central Park under a starry sky, they came across a crowd in the Sheep Meadow gathered in front of giant video monitors. Wendy and James paused to watch Neil

Armstrong become the first man to walk on the moon and listened to the crowd cheer, a peaceful mirage of national unity at a fractious time.

For James this became a romantic memory. For Wendy the evening became material. In 2002, writing about the importance of Shakespeare in the Park for the *New York Times,* she recalled the evening fondly— minus James. He wasn't the only detail Wendy altered. To make her point, she substituted Shakespeare's *Twelfth Night* for Ibsen's *Peer Gynt,* which was actually playing at Central Park's Delacorte Theater that night. And, to serve her story, she changed the time of day Neil Armstrong took that first step on the moon.

James thought he was her boyfriend. His earlier casual attitude had changed to a more intense desire. True to the yin-yang pattern of their relationship, his willingness to become close made her pull away; her withdrawal only made him want to draw closer. Her hesitancy was encouraged by the general tumult and by James's particular neediness and extreme emotional distress. At Amherst, with its ridiculously skewed male-female ratio, she saw his shortcomings more clearly.

She had learned to recognize the signs of infatuation, from men who longed for Mary Jane. No matter how much affection James professed, he never looked at her like that. She still felt the sting of his comments about her weight, even though he now wanted to be with her.

It wasn't that she didn't like him. She did. But he wasn't a dashing iconoclast like Montpelier Pa-zazz, or even her brother Bruce. No matter how much James complained about the System, he was headed to law school—or worse (in Wendy's imagination), his father's textile business. When she told James about breaking into the faculty meeting at Amherst, he didn't take her that seriously.

"Settle down," he said, but then brought it up when she lost interest in him, to coax her back. "What happened to the Amherst Women's Caucus?" he would ask.

She told herself that he was on a conventional path, which—if she married him—put her in danger of becoming a Shirley, à la *Marjorie Morningstar.*

When he had an emotional crisis and needed her help, she wasn't there for him.

She detached; he pleaded.

Dear Wemp,

I'm sitting here trying to do my work which I'm way behind on, but I'm really upset because I haven't been able to talk to you in so long. I must have tried to give you at least 51 phone calls in the last week, but I've never been able to get through. You see I'm having an acute Wemp crisis (and have been all week) and an acute case of James paranoia. I <u>really</u> miss you and love you and really want to see you. Finally I guess after having got a long no answer on your phone for about the fiftieth time I'm taking the unprecedented step of writing you. I don't know why it's so unprecedented, but I feel like it just is. I'm really afraid that because there's been so little communication between us in the last two weeks suddenly I'm going to talk to you and discover that you're on an entirely different wave length and we won't be speaking the same language. I don't know maybe I'm not now.

I hate to tell you why I'm so upset or feel like I'm trying to bother you with my hassles, but then if I can't tell you who can I tell? You see in a way it's like communicating with you makes my life important and when our communication is shut off life no longer is so important. That's why it was so awful at the times you didn't show up to see me when you said you were coming. . . .

I'm really upset because it seems like the whole world is falling around me. I don't want to go into any political bullshit about what's happening in this country or what's happening at Yale. Your roommates told me you were really working on the strike at Amherst. They told me, but I don't know. You see I decided that political events don't affect people in the abstract. They either affect you directly or not at all. That's why it's so much more important to me that I haven't spoken with you, than that Nixon invaded Cambodia. You see I'm really afraid that concurrent with the fall of the external world my private world is beginning to fall as well. I really hope I'm not "a luxury you can no longer afford." But if I am I wish you'd please tell me and not leave me in this damn uncertainty. I guess like you said you had with me, I've come to depend on your love and the thought of losing you really hurts me. I really do love you very much. Maybe I'm just really afraid of uncertainty. Like right now the future is very uncertain.

. . . I really love you and need you. The thing I hate though is the continual uncertainty about our relationship and my doubts about whether what you say is true one day will be true the next. I understand that it's a big hassle to have to pay for a phone call to me, but from now on I promise any time you call me you can call collect. Please call collect, but call me. Love James

PS: How are your dots?

They resumed their relationship, but he wasn't a priority for her when she returned to Mount Holyoke for her senior year. Her primary concern was to figure out what to do next. Lola was pushing hard for law school, and Wendy hadn't found a better idea for her future. She wasn't alone. The women she lived with that year felt anxious about having to face the world. These doubts, unremarkable for seniors about to graduate, were compounded by the enormous flux that made every choice seem questionable. The political climate imposed an inflated sense of self-importance, but also a feeling of great vulnerability. They propped one another up and assumed a pose of bawdy sophistication. It would be years before they managed to stop referring to their dorm as "North *Fucking* Mandelle."

Mary Jane was part of the North Mandelle group, though she almost went the way of Abby Stewart and James Kaplan. Over the summer, home in Glenview, Illinois, she received a letter from Wendy saying she didn't want to room together. "The past year has just been too difficult for me," Wendy wrote. "It's just too hard, I'm putting it behind me."

Before school began, Wendy changed her mind.

Mary Jane saved the letter for twenty years and then threw it away. She hated the way it made her feel. The year at Amherst had been so strange, not least because of all the men who'd paid attention to her. She knew she hadn't handled the situation well. She understood that Wendy might have been jealous, although they'd never discussed it. Mary Jane felt that their friendship really began senior year, when they were away from the odd pressure of being rare specimens at Amherst.

Besides Mary Jane and Ruth, their group included Harriet Sachs, back from a year abroad in Greece.

Harriet was from Montreal and always—to the other girls—seemed very sure of herself. She would become the inspiration for the character Kate in *Uncommon Women and Others.*

Harriet was one of the 1837 "misfits." She saw Wendy as a kindred spirit, a Jewish girl from a big city, out of place in the prim Wasp propriety of Mount Holyoke. Like Wendy, Harriet was younger than the other girls, only sixteen when she arrived at Mount Holyoke, but accustomed to adult freedom. The summer before she started college, she had a job at Expo 67, the World's Fair held in Montreal. She finished work at 2:00 A.M. and then went out to party at discotheques; she dated an "older man," a law student in his twenties.

After freshman year they drifted apart. Harriet became obsessed with another man, and then they took their junior years away from Holyoke— Wendy at Amherst, Harriet in Greece. Reunited senior year at North Mandelle, they once again felt themselves outsiders. The dorm had become a center for the campus black-power movement, and there was tension between the black and white students. Harriet and Wendy felt particularly sensitive, being Jewish, feeling they were being identified with slum landlords oppressing black people. Amiri Baraka, the poet formerly known as LeRoi Jones, had become a potent cultural figure, declaring himself a black nationalist—and he had divorced his Jewish wife, Hettie (née Cohen). With the self-dramatization of college students, Harriet and Wendy saw themselves as aligned with the enemy.

It was a difficult year on all fronts. Wendy took her law boards and scored unimpressively, in the fiftieth percentile. When someone asked Ruth what she planned to do when she grew up, she shrugged and said, "I'm going to be a fertility goddess." Wendy then dubbed her "Fertila T," and Ruth called Wendy "Responsibilia," referring to Wendy's continued arguments with the committee on academic responsibility about long-overdue library books.

For a senior project, Wendy compiled a mock "handbook for seniors," weighing various alternatives for the future. *Great Expectations* was the title; the cover was a full-page picture of a very pregnant woman. Wendy stapled together applications to graduate school, forms for "vocational planning and placement," and ads for wedding rings.

As graduation came closer, Wendy felt panicky. She hadn't gotten into a single law school and dreaded going home to contend with Lola. Harriet was *stoned* when she took the LSATs and got in. But then Harriet was Phi Beta Kappa, whereas Wendy "Responsibilia" was almost denied her diploma because of those library books.

Gretchen Scarry came to the rescue with an invitation to spend the summer in California.

Gretchen was a Smith College student who had performed in many plays at Amherst. After Wendy returned to Holyoke for her senior year, both she and Gretchen continued to spend a great deal of time at Amherst, working on plays. Wendy didn't talk about a career in theater, but it had become a refuge for her, a natural extension of her inclination to inhale the raw material of life and exhale a comedy routine or a story.

The pinnacle of their Amherst theater career came senior year. They became part of an of-the-moment production of *Peter Pan*, reconfigured as a radical treatise, in which the Lost Boys were hippies. Peter Pan was played by a black man, Tinker Bell by a gay man. Wendy choreographed the play; Gretchen was cast as one of the Lost Boys.

Peter Pan had always had special significance for Wendy. There was the obvious connection of her name, the link to Sandy and childhood. She had fond memories of starring in a summer-camp production. The story's magical quality of perpetual innocence continued to be part of Wendy's aura, even though her perceptions about people could be ironic and quite adult.

It was during the Amherst production that Gretchen recognized Wendy's talent—not as a writer but as a choreographer. All those years at the June Taylor dance studio had left an imprint. Gretchen was impressed by the elaborate sequences Wendy plotted out for *Peter Pan* (especially the tap routine she choreographed for a song called "Wendy").

Right before graduation Gretchen was informed that Smith wouldn't give her credit for a class she'd taken at Hampshire College, which had just opened with an experimental program. But Smith would accept credits for a dance course Gretchen found at California State University at Long Beach, California, that she could complete the summer after senior year. She asked Wendy to come along.

It didn't take much convincing for Wendy to exchange the gloomy prospect of rattling around New York, being nagged by Lola while avoiding and pursuing James Kaplan. A summer by the beach, with a continent between all that, seemed perfect. This would become another pattern of Wendy's. If someone invited her somewhere, she went. Like her parents, she kept in motion. (Morris was said to wear out three pairs of guaranteed-for-life ripple-soled shoes a year, probably a Wasserstein exaggeration but accurately reflecting his love of walking.)

She set out for California with Gretchen and Nancy Steele, a friend of Gretchen's who was a dancer, too. The three of them drove across the country—or rather Gretchen and Nancy drove. Wendy didn't have a driver's license; this wasn't unusual for someone raised in New York City.

Wendy was that peculiar breed, the New York provincial—the type who can rattle off the names of Broadway directors and Greek gods and has visited the major European capitals but has never ordered french fries at a drive-in window. For her the California world of fast-food joints like Taco Bell and Jack in the Box was exotic and mystifying. She had a dorm room but spent most of her time at the little apartment that Gretchen rented a block from the beach. They swam in the ocean and entered a go-go-dancing contest at a hotel. They ogled their gorgeous dance professor, William Couser, an avant-garde choreographer who blended primitive, folk, and jazz techniques and used performance to reflect on the condition of the black race.

Wendy liked Gretchen, but it was Ruth Karl who, in absentia, became her partner in misery, as well as an appreciative audience for her adventures and concerns that summer. In long letters they commiserated with each other about their failed attempts at losing weight and their lack of direction. It was hard for Wendy to talk about dieting with lithe Gretchen, who was sympathetic but who could also gorge without noticeable consequence.

When Wendy sent Ruth a detailed explanation of a lecture she'd heard about the relationship between movement, self-image, and the potential for change, Ruth gave a comforting reply:

My dearest Wendella,

Your exercise on self-image and movement was fascinating but I forget what movement means. I've reached unprecedented dissipation. You would have been so proud of me today. I consumed a whole 39 cent Hershey Almond Chocolate Bar, among other things. I've abandoned all hopes of will power. Tomorrow my 3 week supply of super duper time capsule Benzedex diet pills is arriving. Better living through chemistry.

I hope to find a waitress job tomorrow, if I can summon up the energy. Then I'll have a little "bread" for the move to the big city. . . .

<u>*A Mini heavy*</u>

I think life is a pile of shit. I will sell my soul, body and anything else I can get my hands on to construct a safer little world of my own. I don't think I can change the world. Even if I could and did, people would fuck it up again. Have I turned into a no-good capitalist pig? If so, do you still like me? Also, I hate men. And most women.

Love, Ruth

Wendy replied in kind:

Dear Ruth,

Got jealous of your dissipation so Gretchen and I went out and outdid you—a Hershey Almond bar and P'nut butter. Eat Your Heart Out. I am marshmallow woman. Each day I vow to the goddess of thin woman . . . that I will become asparagus queen—and then a sugges-

tion from a friend and I'm back in candy land. To put it bluntly, Lola was right. I'm not a mensch.

Despite her self-flagellation, Wendy enjoyed herself that summer. She said she was happy. "I *am* living the good life," she wrote. "Protein, dance and fun in neon city. It is a bit like being in a health spa with decorations furnished by McDonald's. . . ."

Yet she knew that her romance with L.A. was just a summer fling. As the return home to New York approached, she remained worried about her future.

"Did you ever think you could be great *if only*," she wrote to Ruth. "I live in the fantasy where that *if only* doesn't exist. In reality it looks larger every day."

Part Two

BECOMING A WRITER

1971–80

WENDY'S SIBLINGS SEEMED TO KNOW WHERE THEY WERE GOING,
BUT AFTER GRADUATING FROM HOLYOKE SHE WAS FLOUNDERING.
HERE WITH SISTERS SANDY AND GEORGETTE.

Six

THE FUNNIEST GIRL IN NEW YORK

1971–73

"Wendy, you make me want to blechhh," Lola said to her in exasperation one day. "You know what blechhh is?"

Wendy knew exactly what "blechhh" was, especially after Lola put her hand to her mouth and pretended to retch.

"Why don't you do something?" Lola snapped.

Wendy decided to make a play for maternal sympathy.

"Mother, I'm not feeling well, I've been feeling sad lately."

A futile gesture.

Lola turned to Wendy, ready to pounce. "What have you got to be sad about? Did your husband die? Did your son get sick?"

Up until that moment, Wendy had no idea that Lola had had a first husband, much less one who'd died.

In the torrent that followed, she forgot to ask her mother who that husband was—or knew better than to delve into family secrets, or was afraid to pursue a line of questioning whose answers might be too disturbing.

"No one has put into their children what I put into you, and this is the thank-you I get?" Lola said. "Who knows? Maybe I didn't do the right thing. Maybe I shouldn't have been there. You know, if I was your age—if I had been born when you were born—I could have been a dancer or a designer. I wouldn't have wasted my life putting it all into you!"

Wendy couldn't remember any more of the conversation, except that Lola's hands were shaking, that she was crying, and that she grabbed her bag and slammed the door, yelling as she left, "I have to go kick-kick. I have to work you out of my system!"

It's fair to say that in the fall of 1971, after Wendy returned from California, things were not going well. Despite her persistent self-doubt and her inability to be svelte, she had always felt she held a charmed spot in the family, the delightful child who entertained everyone else. Now she had a new role—the loser. What did she have to show for her Seven Sisters education? No prospects for a job and no husband on the horizon—or not one she wanted.

Look at her siblings! Sandy was remarried, to a man named Peter Schweitzer, who had been a fellow executive at General Foods and had movie-star looks, a Robert Redford type. She continued to rise through the corporate ranks. Wendy always said her sister had invented Tang, the powdered fruit drink the astronauts took to the moon. Actually, she'd managed the brand, less sexy but important enough, a breakthrough job for a woman. Sandy had accomplished all that and had a baby girl, Jenifer, born Thanksgiving weekend, 1969. Her second child, Samantha, was born in 1972, also during the holidays. Each time Sandy returned to work two weeks after giving birth. She subverted her company's mandatory pregnancy leave by renting a hotel room across from General Foods headquarters and installing her secretary there, so she could keep working.

Georgette and Albert were still living in New Haven, where Georgette had provided Lola and Morris with two granddaughters, Tajlei and Melissa.

Bruce, only three years older than Wendy, already had a joint degree from Harvard Law School and Harvard Business School. While he was still in law school, he coedited a book with Mark J. Green, known as a top lieutenant in Nader's Raiders, the collection of disciples who flocked to Washington, D.C., to work for Ralph Nader, the consumer advocate. Bruce himself had worked for Nader one summer while he was at Harvard.

The Green-Wasserstein collaboration, called *With Justice for Some: An Indictment of the Law by Young Advocates,* is an idealistic collection of thirteen essays by law students and recent law graduates, manuscript typed by Bruce's wife, Lynne. In a passionate editors' note, Green and Wasserstein discuss their aim: "The chapters of this book probe the failures of contemporary law, offer proposals for change, and describe some victims—blacks, women, students, servicemen, consumers, the poor."

By the time Wendy returned from college, Bruce had changed course, moving away from worry about institutional injustices toward his future in mergers and acquisitions. He won a fellowship to study law and economics at Cambridge University and spent a year abroad with Lynne. After that he assured Lynne he would be ready to start a family. He wanted no fewer than five children—a dynasty, like the Rothschilds.

No wonder Wendy felt like taking to bed.

"I know I have to leave here," she wrote to Ruth Karl. "The dust on the piano was shaped into 'Wendy get married' when I woke up this morning."

The family got together frequently. Outsiders (and the children's spouses fell into this category) were treated warmly but were aware that they would never be part of the inner circle. "I felt absolutely welcomed into the family," said Peter Schweitzer, Sandra 's second husband. "But it was very difficult. You're in a room where you're almost constantly competing. They're all high achievers, highly intelligent. There wasn't a lot of goofing around playing touch football. You always had to be at your intellectual best. It can be tiring."

None of the children were exempt from Lola's sharp appraisals, although Wendy couldn't help but notice that she was often criticized for flaws that went unnoticed in Bruce. Like Wendy, Bruce was overweight and sloppy, and he had the same flat feet as his younger sister. In his case these attributes—along with his poor eyesight—became pluses, exempting him from the draft. In Wendy's case . . . blechhh.

The previous spring Wendy had been talking to David Rimmer about their post-graduation plans. They'd met at Amherst, where they both were involved in theater. He was shaggy-haired and lanky, with off-center, almost-handsome good looks. After Kent State, and the subsequent eruptions on campus, Rimmer had contacted local high schools and community colleges in the area. He offered to produce some of their Amherst plays about Vietnam and racism and other political issues. Wendy became part of the traveling consciousness-raising dramatic troupe, working as a crew member.

They became even closer friends senior year, when Rimmer directed the *Peter Pan* that Wendy had choreographed.

With graduation weighing on them, the two sat around with a group of friends wondering what they were going to do the following year. Rimmer mentioned a possibility. One of the political plays he'd taken on the road at Amherst was written by Israel Horovitz, a playwright whose work had been making a stir in New York. He'd won several prizes, including an Obie Award for *The Indian Wants the Bronx,* which starred an impressive emerging young actor, Al Pacino, also awarded an Obie for his performance. Rimmer had gotten to know Horovitz, who liked the student director's moxie and took him under his wing. Horovitz was teaching a playwriting workshop at City College in New York in the fall, part of a new master's program in creative writing. He told Rimmer he should sign up.

Rimmer didn't have an agenda beyond "why not?" When Wendy told him she was going to apply to law school, he said, "I've got this playwriting workshop thing with Israel. You want to join me?"

It was an easy decision. She, too, had nothing else to do.

Things were looser then. The English department at City College had just announced the creative-writing program in April, five months before it was to begin. Besides Horovitz's drama course, the teachers included Gwendolyn Brooks, the Pulitzer Prize–winning poet, and Joseph Heller, whose 1961 novel *Catch-22* had become a cultural phenomenon, its wild black humor and antiwar attitude resonating with the Vietnam generation. Only twenty students were to be admitted.

New York City, 1971, was Fear City, dirty and dangerous. The crime rate had been soaring throughout the 1960s; 1,823 murders were committed the year Wendy came home, up from 548 in 1963. Racial and generational tensions were high. Two years earlier Mario Puzo's bestselling novel *The Godfather* elevated the Mafia to mythic status, with its romantic/realistic rendering of the illicit world of drugs and racketeering. Though the story was set in the 1940s and '50s, the book's cynical vision of capitalism and crime meshed with the country's general sense of unease.

As the war in Vietnam dragged on, grit and disillusion had become the cultural norms, in politics and in art. The top-secret Department of Defense documents that became known as the "Pentagon Papers"—which detailed U.S. involvement in Vietnam since 1945—were leaked to the press by Daniel Ellsberg that summer. In November David Rabe's *Sticks and Bones* opened at the Public Theater, about a soldier's return from Vietnam and his family's inability to comprehend what their blinded son has gone through or who he has become. The play was a sequel to Rabe's *The Basic Training of Pavlo Hummel,* the brutal portrait of a young American soldier in Vietnam, written from Rabe's experience. The Oscar for Best Picture that year went to *The French Connection,* William Friedkin's streetwise, nerve-racking action movie about cops and narcotics smugglers

For the new college graduate, New York could be exciting or dispiriting, depending on the day, but in either case it was not the same place Wendy had left behind. Both she and her city had gone through sobering changes. She'd been a girl when she left; now she was supposed to be an adult, or on the way to becoming one.

Through David Rimmer, Wendy had grown somewhat friendly with Israel Horovitz. In addition to taking his playwriting seminar, a couple of times she baby-sat for his three children (one of whom was Adam Horovitz, who later became Ad-Rock, of the band the Beastie Boys). Rimmer had been living at the Horovitz house but then had a falling-out with the playwright, who was in the middle of a grim divorce—and living up to his reputation as a moody character given to tantrums. Rimmer ended up leaving New York a few months into the playwriting program.

In Joseph Heller, Wendy found a kindred spirit. She met him a decade after the publication of *Catch-22.* By then Heller had been declared a genius and *Catch-22* was acknowledged as a landmark work. There had been much critical revisionism since the original mixed reviews that had praised Heller's ingenuity and questioned his craftsmanship, like the verdict issued by the *New York Times Book Review:* "Joseph Heller . . . is like a brilliant painter who decides to throw all the ideas in his sketchbooks onto one canvas, relying on their charm and shock to compensate for the lack of design."

Heller was another Brooklyn Jew who believed that comedy—the nuttier the better—was the way to cope with distress (as well as monumental issues, like the irrational cruelty existing in man and nature). He grasped the flashes of brilliance lurking in Wendy's writing, even though her early sketches were haphazard and occasionally incoherent.

After reading several of her papers, he told her, "Wendy this is fabulous, you've got a real talent here. You should stay with this."

Heller gave Wendy something more important, perhaps, than any single lesson he might have imparted in class or perceptive comment he might have scribbled on a paper. He made her feel that she had something special to offer. This endorsement was a powerful antidote to the sense of failure that weighed on her, a load exaggerated by her having graduated without distinction and being home without any apparent goal in mind.

In future years Wendy would tell variations on an anecdote that indicated how much Heller's approval meant to her. The story, in all its incarnations, also showed how adept she became at turning a memory—real, imagined, or embellished—into an amusing scene with a sly or outrageous punch line that simultaneously promoted and diminished herself:

Version One: Joseph Heller took her to some sort of party and introduced her as "the funniest girl in New York," and Wendy promptly threw up.*

Version Two: She was having lunch with Joseph Heller at a fancy restaurant. Someone stopped by the table, and Heller introduced his student. "This is Wendy Wasserstein, the funniest girl in New York." She responded by throwing up.†

Version Three: She was with a friend who introduced her to the novel-

---

* This version came from Anne Betteridge, a Mount Holyoke friend who became the model for Leilah, the shy anthropologist in *Uncommon Women.*

† She told this story to Christopher Durang, the playwright, when they met at Yale Drama School.

ist Joseph Heller as a brilliantly funny writer. She responded to his request, "Say something funny, Wendy," by barfing on his coat.*

The classes with Horovitz and Heller awakened something profound in Wendy. At City College she began to work on the approach that would become her signature—mingling memory, observation, reality, and fiction. The "Cuisinart method," Bruce called it. "She had perfect-pitch memory for conversations, but then she'd put them in the Cuisinart and they'd come out in random ways," he said. "So if you knew all these things, they'd come out having nothing to do with the particular fact lines."

She began to take herself seriously, relying more confidently on the entertaining voice found in her letters and journals.

It didn't happen overnight. The early experiments led one teacher—most likely Heller—to comment on one paper, "Character is left kind of thin—a habit you have—and without knowing her much better, we don't have much. We've got the wit, we've got the discerning comments about people and behavior, but we don't have any emotional depth. W.W., you've got to decide soon: either fiction or funny essays."

The old maxim sank in: Write what you know. Wendy turned to the material she had used many times in late night gab sessions and letters to friends: The Family Wasserstein. In early fragments of plays and stories, she didn't even bother to change the names. Her characters are named Brucey, Sandy, Georgette, Lola, Morris, Lyn, and Peter—but never Wendy.

Lynne Killin Wasserstein, Bruce's wife, enjoyed Wendy's company and for a time considered Wendy her best friend. They commiserated with each other about mothers who tried to control their daughters' weight. Like Wendy, Lynne was in awe of Lola, without having to directly bear the sting of her criticisms. Lynne admired the intense devotion to family that led

---

* This is almost verbatim the story told by Michael Feingold, chief theater critic for the *Village Voice*, after Wendy died.

Morris and Lola to return early from vacation when Georgette went into labor with her first child, so they could be in New Haven for the baby's birth.

After Lynne and Bruce returned to New York from Cambridge, the couple moved into an apartment at Eighty-second Street and Second Avenue, just a few blocks from Morris and Lola's. Bruce had toyed with the idea of becoming a small-town newspaper editor or practicing law in Alaska. Instead he accepted a position as a starting lawyer at the prestigious firm of Cravath, Swaine & Moore, the epitome of the old-boy network, the antithesis of Nader's Raiders.

During Bruce's flirtation with leftist politics, he demanded justice for all, but that didn't mean he wanted his wife to become a feminist. When Lynne attended a couple of women's-lib meetings in Cambridge, he threatened to divorce her. When he complained that she didn't cook him enough steak—the way his mother did—Lynne bought steak.

Lynne and Bruce often double-dated with Wendy and James Kaplan, who had fallen back into a relationship when Wendy moved back to New York. James was in the city, in his first year at Columbia Law School. Bruce and James had much in common. Both had been involved in liberal politics; in the fall of 1972, James—dogged champion of lost causes—was campaigning for George McGovern, the Democratic candidate for president. Bruce was a law associate; James was in law school. Both had Ivy League credentials—between them Yale, Harvard, and Columbia.

As a Columbia student, James could buy tickets to plays for twenty-five cents each, so they were often at the theater. They prowled the city, having dinner at Umberto's Clam House, where the mobster Joey Gallo was shot. They went to concerts and movies.

It often seemed to Lynne and James that the couple they were double-dating was Wendy and Bruce. Wendy made snide comments about Lynne to James, referring to her sister-in-law as Bruce's cocker spaniel, because she was so docile. Wendy and Bruce were the soul mates, with their own references and secret jokes, their private way of looking at the world. Bruce often called Lynne "Wendy," even when it was just the two of them alone together, Lynne and Bruce.

Bruce's wife said she didn't mind. "I loved Wendy," she said. "I loved Morris, and I loved Lola. The attachment was very strong."

Her feelings toward them never changed—even after Wendy's appraisal of Lynne's relationship with Bruce went public and changed the course of Lynne's life.

Encouraged by her teachers at CCNY, Wendy decided to try earning money from her writing. A longtime fan of television soap operas, she got an assignment from a magazine to do an article about them. After she turned in the piece, before it was published, the magazine went out of business.

She applied for jobs as a copywriter at advertising agencies, with no luck. She sent stories and articles to *Redbook* magazine, the *New York Times,* and the *New Yorker*—all were returned with form rejection notes.

Discouraged with the prospects for a profitable writing career, she took the law boards again. Her new score was still mediocre, but she applied to law schools anyway to satisfy Lola. As before, she wasn't accepted anywhere. She didn't have a chance at Columbia or New York University. After she was rejected from Fordham Law, Lola suggested she lower her sights for a lesser school. Wendy couldn't tolerate this idea, not with Bruce having gone to Harvard, Rita Wasserstein (Aunt Florence's daughter) at NYU, and James at Columbia.

Wendy was ambivalent. Determined not to be rejected from law school yet again, she tested two options, as though asking fate to decide which road she should take. Should she follow her father, brother, and sister into the business world? Or should she pursue the gift that was unique to her, even though it was unlikely to lead to financial security? She applied to both Yale School of Drama and Columbia Business School.

James sympathized with Wendy's struggle to find herself and tried to be there for her throughout this difficult period. He thought they were growing closer, although when he raised the subject of getting an apartment together in Brooklyn, she wasn't interested.

Their families—including Bruce and Lynne—thought they might get married.

Wendy was wary of James's mother. She saw Muriel as a generation ahead of Lola in terms of aspiration and status. Muriel had sent her daughters to Dalton, which had rejected Wendy. Wendy told James that she thought his mother saw her as a schlumpy girl from Brooklyn and not appropriate for her son.

One night James came home after a date with Wendy and woke his parents up. He was shaken. "I don't know what to do," he told them. "I was in the living room waiting for Wendy when her father came out and said, 'Well, Jamey, you've been going with Wendy for a while, how about marrying her?'"

James had been so startled he said to Morris, "Maybe you should ask Wendy what she has to say."

Wendy later apologized for her father. "He's half in the Old World," she said. But she didn't seem concerned that James hadn't taken Morris up on his offer.

James might not have been ready to commit to marriage, but he was disappointed in Wendy's calm reaction, which he took as a sign of indifference. "My sense was that she really wasn't that interested, or she would have been more upset about the whole thing," he said.

Wendy had begun to live two lives. There was the pudgy "loser"—failed law-school applicant, noncommittal girlfriend, unemployed part-time student, unsuccessful freelance writer. And there was the emerging artist, gaining control of her craft as she reconstructed the people who loved her—and who sometimes drove her crazy—into characters whose behavior she could dictate.

The subject that began to occupy her writing most intensely was Bruce's marriage to Lynne. Wendy didn't criticize her brother aloud, but she didn't approve of his attitude and behavior toward his wife. She was also jealous, aware that Lynne provided a sexual connection with which Wendy could not compete—so she belittled it.

She felt Lynne had trivialized herself by her willingness to be Bruce's sex object and helpmate rather than have a career of her own. She considered Lynne's interest in collecting gemstones and making jewelry a hobby, and a lame one at that, though Lynne took her craft seriously.

Wendy was refining her methodology, becoming more comfortable with the process of fictionalization. In a short story called "A Solid Gold Blender," she worked the same familial territory but produced a far more polished result. The wild humor is corralled. She is starting to see the importance of timing.

The story is about a super-brilliant young man named Mark, described thusly:

> Even though he had gained forty pounds to out-weigh the draft, Mark had basically been on his mother's good side ever since he had advance-placed into Yale Law, Economics, and Architecture at nineteen. A truck driver eating Twinkies is a fat truck driver. A genius eating Twinkies is still a genius.

Lynne of Larchmont, Bruce's wife, is cast as Greta of Greenwich, "debutante-in-law," Mark's wife.

> In the past, coming to her mother-in-law's had always given her a headache, and she came equipped with Librium. But today she brought her Rock Rascal polishing machine and was content to concentrate on polishing her booty from a month's rock hounding in Wales. While the counter-culture went to Woodstock, Greta went to rock fairs in Cardiff.

Whenever Greta tries to have a serious conversation with Mark, he condescends: "Princess, hush. Play with your rocks."

Joyce, the Wendy character, is at loose ends:

> Joyce deliberated how to fill the time til "Saturday Night at the Movies." She hadn't read in months. Months, how many "As the World Turns" had passed? Did Jesse have her baby? She resolved the day's possibilities. Today I will try not to think about myself, and not to run into my mother. Today I will go to the museum. No, too intellectual. A movie? Takes too long. A store? Too crowded. An employ-

ment agency? Can't handle it. An apartment agency? No job. A friend? Too parasitic, too many questions, too much dope, too flagellating. Go to Charles.

Charles, modeled on Jamey Kaplan, is the reliable young man Harriet (the mother) wants Joyce to marry, who refers to his girlfriend as "Blimp-child."

This unpublished story contains many themes that Wendy frequently revisited, all revolving around the relationships between spouses, friends, lovers, siblings, parents, and children.

Alone in her childhood room, Joyce reflects, in a telling moment:

There was nowhere to go and she didn't really want to leave. She never wanted to marry Charles, she just thought he'd be good to be divorced from—responsible payments. In fact, she never loved or trusted anyone outside the family. At least they were unique, at least they loved her.

While Wendy was at CCNY reworking the characters and ideas in "A Solid Gold Blender" into the form of a play, Robert Moss was in the early stages of creating Playwrights Horizons, the nonprofit theater that would become Wendy's theatrical home. In doing so, Moss was changing the landscape of New York theater.

It was the era of Joseph Papp, who had become an establishment unto himself as the political climate shifted, and social mores were changing. The counterculture was going mainstream. Papp had become a dominating force in the noncommercial theater, creating the New York Shakespeare Festival, offering free productions in Central Park. At his Public Theater in Greenwich Village, he championed new playwrights and actors and was one of the first producers to put black actors and other minorities into Shakespearean roles. Then he became a Broadway impresario, when he moved the rock musical *Hair* uptown from the Public, where it would become one of Broadway's longest-running shows.

This was the theater world in which Bob Moss came of age. In 1963 he began work as a production stage manager of the Phoenix Theatre, an inventive repertory house. Radiating effusive innocence, he was a nonstop worker and a nonstop booster of theater. His enthusiasm and charm could transform the most devout pessimist into an optimist.

In 1970 Edward Albee asked Moss to run the Playwrights Unit, the theater Albee had established with the profits from his first full-length play, *Who's Afraid of Virginia Woolf?*

The Playwrights Unit offered writers an alternative to Broadway, where the financial stakes were high and led to creative decisions that weren't necessarily based on artistic considerations. At the Unit money didn't matter, because there wasn't any.

Audiences came to see works in progress by new playwrights, some destined for obscurity, others for fame. Among those in the latter category were Sam Shepard, Adrienne Kennedy, Lanford Wilson, and John Guare. Moss introduced every play, explaining that the work shouldn't be judged as a finished product and that the audience reaction was part of the process. "I wasn't apologizing," he said, "just trying to set a lens through which people could look at the plays."

In the spring of 1971, Albee decided to close the Playwrights Unit. A few weeks later, Moss got a call from Louise Roberts, who had been the director of the June Taylor dance school—where Wendy and Georgette had taken dance lessons as a girl.

Roberts had become director of the Clark Center for the Performing Arts, a not-for-profit dance company that was housed in the YWCA branch at Fifty-first Street and Eighth Avenue—the same building where Alvin Ailey started his dance troupe in the 1960s.

Roberts called Moss to say she had an unused room on the second floor that was too small for dance class—about fifteen feet by thirty. She thought it might work as a writing studio for playwrights. "Nothing will come of that," Moss heard himself saying. "Why don't you just give me the room?"

She agreed. That kind of gee-whiz showbiz moment became far less possible in subsequent years, when even Off-Broadway productions required a substantial investment. "I suddenly had real estate, secretarial, janitorial, Con Ed," said Moss. "The only thing I didn't have was money. You didn't need money in those days."

Almost immediately Moss started putting on plays, getting by with rudimentary lighting, makeshift costumes and props, dressing rooms jerry-rigged from janitors' closets by a stairwell. The shows were barely one step up from a rehearsed reading, but they gave playwrights the valuable opportunity to see their work staged and to gauge audience response.

The new theater was named Playwrights Horizons. Moss had taken the mailing list from Playwrights Unit before it closed, a valuable asset. The audience responded: Within six months they were packing the tiny house with seventy people a night. Moss was inundated with plays. At first he scheduled thirty plays a year; each ran for twelve performances. He added a second show at 10:00 P.M. for one-acts and plays he didn't think were as strong; these ran for five performances. Ted Danson, Tommy Lee Jones, and Stockard Channing were among the young actors who showed up on the bill at the Clark Center.

Early in 1973 Louise Roberts called Moss to ask a favor. She'd run into a woman whose daughter used to take classes at the June Taylor dance school. The daughter was studying with Israel Horovitz at CCNY and had written a play. Would he take a look?

He agreed to read *Any Woman Can't* by Wendy Wasserstein, a one-act she described as "the story of a girl who gives up and gets married after blowing an audition for tap-dancing class." Moss liked Wendy when they met. He thought her play was funny but insubstantial. He put it in the 10:00 P.M. slot for five nights that April.

The play was Wendy's response to *Any Woman Can!*, a guide to sexual and personal fulfillment published in 1971 by David Reuben, a physician and "sex expert," who had gained national notoriety two years earlier with the publication of *Everything You Always Wanted to Know About Sex (But Were Afraid to Ask)*. The play's story is essentially "The Solid Gold Blender" in dramatized form. The heroine—Wendy's alter ego—is called Christina. She is a recent Smith College graduate now working as an instructor at a Fred Astaire Dance Studio. Her boyfriend, Charles—modeled

on James—is a straitlaced young man who alternately criticizes and se-
duces Christina, referring to her as "Teeny" and "Pet Tuna." Christina has
an overweight, overbearing boy-genius brother (like Bruce), who patron-
izes his gem-collecting wife (like Lynne).

During the play's brief run, Wendy's family and friends trooped into
the Clark Center to see what she'd been up to at CCNY.

James Kaplan soon recognized himself in Charles. It was like seeing
himself in a funhouse mirror, except that the distortion was not much fun.
It was hard not to feel sucker-punched when Charles's girlfriend, the
Wendy character, yells at him, "I'm not 'ladylike.' I'm not one of those nice
girls all your friends at Princeton kept as masturbating dollies. I hate your
friends, and I hate you."

James couldn't bring himself to confront Wendy directly. He suggested
afterward that maybe the actor hadn't played the role properly. She saw
how hurt he was, so she agreed. She said something about "poetic license."

She told him, "You can't view characters in a play as real." He accepted her explanation, though he knew that changing details like Yale to
Princeton didn't cushion the harsh judgment being rendered.

He wondered what he was supposed to think, when Christina says, "I
was just being cool and biding time in college until something happened
to me. Nothing happened. Look, here I am with you."

They continued to see each other, even though Wendy reported to
James that someone had said to her, with surprise, "You're still going out
with that guy?"

Bruce had read the play and urged Lynne not to go see it, but he didn't
tell her why. She ignored him. She still thought of Wendy as her best friend
and wouldn't miss the production of her first play.

Lynne went to the Friday-night performance of *Any Woman Can't*.
When she saw a version of herself lying on a rug playing with rocks, she
was annoyed. She was a member of the New York Lapidary Society and
considered herself a craftswoman, not some bimbo.

She thought it was pretty silly—until the play struck an essential nerve.
Mark, the Bruce character, has just sent his wife into the kitchen to get
him a Yoo-Hoo, "like a good girl." After she leaves, Christina—the Wendy

stand-in—says to her brother, "I wouldn't let someone treat me the way you treat her."

Over the weekend Lynne couldn't stop thinking about Wendy's evaluation of her marriage—and of her. Bruce was interesting and intelligent and exciting, but what was Lynne? Suddenly she knew. Lynne was unhappy.

That Sunday evening she and Bruce were working on their taxes. They began arguing over who should balance the checkbook. As the fight escalated, Lynne glanced at the television. *Mayerling*, the movie that was on in the background, seemed like an omen. There were Omar Sharif and Catherine Deneuve, playing doomed lovers at the end of the Hapsburg Empire.

Just after midnight Lynne called her parents and asked them to come and get her. Subsequently she told Bruce she wouldn't come back to him unless they went to a marriage counselor.

"He said, 'If you don't like it, get out,'" she recalled. "I didn't like it, I got out. He was not a flexible person."

Wendy would come to hate *Any Woman Can't*. In 1997, in a lengthy interview with Laurie Winer, a drama critic, in the *Paris Review*, Wendy mentioned the play, and Winer said, "I've never seen it."

"And you never will," Wendy replied. "It's an awful play."

Yet she had sent that "awful" play to the Yale Drama School as part of her application for entry in the fall of 1973. By the time *Any Woman Can't* was performed at Playwrights Horizons, Wendy had already been accepted at both Yale Drama and Columbia Business School and was leaning toward New Haven.

After the reading, Bob Moss said to her, "Why do you have to go? You can't learn playwriting in school."

But Wendy believed in the power of pedigree and connections. She chose Yale. The school became an important stepping-stone, though not exactly in the way she might have expected.

CHRIS DURANG AND MERYL STREEP,
SUPERSTARS AT YALE DRAMA WHEN WENDY
WAS THERE, HERE IN A PRODUCTION OF
THE IDIOTS KARAMAZOV, WRITTEN BY
DURANG AND ALBERT INNAURATO.

Seven

DRAMA QUEENS AND KINGS

1973-76

The spring before Wendy arrived at Yale, Christopher Durang had already begun to anticipate her arrival. As a work-study student, then in his second year, he had a job in the bursar's office and sneaked a look at her application. He insisted that he wasn't in the habit of snooping through the files of applicants but confessed he couldn't resist spying on this one. He had heard that Richard Gilman had read a play by somebody named Wendy Wasserstein and liked it. Gilman, a respected critic, was the professor at the school who pretty much determined which playwrights were chosen. This Wasserstein woman was therefore likely to be admitted.

Chris was intrigued, especially when he saw recommendations from Joseph Heller, the bestselling novelist, and from Israel Horovitz, a well-known playwright. Then he looked at her photo. "Her arms were crossed, and she looked really grouchy, not a friendly person," he recalled. "She looked defensive and/or maybe hostile and/or definitely suspicious of the world." The play that was part of her admissions package carried a title Chris thought to be vaguely confrontational: *Any Woman Can't.*

Warily, he began reading the play, anticipating a feminist screed. Everything seemed to be political then. On April 30, 1973, about the time Chris was reading Wendy's application, Richard M. Nixon made his first public reference to Watergate, the political burglary that would end his presidency. The war in Vietnam had shifted to Cambodia, where U.S. bombs were devastating the country. The Supreme Court had, in January, issued a landmark decision, *Roe v. Wade,* which in declaring that women had the constitutional right to an abortion ignited an intractable political battle resonant with biblical ferocity and certitude.

Chris Durang was not apolitical, but he preferred humor to harangues. Descended from a lineage of alcoholics and depressives, many of whom were artists, he began writing plays in third grade. However, the precocious boy didn't start plumbing the darker corners of existence until his freshman year at Harvard, when he wrote, directed, and acted in a play called *Suicide and Other Diversions.* The play that had won him entry to Yale Drama, *The Nature and Purpose of the Universe,* was a comedy based on the book of Job. Howard Stein, the associate dean at the drama school, described Durang's work "as a scream for help in a world he knows provides none. So he keeps on screaming and laughs at it."

As Chris began reading *Any Woman Can't,* he was surprised to find himself laughing, almost from the beginning. The story of a young woman trying to figure out what to do with the rest of her life was told with self-deprecating humor. He found the writer's amusing depiction of the dating scene human, not didactic. His curiosity was even stronger than before.

When school resumed in the fall, he hoped to take a class with Terrence McNally, an up-and-coming playwright teaching a seminar at Yale that year. But McNally was a hot item; his class filled quickly, and Chris was stuck with a teacher he sensed was going to be a bore.

Soon he recognized a possible diversion. There was Wendy Wasserstein, hunkered down with her arms crossed, looking grouchy, just as she had in the photograph he'd seen in her application folder. Despite her forbidding appearance, because he'd read her play and thought it was funny, he felt they might be kindred spirits. "You must be very smart to be bored so quickly," he said slyly, with the cherubic smile that led Robert Brustein, head of the drama school, to fondly refer to him as "a choirboy with fingers dipped in poison."

Wendy responded with the expression Chris would always associate with her. "Her face lit up, and she laughed and laughed, and I felt that I had met Wendy," he said. When she told him that a professor had once called her a "vicious dumpling," he understood why. The rapier intelligence and shrewd wit, which could be delightfully rude, were kept wrapped inside that shy, unthreatening chubby-girl exterior.

The story of their first meeting would become part of their repertoire; Wendy incorporated it into *The Heidi Chronicles*. Her heroine Heidi meets a boy she would fall in love with at a high-school dance. His name is Peter Patrone. Their first exchange:

Peter: You must be very bright.
Heidi: Excuse me?
Peter: You look so bored you must be very bright.

After class Chris invited Wendy for a cup of coffee. When he had to leave, he felt they had much more to say to each other. They met again for drinks the next day

She was a giggler; he was a mischief maker. They shared a cockeyed view of the world but could be quite serious, especially after their friendship deepened, and they began revealing secrets to each other. When Chris confessed that he had peeked at her application, Wendy admitted that before she arrived at Yale she had studied the list of people who were already there. When she saw "Christopher Durang, Harvard College, author of *The Nature and Purpose of the Universe*," she told him, she assumed he would be a scary, smart Harvard jock full of self-confidence. They were both amused by the odd assumptions they'd made about each other and quickly became inseparable.

Wendy was smitten. "She provided 24/7 worship," said Albert Innaurato, a classmate of Chris's, who like Wendy had had an early play produced at Playwrights Horizon by Bob Moss.

Albert was a close friend of Chris's, along with another third year student, Sigourney Weaver, an aristocratic-looking (but messy) Stanford graduate, who shared their zany take on the world. The three made a visual impact separately and together: Sigourney was five feet, ten and a half inches and quite beautiful. Albert was large, and Chris was small. Albert and Chris often worked together, as writers and actors. Their first year Sigourney appeared in one of Chris's early comedies about a dysfunctional family, *Better Dead Than Sorry,* cast as a young woman who was constantly having nervous breakdowns. Chris played her worried brother.

The Idiots Karamazov, a joint creation of Chris and Albert's, a spoof of Dostoyevsky, became a favorite student production of Bob Brustein. Meryl Streep, in the class after Chris's, was cast as the wheelchair-bound "translatrix," whirled around the stage by "Ernest Hemingway," her mute lover. Streep, an ethereal blond beauty, was transformed into an old hag, complete with a wart on the end of her nose. This tour de force was the kind of boundary-stretching phenomenon that might leave ordinary mortals feeling perplexed, even as they laughed, but Brustein adored it, describing it in the loftiest of terms: "*The Idiots Karamazov* hammered away at the most beloved works and authors in literature, leaving Western culture in momentary ruins, like the detritus of a dead civilization."

Both Albert and Chris had large roles in a play the year Wendy arrived. Albert was annoyed to find her always sitting on the steps leading to the dressing room when he arrived for rehearsals. "What are you doing here?" he asked.

"I'm waiting for Chris."

Five hours later, when Albert emerged, Wendy was still there, sitting on the steps, waiting for Chris.

There was jealousy. Albert and Chris collaborated so frequently that they were referred to as "Chris 'n' Albert." Albert felt that he was being edged out by Wendy, a newcomer he didn't quite trust.

Albert didn't exactly dislike Wendy, but he thought the first-year student was a little presumptuous, always hanging around them—make that Chris—all the time. Her devotion bothered Albert, because Chris was gay and Wendy knew it, yet she was behaving like a love-struck puppy.

But was it so strange, given Chris's charming personality and exalted place in the cloistered atmosphere at Yale Drama? Chris had become a superstar at Yale, as both an actor and a playwright. He was a pet of Brustein; the school's dictatorial dean ruled his small empire as if it were the center of the universe. Brustein's teaching philosophy mimicked the brutal distillation process his students would encounter in the real world of theater. Both brilliance and pettiness were fostered by this approach, which nurtured certain dispositions and threatened to destroy others. Brustein saw the drama school as an ancillary program to his passion, the Yale Repertory Theatre. His goal was to produce not academics but working professionals. Brustein had strong opinions—hated the work of Arthur Miller, loved Bertolt Brecht.

He dismissed playwrights and actors who fell below his standard of "poetic consciousness," which he associated with wild farce and dark surrealism. He expected his students to drive themselves to startling, unconventional dimensions; this pressure-cooker methodology produced some genius but even more anxiety and feelings of failure.

Brustein became Wendy's nemesis, a stand-in for Lola, always ready to point out her shortcomings. It wasn't her imagination. "I thought she was a lightweight," said Brustein. "She was witty and funny and a little sitcom-y. In my Puritan way, I was trying to push playwrights in more dangerous areas. What appealed about Chris Durang was his outrageousness. Wendy seemed more domestic and conventional."

The men running the school wanted women to look and behave a certain way. Sigourney Weaver was beautiful but didn't fit Brustein's design; she was criticized in evaluations for looking like an unmade bed. "I had raggedy hippie clothes," she said. "Long, torn, ripped skirts. They saw me as a leading lady, and I thought of myself as a comedienne. When they were going after me about not having any talent, the whole thing was about how I dressed."

Only select women's issues were considered interesting. "The men were very much in charge of defining women's pain," said Susan Blatt, a classmate who became Wendy's closest girlfriend at Yale. "Rape, childbearing, child losing—this was women's pain. Dick Gilman, for example, was especially enamored of a play in which a retarded teenage girl is impregnated by an old farmworker and has an onstage farm-table abortion. Wendy's oeuvre just wasn't on the radar screen."

Chris let Wendy know by their second or third coffee date that he was in a relationship—with a man—and had been for several years. Having made full disclosure, he preferred not to see the obvious. Wendy had a huge crush on him. He combined all the virtues she was looking for in a man. He was smart, funny, ambitious, wayward. He always took pains to compliment her. When they went to a thrift shop and she modeled a clingy evening gown with a marabou collar, he told her she looked "really glamorous"— and meant it—so different from Lola's horrified reaction when Wendy wore the dress to a family function.

Chris wasn't in love with Wendy, but he loved her. As an only child, he was fascinated by her stories of the Family Wasserstein. They amused themselves for hours swapping funny stories about their eccentric families. When he first heard Wendy's anecdotes about Lola pressuring her to marry a doctor or a lawyer, he laughed appreciatively, thinking these were mere comedy routines. But as he got to know Wendy better, he was troubled by the implicit and sometimes explicit message: "If you don't have children and continue the line, your life is meaningless."

Chris's family was repressed and often angry, but he hadn't been belittled by his parents. He had special antennae for adults whose behavior might disturb children. The first time he met Lola—during Wendy's first year at Yale—she was dressed as Patty Hearst (for no apparent reason; it wasn't Halloween), the publishing heiress who was kidnapped by political radicals in 1974.

Though Chris had heard many Lola stories by then, he was still taken aback by the sight of the skinny middle-aged woman, wearing a trench coat, waving a toy pistol and saying, "Guess who I am!"

He understood that it was a joke and thought it was funny, but then he wondered what this exhibition was all about. Coming from a household of alcoholics, he was accustomed to unexpected outbursts and unexplained silences, but it was Wendy's turn to be taken aback when he seemed surprised by Lola's behavior. "If someone is crazy and no one talks about it, you cannot know the truth of something," he said. "The reality testing is off. You don't know what normal is."

He felt protective toward Wendy, and she trusted him. She told him, "I feel like I'm a car that doesn't have bumpers." But with Chris she felt safe—

strong enough to cut the final thread connecting her to James Kaplan, completing the process that had begun with the Playwrights Horizons production of *Any Woman Can't*. When she learned that James had begun to date someone else, Wendy toyed with the thought of telling Chris her true feelings for him. She also wondered what was wrong with her, tossing aside a viable romantic candidate like James and choosing instead to yearn for an impossible relationship.

For the first time since she was eight years old, about to enter the Ethical Culture School, she made entries in a diary—actually a loose-leaf notebook, for just a handful of pages. In early December, three months into her first year, she wrote:

> I have fantasies about Chris as if he were Number 1 in medical school and I dropped to number 9. I also fantasize about James. I want to be held. Maybe he'll be meaner and my masochism will run out. I'd rather be number 9 in med school as long as they knew I was best friends or lovers, difficult in this case, with number 1.
>
> I should tell Christopher. I won't. For future readers, he's very talented. I wish I were nicer or just better, more open. Do I want you to read this and think oh, she was so good and just look at what she thought of herself. Pity. I worry about becoming a bitter spinster or alcoholic.

Even then, with her youthful musings about crushes, Wendy was thinking about a larger audience. She subjected her diary to editorial scrutiny; her periodic journal entries were another way for her to synthesize her life on paper in order to analyze it.

But she wouldn't risk her friendship with Chris. Having a frank conversation—at least about her feelings for him—would run counter to the essential core of her being. Wendy was self-protective. The high girlish pitch of her voice and her giggle were her armor against scrutiny. If she appeared not to take herself too seriously, she wouldn't be a target for other ambitious people who might consider her a threat. Her capacity for making friends reflected her warmth and interest in people but also grew from enormous insecurity. She would go out of her way to befriend people who either intimidated or belittled her, engaging them in conversation, revealing her nervousness by tearing paper or unraveling the braided cords of her espadrilles.

Wendy's open vulnerability kept Sigourney Weaver from getting too close. "There was something about Wendy I found very scary to me," she said. "She was a more naked version of the vulnerability I felt. I wanted to take care of Wendy, to pull her hair back and give her some armor, and that seemed inappropriate, because I was a walking disaster. I resisted the impulse. We didn't become good friends."

Yet there were many others who became friends and putative friends, people Wendy felt she ought to please. "She had a lot of demands on her time, and a lot of it was with people she promised things to," said Susan Blatt. "She would run from place to place, from conversation to conversation. You wished she had closed the door, said no to a lot of people, and just written and gotten by on her merit."

Susan and Wendy met during their first days at Yale; Susan was in the criticism program and took many classes with the playwrights. One day she was sitting on a bench and Wendy came over to her and said, "What's a nice Jewish girl like you doing in a place like this?"

Susan had an impressive résumé—she'd graduated from Princeton in the school's first coed class. She also had a psychologist father who tormented her as Wendy's mother tormented her.

Both of them reported receiving daily wake-up calls at 7:00 A.M.

"Are you married yet?" Lola would ask Wendy.

"You sound depressed!" Susan's father would say to his sleepy daughter.

They became fast friends. There were few women at the drama school, and many of them were in the acting program, women who took pains to make themselves look good. Wendy wore shapeless dresses designed to hide her body and exhibit her shapely legs. "I'm beautiful from the knees down," she told Susan, whose wardrobe was equally unflattering, consisting mainly of baggy jeans and T-shirts.

In New Haven, Wendy lived in York Towers, a high-rise building with a doorman, a place for timid old ladies, not the usual shabby student quarters like Susan's cockroach-infested apartment. They ate almost every breakfast and lunch at Murray's, a standard-issue luncheonette, next door to Superbooks, a shop that specialized in porn magazines and sex toys.

She and Susan often had sleepovers, brewing pots of tea and discussing their latest anguish, always wearing Lanz flannel nightgowns. (Wendy became so known for wearing these nightgowns that when their designer, Werner Scharff, died in 2006, the *New York Times* obituary quoted Wendy: "The entire dormitory, 130 strong in Lanz flannel nightgowns, caroled in the living room while our house mother distributed gingerbread cookies.") They would reveal their concerns and dissect their foolishness. Sometimes after one of these sessions, Wendy called Susan and confessed that she'd called a man she found attractive and hung up the instant he answered. Susan wondered if Wendy was kept awake by demons from Lola, needling that constant refrain, *Are you married yet?*

After he graduated, Chris stayed in New Haven. Brustein decided to stage *The Idiots Karamazov* at the Yale Rep, in the fall of 1974, a major coup for a playwright starting his professional career. The following year Chris moved to New York but still returned every week to New Haven to teach a class; Brustein had chosen him to be the recipient of the same CBS fellowship that had brought Terrence McNally to campus.

Chris's presence and endorsement became even more important to Wendy after a disastrous production of *Any Woman Can't*, directed by one of her classmates.

The main actress was miscast; the funniest lines fell flat. Chris stopped watching the play and started focusing on Richard Gilman's face. Gilman was pale, as if he were thinking, "Oh, my God, this is awful." After the play Gilman was chilly to Wendy, as if saying to her, "I made a mistake letting you in. You wrote a bad play."

Brustein didn't bother to come. He didn't see potential there.

As an actor and writer, Chris had been learning how important casting was, how tone could bring out the wit in a line or kill it. In the play the heroine makes a self-deprecating joke in a throwaway line about her Seven Sisters education, which has earned her a job as a dance-school instructor:

I'm a fucking Smith graduate. I was supposed to be different—
happier than the others. I wouldn't be a secretary, not me.

The actress played it as tragedy. Chris watched her trembling reading
of "I'm a fucking Smith graduate" drain the humor from the line and make
its author seem pathetic.

He made a point of talking to Wendy afterward. "My God, that production was awful," he told her. "What a shame, the play is funny." He wanted
to have the same conversation with Gilman, but he didn't.

Wendy joked about her teachers with her friends, but the coldness she
sensed from Gilman and Brustein left her feeling at sea. "I am very unsure
of myself," she wrote in her journal. "I am not sure of my talent or making
a living from it."

Wendy was not alone in her insecurity at the institution she dubbed "the
Yale School of Trauma." Doubt was intrinsic to the profession she was
pursuing, and Brustein fostered it. Sigourney Weaver never forgave him
for ruining her fantasy of what drama school would be like. "I remember
looking up at one point in my first year thinking, 'This should be the most
joyous place in the world,'" she said. "After years of wanting to do nothing
but theater, we are at this place where we can argue about Chekhov in the
corridors, and everyone is fucking miserable and at each other's throats."

Even Meryl Streep felt the pressure, and she was the school's unparal-
leled darling, the only one Howard Stein could remember an admissions
interviewer declaring, after he'd met her, "She's going to be a star." While
she was at Yale, a new verb came into being, "to Streep it up," meaning find
your light, identify your moment, chew the scenery, activate the space.

Streep recalled:

The competition in the acting program was very wearing. I was
always standing in competition with my friends for every play. And
there was no nod to egalitarian casting. Since each student director
or playwright was casting his or her senior project, they pretty much

got to cast it with whomever they wanted. So some people got cast over and over and others didn't get cast at all. It was unfair. It was the larger world writ small.

I got into a frenzy about this. It wasn't that I wasn't being cast. I was, over and over. But I felt guilty. I felt I was taking something from people I knew, my friends. I was on a scholarship and some people had paid a lot of money to be there.

Finally, I went to the dean, to Robert Brustein. I said: "I'm under too much pressure. I want to be released from some of these commitments."

He said, "Well, you could go on academic probation." Which was the first step to being kicked out.

So I went to see a psychiatrist at the school who said: "You know what? You're going to graduate in 11 weeks and you'll never be in competition with five women again. You'll be competing with 5,000 women and it will be a relief. It will be better or worse, but it won't be this."

He was right. . . .

When they weren't bemoaning their fates to their psychiatrists and one another, or smoldering from being slighted by Brustein, they had fun. The friendships and connections formed at Yale would continue, for many of them, throughout their lives.

William Ivey Long, who became an enduring friend of Wendy's, was a year ahead of her, in Meryl Streep's class. An impish type with a soft southern accent, William had arrived at Yale feeling out of his element after growing up in North Carolina and then attending the College of William & Mary in Virginia.

In his second year, he was doing his first major production, sets and costumes for a production of *Twelfth Night*. William was hysterical and nervous; Ming Cho Lee, a prominent set designer and professor at the school, was coming to see the play. There had been three dress rehearsals; everything seemed ready.

Wendy and Stephen Graham—the son of *Washington Post* publisher Katharine Graham—were working as wardrobe staff. On the day of opening night, Wendy and Stephen were supposed to wash the costumes. Instead of doing it themselves, they decided to drop them off at the dry cleaners and went out to dinner. By the time they'd finished, the dry cleaners was closed. William Ivey Long had his opening night without any costumes. The red set he had contrived to make a bold statement now looked stark, out of place.

The eminent Ming Cho Lee dryly commented, "Well, everyone has to get their red set out of their system."

Ming Cho Lee became his mentor—and William's friendship with Wendy survived this rocky beginning, though it wouldn't be the last time Wendy betrayed him.

William went on to design two of Wendy's productions at Yale: *Montpelier Pa-zazz,* a farce about popular versus unpopular kids, and *When Dinah Shore Ruled the Earth,* a goofy satire she wrote with Christopher Durang, which featured a musical production number called "Welfare Mothers on Parade."

She and William became confidants. He regaled her with his Tennessee Williams–style stories from the South, and she responded with Catskills-style routines about Lola and Morris. William had a sister, Laura, who was disabled; Wendy was intensely curious about Laura, who'd been sent to Duke University for a week of analysis by doctors there. The doctors told his parents his sister should be institutionalized. They ignored this advice.

Wendy peppered William with questions. "She would ask, 'How do you become handicapped? How do you become retarded? What is it based on?'" said William. She didn't say it directly, but he imagined she was trying to understand why his "damaged" sister remained at home while her brother had been banished.

"We talked about it, and I don't think I had the right answers she wanted," he said. "I wasn't hysterical enough about it, so she stopped talking about it ultimately."

But his attitudes toward family made a deep impression. Wendy developed a special trust in William that was evident at Yale and manifested itself more significantly in subsequent years.

One day William told Wendy how when he was in first grade his mother had found out that her father had been married before. That was Wendy's cue to tell him a family secret she'd just learned from her sister Sandra, one that disturbed her far more than the secrecy surrounding Abner and left her wondering, who was her family?

During Wendy's second year at Yale, Lola called to tell her that Sandra was divorcing Peter Schweitzer. "Be a good sister," Lola said, and offered to send her daughters to Maine Chance, Elizabeth Arden's luxury spa in Arizona, which catered to movie stars and other "ladies of fortune," as Wendy called them.

"Don't you think my professors might notice if I'm gone a week and come back tanned and ten pounds lighter?" Wendy asked.

"Sandra needs a rest," Lola insisted. "What is more important?"

Wendy acquiesced but resented her mother's implication that what she was doing wasn't important. She wondered if Lola would have been quite so eager for her to cut classes for a full-body massage if she had been studying heart surgery or torts and contracts.

It wasn't that Wendy didn't love Sandra. She adored her. "If my father invented Velveteen, then Sandra sent Tang to the moon," Wendy wrote, in notes for an unfinished memoir. "At some point in my mind both facts were true."

At age twenty-four, Wendy still regarded her thirty-seven-year-old sister as a supreme being, just as she had as a little girl in Brooklyn when Sandra popped in from England. "Sandra had dinner with men in suits," wrote Wendy. "Sandra ordered cheese for dessert. Sandra was the world's leading authority on sex, career counseling and men. Sandra's weaknesses never occurred to me since my job as 'good sister' was never to see them."

The sisters arrived at the spa and soon found themselves naked in a whirlpool with Clark Gable's widow, Kay. Wendy described the ensuing scene in a notebook:

"Jenifer is the only one with daddy's eyes," I said, referring to Sandra's six year old daughter.

"What?" Sandra moved her head around while our sisterly flesh bobbed in the water.

"Jenifer is the only one of us who has dad's hazel eyes. All the rest of us have muddy brown."

One of the other specialties of my "good sister" entertainment act has always been self-denigrating humor.

"Hmm?" Sandra stared at me. I couldn't tell if I was boring her with the obvious or if she felt this was an inappropriate topic in front of the nude Mrs. Gable.

Here was my chance for a punch line.

"What's the matter? You have a different father than I do?"

"Of course I do," she added matter of factly and shifted her weight.

"What?" I hadn't anticipated this kind of information as part of my sisterly spa obligation.

"My father is George Wasserstein and so is Abner's. He died when I was seven. I thought you knew that."

"No," I giggled. I have a terrible habit of giggling when I'm nervous as if to say this really isn't important, I'm not upset, please don't notice me.

"No. They never told me. And I promise you Bruce doesn't know this, nor does Georgette."

Sandra hardly ever giggles.

"That's ridiculous. She has to know it. She's named for my father George."

"Well, she's never told me about it."

I giggled again.

And that was the end of the discussion.

Even this unsettling revelation, scribbled as an impromptu notation, is written with stage directions and comic awareness. Wendy sees the absurdity of the scene: Two sisters share an intensely personal moment, but it takes place in a hot tub, nude, in the presence of a movie star's wife. She continues:

> I can't remember if Kay got out of the hot tub first or after me and Sandra. But later that night I apologized to my sister for making such a big deal out of the incident in the hot tub. I have a reputation in my family for being "emotional" and "emotional" is synonymous with high strung. The best thing would be not to dwell on the fact that my older sister was suddenly my cousin. The best thing would be never to ask my mother about George because his dying must have upset her enough to begin with. The best thing would be not to figure out who really invented Velveteen.

The order of things as she knew them had been profoundly disturbed. Whatever distress Lola caused her, Wendy had, until that moment in the hot tub, chosen to accept the family mythology as presented to her by her parents. Now she was beginning to see them as mere mortals, with vulnerabilities and concerns she hadn't considered.

She had been aware of George's existence—vaguely—but knowing he was the father of her older siblings raised the specter of Lola's individuality, apart from her position as Wendy's mother or as an outlandish character in a comedy sketch. It also forced Wendy to consider Lola's sexuality, something she didn't like to think about.

Wendy didn't discuss her own sex life much with her friends, beyond confiding her terror of becoming pregnant (she believed that her family was unusually fertile.) When she told Chris about Sandy and *Espresso Bongo*, she didn't yet describe the story with delight but rather embarrassment. The movie's nudity had upset her, she told Chris, and so had the shrimp lunch! Though she was intimate with James Kaplan and others after him, her writing reveals discomfort with the subject of sex.

In *Uncommon Women and Others*, the Holly character, based on Wendy, talks about sex:

Holly: . . . I hate being mounted.

Rita: Holly, pumpkin, life doesn't really offer that many pleasures that you can go around avoiding the obvious ones.

Holly: What kind of pleasure? There's someone on top of you sweating and pushing and you're lying there pretending this is wonderful. That's not wonderful. That's masochistic.

Wendy seemed to take pains to make herself unattractive at times. She wore her clothes until they were unwearable and then shoved them under the bed or stuffed them in the closet. She was often oblivious to basic hygiene. Sometimes she forgot to wear a sanitary pad when she had her period and then walked around with stains on her dress. Uncomfortable with her body, she rarely undressed in front of anyone. She told Susan Blatt that sometimes she worried she might become what was then a sad but common figure on the streets of New York City—a homeless "shopping bag lady."

In later years Wendy talked about "a personal undertow" that began when she was in graduate school. It may or may not have been connected to the revelation in the hot tub. But it was during this period that people began speaking about the sadness they saw in Wendy, underneath the bubbly exterior.

Everything seemed in flux. Her personal history had been abruptly rearranged. The confidence she'd acquired at City College from the endorsement of Israel Horovitz—and, more important, Joseph Heller—was being chipped away at Yale.

Even so, despite the cool reception from Brustein and Gilman, Wendy was acquiring a constituency at the school beyond Christopher and her other friends. Alan MacVey was in the directing program, one year behind Wendy. Not long after he arrived, he wrote music for *When Dinah Shore Ruled the Earth,* Wendy's collaboration with Chris Durang. Later that year Wendy began showing MacVey scenes she was working on for a play based on her experiences at Mount Holyoke.

These scenes were the beginning of *Uncommon Women and Others,* about young women who became friends at a Seven Sisters college during the tumultuous changes of the late 1960s and the beginning of the 1970s. MacVey was assigned by Richard Gilman, head of the playwriting program, to direct the play in a workshop production. MacVey liked the writing and responded to the humor and warmth. He also felt honored to be privy to the secret world of women; there were no male characters.

The themes of the play felt relevant to MacVey. What were highly educated women supposed to do with their diplomas? Could they reconcile careers and family? What was the nature of friendships between women?

MacVey's concerns about the play didn't have to do with the writing or content but with structure and momentum. There was no plot, just a series of scenes, some poignant and some amusing. How did he make the jokes feel organic instead of merely jokes? Wendy had a habit of moving back and forth from the present to the past without figuring out theatrically how to make the shift. When he pointed this out, she quickly understood and "invented" Mrs. Plumm—conjuring up Camilla Peach, her housemother from Mount Holyoke—as a way to connect one scene to the next.

The first read-through with her fellow writers didn't go well. One of the men dismissed it, saying, "I just can't get into all this chick stuff."

Wendy kept plugging away. By her senior year, she expanded *Uncommon Women* until it was seventy minutes long, and it was shown in the school's experimental theater. The audiences at the half dozen performances were receptive, laughing in the right places.

Yet her pleasure in this response was diminished by Brustein's refusal to comment one way or the other. She correctly interpreted his silence as a rejection of her work. "We were almost ideological in our antirealistic view," he said. "She was not touching on things that went deeper than the sociological."

The accumulation of slights and condescension culminated on graduation day. The Wasserstein family descended on New Haven in full force to celebrate Wendy's achievement. They watched as one after another of her classmates received awards, many of them being called back for recognition a second and third time.

They waited for Wendy's turn, but it never came.

Georgette ached for her younger sister. "I was embarrassed for her that there were all these awards, and very few people in her class, and they doubled up on some of them yet she got nothing."

Wendy made light of the snub, but it stung. That summer, back in New York but about to return to New Haven to move out of her apartment, she wrote to Ruth Karl:

> Here I am chez Lola, a graduate of Mount Holyoke, City College and Yale and considering a career in Frozen Yogurt. Has frozen yogurt come to the provinces yet? If not, please let me know. Nothing much is new. I guess I am moving out of New Haven next week, though I can't really say where I am moving to. The last month at Yale was horrible. I felt creeping mediocrity coupled with my new personality bears a strong resemblance to Shelly [*sic*] Winters in the "Poseidon Adventure."
>
> On graduation day playwrighting awards went to 2 women playwrights; not me. Well, that was all right. I felt it was like Amherst College agreeing to accept women after we had left. Speaking of careers, I find myself in the position of having to find work. Oh, the hob globlin[*sic*] of little minds! Why didn't I marry Andy Rosenthal when he was young, Jewish and boring? I am still looking into various writing jobs, but I think I still giggle too much to be taken seriously. Also, Ruthie, in truth I don't think I'm that good, and I guess after these years of educational pursuits I'm far more critical.

In 1981 Robert Brustein's memoir of his years as dean at the Yale School of Drama was published. Called *Making Scenes,* the book makes several references to Christopher Durang, Albert Innaurato, Meryl Streep, and Sigourney Weaver. No mention is made of Wendy Wasserstein.

The seedy stretch of 42nd Street that became
home to Playwrights Horizons in 1975.

Eight

A PLAYWRIGHT'S HORIZONS

1976–77

Wendy graduated from Yale in the spring of 1976, a few months after the infamous headline appeared on the front page of New York City's *Daily News:* "Ford to City: Drop Dead." President Gerald Ford didn't use those exact words as he declined to have the federal government rescue New York from looming economic collapse. But the headline writer succinctly captured the dread provoked by the presidential rebuff—which, some believed, helped him lose the presidential election later that year. (It also forced New York to address its profligate management and begin to repair its abysmal financial system.)

It was the year of *Taxi Driver,* film director Martin Scorsese's mesmerizing pulpy nightmare, with New York portrayed as urban hell, streets paved with prostitutes and pimps. The revitalization* of Forty-second Street was fifteen years away. In 1976 the bright lights of the Great White Way were sickly neon; the bustling show-business world of Oscar Hammerstein, Florenz Ziegfeld, and Billy Minsky had been overrun by sleaze.

---

* Or Disneyfication, depending on your perspective; Disney, Viacom, and other large companies eventually became the backbone of the commercial development that gave new life to the area's theaters while altering its character, with the growth of generic "theme" stores that are not connected to New York culture.

The grand theaters had fallen into disrepair. Porn, drugs, prostitution, and rats prevailed at the "Crossroads of the World."

This was the decidedly unglamorous setting for the resumption of Wendy's embryonic theater career in New York, courtesy of Bob Moss.

Two years earlier, in the spring of Wendy's first year at Yale, Moss's fledgling Playwrights Horizons had almost died. Moss was told that the YMCA branch at Eighth Avenue and Fifty-first Street, where Playwrights Horizons began and where *Any Woman Can't* was performed, was being closed for financial reasons. Moss was devastated. The feisty little theater he'd built on charm and adrenaline had become a respectable enterprise. At the time he heard the Y was being shut down, he had already raised forty thousand dollars for the 1974–75 season, with substantial funding from the New York State Council on the Arts (NYSCA), the Edward John Noble Foundation, and the National Endowment for the Arts (NEA).

Now he had money but no real estate. In the fall of 1974, his grants in jeopardy, he rode his bicycle all over the city looking for a performing space. His program officer at NYSCA told him in December that his grant money would be rescinded if he didn't find a home for Playwrights Horizons, immediately. He had one day to come up with a theater.

Nothing motivated Moss more than a crisis. He held his nose and headed for Forty-second Street, an area he generally avoided because it was so disgusting. At the time a landlord named Irving Maidman owned a large chunk of the street. Maidman had been evicting deadbeat porn tenants, hoping to rent to legitimate theater groups. Not many were interested. The block between Ninth and Tenth avenues was particularly grim. Massage parlors and strip joints were tucked between abandoned buildings. The sidewalks were in disrepair, littered with trash and rubble from crumbling structures.

To Moss the scene resembled Berlin just after World War II. In his history of the area, *Ghosts of 42nd Street,* Anthony Bianco described Moss's encounter with the 400 block:

Winos, derelicts, and even the occasional Gypsy family coexisted here with prostitutes, drug dealers , and their customers.

From the middle of the street, Moss spied a FOR RENT sign on 422. He was appalled by his first look inside the building, which basically was a garbage dump enclosed by walls. But beneath the mounds of refuse Moss could make out the ghostly outlines of the 150-seat Midway Theater. Maidman sweetened the deal by packaging 422 with an office floor at 440 West 42nd Street for a total rent of $1,400 a month.

Moss took possession on January 1, 1975, and announced that the first performance of the season would take place on February 1. The building was small—two stories, twenty-three feet wide—but the task ahead was huge, a total gut job and renovation, all to be done within a month.

He turned for help to his friends—not a plumber or a carpenter among them, but plenty of actors and playwrights. He handed them hammers and nails and told them to improvise.

On opening night the heating system malfunctioned, so the audience sat shivering, but they were there. The hardy theatergoers whom Moss had been cultivating at the YMCA weren't deterred by the aura of danger on Forty-second Street. In fact, the seediness may have been part of the allure.

Within a year of steady attendance, Moss rented additional space from Maidman and formed a not-for-profit corporation called the 42nd Street Gang. His ambitions coincided with the hopes of the 42nd Street Development Corporation, a new nonprofit organization whose mission was described by one official as undoing "four decades of accumulated, renewal-resistant blight."

There was momentum throughout the city to rescue and refurbish. In 1975 Jacqueline Kennedy Onassis had joined the Municipal Art Society's campaign to save Grand Central Station from the wrecking ball—a crusade that coincided with Bob Moss's, on the opposite end of the street. Moss kept a photograph of the elegant former First Lady smiling at him—lean, shaggy, bearded, wearing a T-shirt and a grin—in front of Playwrights Horizons.

Moss acquired the lease to a building that had been a bank's headquarters and had become a strip club. He recognized the public-relations potential. As soon as he signed the lease, he sent a press release inviting reporters to the replacement of the LIVE BURLESK marquee with the Playwrights Horizons banner.

It worked. There was coverage on local television and in the *New York Times,* the *Daily News* and the *Village Voice,* under the headline "Will Bob Moss Become the Next Joe Papp?"

The previous fall Bob Moss had been introduced to a patrician, well-spoken young man with round cheeks, a dimpled chin, a mop of sand-colored hair, and a reserved manner. André Bishop would become a leading figure in New York theater, and one of the most important people in Wendy Wasserstein's life. In 1975, however, when he met Moss, he was floundering around New York, trying to be an actor but mainly waiting on tables and working as a French translator. André was twenty-six years old and a Harvard graduate, but he needed direction; Bob Moss was good at putting people to work—especially those willing to work for no money. André answered telephones, sharpened pencils, cleaned bathrooms—whatever Moss asked him to do, though he wasn't very good at any of it.

"He couldn't do anything," Moss said fondly. "I'd say, 'Paint that wall,' and he couldn't do that. 'Build that,' he couldn't. André was just hanging around, hanging around. He was very smart, but he was helpless."

Moss recognized something in André that touched him, a love of theater that was primal. For André the connection had been made in 1954, not long before his sixth birthday. He'd been taken by a beloved aunt to his first live theater performance, the just-opened Broadway musical version of J. M. Barrie's classic children's story *Peter Pan,* starring Mary Martin. For the little boy, it was an awakening, his future revealed.

He had wanted to go to acting school, not Harvard, but his mother insisted. He became the president of the Harvard Dramatic Club and was considered a promising actor, though he was painfully shy. Once he got onstage, he was fine, but making his way there was excruciating.

At Playwrights Horizons, André found a solution to his dilemma. The peripatetic Moss had been asked to take over a five-hundred-seat theater in Queens, at the former site of the 1964–65 World's Fair. Tickets were

$2.50, and the shows were sold out. Playwrights Horizons Queens, as it was called, specialized in classics and revivals, not the new plays that Moss focused on in Manhattan.

As Moss began to spend more and more time in Queens, not even he, with his relentless energy, could keep up with all the demands on him. André noticed that submissions were starting to pile up unread. One day he approached Moss while carrying a stack of large envelopes, filled with plays.

"What are you doing?" Moss asked.

"These are terrible," André replied. "I'm sending them back."

This kind of editorial astringency was alien to Moss, who felt it was his duty to give aspiring writers a place to experiment, a generous philosophy that led to a wide range of productions, some interesting, some ghastly.

At that moment André became the theater's de facto literary manager.

In making himself useful to Bob Moss, André was on his way to becoming an invaluable fixture at Playwrights Horizons and establishing the course of his career. Though their personalities and styles were in opposition—André was quiet and methodical, Moss gregarious and scattered—they shared a passion for theater and a workaholic drive. Moss was impressed by André's judgment and the way he dealt with creative people: "He had no other activity, so he could call playwrights up and have them come and talk for hours if necessary. Word began to spread that at Playwrights Horizons you had someone who could listen to you, talk to you, care about you. That was crucial."

One of the plays that came across André's desk, in his new capacity as literary manager, was *Uncommon Women and Others* by Wendy Wasserstein. He chose the play along with two others, the first productions that would be "his."

He had already met Wendy. Before she finished Yale, she had approached Moss about staging *Montpelier Pa-zazz*, the little musical she'd written at school. Moss put *Pa-zazz* on, not long after Wendy returned home. André wasn't that impressed with the play, nor with her previous work, *Any Woman Can't*, but he liked Wendy the instant he met her.

When he read *Uncommon Women*, he saw real potential and began to think that the earlier works had just been the plays she needed to get out of her system. They agreed to expand the play, then a one-act, for a fall production and to do a workshop reading that spring.

As Wendy prepared to move back to New York from New Haven, she felt particularly vulnerable, without prospects for either marriage or a dependable career.

She had locked in the small production of *Montpelier Pa-zazz*, but then what? She had no job. Reviewing her rocky path at Yale, and where she stood upon graduation, it was hard not to compare herself with Christopher Durang. The Yale Rep's production of *The Idiots Karamazov*—just after he graduated—received a favorable review from Mel Gussow, writing in the *New York Times*.

A few months later, Chris's *Titanic* played Off-Off-Broadway in New York. In his surreal telling of the legendary disaster, in a production starring Sigourney Weaver, the characters—a bunch of depressives—*want* the boat to sink, and it won't. The play's wacky stream of consciousness won Chris important notice in places that mattered. In the *New Yorker*, Edith Oliver wrote, "From the evidence presented, Mr. Durang is a spirited, original fellow." Mel Gussow declared in the *New York Times*, "Mr. Durang has a ferocious comic talent."

For the summer of 1976, Chris had been accepted at the prestigious National Playwrights Conference at the Eugene O'Neill Theater Center in Waterford, Connecticut. The stars seemed aligned in his favor.

Successful as Christopher appeared to Wendy, he was feeling less than sanguine about his prospects. The positive reception for *Titanic* Off-Off Broadway led to an Off-Broadway production in May, which was trounced by critics, including the same Mel Gussow who had praised it the first time. On reevaluating Durang's "ferocious comic talent," Gussow decided, "There's no ignoring the author's clownish exuberance and malevolence." The *Village Voice* devoted a full page, beginning with the headline "Durang Goes Down with His Ship," noting that some people thought Durang was a major talent but the *Voice* critic didn't see it, concluding that the play

was "self-congratulatory, self-indulgent, numbingly unfunny, and unutterably, *unutterably* stupid."

Chris understood that such was life in the theater, but the personal
nature of the reviews shocked him. His financial situation was precarious,
a pressure Wendy didn't have, thanks to the success of the Wasserstein
brothers.

Chris and Wendy's friendship was built on the yin and yang of insecurity and ambition, and on a willingness to take care of each other as best
they could. For all Wendy's vulnerability, she always surprised Chris with
her ability to get things done and her instincts for using connections to
advantage. When his salary from *The Idiots Karamazov* ran out in the fall
of 1975, Wendy helped arrange a job for him indexing a book about schizophrenia, coauthored by Susan Blatt's father. When Chris moved to New
York shortly after that, Wendy went with him to look for apartments, offering commentary on the safety and specialties of each neighborhood
they visited.

Then Chris's mother, who'd had breast cancer, was diagnosed with a
recurrence and given a dire prognosis; the cancer had spread to her bones.
Relatives were putting pressure on her only child to move back home.
Wendy intervened and introduced him to her sister Sandra's psychiatrist. While Chris didn't find him helpful in most ways, the psychiatrist
gave him one valuable piece of advice: Set clear boundaries with your
mother's relatives. (He didn't know that the same advice was being dis-
pensed to Sandra, who followed instructions to keep Lola on a tight leash,
allowing her to call on Sunday mornings at a certain time.)

Wendy's infatuation with Chris had developed into a true friendship
that was familial, encompassing mundane matters, passing thrills, recur-
ring annoyances, and issues of deepest concern.

Before Chris left for the O'Neill, he went to the Playwrights Horizons
production of *Montpelier Pa-zazz.* Wendy downplayed its importance, just
a ten-o'clock showing in the dregs of Forty-second Street. But she was
excited. She invited her family and friends from her Amherst/Holyoke
theater days and from Yale Drama.

Wendy introduced Chris to André Bishop, who was taking tickets at the door. Chris recognized André from Harvard, having seen him play the character Andrei in Chekhov's *Three Sisters*. That bare-bones undergraduate production had received a rave review in the *Harvard Crimson* from Frank Rich, who became the *Crimson*'s editorial chairman and was now in New York, writing movie reviews for *Time* magazine.

James Lapine was there, too. He had met Wendy at Yale, and they became friends because he lived in New York and had a car. She bummed rides with him and called him "Tats," her version of the Yiddish endearment *tateleh* ["little papa"].

He thought she was adorable, and always thought of her the way she looked the first time they drove to the city together.

"She had a pumpkin outfit on," he said. "Pappagallo shoes and pumpkin tights and a pumpkin dress. I thought it was the chicest thing I'd ever seen."

Lapine had been working as a graphic designer for the theater magazine at Yale when Brustein hired him to join the faculty and do design work for the theater. Theater hadn't been Lapine's interest; he wanted to be a film director. He was twenty-seven years old, trying to get his career going, but not certain which direction to go, frequently getting stoned to avoid thinking about it.

In retrospect it was a remarkable convergence. None of them knew it then, but all of them—Chris Durang, André Bishop, Frank Rich, William Ivey Long, James Lapine, Wendy Wasserstein—would become among the most prominent players in the New York theater scene. Their lives would intersect professionally and personally, with Wendy at the fulcrum of many connections. This was the beginning.

For a year or so after *Montpelier Pa-zazz*, Chris didn't see much of Wendy. After the summer at the O'Neill, he decided to spend much of the fall in New Haven, where his boyfriend lived. He wrote a play, *The Vietnamization of New Jersey*, still subsidized by the CBS grant from Brustein. Then Chris was off to Los Angeles, for a production of *A History of the American Film*, which he had developed at the O'Neill.

But his accomplishments were shadowed by the guilt he felt at being away from his mother, who had endured two bad marriages and was now possibly dying. When he was in the New York area, he spent as much time as he could with her. While he and Wendy spoke frequently by telephone, this made for hit-or-miss contact in the days before cell phones. Their friendship wasn't on hiatus, but there was a lull.

As Wendy's Yale friends landed in New York, many of them discovered, as Christopher had, that the woman who couldn't look you in the eye without giggling was a valuable resource. The impenetrable city was Wendy's hometown, and she could waltz through it as blithely as (a chubby, Jewish) Holly Golightly—and, when necessary, as purposefully as Lola Wasserstein.

When Wendy returned to the city, William Ivey Long—her designer friend and confidant from Yale—had been living for a year at the Hotel Chelsea on Twenty-third Street. The old redbrick building had the kind of romantic history William liked. It was the place where Janis Joplin and Bob Dylan had lived, where Allen Ginsberg had philosophized, and where Dylan Thomas had died. The rent was only two hundred dollars a month, but that was a lot considering William's income, which was nothing.

He had moved to the Hotel Chelsea specifically to meet Charles James, the legendary American couturier. One night, while watching Bruce Jenner win the gold medal for the decathlon in the 1976 Olympics, William came up with a plan.

"As no one would hire me to make costumes, I decided I would make them anyway, on dolls," he said. "I slipped a note under Mr. James's door that explained that I was having trouble re-creating the bodice on a doll of Marie de Médici I made, based on Rubens's coronation portrait; would he help me? Minutes later, ding-a-ling. 'Hello, this is Charles James' . . . and from then on I cooked dinner, I walked the dog—Sputnik—I painted the bathroom, and I learned and learned and learned."

Charles James was willing to teach William but not to pay him. He needed money, and Wendy knew that. When she saw William's growing doll collection—odd, exquisitely dressed interpretations of historical figures, including a court jester—she told him, "I can sell them!" And she did, via a friend who ran an artisans' gallery on Madison Avenue. The jesters were his most popular doll. She sold them for fifty dollars; he got twenty-five. As he saw it, eight dolls equaled one month's rent. Another Yale pal, Paul Rudnick, and Wendy were the delivery people, carrying loads of clown dolls out of the Hotel Chelsea, popping them into the trunk of a taxi, and taking them up to Madison Avenue.

Wendy began dating Douglas Altabef, a good-looking man with wavy hair who fit Lola's specifications—"nice Jewish boy," student at Harvard Law.

They met through his brother, who had taken a summer program in high school with Wendy. Doug Altabef was familiar. He was born in the Bronx and when his family grew more prosperous moved to Long Island. He went to college at Columbia, then to Harvard. He was attracted to show business—took a year off to spend six months on the comedy-club circuit before deciding he was better suited for law school.

He was immediately attracted to Wendy. He liked her sweet smile and the self-effacing way she carried herself, with her head slightly bent. They soon were dating with the kind of regularity that might lead to a serious commitment. They met each other's family, they commuted between Boston and New York while Doug was in school, they traveled together to Canada to visit Wendy's college friend Harriet and to Connecticut where both of Wendy's sisters were living.

Yet she was dissatisfied. Without discussing it much, she was obsessing about her career, working on a play and applying for writing jobs at various places, including *Sesame Street*. In another letter to "My Dearest Ruthie" she confided:

> *I started seeing a psychiatrist. . . . Lola decided that I was indeed disturbed and needed help. Actually, she's been very understanding recently. I don't know if this all brings back a maternal purpose to her, or she just doesn't like to see her youngest of such a proud litter eating dumplings at 10:30 on First Avenue. The shrink is very relaxing. He told me that I didn't have a strong drive for failure but was rather terrified. The thing that's wrong with Erica Jong is she's only scared*

of flying. Baby, that ain't shit! As you know there's food, beaches, sex, buses, going outside, staying inside, writing suicide letters, cutting hair, having sex, not having sex. . . .

Well, anyway, I hope this man can help me a little, or I marry Douglass[sic]. *Actually, I really hope I marry Douglass*[sic]. *For some good reasons, I think I could like him for an extended amount of time . . . and for some bad reasons, I want all this to be settled. . . .*

The days are sort of the same. I spend them waiting for Sesame Street to call me and avoiding calling Douglass [sic]. *It really is nice being obsessed with something besides Christopher. That really was quite a coup.*

Doug Altabef admitted he didn't take her work all that seriously, because she didn't seem to.

"She was dismissive of it," he said. "Denigrating of it. 'I don't know if it's going to go anywhere,' she said. It was private to her, and I didn't try to intrude on it."

He called her "Monkey."

"She liked that," he said. "She loved that."

At least that's what he thought.

Later he would see himself re-created in one of Wendy's plays, *Isn't It Romantic.* He was recast as Marty, a medical student, whose girlfriend, Janie, is a writer trying to get a job working for *Sesame Street.* She has an eccentric mother who dances and pesters Janie about getting married, and a sweet father who doesn't say much.

Janie discusses Marty with Harriet, her girlfriend:

Harriet: He's sweet.

Janie: He's very sweet. Sometimes I look at Marty and think he's such a nice young man, I must be a nice young girl.

Harriet: You are.

Janie: I never meant to become one. Last week, when we were driving up from yet another Sterling Taverne opening on the Island, I had my head in his lap and he stroked my hair and called me

Monkey. And at first I thought, Janie Jill Blumberg, you've been accepted; not even on the waiting list. So he calls you Monkey. You'd prefer what? Angel? Sweetheart?

Harriet: Beauty?

Janie: And I thought, It's settled, fine, thank God. . . . And it was just as we were approaching Syosset that I thought, I can't breathe in this car, and I promised myself that in a month from now I would not be traveling home from the Island in this car with Marty. And as soon as I thought this, and honestly almost pushed open the car door, I found myself kissing his hand and saying, "Marty, I love you." I don't know.

sn't It Romantic reveals Wendy's fundamental insecurity, her belief that someone could love her only in default mode, as a backup plan. When Marty meets Janie, she is with her attractive friend Harriet, whom Marty describes as "a beautiful girl." He says to Janie:

I remember you. I saw you and Harriet together in Cambridge all the time. You always looked more attainable. Frightened to death, but attainable. I'm not attracted to cold people anymore. Who needs that kind of trouble?

Janie replies with a joke. From the outset she distrusts Marty's motives, unable to believe he is truly interested in her. When she begins to believe that he might want to marry her, she worries that she will be stifled by him. Echoing Wendy's recurrent theme, Janie wonders who she is and what she wants.

I like my work. I may have stumbled into something I actually care about. And right now I don't want to do it part-time and pretend that it's real when it would actually be a hobby. But I want a life too. Honey, my mother takes my father skating every Saturday. . . . I'm their daughter. I want that too.

✦ ✦

At age twenty-six, Wendy found herself in the odd position of being a grown-up in some ways but still a child, dependent on Morris for money, unattached, uncertain about her career.

But things were about to change.

She was preparing for the workshop production of *Uncommon Women,* and she had a job in theater—sort of. Nancy Quinn (sister of Pat Quinn, a Yale friend) hired her as an assistant for the National Playwrights Conference at the O'Neill Center; her primary responsibility was delivering scripts to the members of the selection committee. She quickly acquired a reputation for being fun to have around and for her habit of sweetly accepting subway fare and then taking cabs to her destination. While she was working there, Wendy submitted *Uncommon Women* for consideration at the O'Neill.

Meanwhile she and André began spending a lot of time together, discussing ideas for the workshop production of *Uncommon Women* at Playwrights Horizons, scheduled for March, and how to expand the play for full-blown presentation in the fall. During this period André began to see that Wendy took her craft far more seriously than appearances would suggest. "She would often appear quite disheveled and wear her nightgown to rehearsals and that kind of thing," he said. "She was funny but also hardworking." She always brought a college-ruled spiral-bound notebook (or a yellow legal pad, or the back of a calendar) to meetings, scribbling notes in her loopy handwriting.

The main characters had evolved since the Yale production of the play, three years earlier. They still bore strong resemblances to Wendy's friends from Mount Holyoke but benefited from the intervention of time. Wendy presented the women as they were when they were in college, and as they had become six years after the fact. Experience had added depth to the characters and resonance to her writing.

As she expanded the play from its earlier incarnation, Wendy incorporated new details gleaned from her friends' lives. Harriet Sachs, her friend from Canada, had become a lawyer (like the character Kate) and was in a married-like relationship with her boyfriend, another lawyer, though they agreed they didn't want to marry. Mary Jane Patrone (Muffet)—to Wendy's surprise—hadn't settled down with a man and was working in the promotions department at the *Boston Globe*. Ruth Karl (Rita) had moved in with her boyfriend and was living in the Berkshires, where she continued to assess her possibilities and the meaning of life.

The workshop took place on March 19 and 20. The readings went well; the audiences were enthusiastic. André continued Bob Moss's practice of explaining the mission of Playwrights Horizons at every performance, hoping to raise money, and did so on those evenings. As the room emptied, after one of the *Uncommon Women* workshops, he met Wendy's family. Morris Wasserstein, perplexed as to why the nice Harvard graduate was stuck in a theater next to a massage parlor, went up to André and put an arm on the young man's shoulder. He was muttering "tsk, tsk, tsk" as he withdrew his wallet and proceeded to take out everything in it, more than fifty dollars, a significant sum for Playwrights at the time.

"André," he said, "if you want to continue a life in this not-for-profit theater business, you're going to need a lot more of this."

André appreciated the donation but was far more moved by the spontaneous kindness of the gesture.

On May 3, 1977, Wendy received a letter from Lloyd Richards, artistic director of the O'Neill, telling her the play was accepted, chosen from more than eight hundred submissions, for the National Playwrights Conference taking place in Waterford, Connecticut, between July 10 and August 7.

André was excited when he heard the news—for her but also for himself. He thought *Uncommon Women* could help launch his career as literary manager at Playwrights Horizons. Having the play chosen for the O'Neill confirmed his judgment and would make their production in the fall more momentous. Significant producers went searching for material at the O'Neill, and André already had laid claim to this one. Or so he believed.

Wendy's summer at the Eugene O'Neill
Theater Center changed everything.

Nine

TRYOUT TOWN, USA

Summer 1977

The Eugene O'Neill Theater Center had theatrical romanticism built into its foundation. Eugene O'Neill—the great American depressive, playwright, author, and Nobel laureate—used to spend summers in New London, Connecticut. When O'Neill was twenty-six, he wrote a poem for his girlfriend, titled "Upon Our Beach," referring to the secluded cove in nearby Waterford, where the playwright regularly trespassed. This beloved stretch of beach belonged to a local railroad tycoon, Edward Crowninshield Hammond, who chased O'Neill and his girlfriend off his property. O'Neill took his revenge as writers do, by modeling characters—the wealthy sluggards in *A Moon for the Misbegotten* and *Long Day's Journey into Night*—in part on Hammond.

The Hammond farm was bought by the town of Waterford in 1961, eight years after O'Neill's death. Town officials had plans to turn the estate into a park and to destroy the property's buildings, including the rambling house and the large old barn. George C. White, a Yale School of Drama graduate, had grown up in Waterford. When he heard of his hometown's plans, he conceived of the idea—with other graduates from Yale Drama— of a nonprofit center aimed at developing American theater outside the Broadway establishment. It was the same impulse that had motivated Joe

Papp, and which led Edward Albee to begin his Playwrights Unit, where Bob Moss got his start developing new plays.

In 1965 the National Playwrights Conference at the O'Neill was established. The O'Neill Center quickly became a place for new playwrights to rail against the theatrical establishment, in an idyllic setting paid for largely by the establishment, including major grants from the Rockefeller Foundation and then the Ford Foundation. Soon producers, from both Broadway and Off-Broadway, were prowling the grounds looking for talent. In 1967 the *New York Times* deemed Waterford, Connecticut, "Tryout Town, USA."

In 1968 White asked Lloyd Richards, who had worked as a director at the conference, to take over as artistic director. Under Richards's leadership, the O'Neill tried to balance the founders' desire to develop new works free of commercial pressure with the playwrights' need to make a living. The compromise, as White put it: "Producers and agents continued to be welcome at Waterford, but rigorous efforts were made to keep negotiations off the grounds."

These rules were still in place almost a decade later, when Wendy arrived at the O'Neill. The focus was on the playwrights. Each play was assigned actors plus a director and a dramaturge, a literary adviser who acted as a mediator between the directors and the writers. That summer there were sixteen plays divided among four dramaturges and four directors.

Wendy thrived on both the work and the summer-camp ambience at the O'Neill, located on ninety acres sloping down to Long Island Sound. Meetings took place underneath picturesque copper beech trees and on the beach. The actors and playwrights lived off the premises at Connecticut College a few miles away, in a bare-bones dorm designated "The Slammer." They were transported from their "prison" by buses to the O'Neill, where they took all their meals, cafeteria style, in the big house they called "The Mansion."

Wendy became the resident social butterfly. She took it as her duty to provide comic relief, in surroundings that were both magical and fraught.

The creative spirits gathered at the O'Neill understood that while they might be soul mates in that shimmering enclave on Long Island Sound, once they stepped outside the O'Neill they would be competitors in the fractious domain of the show-business professional.

The injection of nervous tension into the bucolic landscape created an atmosphere conducive to late-night talks and personal revelation. They discussed their anxieties. There were flirtations and romances, gay and straight. Some crossed over, leaving wives for boyfriends.

Peter Parnell was also workshopping a play at O'Neill that summer. He was twenty-three years old and, like Wendy, was consumed with self-examination. Like Chris Durang, he was gay and an only child. Parnell soon felt that his relationship with Wendy had a familial quality, as though they were sister and brother. Parnell would become part of Wendy's growing cast of confidants and colleagues who would remain friends as their lives changed.

The O'Neill clarified what Wendy already knew: She had no intention of settling down with Douglas Altabef, even though he understandably believed that their relationship had been moving in that direction. He took Wendy to the bris of his older brother's son and to the party for his parents' thirty-fifth anniversary. After he graduated from law school in June, he returned to New York from Cambridge; he had a job with a prestigious law firm (Stroock & Stroock & Lavan) lined up for the fall. Though he and Wendy weren't officially living together, he had essentially moved into her apartment. They discussed getting a place together in Brooklyn, where the rents were more reasonable for more space.

While he looked through the real-estate ads, she agonized. There were many factors at play, but the proximate cause of her final, internal estrangement may have been a roast chicken.

Aimee Garn, a friend of Wendy's who had studied design at the Yale University School of Art while Wendy was a drama-school student, was going to the theater with Wendy and Doug one evening. He told Wendy he'd rather eat at home than go out to dinner. Could she cook a chicken?

The question upset Wendy. It wasn't that she didn't know how to cook a chicken.

The chicken symbolized the dilemma she delineated starkly: Would she become part of the theater world or would she become a homebody?

"Wendy's drive was to be visible, to be connected with important people and included in the social scene," Aimee said. "I think Wendy saw the whole picture then—that she was choosing between the domestic plans of Doug and the theater and social worlds."

The roast chicken would become the centerpiece of a scene in *Isn't It Romantic*. In this fast-paced bit of slapstick, Janie Blumberg, the Wendy character, contends with her boyfriend Marty's desire to have her cook a chicken instead of ordering in.

In the play the chicken represents Janie's indecision, her insecurity, her inability to be honest with Marty—deep, troubling questions, but it's hard to take them *too* seriously when they revolve around a chicken dinner. Still, at the end of the scene, there is undeniable poignancy when Janie cradles the chicken according to Wendy's stage directions: "like a baby."

In real time, summer of 1977, Doug wasn't aware of the tsunami of angst unleashed by his request for a roasted chicken. He wasn't aware of much of anything apart from the vast assemblage of legal data he was memorizing in order to become a member of the New York State Bar Association. When Wendy left for the O'Neill, he barely noticed. He remained in her apartment, immersed in studying for the law boards, oblivious to anything else.

Doug missed the production of Wendy's play because of the bar exam but then went to visit her at the O'Neill, still in a fog from his ordeal. They planned a trip to London for later that summer. Doug told Wendy he'd found a terrific apartment—a huge duplex with a garden—for them in Cobble Hill, a quiet residential Brooklyn neighborhood where rents were cheap. He took her lack of a response as an affirmative, and when he returned to New York, he signed a lease for occupancy in the fall.

He didn't realize that Wendy's summer at the O'Neill marked a turning point in her career and in their romance.

* *

Wendy's play was one of four that Swoosie Kurtz had been assigned to act in at the O'Neill. When she began reading *Uncommon Women and Others* by Wendy Wasserstein, she was stopped by a line her character— Rita, based on Ruth Karl—was supposed to say.

I've tasted my menstrual blood.

Kurtz was surprised by her own squeamishness. She was thirty-two years old and was accustomed to exploring the dark realms of human consciousness at the O'Neill, where she had first begun spending part of her summer four years earlier. Death was a frequent subject for the playwrights invited to test and refine new works. Menstruation was not. Men were encouraged to ponder the emotional trauma they might have endured as masturbating youths or homosexual adults. But women were supposed to keep their hormonal imbalances and vaginal business to themselves. Until 1972, just five years before Swoosie Kurtz confronted Rita's line about menstrual blood, the National Association of Broadcasters had forbidden the advertising of women's sanitary products on television or radio.

Kurtz's hesitation was momentary.

"The part just went, boom! Off the page. I knew I could soar with this, I could fly," she said. "The play said things to me about women that I'd never thought of."

Kurtz was a military brat who had always felt more comfortable around boys. "I sort of mistrusted women because they gossiped, maybe they had ulterior motives," she said. "I felt with guys, even in grammar school, they were more direct, they said what they mean, you knew where you stand with a boy."

Uncommon Women and Others forced her to think about her attitudes and relationships toward women and female friendship. Having moved around so much, she'd become accustomed to being a loner. She was a reclusive, private person who had never been part of a group like the one depicted in Wendy's play. The Seven Sisters–college world of the characters was also alien to her—but the women's relationships and insecurities felt familiar. She understood what Rita, her character, meant when she said, "I figure if I can make it to forty, I can be pretty fucking amazing."

Kurtz had appeared on Broadway, but she was still waiting to be discovered. While she was tiny and could pass for a scrappy little gamine, she was in her thirties, geriatric for an ingenue. Her part in *Uncommon Women* had the potential, she hoped, to help her get noticed in a way she hadn't been before.

It was customary at the O'Neill for the participants to gather for a critique the day after each play had its second performance. Everyone staggered outside after breakfast, clutching cups of coffee, to the rough-wood-and-bleachers setting they called the "instant theater," just behind the back porch of the Mansion. The playwright, dramaturge, and director joined Lloyd Richards, artistic director of the O'Neill, on metal folding chairs on the small stage at the center and listened to comments from the other conference participants. Richards instructed the group to give honest feedback. Which characters did you identify with? What themes did you recognize? The dramaturges took notes, to review later with the playwright.

During the critique Marilyn Stasio—the dramaturge assigned to *Uncommon Women*—saw that Wendy's play created the kind of stir that happened once or twice each season. "It was the hit of the summer," she said. "It was a charmed show."

Kathryn Grody, who played the role of Holly—the character modeled on Wendy—felt the buzz. "We felt we were the stars of the O'Neill that summer," she said.

There were reservations. One man said at the critique that he thought it was peculiar that more men than women laughed at the show.

A woman director said she felt that the playwright trivialized female experience, though someone else disagreed. "We have to have farce as well as tragedy about women's lives," she said.

Honor Moore watched *Uncommon Women and Others* at one of the public performances. Just a few years older than Wendy and a Radcliffe graduate, Moore described her reaction in an article for the December 1977 issue of *Ms.* magazine, where the name Wendy Wasserstein first appeared in a national publication:

Seven young women, portraying students at Mount Holyoke in the sixties, dance to a bouncy calypso beat. It is strange at first and then moving to see these women—who throughout the play have been competing, waiting for phone calls from men, examining a first diaphragm, wisecracking ("I think all men should be forced to menstruate . . .") and otherwise comically demonstrating white middle-class female paralysis—dancing together so happily. The playwright's choice of dance tune—"If you want to be happy for the rest of your life / Never make a pretty woman your wife"— illuminates that contradiction with poignant irony. This and other moments in Wendy Wasserstein's hilarious *Uncommon Women and Others* make me weep, not laugh.

Only one reaction truly mattered to Wendy, however—that of Daniel Freudenberger, artistic director of the Phoenix Theatre. He was so impressed by the staged reading that he offered Wendy a full production, with her O'Neill director, Steven Robman, as part of the package. The Phoenix was a venerable Off-Broadway institution, begun in 1953 on the site of the old Yiddish Art Theatre on Second Avenue. Over the years the theater had gone through several incarnations, with different aspirations and in different locations. Nevertheless it was a significant organization, which had nurtured talent—including Montgomery Clift and Meryl Streep—and was a respected producer of classics as well as new works.

The year before, in 1976, the Phoenix had taken up residence at Marymount Manhattan College on the Upper East Side, in a 250-seat theater dedicated to the work of new playwrights. It was a place to be noticed. Critics would come.

Following the success of *Uncommon Women*, Wendy left the O'Neill with two pressing problems to contend with.

She had to tell André and Bob Moss that she was taking her play back and having it produced somewhere else.

And she had to let Doug Altabef know that she wasn't going to move to Cobble Hill with him.

She waited to deal with both these matters until she returned from the planned trip to England with Doug. The vacation went splendidly, from his point of view. They enjoyed their stay in London and their travels through the English countryside, keeping each other amused with their usual nonsensical wordplay. They rented a car, even though Wendy didn't drive and Doug had no experience driving on the left side of the road. His confusion led to a series of riffs about which side of the road was wrong. He believed they were having fun.

Somehow they managed not to discuss whether they were moving to Brooklyn as a couple. Or possibly he thought there was nothing to discuss. He thought she'd said yes to their renting an apartment together when she actually hadn't said anything definite.

So when they returned to New York and Wendy told him she didn't want to move, Doug felt blindsided.

He left for Brooklyn—alone. The borough hadn't yet evolved into the postgraduate paradise it would become a generation later. It was very quiet at night when he returned from his new job as a law associate. He had imagined a snug existence with Wendy in the attractive garden apartment he'd found for them. Instead he felt as though he'd been exiled. Within six weeks he moved back to Manhattan and a few months later began dating a paralegal at his firm. When he told Wendy, he sensed she was bothered not by his transfer of affection but rather by his new girl-friend's profession.

"She was mortified," he said. "How could I go from her to this regular old person?"

There it was again: superior-inferior.

While Wendy allowed her relationship with Doug Altabef to drift into oblivion, she was far more direct with André and Bob Moss, and the matter of where her play would be produced.

She asked them to meet for breakfast at a diner, near Playwrights Horizons.

The little-girl affect was gone. She was warm but businesslike. She told them the Phoenix wanted the play and that she had to go there. The Phoenix would attract better actors; it would give her visibility in a way they couldn't. The critics would come.

Neither man offered an argument. Both of them had been at the O'Neill for the performance, squeezed in between other producers. "They were all laughing uproariously at this play," said Moss. "André and I looked at each other and realized we lost it. We didn't say anything to Wendy."

But when she asked them to breakfast, they knew what was coming. "We were all crying, the three of us," said Moss. When Wendy said, "Can we still be friends?" she already knew that the answer was yes.

"We weren't fools," said Moss. "We thought we could do a better job with the play artistically, because we were so in tune with Wendy and new plays were what we did. But we knew everything she was saying was true."

They vowed they would love each other and be friends forever. "We had this incredibly loving, heartbreaking but wonderful breakfast," said Moss. "That breakfast was about loyalty, friendship, art, business, it was about everything."

For André Bishop that breakfast marked a seminal moment in his thinking. He knew that Wendy had made the right decision for the play and for her future. In plain terms, she got a better offer and took it.

Her decision accentuated the annoyance he'd been feeling for a while now, about the amount of time Moss had been spending at the theater in Queens. He felt that Moss's attention had become too focused on the revivals that were the bread and butter in Queens, not the new plays that were Playwrights Horizons' raison d'être.

Indeed, shortly after the workshop of Wendy's play at Playwrights Horizons in March, André had scribbled a note in pencil on the back of the program for *Uncommon Women and Others,* venting his frustration.

> *Bob,*
>
> *I strongly _feel_ that you must direct _not_ revivals but new plays—I'm convinced that you have so much to give to _living_ playwrights (your Wasserstein comments for ex.), why waste this, yes, talent, I know you love Queens but anyone can direct an ok revival but not anyone can*

direct an ok new play. Plus because you are <u>BOB</u> <u>MOSS</u>, *a stubborn playwright might listen & act because of you instead of not listening to a young director.*

Next year. This is important.

XX André

André Bishop didn't appreciate it then, but Wendy had done him a huge favor. Her defection to the Phoenix made it clear to him that the need to change course was urgent. "We had lost a play that we had worked on a lot, and we lost it to a bigger and publicly 'better' theater," he said. At that moment he determined that Playwrights Horizons was going to change. The theater was no longer going to fan every flame, but rather focus on fewer, better plays that would be more professionally produced and attract larger audiences. Thanks to Bob Moss, who had turned the theater over to him, André was no longer floundering. He knew, very clearly, that he wanted Playwrights Horizons to become a real presence as a New York City theater, and—though he never forgot his enormous debt to Moss—André wanted to be in charge of its destiny.

It was his Scarlett O'Hara moment. He vowed to himself that his theater would never lose a play again.

WITH THE SUCCESS OF *UNCOMMON WOMEN AND OTHERS*,
WENDY BECAME A FORCE IN NEW YORK THEATER.
HERE'S THE CAST FROM THE PBS PRODUCTION,
INCLUDING MERYL STREEP (STANDING CENTER),
JILL EIKENBERRY (LEFT ON COUCH SEATED),
AND SWOOSIE KURTZ (FAR RIGHT, SEATED ON COUCH ARM).

Ten

THE EMERGENCE OF WENDY WASSERSTEIN

1977–78

Things moved quickly after Wendy returned from the O'Neill and her trip to Europe with Douglas. *Uncommon Women* was set to open at the Phoenix on November 21, 1977, in less than three months. There was much at stake for everyone. Wendy and Steve Robman, the director, knew that this was a chance to get noticed in New York. The powers-that-be at the Phoenix wanted to prove that this latest shift in the theater's identity—as incubator of new plays—would be the one that fulfilled the dreams of its founders.

For all its renown and longevity, the Phoenix had never quite found its place. "The dream kept almost materializing—there were many nights when the stage was bathed in unexpected glory—and then vanishing backstage somewhere, or perhaps escaping by the alley door," wrote Walter Kerr, *New York Times* theater critic.

When the call went out for a new play with parts for nine actresses, the response was huge. Wendy introduced actresses who were her friends to Robman and to Bonnie Timmermann, the casting director. They included Alma Cuervo from Yale, for the part of Holly Kaplan, the Wendy character.

Cuervo's audition hit every mark. She grasped how to convey Holly's insecurity and indecision with poignancy but without making her seem pathetic. As important—and different from Kathryn Grody, who played the part at the O'Neill—Cuervo's physical appearance more closely matched Wendy's description of Holly Kaplan, the playwright's alter ego: "a relier for many years on the adage 'If she lost twenty pounds, she'd be a very pretty girl, and if she worked, she'd do very well.'"

Grody was devastated when she learned that Cuervo had been chosen for "her" part. She kicked herself for her outburst about Robman at the O'Neill, when she'd sat on a bench with Wendy and unleashed a litany of complaints about the director. He projected a laid-back sense of certainty that comforted some people, annoyed others. Grody found him aloof and difficult.

Wendy had listened but didn't reveal her feelings about the director. Now Grody wondered if she had insulted Wendy by criticizing Steve Robman. But she wasn't picked for a more straightforward reason. Both Wendy and Robman agreed that Grody was too petite to be fully convincing as Holly. Her size didn't jibe with the text. They didn't tell the actress their reasoning, allowing her imagination to roam free across all her shortcomings and settle on her indiscretion at the O'Neill.

If Grody had offered her theory to Wendy, she might have heard the playwright's true feelings about the director. (Instead Wendy would tell her about them thirty years later.) Wendy agreed with many of Grody's criticisms of Robman. She, too, thought he could be brusque, arrogant, insensitive—and complained about him to her closest friends.

Chris Durang saw the problem as a clash of temperament and style.

As he perceived it, Wendy's gift and weakness was dialogue. The freeform conversations that made her such a popular friend helped her create characters overflowing with youthful exuberance and introspection. But there could be too much of a good thing. Her drafts were too long, and there wasn't much time to shorten them. After working on the play for almost three years, Wendy now had less than three months to get it right. Robman didn't bother with niceties. "Steve had that gruff, regular-guy attitude of being blunt and was always telling Wendy to cut," Chris said, "but not in a nuanced, careful-of-feelings way."

Even though *Uncommon Women* had gone through many incarnations since that first student production at Yale, Robman was confronting the same mechanical problems that had plagued Alan MacVey at Yale, and which Wendy had worked on with André Bishop, and then again with the group at the O'Neill. The play was written as a series of episodes, which created production obstacles when it came to making transitions from scene to scene. Shrewd though the dialogue and characterizations were, the scenes often dragged and were shapeless.

Robman was oblivious to Wendy's irritation toward him, because she didn't reveal it. He remembered the preparations for *Uncommon Women* as an idyllic period, a feeling echoed by many of the actresses and crew. "Wendy was wonderful to work with, because she was patient in listening to suggestions from actors but by no means a pushover," he said.

He acknowledged that he didn't understand either Wendy's world or her contradictions. He was from Los Angeles, not from the East Coast universe of sophisticated girls in fancy private schools. He genuinely admired Wendy's intelligence and talent but was perturbed by her lapses in hygiene and her tendency to eat cookies on the set. It wasn't unusual for her to show up at rehearsal unshowered and uncombed. "Why doesn't Wendy pull herself together?" he asked a mutual friend. "She has so much going for her."

It was hard to reconcile the unkempt nosher and undisciplined writer with the cool businesswoman who emerged when the situation demanded. As they discussed making changes from the cast at the O'Neill, they knew there would be hurt feelings. Kathryn Grody wasn't the only one who didn't make the cut; only three actresses from the O'Neill—Swoosie Kurtz among them—were hired for the Phoenix production. Wendy never hesitated to make a difficult choice when she thought it was for the good of the play. "Beneath that giggly wit were shark's teeth," Robman said. "That's a terribly mixed metaphor. But somewhere inside there was a sharp ambition."

Some of the most promising young actresses in New York showed up at auditions, including Glenn Close—three years before *Barnum*, the musical that made her a Broadway star, and five years before *The World According to Garp*, which launched her film career. She won the small role of Leilah, the friend who is a bit distant, the academically minded young woman who ends up studying anthropology in Mesopotamia.

Another was Jill Eikenberry,* who had already appeared on Broadway and, at thirty, had the beginnings of a reputation in the New York theater.

Eikenberry had come to the tryouts to read the part of Samantha, the pretty coed destined for marriage. When she finished, Wendy asked the actress to try the role of Kate, the cool customer who becomes a lawyer and always seems to have everything under control. Kate's outward imperviousness to doubt was familiar to Eikenberry, a beautiful woman who had been raised not to reveal any insecurity that lay behind her elegant mask of self-assuredness.

What struck Eikenberry most vividly about that day was how comfortable the experience was—because of Wendy. Usually, at an audition, the actress felt that she was the most vulnerable person in the room. But Wendy's vulnerability was so palpable that Eikenberry read with unusual confidence, exactly what the play demanded of her character. After she was hired and they began rehearsals, Eikenberry found insights into herself as she analyzed the chinks in Kate's armor of competence. She recognized the strain of always being the person who refuses to be less than perfect. The actress felt understood by this playwright she'd just met.

"Wendy made me feel like she was extremely grateful that I had come in," she said. "I remember thinking there wasn't any of the usual feeling of 'What am I doing?' or 'Am I going to be okay?' Right from the beginning, it felt good."

As opening day approached, uncertainty crept into the charmed atmosphere. Steve Robman began to see only the flaws: the awkward transitions, the caricatures, the absence of a defining plot. The characters no longer seemed like an endearing ensemble representing the concerns and confusion of contemporary, educated young women, but like spoiled, self-involved shallow creatures with no wisdom to impart.

---

* Nine years later she became famous as Ann Kelsey, a lawyer on NBC's *L.A. Law,* a series that dealt with the social issues of the day, including abortion, late-in-life pregnancy, gay rights, and the like.

He ran into André Bishop and Bob Moss at the bumpy first preview. Robman didn't have to ask what they thought when he saw the grim looks on their faces.

Bob Moss said to him, "You've got to tell the actresses to love the play."

The performances improved. As the actresses got better and better in subsequent previews, Wendy's anxiety increased proportionately. She was worried about the reaction of her Mount Holyoke friends; she also made sure they knew about the play.

Wendy invited Mary Jane Patrone, her Mount Holyoke friend considered a "hottie" at Amherst, to come to previews the weekend before opening night. The two women had remained close, though Mary Jane lived in Massachusetts. When she asked what the play was about, Wendy replied, "Oh, it's about my sisters."

On Friday night Mary Jane stood in the back with Chris Durang.

As the play got under way, she began to realize that many of the words she was hearing were familiar. They were *her* words—coming out of the mouth of the character called Muffet DiNicola. Then she heard other familiar echoes, as though the actresses were projections from the not-distant past—*her* past.

"Whoa," she thought, "wait a minute."

Then she realized that Chris Durang wasn't watching the stage, he was watching her.

It rapidly dawned on Mary Jane why Chris was looking at her. The *Uncommon Women and Others* of the title weren't metaphorical. Wendy was writing about her friends and their experience at Mount Holyoke.

Mary Jane felt overcome by an uneasy sensation, not quite betrayal but something unpleasant, as she watched Wendy's recapitulation of their communal life. It was as though her memories had been stolen and altered. The play was rooted enough in reality that when there was a deviation, Mary Jane found herself thinking, "Oh, she didn't get that character right."

In Rita, the disaffected woman searching for her place, once again played by Swoosie Kurtz, Mary Jane saw Ruth Karl—exaggerated, more extroverted, and funnier, but recognizable. Leilah, the anthropology student who goes to Mesopotamia, was Annie Betteridge, who had gone to Iran after graduation. Kate, the attractive lawyer who had it all pulled together, bore a close resemblance to Harriet Sachs, their Canadian friend, now back in Toronto practicing law, settled into a relationship with her longtime boyfriend. Holly was Wendy.

It would take some time for Mary Jane to gain perspective on the strange ability she hadn't realized Wendy possessed. "She takes things she knows and characters she knows and Wendifies them, probably making them more interesting than they are in real life," she said. Eventually Mary Jane saw some advantage in being part of the process. "It was cool in a way to be immortalized," she said.

That night, however, she was quite disturbed, and she told Wendy as much. After the play they returned to Wendy's apartment and talked. Wendy told Mary Jane, "It's not really you. All the characters are me." The rest of their conversation dissolved into a blur. Mary Jane was still in shock.

She saw *Uncommon Women and Others* two more times that weekend, and began to understand what Wendy was saying. She needed to understand Wendy's reasoning, for the sake of their friendship. It had been tested before—the awful letter Wendy wrote to Mary Jane after their junior year at Amherst, telling her she didn't want to live together (and then changing her mind).

Mary Jane forgave Wendy but never forgot how mortified she felt. "I hated that play," she said.

Opening night: November 21, 1977.

A sense of momentum had been building all day. Western Union telegrams began arriving at the theater. There was one from Lloyd Richards on behalf of the O'Neill and another from Howard Stein at the Yale School of Drama. Even Bob Brustein, who had previously dismissed *Uncommon Women,* chimed in: BEST WISHES TO ALL YOU UNCOMMON PEOPLE FROM YOUR FRIENDS AT YALE.

Just as Wendy had hoped, the Phoenix generated buzz. Major critics from the New York press showed up for the opening. That night, whatever their differences had been during production, Wendy and Steve Robman were united in their nervousness and excitement. This was a major debut for both of them. How would their efforts be received? The actresses seemed to be electrifying and endearing; the audience laughed and sighed in all the right places. Or did they? Wendy had experienced enthusiastic audiences at Yale only to find that the official response to her work was icy silence.

Besides, she knew that this was a friendly audience. Ticket sales had been slow for the unknown playwright's debut. It could be deadly for critics to sit in an empty theater, listening to laugh lines drop into a silent void. Shortly before opening night, Jim Cavanaugh, a drama professor at Mount Holyoke, received a telephone call from the house manager, a Smith graduate who had taken a directing course with him. "Since nobody knows Wendy, we've got an awful lot of empty seats for the opening," she said. "I'll give a comp ticket to any alum from Wendy's years at Mount Holyoke you can round up."

He got on the telephone and found about a dozen Mount Holyoke graduates willing to paper the house, enough to fill the fourth row—which happened to be right behind Richard Eder, the *New York Times* critic.

Cavanaugh's group became politely rowdy as they realized what the play was about. "There was much whispering and giggling back and forth down our row," he said, "as real names or easily decipherable noms de plume came sailing across the footlights."

The Wassersteins showed up in full force—not just the adults, but Wendy's two oldest nieces: Tajlei, age ten, and Jenifer, one week away from her eighth birthday.

None of them was prepared for what they were about to see.

At the end of the play, Jenifer looked sadly at her mother. "Wendy's really unhappy, isn't she?" the little girl observed.

For Georgette the play took a raw turn when Holly, the Wendy character, puts a melancholy song on the record player (James Taylor's "Fire and Rain") and pulls an old raccoon coat over her head while she lies on her bed, smoking. Holly telephones a young doctor she met briefly in a museum and proceeds to deliver a prolonged, unfiltered catalog of her insecurities and deficiencies. With wit and poignancy, the monologue strips the character—an intelligent, searching young woman—to her painful, unformed essence.

First Georgette recognized the coat—it was Wendy's—and then came to a realization about her sister. "She revealed so much of herself, she went so deep, that I felt uncomfortable," said Georgette. "I didn't know that part of Wendy."

Lola and Morris stood and clapped for their daughter, but Lola was not altogether happy. She was proud of seeing Wendy's name in the newspaper, but she wasn't thrilled to sit next to her granddaughters watching a frank discussion of diaphragms and sex. Shortly afterward Lola said to Tajlei, "Ah, sweetheart, the girls in the dance class were talking about Wendy's play." Her tone indicated that she liked the attention but was embarrassed to have a daughter who used dirty words in public.

Pride prevailed. It wasn't unusual to find Lola standing outside the Phoenix accosting people as they left the theater. "So did you like the show?" she asked. "The playwright's my daughter, you know."

Just as *Uncommon Women and Others* had revealed hidden truths and suppositions about Wendy's friends, the play exposed aspects of Wendy she tried to conceal. Beneath the giggles and lowered head lay a questioning, rebellious soul. In addition to the empathy, sincerity, and uncertainty she radiated, Wendy Wasserstein was filled with angry frustration at society's expectations and life's vagaries. She wanted to be heard.

And she was.

"Dramatic Wit and Wisdom Unite in 'Uncommon Women and Others'" was the headline on Richard Eder's review in the *Times*.

Eder, who had become the paper's chief critic just a few months earlier, praised the "inventive direction" and "splendid acting," elaborating with specific instances of memorable portrayals, offering special plaudits for Jill Eikenberry, Swoosie Kurtz, and Alma Cuervo. He admired the peek into a woman's world but was also somewhat offended by the vulgarity. He ended the review on a note of disapproval, wagging an editorial finger at the unladylike language and offering a veiled warning to the playwright, as though telling her not to get an overinflated sense of her own importance, to be careful with her talents.

"Uncommon Women" contains enough specific sex talk to cover the walls of every women's lavatory in the World Trade Center. It is believable, sometimes funny and sometimes touching, but it becomes excessive. One has only to imagine this to be a play about men to realize just how excessive.

Three weeks after her twenty-seventh birthday, Wendy Wasserstein became a public entity. Less than a year had passed since she wrote to Ruth Karl in frustration, speculating on whether she should make yet another attempt at applying to law school. Now her play was the subject of lively and largely favorable discussion in the *New York Times*—and the *Daily News* and the *New York Post*. Soon followed more positive notices in *New York* magazine (where the notoriously tough, even cruel, John Simon offered high praise) and the *New Yorker* (from Edith Oliver, already a fan of Wendy's from the O'Neill).

There was criticism focused on the play's lack of structure, questions of substance, vagueness of time and space. But the general tenor, even the objections, conveyed the sense that this was a playwright to be reckoned with.

Uncommon Women and Others was getting attention everywhere that mattered, but the praise didn't translate into making a living. The run at the Phoenix couldn't be extended past December 4, no matter that the reviews attracted sellout audiences. The theater was already committed to the next new playwright's work. Not-for-profit theater was just that: no money. Wendy had been paid fifteen hundred dollars for her weeks of work, same as Steve Robman. This was Off-Broadway; it was possible to be a one-play wonder.

Still, despite all that, there was no denying the thrill of this moment in the sun.

Within weeks, Thirteen/WNET in New York picked up the play for its series *Great Performances: Theater in America*, which meant national exposure on the Public Broadcasting System (PBS). The producers approached the Mount Holyoke administration about providing some props and then helping to publicize the broadcast:

January 12, 1978

Memorandum

Subject: Production of "Uncommon Women and Others" on Public Television in June

    To: David B. Truman (president, Mount Holyoke College)

    From: Irma L. Rabbino (director, public relations, MHC)

I have just had a conversation with Phyllis Geller, producer at WNET in New York, who will be producing the play by Wendy Wasserstein '71, on the public television network in June. The play, "Uncommon Women and Others" will be produced by Theatre in America. . . .

    As you know, I saw the play in New York, and although my reaction may have been intensified by the seating arrangements—I sat between my mother and father—I did find that some of the explicit sexual references, descriptions, gestures and language, left me with some deep concerns about what the play did for Mount Holyoke.

    Mount Holyoke is very clearly the college . . . we are caricatured e.g. napkin folding was an important skill to be learned in the late '60s. We are stereotyped. . . . But this kind of thing has been done before to all of "the seven" and we have seen it less skillfully portrayed on our stage in many a Junior Show.

    Phyllis Geller tells me that they have taken out the four letter words and "overt obscenity" and any "gratuitously pornographic discussions" but have left in most of the "graphic sexual things." "We're not discussing anything that isn't frequently discussed on talk shows," she said, "and if Dinah Shore can say it, why can't a dramatist?"

    I told her about the problems that I had with some of the language, and that I was concerned about the potential embarrassment to one of our faculty members. She will discuss this with Wendy Wasserstein.

    Jim Cavanaugh has seen the play and thinks it's terrific, as did the group of Wendy's contemporaries with whom he saw it.

    The play certainly helps to dispel our image as "a small Catholic college somewhere" or as "a convent," and although it seems to hit most other sexual concerns and activities, it does not mention the lesbian issue.

We have also gotten miles of coverage in publications we do not normally appear in, e.g., the New Yorker, Time magazine, New York magazine, the Associated Press wire service, Ms., etc.

The questions that arise relate to our "endorsement" of the play.

My feeling is that we should not supply our mailing list (although the directory is available for $3.00) and, whether we agree to lend a few pieces of furniture or not, insist that we receive no credit line on the screen. . . .

As the Mount Holyoke pooh-bahs contemplated how to capitalize on the PBS broadcast without alienating too many alumnae, the theater people confronted the realities of television. A codirector with video experience, Merrily Mossman, was brought in by PBS to work with Steve Robman, a novice at staging scenes in front of cameras. The producers ordered the playwright to cut all curse words—"fucking amazing" wouldn't fly on television—and to remove certain sight gags, considered too daring for the mainstream viewer, like Holly pouring piles of spermicidal cream into a diaphragm. Wendy saved the message she found on her answering machine, from a PBS executive: "We've okayed the script, everything's fine except for clitoral orgasms."

There was also a last-minute cast change. Glenn Close couldn't play Leilah; she was in Buffalo playing the female lead in *The Crucifer of Blood*, a Sherlock Holmes story that was headed for Broadway. Both Steve Robman and Wendy knew Meryl Streep from Yale and decided to ask her to fill in. Wendy made the call.

Streep hadn't spent much time with Wendy at the drama school, except a brief time they'd shared on crew sewing costumes—not getting much done because Wendy kept making jokes with Chris Durang and Albert Innaurato. The hyperintuitive actress enjoyed being around Wendy but couldn't get a grip on her. "To me she always seemed lonely, and the gayer her spirits and the more eager her smile, the lonelier she seemed," Streep said.

Streep had already made an impression in the New York theater world; she had appeared onstage at Lincoln Center in Chekhov's *The Cherry Orchard* and in *Measure for Measure* at Joe Papp's Shakespeare Festival. She had received a Tony nomination for her work in Tennessee Williams's *27 Wagons Full of Cotton.* Her movie career was just taking hold; the previous year she appeared briefly in *Julia,* which starred Jane Fonda and Vanessa Redgrave, and had filmed *The Deer Hunter,* Michael Cimino's epic Vietnam movie, scheduled for release later in 1978.

Personally, it was a difficult period for Streep. Her fiancé, the actor John Cazale, best known for his role as the doomed Fredo Corleone in Francis Ford Coppola's *Godfather* series, was dying of bone cancer. (Cazale's final film was *The Deer Hunter,* released nine months after his death on March 12, 1978.) But the PBS film would take just a few days, and though Leilah's role was small, the character was opaque enough to be interesting. She agreed to take the part.

Streep's participation became a significant component of the marketing of *Uncommon Women and Others.* In April, a month before the play was shown on PBS, the actress appeared in a leading role on national television, in the NBC miniseries *Holocaust.* (It received huge ratings and she won an Emmy. When the video of PBS's *Uncommon Women* was released a year later, Streep's picture appeared on the box.)

Even with all the cuts and changes, the PBS taping went smoothly. "Wendy seemed very happy during that shoot. She seemed to get a big kick out of the whole thing," said Jennifer von Mayrhauser, the costume designer. When Wendy was alone, however, the old demons returned. Despite the huge wave of acclaim, she hadn't yet convinced herself that she was Wendy Wasserstein, Promising Playwright. There was the dismissive review in *Time* magazine, which called her play "stereotypical" and suggested that the "well skilled" actresses "might be better employed." The check she received from Avon Books for the book version of *Uncommon Women and Others* was equally deflating: For the U.S. and worldwide rights, she was paid $750.

Not long after the PBS taping but before the play was shown on television, she described how she was feeling in a letter to Ruth Karl, her Mount Holyoke friend:

> *My dearest Ruthie,*
>
> *What a strange year this has been. I feel as if I've aged around 8 years and had no intention of doing that. It's as if the girl who wrote* Uncommon Women *is different than the sort of average looking woman who is writing this letter. Well, some things are the same. As I sit here near Zaro's Bread Basket (new bakery in Grand Central), chocolate chip cookies are dancing a tango with a Barton's white chocolate rabbit possessing my anxiety and imagination with desire and guilt.*
>
> *God I love to eat and smoke and I know it's all about avoiding relationships and oneself and all this energy should be chanelled [sic] into something creative, useful, not to mention monetarily gainful but when I think of a chocolate Godiva egg it only brings a smile or a tinge of pleasure to me. Oh well.*
>
> *I thought I would devote this year to becoming a "woman" whatever that is. You know a lovely person who writes, is understanding, lives in a house with flowers and a man who she respects and can make her laugh and they will have children and do good work and someone else will fill out the tax forms while she remains interesting and he stays kind and loving.*
>
> *Well, these images have led me on a road to isolation and I suppose feeling as lost as I've ever been. . . .*

Their friendship had been strained by *Uncommon Women*. Wendy had invited Ruth and her boyfriend to see the play, but when Ruth tried to get in touch to nail down details, Wendy became elusive. Ruth had the feeling Wendy didn't want her to see the play.

Finally Wendy called Ruth and told her she'd arranged tickets for the Saturday matinee, the play's final weekend. Ruth drove from the Berkshires with her boyfriend (who became her husband the following year).

It was a difficult trip. They had just moved into a house together and had stopped to visit his parents in Connecticut on the way to New York. This was Ruth's first visit to their house; everyone was apprehensive. On the way to New York, still feeling the tension, her boyfriend drove sloppily, and they almost had an accident.

By the time Ruth settled into her seat at the Phoenix, she was already frazzled. Like Mary Jane Patrone, she didn't know what the play was about. Wendy hadn't told her anything, and, living in Massachusetts, in those pre-Internet days, Ruth hadn't seen the New York reviews.

Like Mary Jane, Ruth didn't take long to feel recognition, then shock, then betrayal. Ruth wasn't flamboyant or outrageous like the character Rita, but Rita's confusion and insecurity were recognizably Ruth's. She felt naked as she listened to Swoosie Kurtz say words Ruth had said in private to Wendy, never imagining that those conversations would become public. They'd told each other deep, dark things they didn't tell other people—or hadn't until now.

She would retain "a vivid and visceral memory of sitting in the darkened theater, feeling it was not nearly dark enough, and wanting to disappear altogether."

After the play was over, Wendy introduced Ruth to Swoosie Kurtz, who thanked her for providing the life that had led to this huge break for the actress. Ruth appreciated her kindness but was overwhelmed by emotion and needed to get away from the suffocating mob scene in the theater. She left quickly, not knowing how this play was going to affect the friendship that had been so central to her for many years. She and Wendy didn't see each other often, but their letters and telephone calls had had the intimate, dissecting quality of therapy sessions. Clearly, though, the same rules of confidentiality hadn't applied.

Ruth knew that Wendy preferred to avoid conflicts, hoping they would go away. A couple of months before the play opened, they'd had a conversation about Doug Altabef. A month after she'd refused to live with him in Brooklyn, Wendy told Ruth, "I *think* I am breaking up with him."

Wendy allowed Douglas to slip away, but she called Ruth to reconcile.

"You have to look at this character, and she is written with much love," Wendy said. She told Ruth she had received letters from young women who were inspired by the character of Rita, knowing that this would be important to Ruth.

Eventually Ruth came to a realization about her friend. "Wendy was a very driven person, and yet she was a very warm person," she said. "Sometimes those things came into conflict."

The correspondence between Ruth and Wendy dwindled over the next two years, and their phone calls became more infrequent. Ruth was married by then, renovating her house, gardening, baking, feeling depressed and bored. She wrote to Wendy:

> *Waiting in line in a dirty place with the paint chipping off the walls makes me feel like a junkie. Then they send me to a state job service where a nice old man told me I was a Mount Holyoke graduate and he didn't have any jobs for me and never would have.*
>
> *I have really been caught up in housewifery. Don't get married! It's not the housework, it's the role that comes with the ring. . . .*

Ruth tried to reach Wendy by telephone—unsuccessfully—for a long stretch of time. When they finally connected, Wendy spoke to her briefly and said she couldn't talk, that she was meeting Meryl Streep for lunch. Ruth was wounded. She knew then that their friendship had run its course.

When she told another friend the story, the friend had only one thing to say:

"Wendy knows Meryl Streep! What's she like?"

Within the small world of Mount Holyoke, Wendy vaulted from obscurity to notoriety. The Spring 1978 edition of the *Mount Holyoke Alumnae Quarterly* contained a friendly article about the alumna playwright, pegged to the PBS airing of her play. By the time the Summer 1978 edition appeared, *Uncommon Women and Others* had become available to Mount Holyoke graduates throughout the United States, via their television sets.

The letters to the editor, which occupied almost a full page, gave the impression that not one of those who had watched Wendy's play on PBS was happy with her portrayal of Mount Holyoke.

From Mary P. Smith Dillingham, '16, of Bridgeport Connecticut:
I sat through 90 minutes of disbelief that any graduate should so sully the name of her alma mater. I was shocked and angry. Does the author realize that she has antagonized other alumnae, probably not of her generation, but of the graduates who for so many years have raised money for the college, worked to inspire young women to select Mount Holyoke who in great numbers have gone on to make important contributions to society and the educational world? And I don't mean by writing revolting plays.

From Helen Duff Conklin, '22, of Washington, D.C.:
Is it possible that these self- and sex-obsessed, nasty talking and thinking characters are representatives of the new breed of uncommon women being educated at Mount Holyoke?

From Muriel W. Riker, '29, Rockville Centre, New York:
She writes like an adolescent who has just discovered sex and wants the world to see how knowledgeable, experienced and sophisticated she and her friends were.

From Sylvia Smith Hawkins, '33, West Redding, Connecticut:
It is my fervent hope that the uncommon women whom I saw on Theatre in America are so uncommon that there are no more of them—at least at Mount Holyoke.

From Susan Breitzke Dunn, '60, Atlanta, Georgia:
We alumnae in Atlanta, who are making a special effort to recruit candidates for admission to Mount Holyoke, now really have our work cut out for us.

Et cetera.

The *Quarterly* responded with a carefully worded defense:

Editor's Note: The television production of Uncommon Women and Others *was filmed in the PBS studios in Hartford. The exterior scenes were taken on the campus of Trinity College. Mount Holyoke, which has no control over the use of its name in literary forms, did not sponsor or endorse the play. While it was distasteful to many viewers, including many connected with the College, there are many others who regard it as an excellently-written play, touching concerns with which young people today are dealing. Among those who admire the play are those who deplore the language. The editors feel that Wendy Wasserstein's success as a young playwright is worthy of coverage in the magazine. Her play was selected for production from among 800 plays submitted to the Eugene O'Neill National Playwriters [sic] Conference and has had, with only reservations here and there, excellent reviews in* MS, The New York Times, The New Yorker, Time *and* New York *magazines.*

This intramural controversy over Wendy Wasserstein and *Uncommon Women and Others* continued for more than a year. The *Quarterly* received an outpouring of opinion—pro and con—from several generations of Mount Holyoke graduates. The play became the vehicle for them to vent, defend, question, and contemplate their feelings about what it means to be an educated woman.

"I am not just a 'student' nor just a 'career-woman,' and I resent being reduced to just those aspects of my womanhood," wrote Nancy Robertson, '78. "In my life there is a tension between my need for a career and my need for friends and family. Precisely this complexity in a woman's life is what Wasserstein's play addresses."

In other words, if the old rules no longer apply, what does?

With her funny little Off-Broadway play, Wendy Wasserstein had hit a nerve located smack in the center of the zeitgeist, landing with special force on the subregion occupied by privileged, ambitious, educated American women born after World War II.

She expressed the often-unspoken, conflicted desires of her peers. Many women like Wendy rebelled against social constraints but were driven toward conventional notions of success. They wanted power and respect—and had begun filling newsrooms, law schools, management-training programs, and medical schools in significant numbers. But they still measured themselves by how much they weighed, what they saw in the mirror, and whether or not they were married.

Wendy recognized the inherent tension for women who wanted professional achievement and a family. She resented feeling forced to make choices that men hadn't been obliged to make, because they had wives to take care of their children. The characters in *Uncommon Women* keep postponing the age by which they will be "pretty fucking amazing," because the goal seems both impossible to define and unattainable.

"I keep a list of options," says Holly, the Wendy character, at the end of the play. "Just from today's lunch, there's law, insurance, marry Leonard Woolf, have a baby, birdwatch in Bolivia. A myriad of openings."

Lest Wendy become complacent, now that her play had been acknowledged, Lola was there to remind her of her shortcomings. Wendy might have been reviewed favorably in the *Times*—the clipping was placed on Lola's wall of pride—but she remained single, plump, and childless.

There were many more ways to succeed—and even more ways to fail.

As Wendy became the social nexus for her group, she created "Orphans' Christmas," for friends who needed somewhere to go at the holidays. [l to r André Bishop, Wendy Wasserstein, Stephen Graham]

Eleven

ORPHANS' CHRISTMAS

1978–79

Following the success of Uncommon Women, Wendy found her way to the epicenter of the overlapping circles of young aspirants milling around New York trying to break into show business.

Wendy and her contemporaries—many of them from Yale—were emerging into the spotlight as a cohesive force in the theater (and film and television), forming a loosely connected Baby Boom sensibility. They were preoccupied with questions of personal identity and a desire to shake up the post–World War II conformity that had defined their childhoods. They were the first generation of playwrights to grow up watching television, which influenced their language and sense of timing.

It was a heady time, tempered by jolts of show-business reality. After her success at the O'Neill, Wendy was signed by a William Morris agent, who immediately relegated handling the novice writer to an assistant, and so Wendy was inducted into the weird ways of show business. Some of the early meetings were so strange that she wondered whether the agent had an inkling of what her work was about.

One meeting was to discuss a film adaptation of *The Total Woman,* Marabel Morgan's 1974 book for Christian wives that became a huge bestseller, its essential message being that women could keep their marriages happy by catering to their men. Wendy and Chris Durang read parts of the book together, howling at various passages, like the one advising women to greet their husbands at the door wrapped in clear plastic wrap and nothing else. The two friends tried to imagine the logic that had led the agent and publisher to match Wendy with this book. They decided that the business people must have seen "Woman" in one title and "Women" in the other and concluded, "Aha! A meeting!"

She switched agents, moving to International Creative Management, where eventually she was represented by Arlene Donovan, who worked closely with Sam Cohn, a powerhouse agent in movies and theater.

Wendy Wasserstein was becoming known as part of the New York vibe. The Phoenix commissioned an original play, the development of which would preoccupy her for the next three years. WNET asked her to adapt a John Cheever story about suburban despair called "The Sorrows of Gin" for public television. Within two years she began work on *The Refugee,* a television adaptation of a book. She and Christopher Durang were hired to write *House of Husbands,* a movie based on a *New Yorker* short story by Charles McGrath.* Jane Rosenthal, a hotshot young television producer at CBS, hired Wendy and Peter Parnell to write a pilot for a comedy. The show wasn't produced, but Wendy and Jane became friends.

As the projects accumulated, Wendy had to stop prospecting and start writing. Most pressing was "The Sorrows of Gin," the only one of the non-theater projects that had developed into a firm commitment. As always, she found that the best way for her to work was to remove herself from her apartment and the lure of the telephone and the refrigerator. The Yale Club Library became her refuge of choice—and even there she managed to distract herself, by writing a letter (on lined yellow legal paper) to her friend Aimee Garn, a document that provides insight into Wendy's work habits:

---

* Called "Husbands," the story (which appeared in the October 22, 1979, edition) is about a group of twenty-two husbands who live together after separating from their wives. The wives begin dating and taking classes while the husbands despair and sit around moping and reading *Madame Bovary,* trying to understand their wives' psychology.

*I am sitting in the Yale Club Library having completed Town and
Country and People Magazine where John Houseman is referred to
as John Paper Chase Houseman* and I'm waiting for the Cheever
story to start writing itself.*

*Keep telling myself if only I could write an outline for a movie or
sit still for 15 minutes then there could be a future of second homes
and peacefulness instead of back at the Yale Club.*

Her lack of enthusiasm for the project was duly noted. The *Times* reviewer dismissed her adaptation of "The Sorrows of Gin," which aired on
October 24, 1979. "The Cheever subtlety is lost in a torrent of obvious
references," he wrote. "Wendy Wasserstein's script and Jack Hofsiss's directing keep emitting traces of contempt for the characters." The few kind
words are reserved for the cast, which included Sigourney Weaver, the only
time she worked with her fellow Yale graduate.

As Wendy's career progressed, albeit with setbacks, the Yale group of
her era was making itself known in the entertainment world. When Sigourney Weaver was filming "The Sorrows of Gin," she and Chris Durang were
reworking *Das Lusitania Songspiel,* a musical spoof of Brecht and Weill,
which they had written and performed together earlier. The play became a
cult hit Off-Broadway in the 1979–80 season and won both of them Drama
Desk Award nominations for Best Performer in a Musical. Christopher had
already been nominated for a Tony in 1978, for *A History of the American
Film,* which had been his O'Neill summer project two years earlier.

That year Meryl Streep received her first Oscar nomination (for Best
Supporting Actress in *The Deer Hunter*); she won the following year, as
Best Supporting Actress in *Kramer vs. Kramer.* Also in 1978, after working as an apprentice for Charles James for three years, William Ivey Long
launched his career with the costumes he designed for his first Broad-

---

* The British-American actor was known as collaborator with the great Orson Welles but in 1973
became more famous as the demanding law professor in *The Paper Chase,* a popular movie about the
tribulations of first-year students at Harvard Law.

way show, *The Inspector General*. Stephen Graham had gone through substance-abuse rehabilitation after being kicked out of the drama school. Now he was in New York, making a place for himself in the theater world with Stephen Graham Productions. In 1979 he joined the expanding universe of nonprofit theater and established the New York Theatre Workshop in the East Village.

As she had at the O'Neill, Wendy became a hub of social connections for her friends and acquaintances. It was in this period that she became friendly with Frank Rich, then still at *Time* magazine reviewing movies and television. He was soon to become the chief theater critic of the *New York Times,* the most powerful person in the New York theater universe.

Chris Durang began to understand that Wendy had an uncanny gift for mixing business and pleasure. She was a born networker. "Wendy would go to all these parties and then say, 'Oh, I got a sitcom deal.' And I'd say, 'How did you get a sitcom deal?' She'd say, 'Oh, I met So-and-So at this party.'" Christopher was uncomfortable at parties, but he was ambitious and so would ask Wendy to bring him along.

Soon he began to get script jobs. "I don't know if I literally got jobs from these parties, but all of a sudden I knew all these people," he said.

After *Uncommon Women,* Wendy began inviting friends at loose ends to her apartment for what became her annual "Orphans' Christmas for the Jews" (being Jewish was not a requirement, and sometimes Orphans' Christmas took place Thanksgiving weekend). Yale friends like Stephen Graham and James Lapine were part of the group, and so were André Bishop and Aimee Garn, honorary inductee into the theater world. With these informal gatherings, Wendy began creating a family of her own, made up of her contemporaries, people in flux, who were—like her—scrambling to make their way in the world.

They weren't oblivious to the harsh realities of adulthood, just eager to keep them at bay. Wendy and her friends turned themselves into Christmas trees, hanging "ornaments" cut out of cardboard boxes around their necks. "It was really infantile," said Lapine. "We had a great time, gave each other presents."

During this period, between 1978 and 1979, Wendy dated Edward Kleban, lyricist for *A Chorus Line,* which would hold the record for many years as the longest-running musical on Broadway. The show had a fairy-tale success story: It began as a downtown workshop production, opened at the New York Shakespeare Festival in 1975, and a year later moved to Broadway, winning nine Tony Awards and a Pulitzer Prize. The songs in *A Chorus Line* spoke directly to the fragile longings of youth and everything else that was significant to Wendy—above all the yearning and hopefulness that made the theater a repository of disappointments and dreams.

Wendy was infatuated, unable to resist the man who wrote lyrics she felt spoke directly to her, such as:

Different is nice, but it sure isn't "pretty."
Pretty is what it's about.
I never met anyone who was "different."
Who couldn't figure that out.

Kleban kept out of the spotlight, preferring to have attention directed at Marvin Hamlisch, his musical collaborator, and Michael Bennett, *Chorus Line*'s director and choreographer. Kleban had a reputation for being funny, charming, and romantic—as well as a hypochondriac and a neurotic hothead. He called himself a "quackster," referring to his tendency to emit critical comments, which he called "quacks." When he went to the theater, he had to sit by the aisle (he was claustrophobic) and then leave before curtain call so he wouldn't bump into a critic. But he was also generous to young writers and composers. He was a gifted teacher, a rousing success (*Chorus Line*) en route to becoming a one-show wonder (he never wrote anything that memorable again).

In the fall of 1978, Aimee Garn, who often felt like an outsider in Wendy's theater crowd, worked up the courage to throw a party for Wendy's twenty-eighth birthday. She invited all Wendy's friends, including Chris Durang and Albert Innaurato, as well as the Orphans' Christmas group. On October 21 everyone gathered at Aimee's apartment, where they waited for Wendy and Ed Kleban to arrive.

Two hours later they were still waiting. Aimee felt humiliated, berating herself for organizing the party, concerned that she'd been presumptuous, thinking she was part of the inner circle. Then Wendy arrived—alone—in a state of agitation. She immediately whisked all the women into the bedroom to tell them about Eddie Kleban's latest "quacks"—how he badgered her to diet and insulted her in bed, assuring them that she was definitely breaking up with him this time (she didn't—not yet).

When Wendy apologized to Aimee—by letter—she recalled the lie she'd told Lola in second grade, at the Flatbush yeshiva, about the wonderful play she was starring in—the play that didn't exist. She told Aimee about Lola showing up at the school and being told there was no second-grade play, and how Lola had protected Wendy by saying, "It must be one of my other children." Wendy recounted how embarrassed she'd felt as a child, her unwillingness to accept the consequences of her own actions.

She connected the story to Aimee's party. "I cannot think of that night at your house without a similar embarrassment," she wrote. "For myself because I would never want to hurt you or have the trust we have dissolved. Sometimes I feel guilty because I rely on you so much and maybe I think that doesn't give you space to find a different sort of life than mine. What if you went to Milan? Or married some vivacious count? Maybe I would feel stranded."

She continued in this vein and then revealed a crucial aspect of their friendship—perhaps of all her friendships. "The thought that I rely on you so much, that you are my family, makes me think for your sake to give you distance," she wrote. "But then I think that would be an enormous loss."

For Wendy, loyalty was a paramount virtue; she had difficulty separating from anyone she once held dear.* True friendship required the intensity of emotion she equated with familial love. "A person has only so many

---

* After she and Ed Kleban finally broke up, they remained friends. After he died in 1987 at age forty-eight, of cancer of the mouth, Wendy spoke at his memorial service and then served on the board of the Kleban Foundation, which the lyricist established to give an annual hundred-thousand-dollar award to promising songwriters.

close friends," she would write in *The Heidi Chronicles*. "And in our lives, our friends are our families." This was a philosophical break from her parents, who regarded family as paramount, an inviolable enclave.

Yet Wendy never overcame the powerful force of family expectations. At an age when her contemporaries were declaring their independence, she remained stuck in childhood struggles for approval. Even as she created an alternative family of friends, her parents and siblings remained the standard-bearers for success. They continued to influence, unnerve, exasperate—and to comfort her.

After the playwright Terrence McNally became a close friend of Wendy's, he observed, "A lot of people in theater came to New York to get away from family," he said. "but if your family lives in New York and you want to live in New York, you can't escape very far."

Wendy hadn't made much effort to distance herself. Throughout Yale, and before that at Mount Holyoke and Amherst, whenever Wendy took part in a play—as actor, choreographer, or playwright—a Wasserstein contingent would almost always be in the audience, applauding vigorously. Lola may have needled Wendy mercilessly about being single, but she and Morris rarely missed a performance.

To the family's command performances—the gatherings for Thanksgiving and Passover—Wendy usually brought a friend, in part to prove that the stories she told were true and partly for self-protection. Bringing someone home was also a sign of real affection.

Even as the children became adults—and husbands, wives, and parents—their most intense bond remained with one another. "Bruce was his most human and humane with Wendy," Doug Altabef remembered, long after he was out of the picture. "They would get very silly together. That was probably the only relationship where he let his guard down, back to being the kid at Yeshivah of Flatbush, riffing, letting his hair down."

When Wendy had been trying to decide between Columbia Business School and Yale Drama, and her parents had been pushing her toward business, it was Bruce who encouraged her to go to Yale, to take a risk on her talent and do something she loved.

"It was a very tight family," said Peter Schweitzer, Sandra's former husband. "God forbid you should ever criticize one of them to the others—the old thing about blood."

In 1976, the year Wendy returned to New York from Yale, Bruce remarried, to Christine Parrott, a willowy redhead. She'd met Bruce in a bar three years earlier, shortly after he separated from Lynne. Christine, who owned a preschool on the Upper West Side and later became a psychoanalyst, was impressed with his intelligence and his dedication to public service; he told her he'd been a Nader's Raider and that he'd edited books with Mark Green. He was working at a corporate law firm, but she believed that he was an idealist who cared about people. "I thought he certainly had that side to him," she said.*

Soon after they met, he took her to meet his family, at a Saturday-afternoon swim party at Sandra's house in New Canaan, Connecticut. Even though Christine had lived in New York for two years by then and her training was in psychology, she was startled by the Wassersteins.

"Sandy had the two darling little girls and this high-powered executive position," said Christine "All of them were so talkative and vivacious and outgoing—not Morris, but Lola, Bruce, and his sisters. I was really intrigued by them, though, for those reasons, because it was so different from my own upbringing. They just said whatever came into their minds as far as I could tell."

Lola's critical outbursts felt like an assault to the gentle young woman. She had grown up in New Castle, Pennsylvania, in a middle-class Presbyterian family. "We were taught to be nice. 'Don't throw stones,'" she said. "I was shocked by the things Lola would say to Bruce—'Pull your pants up! Tuck your shirt in!' I don't think he experienced much in the way of empathy from his mother."

---

* He was a first-year associate at Cravath, Swaine & Moore, one of New York's leading corporate law firms when he met Joseph Perella, the sole operator in the new mergers and acquisitions department at First Boston Corporation, a prominent investment bank. Perella was so impressed by the smart, blunt young man that a year later, 1977, he hired Bruce, doubling his salary to the then-enormous sum of a hundred thousand dollars a year and changing the course of his career.

Wendy was cordial enough, but Christine always felt that her sister-in-law was wary of her. "She probably felt ambivalent toward me," she said. "In some sense I took her brother away from her."

As for Sandra, Wendy's reliance on her older sister had become even stronger over the years. Sandra could be aloof but was comforting. "She was maternal in her own, always-in-control sort of way," said Jenifer, her older daughter. "She was the kind of person who, if you showed up at night upset, she would cook you something and sit you down and give you a glass of wine."

Sandra's home in Connecticut had been a refuge for Wendy when she was at Yale. Several times she called Sandra at midnight to ask if she could come to stay for the weekend, when the pressures at school became too much for her. She was a constant presence in the lives of Sandra's daughters, Samantha and Jenifer, instilled in their earliest memories.

Even before that, while she was at Mount Holyoke, she had come to relish the role of Aunt Wendy to Georgette's daughters, Tajlei and Melissa, who were born while Wendy was still in college. On trips to New Haven to visit James Kaplan, Wendy had often stayed at Georgette's house, amusing her nieces with her endless store of games, delighting them with marvelous gifts, like the little illustrated books she made for them.

By the time Wendy resumed life in New York after Yale, Sandra had divorced Peter Schweitzer and moved back to the city. The two sisters began talking on the telephone almost every day, a routine that became a lifelong habit. They discussed everything: what shoes to wear, their weight, their mother, their careers, their dates or would-be dates. Wendy called these conversations "Opinions with Sandra Meyer." Sandra had firm ideas about almost everything, and Wendy accepted her authority (bridling only when she disagreed with Sandra's editorial comments on her work). Although Sandra took pains to keep Lola at bay, she, too, relied on her family. Often Lola and Morris would baby-sit for Jenifer and Samantha during her frequent business trips, but sometimes the job would be Wendy's.

If Sandra had a business dinner nearby, she would sometimes leave Jenifer alone with Samantha for a few hours, knowing that their building had a doorman. Jenifer remembered feeling terrified, worrying that someone was breaking into the apartment. Just as Wendy had called Sandra when she needed help at Yale, Jenifer called Aunt Wendy. "She would sit there for hours and talk to me, about how somebody couldn't crawl up the side of the building," said Jenifer. "She would totally take it seriously and have real conversations about it."

Even then Wendy approached life with a sense of urgency, and with good reason. Despite the outward image of unstoppable success, the Wassersteins suffered. The family Bible might have been the *New York Times,* but their story was rooted in the book of Job.

While Wendy was enjoying the acclaim that greeted *Uncommon Women,* she watched Sandra fall deeply, madly in love. The object of her passion was Andrew G. Kershaw, chairman of Ogilvy & Mather, one of the world's largest advertising agencies.

Kershaw fulfilled Sandra's strict demands. He was brilliant, dashing, larger than life, a Hungarian-born World War II marine commando, fearless businessman, and pugnacious debater. When they met, she was almost forty, twice divorced; he was fifteen years older and still married. While his divorce was pending, they made plans to marry and began to live together.

They were smitten, necking in the backseats of cars like teenagers. On October 28, 1978, they were together at home in Pound Ridge, an affluent New York suburb, when he came in from the yard, where he'd been trimming tree limbs. Twenty minutes later Sandra found him dead of a heart attack.

A few days after his death, she appeared, stricken but composed, at Alice Tully Hall, where twelve hundred people had gathered for a memorial service. Even when submerged in grief, Sandra maintained a surpassing ability to coolly appraise a situation.

"If I do say so myself—Andrew would have been proud of me and the girls," she recalled, writing about that day. "We looked exactly right: I was wearing a stunning, very classic black suit (bought the day before with my sister, Wendy), with a wine coloured silk shirt and one rope of pearls. The girls, with their very blond hair, dress-up clothes, and solemn manner, walked into the hall with me after almost everyone else was seated— escorted by one of Andrew's partners. I'm sure we looked admirable. . . .

"How Andrew would have laughed at Jock's obvious inability to admire him—right to the end," she said of the eulogy delivered by John "Jock" Elliott, chairman of Ogilvy & Mather's worldwide operations. "If you really analyze the eulogy, Andrew was being credited with immense energy and the ability to work hard . . . not with the extraordinary qualities of mind and character that were really his. . . ."

She revealed the complex mixture of qualities that made her such a grand and intimidating presence in Wendy's life. "I loved him—really," Sandra wrote. "And from me that's saying a great deal. I've never loved any man, or even admired any man before. In fact, other than my children, my sisters and brother and in a way, my parents—I don't suppose I have ever loved anyone. In fact, most people who know me would wonder if I was capable of loving."

Passion was the overriding theme. "I've lost my man and I feel I've lost my life," Sandra confessed.

Small wonder that Wendy often found herself in emotional turmoil and unable to deal with mundane reality. In her family, relationships were writ large or erased. Her sister's doomed, no-holds-barred love for Andrew Kershaw set an impossibly high standard for romance. Yet even at this moment of supreme loss, Sandra—whom Wendy trusted more than anyone— joined the family's unspoken conspiracy of silence about Abner, their absent brother. As Sandra spoke about people she loved, she chose to delete him from memory ("my sisters and *brother*").

Wendy's inability to forget was both a blessing and a curse. Memory fueled her work, but her family's past nagged at her. She was haunted by Abner and what he represented. Her older siblings had known him, had witnessed his seizures and been frightened by his behavior. None of them questioned their parents' decision to send him away. For Wendy, Abner became mythic, a symbol of what might happen to children who didn't meet Lola's standards. They could be banished. Wendy could never shake that empty feeling, the sense that love, like life, was precarious—parents abandon their children, husbands and lovers die, and sisters are left to wonder, are they their brother's keeper?

She never stopped wondering about the figure long missing from Wasserstein family portraits. When *Uncommon Women and Others* was published in book form, she dedicated it "To my brothers, Abner and Bruce." Was this a rebuke to Lola and Morris, for separating Abner from his family, or was the dedication simply an expression of Wendy's urge for fairness, or a bit of both? If she was going to pay homage to the brother she adored, she would also acknowledge the brother she never knew.

A bner was not a ghost. He had become a man. When Wendy turned thirty, he was forty. He was easily recognizable as a Wasserstein; he had the same broad features as Bruce and Wendy and a thicket of dark, curly hair, just like his younger sister's.

His had been a long, lonely journey. After he was too old to remain at the Devereux School, Morris and Lola moved him to a state-run institution in upstate New York, for people who suffered from epileptic seizures. Even the best of these institutions were grim places, known as human warehouses. In the 1970s, spurred by the civil-rights movement, there was legal and political momentum to deinstitutionalize mentally ill people and move them into smaller halfway houses that were—theoretically—more humane. Abner lived in one of these for a few years, in Rochester, New York; when it closed, he moved into a group home in Penfield, a Rochester suburb with a utopian motto: "A Town of Planned Progress."

Eleanor and Ray Newell met Abner at the Downtown United Presbyterian Church in 1978, shortly after he began attending the church's monthly Joy Class meetings for developmentally disabled adults. During regular services the Joy Class met in the church assembly room for informal prayer and discussion. The Newells were volunteers who helped lead the talks, encouraging the participants to go to the microphone and read stories and poems they'd written.

When it was Abner's turn to speak, everyone settled in for the long haul. It took him several minutes to collect his thoughts, which he delivered with awkward precision, punctuated by numerous pauses. As Eleanor Newell—a high-school math teacher—listened to his painstaking stories, she realized that Abner's ability to reason far surpassed his speaking skills. "Abner often would use a mike and give us his ideas," she said. "It might be a long, tedious wait until he had something to say, but it was always something worth waiting for. He thinks things through and analyzes things and makes observations that are well thought through."

When the Newells learned that Abner's sister was a writer who was becoming known, they began collecting newspaper clippings about her for their friend. He watched "The Sorrows of Gin" on television. Unlike the critic at the *New York Times,* Abner was deeply impressed by the show.

There is a record, however imperfect, of his reaction. The Newells and other volunteers began writing down what Abner had to say. Eleanor saved his poems and articles, which represented Abner's thoughts as dictated and transcribed, perhaps edited and embellished, by the various people who recorded his halting words. There is no way to authenticate the accuracy of these typed documents, word for word, but they offer insight into what was on Abner's mind.

After he saw "The Sorrows of Gin," he dictated a review of the show in which he expressed his anger at being separated from his family:

In the world today, instead of putting people away (like the handicapped) let them show how they can help when they are helped.

An example of "putting people away" happens in families. Parents who leave their children each day, ignoring them and refusing to show them love, cannot expect to receive any respect from those children. Caring parents will stay at home with their family more often, paying attention to their children and learning what those children are like. They must realize how delicate and important children's feelings are. . . .

Whether a child is handicapped or normal, his feelings are hurt when he is left alone. A true friend would not do this—he would help a person try to make him understand what's happening. Parents—and others—should look into themselves first before they turn away from a child or a handicapped person who has been "brought down." It might be their own treatment that was the cause.

(Most parents do not see that; they see only the child's fault, and yet they themselves are tearing the child apart, hurting him more and more each time he is left alone.)

Lola and Morris visited Abner two or three times a year. During those visits they kept him informed on what his siblings were doing and how the family was growing. He wanted to be connected, even from a distance. Sometimes he called Morris at the office. That's how Jenifer, Sandra's daughter, learned that he existed. At age thirteen she was working at her grandfather's business during a school break, when a man called. "Can I talk to my father?" he asked.

His niece had no idea who he was. They talked past each other for a few minutes. When Jenifer explained that she was Sandra's daughter, the man on the other end was equally baffled. Then an aide took the phone from Abner. Jenifer immediately called her mother, who filled the canyon-size gap in Jenifer's family history.

When Georgette's younger daughter, Melissa, was eight years old, Abner sent her a gold stickpin inscribed with her name. She told her mother she wanted to send her uncle a thank-you letter.

"Don't," Georgette said. "It upsets him." She had encouraged her children to write to Abner until she'd received a letter from a social worker telling them to stop. The letters agitated him, making him aware of what he was missing, she was told, and the awareness sometimes triggered a seizure.

Georgette didn't question the social worker's instruction, nor did she discuss Abner with either of her sisters or Bruce. Lola sometimes gave Georgette a report, returning from Rochester either in good spirits because Abner said he had a girl friend or depressed because he'd had a seizure.

There was a recurrent theme. "Abner wanted to come home to the family, but the family wasn't there," said Georgette. "What house? What family?"

The lives of the other Wasserstein children had continued. The Brooklyn home Abner longed for was part of their past. His brother and sisters were adults, with concerns far removed from the isolated world he inhabited. For Abner, however, time had stood still. He was a middle-aged man equipped with the mind and heart of an inquisitive youngster, understanding that a larger life was passing him by but powerless to do anything about it. His lot was to feel, forever, the pain of a lost boy.

Part Three

ISN'T IT ROMANTIC

1980–89

André, Wendy, and Gerry during their
Noël Coward vacation in Jamaica.

Twelve

DESIGN FOR LIVING

1980–83

For years there was only one photograph Wendy Wasserstein felt worthy of a Tiffany frame—a snapshot, taken at sunset on a Jamaica beach, at Firefly, the Caribbean home of Noël Coward. Wendy is sitting on a bench between two handsome young men, their arms intertwined. She is wearing a flowing Laura Ashley dress and looks tan and happy, face lit with a huge smile, kicking her feet (clad in red espadrilles) in the air.

It is the summer of 1982. To her right is André Bishop, smiling shyly at the camera, rosy-cheeked, wearing deck shoes and white slacks and a light T-shirt. To her left, Gerald Gutierrez, a rising young director and a new friend of Wendy's, strikes a theatrical pose.

In memory the vacation became mythic, the moment that bonded the three of them for life. "In the theater one always forms instant families, but the next family forms with the very next rehearsal of the very next show," Wendy wrote. "However, in Jamaica, Gerry, André and I became one another's permanent artistic heart and home. During those nights . . . we formed with one another the opinions—and in the theater all you have is your opinions—which would always count, which would always matter."

The three friends were about to collaborate on a project. The following year Playwrights Horizons was going to produce a new version of *Isn't It Romantic,* Wendy's play about a clever, overweight Jewish girl trying to break from her parents and find her own path. André was now in charge of Playwrights Horizons; a year earlier Bob Moss had officially handed the mantle of artistic director to his protégé. Gerry Gutierrez, who had just had a hit at the theater, was going to direct. (In May 1982 Gutierrez directed *Geniuses* by Jonathan Reynolds, which was well reviewed and then ran for a year.)

They were all in their early thirties and unattached. Both men were gay. Wendy called their three-week trip to Jamaica their *Design for Living* holiday, a nod to the Noël Coward play about three people "diametrically opposed to ordinary social conventions"—Otto, the painter; Leo, the playwright; and Gilda, the golden girl they both loved.

Later she gently mocked her own romantic vision. "None of us really opposed social conventions," Wendy wrote of her budding relationships with André and Gerry. But their friendship was emblematic of the new social order. Just twenty years earlier, 25 percent of women between the ages of twenty and twenty-four were single, compared with 50 percent in 1980. As women delayed marriage, they created more intimate connections with friends, male and female.

They rented a villa, equipped with a pool, a kitchen, three bedrooms, and two maids, called Mrs. Henry and Julia. The housekeepers did not seem to approve of their guests and their high-spirited enthusiasm for one another.

Every night Mrs. Henry and Julia prepared specialties like callaloo and saltfish, local dishes that went unappreciated by their guests. As Wendy wrote, "André is allergic to fish, I prefer candy, and Gerry is a vegetarian." They stayed up all night drinking beer and eating saltines covered with Velveeta cheese spread, arguing about the theater.

They paid homage to the playwright at his gravesite overlooking the ocean, by smoking cigarettes and drinking the dry gin martinis they'd brought in a thermos and calling one another "darling" as they imagined Sir Noël would if he were there. The sun and booze made Gutierrez extra buoyant. He quoted Leo, from Coward's *Design for Living:* "The actual facts are so simple," he said to André and Wendy. "I love you. You love me.

You love Otto. Otto loves you. There now! Start to unravel from there."
Someone snapped their picture.

Gerry Gutierrez, enchanting and volatile, reminded Wendy of the parts
of Lola she liked, the lively, funny, unpredictable parts, the go-go without
the meanness. (She hadn't seen his moody side yet, the impatience that
expressed itself in emotional outbursts, the demons that sent him into
hiding.) André was sensible and sweet, glad to go along for the ride, reserved, supportive—reminiscent, perhaps, of Morris.

They swapped stories about their families. Gerry's father was a police
detective. Gerry had grown up in Brooklyn and attended Midwood High,
the same school as Georgette, and received training in classical piano at
Juilliard in Manhattan. After attending the State University of New York,
he returned to Juilliard, where he studied drama with John Houseman,
first as an actor but then finding his calling as a director. His mother
worked as the office manager for Elizabeth Holtzman, a prominent New
York politician, but—like Lola—Obdulia (called Julie) Gutierrez was a
dancer; flamenco was her specialty.

Wendy and Gerry were familiar to each other. They were Brooklyn-
born children from ethnic families to whom they remained attached. The
two of them were captivated by tales of André as a child, a rarefied creature, descended from the world of Edith Wharton. As he traced his DNA
back just a generation or two, they felt directly connected to the gilded
society found in Noël Coward's plays.

André patiently explained his complicated background. His mother,
born Felice Rosen, was the child of New York Wasp royalty (her mother
was Mary Bishop Harriman) and a wealthy immigrant Jew (Felix Rosen).
Mary Bishop Harriman Rosen left Felix and their daughter to marry Pierre
Lecomte du Noüy, a distinguished French philosopher and scientist, with
whom she lived in France.

Felice remained with her father in New York, raised by governesses and
attending a private school where girls named Rosen were not made to feel
welcome. She rid herself of her Jewish-defining surname as quickly as she
could, by marrying a southern Protestant named Hobson. They had a son,

George, and then divorced. Felice next married a Russian émigré, André V. Smolianinoff. They named their son André Bishop Smolianinoff. They divorced; Felice remarried again. She then deposited young André, age seven, in a Swiss boarding school, less than a year after his father died, at age forty-five. She enrolled her son as André S. Bishop, sparing him the potential for insult embedded in the foreign, unpronounceable Smolianinoff (even his father had jokingly referred to himself as "André Smiling On and Off").

What could be more sophisticated? André came from a world populated by railroad barons and dashing heiresses who defied their families by marrying Jews (his grandmother's path) or fleeing to Europe and having tragic affairs (as his mother did, before her first marriage). He had grown up among the New York gentry. His summers were spent on Martha's Vineyard with regular visits to Caramoor, an hour's drive north of Manhattan, the ninety-acre estate surrounding the Mediterranean-style mansion built by his great-uncle Walter Rosen (the railroad baron) and his wife, the former Lucie Bigelow Dodge.* But as a boy he was often on his own, and unhappy, having lost his father and not caring much for his stepfather. André was educated at boarding schools, ultimately graduating from St. Paul's in Concord, New Hampshire, an upper-crust Episcopal school, (alumni include Senator John Kerry and Garry Trudeau, the *Doonesbury* cartoonist) before following the prescribed path, to Harvard.

André was dimly aware of his Jewish ancestry, far more conscious of his mother's aversion to her own Jewishness. He was surprised at how attached she became to Wendy. Felice "Fay" Harriman Francis, as she ultimately called herself (after yet another marriage), also didn't approve of overweight women, but she came to love Wendy and admire her. André felt that in Wendy, his mother—who hadn't gone to college—saw everything she hadn't accomplished.

After the Jamaica vacation, everything merged, the personal and the

---

* Walter and Lucie Rosen began entertaining their friends with musical evenings when the house was completed in 1939. After their only son died flying over Germany in World War II, they decided in 1946 to establish Caramoor as a performing-arts center; which it remains today.

professional. So it seemed natural that, when the time came to promote the play, it became a family affair. The radio ads for *Isn't It Romantic* featured their mothers, Lola, Julie, and Fay—formerly Liska, Obdulia, and Felice—bragging about their children.

André's decision to produce *Isn't It Romantic* was regarded as a rescue mission by Wendy's friends. The play had been commissioned by the Phoenix in 1979, the follow-up to *Uncommon Women and Others*. Steven Robman had become the Phoenix's artistic director, so he had even more reason to hope for a repeat success with the playwright.

Wendy's first version of *Isn't It Romantic* opened at the Phoenix on May 28, 1981. While *Uncommon Women* was remembered as an auspicious production, the Robman-Wasserstein collaboration on *Isn't It Romantic* became a sore subject for many people, for different reasons.

Wendy had struggled to find a workable idea for a new play. She wanted to write about her family; she was also drawn to the questions raised in *Uncommon Women,* now perplexing her in a different way. "I was 28 or so, and suddenly there was this question of all these biological time bombs going off," she told an interviewer. "I had never thought about it before, because there was this pressure when I was getting out of Holyoke in 1971 to have a career. If you said you were getting married back then, it was embarrassing. And then suddenly, all these people were talking about getting married and having babies. Things had somehow turned around and I was trying to figure it all out."

Her notebooks in 1980 and 1981 are filled with character sketches and snatches of dialogue, more crossed out than not.

The Phoenix production of *Isn't It Romantic* seemed jinxed from the moment the sprinkler system went off onstage, right before a matinee performance. The performance was canceled. A frantic Robman went to the yellow pages and found Disaster Masters, a company that promised to quickly deal with the damage.

When Wendy arrived at the theater, she howled with laughter when she learned that Disaster Masters was coming in to save the day. By the evening performance, everything was up and running. After that, every time something went wrong with the show, Wendy giggled and said, "Let's call Disaster Masters."

For Steve Robman, however, Disaster Masters came to sum up the entire experience, and it wasn't funny. Unlike *Uncommon Women,* which Wendy had spent years writing and revising in workshops at Yale and then the O'Neill, *Isn't It Romantic* went into production direct from the page. And the pages kept changing; Wendy was rewriting throughout rehearsals, until the day the play opened.

"Wendy was bubbling over with humor and information and insights," said Bob Gunton, the actor playing the Wasp boss having an affair with his employee. "I had the feeling she was trying to cram it all into this already fairly slenderly plotted play. She trusted Steve to help her shape this into a viable evening of theater."

Robman realized later that they should have taken more time. "I was young and hardheaded or stupid or naïve, thinking we could get the work down in rehearsal," he said.

Always blunt, Robman had become more critical as time ran out and the pressure built. Now he was no longer a director-for-hire but in charge of the long-running theater company's artistic destiny. He was counting on Wendy to come up with a success like *Uncommon Women.* He told her to spend less time eating cookies and more time cutting and revising—in his mind a joke, in hers a jab.

Expectations were high. The *New York Times* ran an affectionate Sunday preview piece, a profile of Wendy, in which she is described as "one of a growing number of women playwrights currently making their mark on the theatrical scene—and, in the process, broadening its scope."

Opening night, however, was not a repeat of the joyous celebration that had accompanied *Uncommon Women.* Steve Robman was tense, already upset with Wendy, who'd told him less than a month earlier that she planned to leave the Phoenix and do her next play at Playwrights Horizons; André Bishop had been building a cadre of writers and asked her to be part of it. He wanted Wendy back in his fold.

Robman and Wendy complained about each other to their friends but maintained a surface of cordiality at work. Following theater custom, Robman gave her an opening-night gift—a gift he would forget about but one that she always remembered. To memorialize his persistent request for cuts, the director presented her with a pair of scissors.

The playwright was not amused.

Wendy never forgave the scissors. Eleven years later, speaking before an audience of theater people and others, Wendy said, "There was this director who shall go nameless who gave me a pair of scissors on opening night because he thought the play was too long," she said. "My advice is, 'Don't work with directors who give you scissors on opening night.'"

Walter Kerr, the influential Sunday critic, offered his assessment, on June 29, 1981, the day of the final performance. He began with a disarming preamble, praising the writing for several paragraphs, making it clear that he saw depth beneath the humor." If the playful little bypass is fun, it's more than that," he wrote of one exchange. "Its implications—the gap between the lines, the stammer at the heart of things, the tumble into uncertainty— is precisely what author Wasserstein means to write about."

Except for a zinger calling Janie's parents "disappointingly clichéd," the review was complimentary until paragraph eight. There Kerr tossed a dart directly into Wendy's most sensitive spot, the place where Bob Brustein still lived, whispering that she was nothing more than a witty poseur.

"The one thing I'm not sure of is whether Miss Wasserstein is in any special sense a dramatist," wrote Kerr. "An explorer, a researcher, a reflective observer, yes." But a playwright? The review's title indicates that the answer is no: "Does This Play Need a Stage?" He concluded with praise that felt like a slap. "It seems to me that Miss Wasserstein should think seriously about the future and about the particular literary form—whatever it may turn out to be—that is most congenial to her. She's too good not to get to the other side."

While Steve Robman's career as artistic director at the Phoenix was flailing, André Bishop was turning into the new golden boy of Off-Broadway.

Before he officially became artistic director, he had already begun creating a sensibility for Playwrights Horizons by picking plays that reflected his own. André liked plays that set off what he called an "unconscious click" in his brain. "It's very personal," he said. "Someone was once analyzing the plays I like, and said rather cruelly that I choose only plays whose lead characters are variations or projections or fantasies of myself. It may be true."

Between 1980 and 1982, he produced a steady run of successful shows, by writers who were just becoming established. These included *Gemini* by Albert Innaurato, *Table Settings* by James Lapine, *Coming Attractions* by Ted Tally, *Sister Mary Ignatius Explains It All for You* by Christopher Durang, and *March of the Falsettos* by William Finn (directed by James Lapine).

Many of the playwrights André produced were friends of Wendy's, either people he'd met through her or had found in the places where talent gravitated, like the O'Neill. There was also a commonality of age (these playwrights, like André, were almost all in their thirties) and of background (there was a heavy, if not exclusive, bias toward the Ivy League).

"We were sort of a gang," said Lapine, who became—along with Bill Finn—part of Wendy's inner circle.

Because of Lapine's connection there, Playwrights Horizons became the workshop venue for *Sunday in the Park with George,* by Broadway's premiere composer-lyricist, Stephen Sondheim, collaborating with Lapine.

"Why am I working off Broadway?" Sondheim echoed a reporter's question. "Basically, I wanted to write something with Jim Lapine. He's associated with Playwrights Horizons, so naturally he wanted to do it there."

As the Reagan era of deregulation and gentrification was beginning, Playwrights Horizons reflected not the ballyhooed 1960s political consciousness of Baby Boomers but the self-involvement that was emerging as a dominant characteristic. "Our 'social concerns' really have to do with the quality of our own lives," said John Lyons, the theater's casting director. "We tend to want to live well and we're unhappy when we can't. Sometimes I feel a twinge about that."

Lyons further elaborated. "We're after intelligence, verbal facility, so-

©Jack Mitchell

IN 1983 *THE NEW YORK TIMES* ANOINTED PLAYWRIGHTS HORIZONS AS THE NEW STAR
OF OFF OFF BROADWAY. [THE THEATER'S PLAYWRIGHTS, L TO R: JONATHAN
REYNOLDS, CHRISTOPHER DURANG, JAMES LAPINE, TED TALLY, WENDY
WASSERSTEIN, WILLIAM FINN, ALBERT INNAURATO]

phistication, freshness," he said. "Many of us got into theater in the first
place because we wanted some wit, style and, yes, glamour. Put it this way:
If Noël Coward and Sam Shepard were both young playwrights submitting
to this theater for the first time, we'd produce Coward."

André Bishop became a darling of the *New York Times,* no small matter for a producer building a reputation. In the summer of 1983, an article
in the *New York Times Magazine* declared Playwrights Horizons "the most
critically acclaimed Off Off Broadway group since Joseph Papp's Public
Theater began in 1967." A year earlier André had been the subject of an
admiring *Times* profile, under the heading "He Nurtures the Gifted
Playwright."

There he explained the common thread in the plays he produced. "I'm
often drawn to work that is not all neatly tied up and beautifully struc-
tured," he said. "I like plays that are lucidly framed, but within that frame,
I'm drawn to writing that is unpredictable, that comes at you in strange
ways, that astonishes you verbally by expressing strange thoughts."

The reporter asked André what he thought "drove playwrights to continue at their often unrewarding craft."

The answer belied a gentle soul. "My feelings about the world are so confused," André said. "I don't know why anybody does anything, much less sit alone in a room with pen and paper. I admire them, though. There's a part of me that's very much a loner. I mean, in my free time, I have a couple of friends, I have dinner with them, and I love to go out and see other plays. But basically when I have nothing to do, I come home and take bubble baths, and that's pretty much it."

Just as Wendy masked her ambition with giggles, André hid his beneath a shy, courtly manner. But when he wanted something, he could be relentless, and he wanted Playwrights Horizons to be noticed.

On December 26, 1982, Walter Kerr wrote an assessment of the past year, in which he drew up a list of the season's ten theatrical achievements. He began with a eulogy for the Phoenix Theatre, which two weeks earlier had ceased operations after a run of thirty years.

Number five on the list was André Bishop.

"If you are a natural wonderer, and have begun to wonder why a group known as Playwrights Horizons should be proving so much more successful than any other Off Broadway house on 42d Street's Theater Row, you will probably conclude that there's a hidden achiever stashed away backstage somewhere, picking the play scripts and putting together the production units," wrote Kerr. "Your conjecture will be entirely correct, and the name of the artistic director is André Bishop. . . . Hereafter the name should be writ large."

Wendy, too, was working hard to advance her career. In April 1983 she won an eighteen-thousand-dollar playwright grant from the prestigious John Simon Guggenheim Memorial Foundation. (She was one of 292 scholars, scientists, and artists chosen from 3,571 applicants.) She wrote a one-act play called *Tender Offer,* a slight, sweet story about a busy father who misses his daughter's dance recital, for the Ensemble Studio Theatre's annual festival of short plays. There were offers to write television and movie scripts.

Even before she read Walter Kerr's advice about trying new literary forms, she had been considering her options. Three years before the Phoenix production of *Isn't It Romantic,* she met with an editor at Atheneum Publishers, who followed up with an enthusiastic note: "Have you decided to try your hand at a novel yet? . . . I thoroughly enjoyed our meeting the other month."

She hadn't attempted a novel, but she had begun writing the journalistic essays that would become a significant aspect of her career. One of the first, a tongue-in-cheek piece called "The Itch to Hitch" (for which she was paid twenty-five hundred dollars) appeared in the November 1981 issue of *Mademoiselle* magazine. Peppered with skepticism, sarcasm, and longing, the essay begins:

> If I were married, the following problems would be solved: loneliness, insecurity, the difficulty of meeting new people, the OPEC crisis and the real whereabouts of the lost ark of the covenant. Furthermore, I would no longer have $200 phone bills, bad plumbing, any friction with my mother or a compulsion to watch *Tomorrow Coast to Coast* even though I don't really like it. If I were married, all my needs would be met by my husband. All my inadequacies would disappear.

For Wendy, now in her thirties, marriage loomed larger as a concern. She addresses her fears—and Lola's—in *Isn't It Romantic,* via Tasha, the character based on Wendy's mother:

"Unfortunately, Janie, the clock has a funny habit of keeping on ticking," Tasha tells her daughter. "I want to know who's going to take care of you when we're not around anymore."

But Wendy may have identified more with Lillian—modeled after Aimee Garn's mother, the publishing executive.

"When I was your age," Lillian tells her daughter Harriet, who is twenty-nine, "I realized I had to make some choices. I had a promising career, a child, and a husband; and, believe me, if you have all three, and you're very conscientious, you still have to choose your priorities. So I gave some serious thought to what was important to me. And what was important to me was a career I could be proud of and successfully bringing up a child. So the first thing that had to go was pleasing my husband, because he was a grown-up and could take care of himself."

Wendy avoided the dilemma by specializing in impossible relationships with inaccessible men. As she began to revamp the play, the Firefly bond with André and Gerry grew stronger. "My husbands," she called them, as Gerry became involved with Peter Evans, a talented and versatile young actor.*

Her friendship with Frank Rich had quickly evolved into a serious infatuation, though he was married and his older son had already been born. "My relationship with Wendy was very intense during my first marriage," he said. "I was essentially not terribly happily married, and [my wife] Gail didn't want to go to the theater. I had two friends, Rafe Yglesias [a novelist and screenwriter] and Wendy, with whom, together or separately, we went to the theater all the time. They became surrogate spouses."

Rich understood that Wendy approached her role as surrogate spouse differently than Rafael Yglesias did. "She definitely had a crush on me, and I had sort of a crush on her," he said. The critic and the playwright had much in common. Both were bright, charming, verbal Jews, driven to be exceptional, using the theatrical arena to do battle with childhood traumas as well as adult demands and desires.

She gave him her scripts to read, and he discussed plays with her. They delighted each other, exchanging gossip and piercing observations about their overlapping worlds. He had someone to endure awful productions with him, who could inject some fun into a dreary evening.

"At one long-forgotten fiasco, we returned from intermission to discover a 'real' swimming pool displayed on stage, with an invalid perched in a wheelchair at its edge," he recalled. "Wendy turned to me with a con-

---

* The two had met in the late 1970s, when Gutierrez had directed Evans in *A Life in the Theatre* by David Mamet, and then they'd worked together during the Playwrights Horizons production of *Geniuses* in 1982.

spiratorial grin. 'Honey,' she said in that husky tone that signaled a punch line was on the way, 'by the end of this play that woman in the wheelchair will be in that pool.' (We were not to be disappointed.)"

Many of Wendy's theater friends disapproved of her relationship with the critic, though he recused himself from reviewing her work. Rich was doubly influential, as chief critic for the *Times* and as a Baby Boomer who paid special attention to the burgeoning voice of his peers. He was key to the resurgence of Off-Broadway, putting his stamp on what new theater should be. This made him friend and foe, builder and destroyer.

Chris Durang said to her, "How come you're hanging out with Frank Rich?" It seemed odd to him. "I wasn't used to playwrights hanging out with critics, and she just said she liked him, and I sort of accepted that," he said.

Acceptance was not the same as liking, especially after Durang's work didn't fly with Wendy's powerful theater companion. Wendy was caught in the middle when Rich skewered her friend, as he did when Durang's screwball comedy *Beyond Therapy* opened on Broadway in the spring of 1982. The review began:

"Some day, I swear, the explosive comic brilliance of Christopher Durang will erupt on Broadway. The only question is when. It didn't happen in 1978, when this playwright's 'A History of the American Film' capsized in a spectacularly ill-conceived production. And it didn't happen last night, when Mr. Durang's latest play, 'Beyond Therapy,' pretty much wilted of its own volition at the Brooks Atkinson. But we must be patient with this gifted fellow—he'll get there yet."

Rich was aware via Wendy that Chris was angry at him. But it had always been clear to the journalist that while his friends could become hers, Wendy's theater crowd was off-limits to him. "When I was theater critic, I wasn't in touch with those people," Rich said. "I'm sure she had to defend me right and left." Their friendship was not secret, but it was separate.

With prominence came a kind of scrutiny Wendy didn't like. Old friends like Aimee Garn noticed that she began to compartmentalize people rather than try to mesh her groups as she once had. "She was critical of others, often in a humorous way, but she was highly sensitive to other people's reactions to her," said Aimee. "She didn't like to be gossiped about or to be called on inconsistencies. The way to avoid that was to keep everyone separate and not able to share information."

She also didn't like people to cross boundaries without her blessing. After she and Doug Altabef broke up, he sent André Bishop a script he'd written. Wendy was not pleased.

André was astonished by the number of friends Wendy seemed to have. If she wasn't out with a classmate from elementary school, middle school, or college, she was at a party or having dinner with Chris Durang, or at the theater with Frank Rich, or at a Wasserstein relative's child's bar mitzvah.

It was the era of *Bright Lights, Big City,* the 1984 bestselling novel by Jay McInerney that came to epitomize Manhattan in the 1980s. *Bright Lights* portrayed the city as an unending hedonistic party of yuppies on the prowl, avoiding responsibility, seeking something elusive, snorting cocaine to help them find it.

The Culture of Indulgence was in full swing, and Wendy was in the middle of it, always game for a night on the town, though she preferred martinis and candy to drugs.

Her friendships took her to glitzy parties, but also to parts of New York that were unfamiliar to the pampered ribbon heiress, the delivery girl who took cabs instead of subways. Through Playwrights Horizons, Wendy met Harry Kondoleon, whose play *Christmas on Mars* was produced in 1983. Wendy was riveted by the play's bright chatter and went to see it three or four times. She became fixated on a scene in the second act, when a mother says to her pregnant daughter, "Walk on me if you think it would help."

The daughter, wearing pink bedroom slippers, steps on her mother's back, using it as a treadmill.

Each time Wendy thought, "How did Harry know how much I want to walk on my mother?"

After noticing Wendy in the halls after one performance, Kondoleon invited her to his home in the East Village for lunch. The neighborhood was seedy. As Wendy walked past the Turkish-Russian bath across the street from his walk-up tenement building, she wondered if Harry could really live in a place like this.

After climbing three long flights of stairs, she was greeted at the top by an unexpected vision. There was Harry Kondoleon—a slight, beautiful, vaguely Victorian-looking young man—elegantly dressed, as if they were going to Rumplemeyer's for ice cream with their grandmothers. He invited her in for the studiously formal meal he had prepared—chicken curry and poached pears served on perfect blue-and-white china.

She often returned for those poached-pear lunches and long conversations about theater and their love lives, or lack thereof. Kondoleon's imagination overflowed, leading him to write plays and poetry—and to draw pictures and write fiction—that mingled camp and sentimentality, homosexual themes and fairy-tale innocence, acerbic wit and flatfooted shtick. He was another of Wendy's friends who would be praised and then dismissed by Frank Rich.

"Are we eternally doomed to admire this man's talent while fighting off boredom?" the critic asked in one review.

By the 1980s, as Boomers themselves were moving into their thirties, boredom had replaced people over thirty as the enemy. The age of adulthood was pushed back still further, to some later date, no longer specified.

Unlike many artists, who claim they don't read their reviews, Wendy studied the criticism of *Isn't It Romantic*—so much so that every time she sat down to write, she heard Walter Kerr say, "You aren't really a playwright." Finally Chris Durang told her, "You have to open the window, push Walter Kerr out, and close the window." In the summer of 1983, Wendy and Gerry Gutierrez worked together to revise the script.

Wendy secluded herself in a place she rented in Bridgehampton—an apartment over a garage—the only way she could get work done. She liked working in small rooms with no telephones; another favorite spot was a little typing room at the New York Society Library in Manhattan on Seventy-ninth Street. Gerry visited her in Bridgehampton and told her to read the play to him, line by line, his routine with every playwright he worked with. "It's the perfect time to look at anything swept under the rug," he explained. Together they cut, added, and rearranged.

She managed to write at least seven new versions, paying particular attention to the portrait of the parents, which had been singled out by the critics as caricature. She softened Tasha (the Lola character), adding emotion and depth to the nudging and cajoling. To her complaints about her daughter, Tasha adds a wistful lament. "You know what's sad?" she asks. "Not sad like a child is ill or something. But a little sad to me. My daughter never thinks I call because I miss her."

With Gerry's guidance Wendy gave more of a narrative arc to Janie, the main character. In the original production she ended as she had begun: indecisive, rebellious, but complacent. Wendy couldn't decide whether to let Janie marry the doctor she was dating; at one point she found Peter Riegert—the actor playing him—so attractive she changed the script to have the couple reunite at the end, then changed it again. Now, in the rewrite, Wendy felt secure enough to give Janie a mind of her own. When she decides to reject her boyfriend, she knows why she's doing it. She would rather be alone than live a life that compromises her ideals. The curtain closes on Janie alone, dancing to the nostalgic strains of "Isn't It Romantic?" the 1930s standard by Rodgers & Hart.

Despite this emboldened statement at the end of her play, Wendy's ambivalence about her own destiny remained intact. "There's as much of me in Harriet [the character based on Aimee Garn] as there is in Janie," she told an interviewer. "When Harriet says I want to get on with my life, have a family and children—I understand that. It is time to move on: I mean the other day I got the Mount Holyoke alumnae magazine and for my class there was a list of 10 people who had had their second child, and at the end of the list it said, 'Wendy Wasserstein won a Guggenheim.' It does make you think."

The new version of the play opened at Playwrights Horizons on December 16, 1983. Reviewers approved of the changes. In the *New Yorker,* Edith Oliver commended the playwright. *Isn't It Romantic,* she wrote, was no longer "listless" but now had "momentum and a sense of purpose." Susan Bolotin, writing in *Vogue,* liked "the honesty with which Wasserstein treats her characters." In the *New York Times*, Mel Gussow praised the "new, improved version," his only significant reservation being "there are still too many scene changes." Walter Kerr's review was written with almost fatherly pride, commending the playwright for taking his advice and transforming her flawed work into a play well done.

Not all the critics were enthralled, especially those looking for a political statement. In the *Village Voice* and the *Nation*, reviewers compared the play to a television sitcom. The *Nation* reviewer went further, seeing in the play "ugly reverse bigotry" perpetuating an "old racial myth" that establishes Jews as "warm and emotional" and Wasps as "cold fish."

Her most valued review came privately, from Frank Rich.

Dear Wendy,

It was impossible to tell you at La Rousse how overwhelmed I was by your play. Partially because of the circumstances—but just as much because of the strong feelings the play aroused. Indeed comparisons between the old Isn't It Romantic? and the new are ludicrous—for it seems to me that the cuts, narrative changes and so on (the improved carpentry of the play) are beside the point. What's really important about the new version is that you said honestly and exactly what you wanted to say—and said it so eloquently that the play hit home to me in a way it never had before. Which is to say that I now really understood what Janie wants—and who she is—and what Marty wants—and who he is. And in that conflict you've hit on something fundamental about the choices we all make. I found it devastating—just as I did the conflict between Janie and Harriet, which crystallized and moved me in a more forceful way than it did before. I really think "Isn't It Romantic?" (excuse me for adding the question mark—I'll stop) will speak to everyone, or at least everyone sensitive, quite apart from their feelings about nouvelle cuisine.

I know it isn't easy for you to be my friend, given the odd paths of our respective careers. I value your friendship so much I cannot tell you. I hope you know that I love you, and it was killing me to have to contemplate all the gloomy faces (yours excepted and possibly Herbert

Levine's) as Mel's review came in. His piece was by no means bad, objectively speaking—save for his shortchanging Gerry—but I do know that, as low [an] opinion as I have of my own work, I could have done better. I wish I could have. But I guess what the whole scene brought home to me is how silly my job is—whether it's executed by Mel, me, whoever—and how unfortunate it is that our theater lives or dies by a single article in a newspaper. It's ridiculous, and a critic's words should have nothing to do with an artist like Gerry's self-esteem. (But I know that is easier said than put into practice.)

Still, that's another subject—which I must start to deal with in my own way. The point of this letter is to say how proud I am of you, how much in awe I am of your talent, how much I treasure being your friend.

Frank

Isn't It Romantic found a large audience at Playwrights Horizons—and substantially altered Wendy's financial status. Up until then her biggest paycheck had been for *House of Husbands;* she and Chris divided the twenty-five thousand dollars between them. Otherwise she had earned relatively small, sporadic sums of money. Her advance for *Isn't It Romantic* was twenty-five hundred dollars. Then Playwrights Horizons moved the play to the 299-seat Lucille Lortel Theatre in Greenwich Village, where it ran for 733 performances. The play was picked up by theaters in Los Angeles and San Diego; there was interest from Hollywood in a screenplay. Betty Friedan asked her to write a TV miniseries dramatization based on her books, beginning with *The Feminine Mystique* (that didn't happen). Suddenly Wendy was making a sizable income from royalties, between $2,000 and $3,000 a week for almost two years, just from the Lortel. She could stop depending on Morris for money.

Her success also benefited the bottom line at Playwrights Horizons, where ticket prices were low—ranging from $9 to $14 in its two theaters, compared with $45 for a Broadway show. Admissions covered only 25 percent of the operating expenses, with the rest coming from grants and donors. Salaries were meager. André Bishop earned about $30,000 a year. Actors were paid a smidgen above minimum Equity rates.

The organization maintained financial health by keeping control over its productions instead of licensing plays to the highest bidder. When successful plays, like *Isn't It Romantic* moved to other houses for commercial runs, rather than licensing plays to other producers, Playwrights Horizons put up the money and then kept the profits, a strategy that allowed the production budget to increase almost fivefold between 1980 and 1983, to $3.5 million.

André made sure Wendy understood how much he valued her, in every way. "You have that rare quality of making people happy in your life as well as through your work," he wrote to her on December 15, 1983, the night *Isn't It Romantic* opened. "I want you to know, once again, how deeply I love *and* admire you and hope we have many more plays and vacations together as we stagger on through this crazy life—Thank you. Love André."

He and Wendy had already begun spending more time together, sometimes to go over rewrites, often just to giggle and gossip over martinis. Wendy forced André to be more spontaneous. "She was just up for anything," he said. "Let's drive to the beach tonight! Great! We did all that."

The steady companionship they fell into felt natural. André had had boyfriends but hadn't been able to sustain a relationship. He told himself he had enough friends to satisfy him, and besides, he was preoccupied with Playwrights Horizons. An admitted workaholic, he found it easier to concentrate on plays than to think about why he was alone.

Wendy was looking for an idealized love and hadn't found it. Or, rather, she kept finding it and then was disappointed when Prince Charming jumped off his steed and revealed himself to be distressingly human. Or he was gay. Or he was married to someone else. She had been in therapy for years, with at least three different therapists, and still hadn't determined why she always chose impossible men.

André, like her, was a romantic, willing to overlook practical concerns such as sexual compatibility. Most important, André believed in her, the way Chris Durang always had. Just as Chris had been a powerful presence at Yale, André was becoming part of the New York theater elite, and

Wendy always gravitated toward power. It wasn't as though she were trading Chris in—she and Chris remained close, but after their screenplay, *House of Husbands,* failed to make it past development, they didn't have a reason to see each other as regularly. Chris had a boyfriend—the same one, now living in Washington, D.C.—and was often out of town on weekends.

André was becoming the person Wendy turned to when she felt impending doom, regardless of the hour. One night, after she had moved into a co-op apartment that Bruce owned on Eighty-second Street, near the East River, she called André in hysterics, telling him she was sure someone was trying to break in through a window. Without hesitation André told her to come to his apartment, in Greenwich Village. She arrived at Waverly Place, her hair a tousled mass of curls, wearing her nightgown under the mink coat her father had given her, clutching her passport, terrified but laughing—an endearing, ridiculous figure, full of warmth and love and life.

André made her laugh even more. "You look like you're fleeing from the Cossacks," he said.

André had never had a friend like that, who touched him so deeply and made him feel that he truly mattered to someone.

WENDY ALWAYS FELT NOSTALGIC ABOUT
FAMILY TRIPS TO MIAMI BEACH. HERE SHE IS
WITH BRUCE AND GEORGETTE.

Thirteen

MIAMI

1984–86

Wendy's next play, *Miami*, took her back to childhood and her relationship with her brother Bruce. Perhaps inevitably, given the complexity of their relationship, she was never able to get the play to work.

Wendy had never stopped loving Bruce, but sometimes she wasn't sure she liked him anymore. The two of them emerged into the spotlight together, as they ascended into the top echelons of their hometown to become representatives of New York's lifeblood industries, culture and commerce. Wendy became known for her openness, Bruce for his secrecy. Both of them sought attention, in very different ways. Neither was as clear-cut as they both seemed.

In late 1983, as *Isn't It Romantic* opened at Playwrights Horizons, Bruce was orchestrating the largest takeover in American corporate history, Texaco Inc.'s $10 billion acquisition of Getty Oil Company, which had already announced it was going to merge with Pennzoil. With this deal, as codirector of mergers and acquisitions at First Boston Corporation, he could claim the distinction of being the investment banker involved in the four largest mergers in U.S. history.

By then Bruce had frequently been quoted in articles in the *New York Times* and the *Wall Street Journal* and had developed a reputation for eccentricity and arrogance, showing up for meetings wearing decaying sneakers, no socks, and faded jeans with a hole in the seat. In a financial journal, he explained the difference between him and Joseph Perella, co-director of M&A at First Boston, the man who'd hired him. "If the company is run by a 65-year-old self-made type who doesn't want to have people telling him what to do, he's usually more comfortable dealing with Joe," said Bruce. "If he's a 45-year-old boy-genius type, he may be more comfortable with me."

Wider recognition, outside the business pages, came in May 1984, with a long profile in *Esquire,* under the title "The Merger Maestro," with an ego-inflating subhead: "At thirty-six, Bruce Wasserstein plays in the high powered world of corporate mergers, where the prizes can be worth billions. No matter who loses, he always wins."

Two months after the *Esquire* article appeared, Tom Wolfe began writing installments of a novel in *Rolling Stone,* as Charles Dickens and William Makepeace Thackeray had done a century earlier. Eventually these installments were reconfigured as Wolfe's hugely popular 1987 novel *The Bonfire of the Vanities,* which chronicled Wall Street excess in the 1980s and then came to represent it. In *Bonfire,* Wolfe created the designation for men like Bruce Wasserstein, who treated the world's financial markets as an extension of boyhood Monopoly games. They were, Wolfe wrote, "Masters of the Universe."

Their motto was succinctly stated in *Wall Street,* Oliver Stone's 1987 movie: "Greed is good."

As the Wasserstein siblings gained prominence, strangers wondered how the two could have emerged from the same gene pool: the warm, lovable playwright, trying to find a resonant message for her peers, and the ruthless banker, concerned with making himself and his business partners rich without apparent regard for the repercussions on the larger society.

Their lives had diverged. Wendy lived in a series of sublets, while her brother moved from a ten-room Fifth Avenue apartment to one that had fifteen rooms (and six bathrooms, four fireplaces). She escaped to the Hamptons to write in an apartment over a garage; he bought a sixteen-acre beachfront estate, eventually becoming one of the biggest taxpayers in East Hampton, a community with a disproportionate allotment of millionaires and billionaires.

Yet the siblings were as similar as they were different. They were smart and ambitious and had gargantuan personalities, hers projecting warmth and his, gruff superiority. Despite appearances Wendy was as guarded as Bruce, but she used selective revelation to deflect outside probing. They were drawn to fine things but were often unkempt. They struggled with their weight and shared a particular look; strong, expressive faces notable for character, not beauty. They gravitated to power and were fiercely loyal to people they cared about. But Wendy's circle seemed to endlessly expand while Bruce's affection was tightly controlled. He extended it lavishly to his immediate family and more modestly to a very select number of friends and relatives.

Bruce was not happy with Wendy's public disclosure of personal detail. He took Lola's childhood lessons to heart and was intensely private about personal matters. In his business the control of information determined success or ruin; Masters of the Universe must be infallible. He found his sister's plays to be too revelatory, too poignant, too Jewish. He felt she turned their parents into caricatures. He didn't appreciate the inside joke in *Isn't It Romantic,* when Tasha Blumberg refers to her non-Jewish daughter-in-law as "Christ." His wife, Christine, looked stricken, when she first heard the line but took the poke in stride.

Bruce was competitive by nature. Decades after he and Wendy had applied to the Ethical Culture School, he discovered his little sister's diary entry: "For the first time I got a higher IQ score than Bruce!"

Bruce was sixty years old when he learned what his then-eight-year-old sister had written.

Almost a half century had passed, but his answer was instant. "That's not true," he said. "I know the test, I know the scores. . . . It's not true."

Still, they were bonded by memories no one else shared, even if their versions of the past didn't always jibe.

"We were very, very close," said Bruce, no elaboration.

Elaboration was Wendy's forte. "Sometimes I wonder whether many of my current friendships with men aren't influenced by those years with him," she wrote in a largely affectionate article. "Not that I've ever again latched onto anyone who wanted to carve a B onto my pajamas. But I derive great comfort from long-term friendships with men—brother figures actually. We don't play emotional games with each other, and I don't worry about whether they'll ever call me again. Nonetheless, I still fall into the trap of thinking, 'Oh, he's brilliant, he's smarter than I'll ever be.' And they no doubt get pleasure of a sort out of being around someone who feels this way."

The divergence of their paths bothered her. "We travel in orbits that rarely intersect, and in some ways we've become enigmas to each other," she wrote. "There's little I can say about my life that I think he will easily understand—I'm not making mega movie deals or marital deals, and I don't have a game plan, a strategy. His secretary still places his calls to me; when he gets on the speakerphone he inevitably bellows 'What's new?' And I can't help wondering whether what I say has any relevance for him at all."

She might criticize him, but no one else should dare. While Wendy was in the New York University library, working on the screenplay of *Isn't It Romantic* (never made into a movie), she diverted herself by thumbing through *Powerplay*. The bestselling memoir by Mary Cunningham, an attractive executive, described her rapid ascent at the Bendix Corporation and then her public humiliation after being accused of having an affair with her boss, the company chairman William Agee, whom she later married. A reference to Bruce prompted Wendy to write a huffy letter to Cunningham—not to proclaim sisterhood but to defend her brother, who had been hired by Bendix for a takeover play:

> I doubt very strongly that my brother ever said, "It must be nice to have a wife who does more than cook" and furthermore question the claim you influenced Bruce's late awakening to feminism.

Let me tell you a little about the women in my brother's life. I am a playwright, my play Uncommon Women has been performed at over 1,000 colleges and my play Isn't It Romantic is running in its 8th month off Broadway at the Lucille Lortel Theater. My sister Sandra Meyer is president of the communications division of American Express. My sister-in-law Chris Wasserstein is a psychotherapist . . . and my mother is a dancer who at age 65 still dances at least 5 hours a day. Furthermore, none of the above women cook, except my sister who can make an extraordinary cassoulet.

Bruce has never, in fact, been around a wife who only cooks (and if he were, what an extraordinary cook she would be!). Because Bruce, in a very exceptional way, has always supported the women around him. . . .

Miami began after Wendy told her ex-boyfriend, Ed Kleban, that she was interested in writing a musical. The story would be inspired by the Wasserstein family's Miami Beach vacations in the 1950s. Kleban recommended a songwriting team, Jack Feldman and Bruce Sussman, fresh off their success with the 1978 Barry Manilow hit disco song "Copacabana."

Wendy and the songwriters understood one another. "We grew up in a similar world and all had the same Miami experience," said Sussman. He was from a middle-class neighborhood in Queens; Feldman's family had made it to the more affluent Five Towns of Long Island. As Wendy talked about her childhood winter vacations, Sussman was flooded with memories from his own childhood, when his family used to drive to Florida from New York over the Christmas school break.

It was easy to mock the pretensions of the Miami Beach crowd—the women dripping jewelry, the men dripping sweat, all of them broiling themselves mercilessly to acquire the souvenir tans that signified they were rich enough to vacation in Florida. But Wendy and her collaborators remembered how glamorous it seemed to them as children, a giddy interlude—let's rumba!—in lives preoccupied with work, a break from the perpetual climb toward elusive aims.

"The holidays were a time for the family to catch Harry Belafonte, build sand castles on the beach, avoid jellyfish, and dance with Dad under the stars to a Latin combo," Wendy recalled.

They traded anecdotes from their youth. Sussman had a younger sister who always complained that he was the prince, just as Wendy complained about Bruce. One day Wendy burst into tears and told her collaborators about Abner. "She just talked about how difficult it was, the choice the family made," Sussman said. "She just sobbed."

For a couple of years, while Wendy worked on *Isn't It Romantic,* the three of them met sporadically. Wendy became fascinated by a comedian named Belle Barth, a transplanted New Yorker who became a Miami Beach character, known as the raunchiest female comic of her day (live recordings of her acts were released as record albums, including the titles *If I Embarrass You Tell Your Friends* and *I Don't Mean to Be Vulgar, But It's Profitable*). Wendy saw dirty-mouthed, rule-bending Barth as a pioneer in her field and good material for a musical. She began to see the comic's story as a way to revisit her own childhood, by having a close-knit, ambitious New York family confront the larger world represented by Barth and Miami Beach itself.

Gerry Gutierrez joined the project after the Playwrights Horizons' version of *Isn't It Romantic* became a hit; both he and Wendy wanted to work together again, and both were eager to do a musical. They'd survived a disappointing experience with a CBS comedy series, a failed summer replacement show called *The Comedy Zone.* Wendy was one of the writers; Gutierrez had been fired as director halfway through taping. Their shared misery made them even closer than they had grown during the Los Angeles run of *Isn't It Romantic,* when they were together so much that Gutierrez joked, "We might as well be married." Whenever he called Wendy, he greeted her with a lyric from *Fiddler on the Roof:*

Do you love me?

She would sing back:

I'm your wife!

André was ready to produce their new work and scheduled a workshop production of *Miami* for the end of 1985. With a deadline now looming, Wendy's sporadic meetings with the songwriters intensified to a regular schedule, usually five times a week.

At first Feldman found the playwright's work habits annoying. "She would come in late to a meeting with notes and dialogue scrawled in a spiral notebook, that she had written on the bus, on her way over," he said. "It seemed like she hadn't really given a lot of thought to what we were going to deal with that day." Over time he realized that her sloppiness was a front for her insecurity. "This was a way of saying, 'Well, if it isn't good, it's because I really didn't have time to work on it,'" he said. "She was so sweet and personable and *heymish* [Yiddish for cozy, snug] that it was very hard to—and this may have been more deliberate than I knew at the time—it was very hard to reprimand her or get angry. But it could be frustrating."

The collaboration grew strained as the months dragged on and it became evident that the songwriters and the playwright had different interests. Sussman and Feldman were enthusiastic about Belle Barth, who Wendy fictionalized as Kitty Katz. They could hang a show on Katz and the pretensions of the nouveau riche New Yorkers who flocked to Miami Beach. The overdone hotels and their overeager patrons were ripe for satire.

Wendy didn't disagree. She loved the untamed impropriety of old-time show-business characters. But her real passion lay in developing the relationship between Jonathan and Cathy Maidman, the children who represented her and Bruce.

As the songwriters argued for more Catskills humor and broad comedy, Gerry Gutierrez pressed her to probe the darker vein of her family story. Wendy tried, writing and revising scenes and dialogue designed to reveal the pressures beneath the surface of the happy family: The mother can't enjoy her vacation until she hears whether her son has been accepted to Harvard. The son can't wait to fulfill the larger destiny he sees for himself. "I know I won't grow up to be like Daddy," Jonathan says. "He's a very good man, but he's not going to change the world." The daughter wants to be loved. The father just wants them all to relax and have a good time.

But Wendy wouldn't break the Wasserstein family's unspoken pact of silence, not even behind the shield of fiction. In *Miami,* Cathy Maidman, speaking for Wendy, explains, "My mother told me never to tell our family secrets." The play avoids conflict, culminating in a warm reconciliation between brother and sister in a heartfelt scene that reflected Wendy's yearning but didn't solve essential structural and thematic problems.

The reaction at readings was discouraging. Some of their Jewish friends were offended, thinking their ode to bad taste was mean-spirited and possibly anti-Semitic. Others thought the musical was funny but disjointed. Others agreed with Stephen Sondheim, who had come to one of the readings at Sussman's invitation. "The tail is wagging the dog," he told the songwriter. In his opinion they should focus on the raunchy nightclub singer and cut back or eliminate the rest.

Dissecting a failed play is like analyzing a failed marriage. Everyone has a point of view; no one has a satisfactory answer. But one thing became clear: As time wore on, everyone besides Wendy ran out of steam. She continued to write furiously, bringing in new scenes and revisions every day. But the songwriters didn't keep pace, and the director seemed to have checked out. Feldman and Sussman had been counting on Gutierrez to do what he'd done with so many other shows, including *Isn't It Romantic*—to dazzle with stage design, pacing, whatever it took to set a piece spinning.

But he couldn't do it. Unable to find a way to make *Miami* work, ashamed of failing Wendy, Gutierrez fell into one of his periodic funks. "It was always a roller coaster with him, part of the 'contract' when doing his shows," said Scott Lehrer, the sound designer. "He was an absolutely brilliant but difficult human being. This was a show that was not jelling for him, and he had a hard time dealing with that."

For the entire month of January 1986, Playwrights Horizons presented

Miami as a musical-in-progress, a workshop that was closed to the press. The entire run was sold out, partly because of the popularity of *Isn't It Romantic* and also because Sondheim's *Sunday in the Park with George* had been tested at Playwrights exactly that way and had gone on to become an esteemed artistic triumph on Broadway.

It was clear, by the end of the run, that *Miami* wasn't going to follow in the footsteps of *Sunday in the Park with George.* On the final night, Ira Weitzman, director of musical theater at Playwrights Horizons, tried to inject a celebratory note into the subdued cast party. He brought in a flamingo he'd designed out of chopped liver, an homage to the outlandish culinary touches that had prevailed at the Miami hotels of Wendy's youth. Weitzman knew that it was a futile gesture. While musicals could find their spark just when it seemed everyone was exhausted, that wasn't likely to happen this time.

"If your energy has been spent leading up to that point, a show can flounder," he said. "That's what I remember about *Miami.*"

Subsequently André, Gerry, Wendy, and the songwriting team met at a restaurant in Chelsea, to contemplate the various pieces of advice they'd received. They emerged from lunch with a vague plan on how to move forward. But the momentum, already flagging, stopped altogether when lawyers and agents weighed in. The project died.

Wendy was deeply disappointed. "I guess I do have some pain about Miami," she wrote to André two months later. "But that's not the real pain. I guess it's that in some way I feel that Gerry and Jack and Bruce [Sussman] didn't come through for me, and I, therefore, couldn't come through for my play or for the theatre. It's a frustration."

Wendy never worked with Gerry Gutierrez again, though they remained close friends. Bruce Sussman and Jack Feldman remained a team a while longer, and then they, too, went their separate ways. As for André, he blamed himself. "I wasn't really the captain of the ship," he said. "The problem was that nobody was the captain of the ship."

After four years of effort, and a brief run as a Playwrights Horizons workshop production, *Miami* was put into storage, where it remained.

Its failure continued to nag at Wendy. At thirty-five she remained in flux. "I feel that things are changing, or rather, I haven't decided how they would change," she wrote to André. *Miami*'s unsatisfactory denouement represented her feelings about Bruce, family, heritage, ambition, the future. For her, she said, "it seems unfinished business."

Wendy and her producers accepting the Tony for *The Heidi Chronicles*, which André [second from right] knew, the moment he read it, would be an "American Important Play."

Fourteen

ROOMS OF HER OWN

1986–87

On June 2, 1986, Newsweek magazine terrified the women of Wendy's generation. The cover story—headline, "The Marriage Crunch"—informed readers that for female college graduates still unmarried at thirty, the chances of finding a husband were one in five. At age thirty-five their chances were almost nil, 5 percent.*

By then Lola Wasserstein had nine grandchildren, each offering a fresh opportunity to remind her youngest (still-unmarried) daughter, "Your sister-in-law is pregnant, and that means more to me than a million dollars or any play."

The pressure came from every quarter. While the Wassersteins proliferated, Wendy's friends and acquaintances had also begun coupling and were beginning to have children. That summer Chris Durang had a small part in a movie (*The Secret of My Success*), where he met a young actor named John Augustine; they became lifelong partners. Sigourney Weaver was married. James Lapine had married and in 1985 had a daughter with Sarah Kernochan, a versatile woman who wrote, produced, and directed

---

* The article was based on a study by a Yale sociologist. On November 11, 1989, the *New York Times* reported, "Marriage Study That Caused Furor Is Revised." As usual, the correction came late and received far less notice.

films and was an accomplished musician as well. Meryl Streep gave birth to her third child that year (there would be a fourth).

Wendy took steps toward acknowledging her independence, or spinsterhood, depending which generation was talking. In 1985, at age thirty-five, she finally got her driver's license and bought a car. After years of rentals and sublets, she moved into a home she owned, an airy sixth-floor apartment at One Fifth Avenue, an Art Deco tower just north of Washington Square, an enviable address for anyone and perfect for her: Greenwich Village, to satisfy her bohemian urges, but definitely not a walk-up. One Fifth bespoke elegance and accomplishment. It was a doorman building equipped with uptown perquisites, including a grand, wood-paneled lobby and the bragging rights that came with neighbors like Brian De Palma and Paul Mazursky, celebrated filmmakers, and Michiko Kakutani, book critic for the *New York Times*.

Perhaps the most attractive feature was proximity to André Bishop, who lived on Waverly Place, a short walk away.

During *Miami* the producer and the playwright had begun spending even more time together. André appeared frequently in Wasserstein family photos. He and Wendy had traveled to Oxford, England, to meet his half brother, who was studying to be an Anglican theologian. There Wendy experienced her first traditional Christmas celebration—nothing like previous Christmases spent at Miami Beach nightclubs, or watching the Radio City Rockettes, or her Orphans' Christmas in New York. Before she left for England, she consulted friends about what gifts to bring and what to wear. During Yuletide at Oxford, Wendy ate lobster Newburg and drank champagne, according to André's family custom, listened to medieval carols, and then everyone gathered to trim the tree with tinsel and lights.

Wendy was both moved and terrified, not quite knowing what to do when Fay, André's mother, handed her an ornament and encouraged her to hang it.

"I was seized with panic," Wendy wrote. "How could I tell this woman that I'd never done this before? How could I explain to her that when I put the ornament on the tree, a flying ham, all the way from Flatbush, might come crashing through their Oxford window?"

Muttering "Oy," she took a deep breath and found an empty spot to hang the ornament, right in the center of the tree.

"The house remained standing," she noted gratefully. "The carols went on playing. No bushes spontaneously combusted and no flying hams pelted the window."

In subsequent years she and Fay became Christmas regulars—not in England but on Park Avenue in New York. Lunch at the Colony Club became an annual Christmas event for Fay, Wendy, and André. Every year Fay—wearing her customary gloves and Schlumberger brooch—presented Wendy with an elegant handbag. Every year Fay's escort introduced Wendy to General MacArthur's widow. Every year they ate plum pudding.

Being embraced by André's family gave Wendy entrée into the world that had seemed far out of reach when she was a student at Calhoun, envying the Brearley girls and their apparent ease. André's elegance wasn't learned, it was inbred. He had begun wearing Brooks Brothers in prep school; now Wendy accompanied him when he purchased his annual supply of fifteen oxford button-downs, the heavier weight.

She regarded his fastidiousness with tender amusement. "Seized by a moment of wild-and-crazy abandon, he also purchased two striped Egyptian-cotton shirts without collar buttons," she wrote. "Following this act of unrestrained depravity, poor André was troubled for at least three hours."

Whenever he needed a new suit, he asked Wendy to go shopping with him. Unlike Chris Durang, a reluctant shopper who liked thrift shops and bought his slacks at the Gap, André happily followed Wendy to Saks and Barneys. Wendy wanted to buck social convention, but she was comfortable in the class to which her family had climbed. Her feminism was not commingled with egalitarianism. She liked cabs, dry cleaners, doormen, and Bergdorf's—though she would show up at parties wearing high-topped sneakers with a designer dress.

After Wendy moved into One Fifth, she and André spent almost every weekend together and often went out to dinner during the week. Her day began with a call to him, to catch up on gossip or just to say hello. It was André who converted Wendy into being a cat lover. "He convinced me to drop my fears of becoming a L.S.W.W.C.—Lonely Single Woman With Cats—and replace them with the joy of having a warm, intelligent feline by the fire," she wrote.

André was besotted with his own Aristocat, an elegant feline named Pussers. He dragged Wendy to the ASPCA, where they visited the back room that Wendy called "kitty skid row." André discouraged her from taking home the lumpy furball she was inclined toward. Wendy told André she wanted a hot-water bottle of a cat, one that considered cuddling a form of exercise.

He ignored her and looked at the forlorn rejects imprisoned in their cages. He spotted a mature orange calico and asked the manager to release her. The cat strutted slowly out, with a regal lift to her tail. André picked her up and began to pat and tickle her head.

"I think she's the best cat," he said, nuzzling her ears.

When Wendy hesitated, André said, "I'm telling you, this is the best all-around cat. She's older, she's pretty, and we know she didn't come from the street."

The ASPCA person noted Wendy's anxiety and asked, "Are you sure you know how to take care of a pet?"

André answered. "She does," he said.

Wendy named the cat Ginger Joy. She later wrote about that day, from the cat's point of view. In an unpublished story, "A Happy Story" by Ginger Wasserstein, Ginger describes André: "He is my guardian angel, my knight in shining armor." Wendy may have put the words in her kitty's mouth, but the feelings were hers.

André had become, quite simply, the love of Wendy's life, though nothing else about their relationship was uncomplicated.

They spent summer weekends in his house in East Hampton, a modest place notable for its previous owner, Alger Hiss, the diplomat and government lawyer accused of being a Soviet spy during the Cold War. When André won grants to go to London to see theater and meet people, Wendy went along. They sailed together on the *Queen Mary* and traveled to Maine. They were intimate, holding hands and often sharing a bed but not sex.

André had a calming affect on her. When she was frazzled by having too many things to do, or jumped to weird conclusions, or worried about things not worth worrying about, he told her, "That's totally insane." That particular phrase became an inside joke, but it was also reassuring.

Discussing Wendy with his therapist, André came to understand that he was drawn to her because of his mother, toward whom he felt both love and anger. "She really didn't bring me up very well," he said. "She wasn't careless or cruel, she didn't not provide for me. She just wasn't that interested. She wanted her new husbands, and I shut her out. She wasn't the warmest, most sympathetic person in the world unless you really dug down. Wendy was kind and generous. I always gravitate toward warm, caring women, the mothers I never had, the sisters I never had."

When marriage entered conversations between him and Wendy, André was interested, even though he was openly gay—with one major exception. He hadn't discussed his sexual preference with his mother. Her prejudices and fears ran deep, and André preferred to avoid confrontation.

Fay let him know she would be pleased to have Wendy as a daughter-in-law. Her endorsement wasn't the main reason he seriously considered marriage, but it lent weight to the idea.

"Wendy always tried to say, 'Oh, let's get married, let's have children,' and be sort of lovey-dovey," said André. "I think she thought, 'At some point he'll marry me and we'll have a strange but happy relationship.' I thought it, too. Seriously. I had nothing else in my life. It wasn't like I had all these boyfriends and then there was good old Wendy. It wasn't like that. She was the primary relationship in my life for a number of years . . .

"I deeply loved her," he said. "Probably in my life she was the closest person ever to me."

There would come a time when he wouldn't be able to clearly remember the details of those carefree days of wandering around Greenwich Village without a destination, having dinner at two in the morning. He never forgot, however, why Wendy was so important to him. "I was always mopey and unhappy, or anxious, and Wendy was very, very sympathetic," he said. "We were helping each other grow up."

The idea of marriage between him and Wendy, which seemed improbable to others who knew them, seemed fairly straightforward to him. "I thought about marrying Wendy because I loved Wendy," he said. "There was no real mystery."

Wendy performed many functions thought of as "wifely." Not just shopping and providing companionship and encouragement, but setting the social agenda. "I was very clear all the time about what I wanted to do in theater but very unclear about everything else," said André. "I was insecure and uncertain and shy." Wendy cleared the path, plunging in, making introductions. "I had someone to go places with, and it was wonderful," he said.

He saw many reasons for them to be together. "I cared deeply about her success, because I believed deeply in her as a writer," he said. "We had wonderful times together. We had a lot of friends together. She made no demands on me. She was sympathetic and cozy, and I was also there for her. We were very, very compatible. Stranger marriages have happened."

To a later generation, raised on open discussion and increasing acceptance of gay rights and same-sex marriage, this romance might seem quite peculiar (or not). Certainly in the eighties, everything was up for grabs. More and more people were coming out of the closet, but just as many remained inside. Gay men and women had historically married straight partners, for propriety's sake; both Wendy and André knew people with secret lives. Old customs die hard.

In early 1987, infatuated with André, Wendy began mapping out a screenplay for *The Object of My Affection,* a novel by Stephen McCauley about the relationship between a gay man and his best friend, an eccentric young woman. Wendy worked on the project, on and off, for years. The story—encapsulated by McCauley in a poignant reflection by the main character, the gay man—must have struck home:

There isn't much to say about my relationship with Nina except that we loved each other and took care of each other and behaved a little like best friends, a little like brother and sister, and a little like very young and very tentative lovers. I suppose the best way to describe our friendship is as a long and unconsummated courtship between two people who have no expectations. Sometimes when we came home late from dancing or a double feature, there was an awkward moment of hesitation as we said good night and each went off to our separate rooms, but that was only sometimes. I think we both valued our friendship too much to make any overtures at exploring the murky and vague desire we felt for each other. I think we were threatened and excited when we were mistaken for a couple by the neighbors. . . .

Wendy began pushing André for answers about their future, leading him to a realization. She wanted children, and he firmly believed he couldn't do that. "I didn't think I would be a good father," he said. "I had such an awful, remote family life that I was afraid of inflicting whatever I had inherited, or learned, on a child."

André was gay and a worldly man of the theater, but in many ways he was conventional, with old-fashioned ideas of what a marriage should be. He realized that he and Wendy were too young—still in their thirties—to commit to a life without sex, and an "arrangement" seemed too cold-blooded.

Inevitably, there was a confrontation. One evening as they were having a drink at the West Bank Café, across the street from Playwrights Horizons on Forty-second Street, the conversation turned, as it often did in those days, to the subject of marriage and children.

When Wendy asked him directly if he was willing to try, André could have kicked himself for his answer. The only thing the erudite Harvard-educated producer and literary adviser could come up with was an utter cliché. "I don't think you should put all your eggs in one basket," he told her.

She didn't record her reply, and André couldn't remember it, or didn't want to.

Their "breakup" was followed by heartbreak, a brief period of separation, awkward moments, tears. They didn't see each other all the time anymore, nor did they talk as frequently as they once had. Resilience being a dominant Wasserstein family trait, Wendy then resumed her friendship with André, the same as it had been but different.

They continued to take trips together, although hard feelings lingered. On an excursion to the Berkshires, the two of them were supposed to meet at the Red Lion Inn in Stockbridge, at a time that turned out to be unpropitious: André was late. Wendy had a toothache.

While she waited, she wrote him an angry letter that made it clear she hadn't taken their separation as a couple as easily as André had wanted to believe.

4:00 Red Lion Inn

André—

. . . It is 4:05 and I am placing a bet with myself that you will arrive at 4:30 or later.

Frankly this makes me furious! I have seldom to experience a meeting with you for which you are not at least twenty minutes late. Yes plays are important, deficits are important . . . but the consistency is irritating and insulting. . . .

. . . .I don't know why I am so angry at this moment. Maybe it's because I am angry at myself for letting you play such a large part in my life. You are at the moment my major attachment, who I call when I get a tooth extracted.

And though I know you love me very much, there is something wrong here. Or I'm feeling not enough coming back. Or I have invested too much.

André, I don't want to marry you. I did two years ago, maybe six months ago. I don't anymore and sometimes I think I would like to have children with you. I would like us to reproduce, I would like to bring them up at One Fifth near you. But that fantasy, too, fades. Has faded.

I am very sad about this. Not actually as sad as I was in January when Linda told me André told Rachel he's seeing someone. It wasn't jealousy. It was just the thought we don't know each other very well. We're not such great friends.

Sometimes I feel like a convenience for you. Someone to travel with, spend weekends and few demands or commitments. Because the ultimate answer is, Wendy I love you but I'm gay.

. . . André, I want to marry and have children. Or at least I want to feel some personal vitality or possibility. If I hide with you and you are not stopping me from pursuing others, I won't.

I so wish you weren't late. I so wish I wasn't angry. . . .

Wendy

P.S. André, your family is your theatre. Your vitality is your productions and I believe liaisons not obsessive come easier for you. . . .

Wendy did not sit home pining alone. After she moved into One Fifth, her circle came to include Michiko Kakutani, now her neighbor. Kakutani, just a few years younger than Wendy, also had a Yale (undergraduate) degree and was a friend and colleague of Frank Rich. The two women already knew each other; in 1984, Kakutani interviewed Wendy for an article about the lessons the playwright had learned from the first production of *Isn't It Romantic*. Kakutani seemed to empathize with the dilemmas Wendy had been writing about.

They treated One Fifth as a kind of upscale dorm for grown-ups, with the world of New York culture as their campus—though they tended to talk on the telephone more than anything else. André and Kakutani became friends; even Ginger the cat grew fond of her "Aunt Michi," as Wendy referred to her on Ginger's behalf.

After Kakutani became the *Times'* chief book critic, her judgments—acid or admiring—made her a favorite target in the publishing world. The small woman wrote with a critical swagger that drew the wrath of literary heavyweights such as Susan Sontag, Salman Rushdie, and Norman Mailer. With Wendy, Kakutani could be just a girlfriend, receiving silly messages on her answering machine from her "niece," Ginger the cat. They could be serious or mischievous as they contemplated world affairs and romantic liaisons, handbags and handmade chocolates, celebrity gossip and personal sorrow. Wendy talked about people who had "nut-juice," Kakutani explained, "by which she meant a heightened sense of the absurdities of life, an ability to see the humor in a painful situation, the ridiculousness beneath the solemn or pretentious. . . ." As with many of Wendy's friendships, their relationship was known but somehow secretive, cozy, special.

Wendy also continued her habit of transforming get-togethers with friends into theatrical occasions. Monthly drinks at 5:00 P.M. at the Parker Meridien Hotel with Heidi Ettinger and Carole Rothman evolved into the "Red Meat Society," dinners, focused on steak and red wine at different restaurants around the city. Ettinger—namesake of Wendy's title character in *The Heidi Chronicles*—was a Yale classmate and was becoming a prominent set designer. (She was the first woman to graduate from the school's set-design program; managing contruction crews had been considered too rugged a business for women.) She was married, at the time, to Rocco Landesman, a theater producer who knew Rothman from their hometown, St. Louis, Missouri. Rothman was André Bishop's counterpart at Second Stage Theatre, one of the small nonprofit theaters that had sprung up in the Public Theater's wake.

At the Red Meat Society, they talked some shop, but it was more of a treat to indulge in what they referred to as "girlie" matters, say, manicures or visits to spas like Canyon Ranch. "Girlie is both to Wendy and to me not a place we gravitate to naturally," said Ettinger. "We created a girlie language because it created a certain comfort level or [filled] a certain missing blank. We were in professions that did not allow that at all. With each other we could do cutesy messages and funny voices and go shopping and have facials and do that part of our lives we really weren't allowed to express in any other way. At the time we were women competing with a lot of men who were very serious."

None of Wendy's other friends were invited to take part in the monthly dinners. "Wendy kept people in certain boxes," said Rothman. "Wendy, Heidi, and I were in one box, and [Heidi and I] didn't know what was going on in the other boxes."

One of those other boxes contained Rafael Yglesias, Frank Rich's novelist friend and, besides Wendy, his other regular theater companion.

Yglesias lived a couple of blocks from One Fifth, at Tenth and Univer-

sity, and was married with one child (the first of two) when he and Wendy
became close. Sometimes Wendy went to his apartment, to have take-in
Chinese food with him and his family. His wife, Margaret Joskow, deputy
art director at *Newsweek,* enjoyed Wendy's company; the two women were
both obsessed with Princess Diana and relaxed by watching (and mocking) beauty pageants. But usually Yglesias and Wendy met three or four
times a week alone for lunch—breakfast for her—at a local deli. They discussed their work and complained about the unfair success of unworthy
(in their opinion) colleagues. This subject could fill hours, so when Yglesias
had lunch/breakfast with Wendy, he didn't count on getting much writing
done that day.

Yglesias, like Wendy, was a born-and-bred New Yorker, persuasive yet
insecure, confident yet neurotic. He was imposing—tall and smart, with a
cynical charm. Four years her junior, son of a Jewish mother and a Cuban
father, he was both familiar and exotic. He managed to simultaneously
rebel against and succumb to pressure to succeed—dropping out of prep
school but then having his first novel published when he was seventeen.
Like Wendy, he'd had an early success and now felt the pressure to follow
up. Both of them had begun writing screenplays; hers included a script for
Isn't It Romantic that went nowhere. They exchanged gripes and gossip
about Hollywood.

He recognized her ambition. In fact, Yglesias began to think that she
was the most ambitious person he'd ever known, and he knew many people with large dreams, including himself. As they got to know each other
better, Wendy frequently mentioned that her sister was a big shot at American Express and her brother was a prominent investment banker.

"She would say she was in competition with them, and if she had any
hopes of being acknowledged in her family, she would have to win a Pulitzer Prize, have a hit on Broadway, and even that wouldn't be enough,"
he said. "She would say it over and over again."

When Wendy said these things, they came out as comedy, not melo-
drama, but Yglesias saw the psychological implications. "She was climbing
the highest mountain; she was going to top her brother and sister the only
conceivable way she could," he said.

He was appalled—not at her ambition but at her glorification of Sandra and Bruce. "I didn't think what her brother and sister had accomplished was anything compared to writing a good play," he recalled telling her. "'You've got to be kidding. Your brother and sister are nothing. They're just part of this huge machine designed to make money. Somebody's got to float to the top of it. They're nobody!'"

He made his point with brutal emphasis. "They're nobody," he repeatedly told her. "You're an artist."

His feelings about her family were confirmed one night when she invited Bruce to join her, Yglesias, and Frank Rich at Elaine's, the Upper East Side show-business hangout. Bruce's awkward avoidance of the group was so profound, Yglesias said, "I thought he had Asperger's syndrome."

Wendy met Yglesias for breakfast the next day and announced, "Bruce said you're all idiots."

"Why?" he asked.

"Because we should right now—you, me, Chris Durang—we should form a corporation and sell shares in ourselves," she explained. "Only a few of us are going to make it big, and whoever makes it big will just share all the money. If we buy shares now, we'll make more money than we would individually. We're idiots if we don't incorporate."

That idea seemed far-fetched, but Yglesias was impressed by Wendy's other strategies for developing her career. "We would discuss how the New York theater audience was largely Jewish, suburban, read the *Times* as though it was the Bible, so the more you were beloved and appeared in the paper, the more the audience would come and see your work," he said. "The most important thing a writer can have is a loyal audience. A loyal audience makes you invulnerable; no matter what the world tries to do to you, you can survive. We talked about public appearances, writing for magazines, being in the *Times* as much as possible."

Wendy was a natural at self-promotion. By the time she was discussing *Miami* with Rafael Yglesias, her name had been in the *New York Times* eighty times—in reviews and articles about her plays or about theater. Even though Frank Rich couldn't ethically review her plays, he could—and did—refer to her work when he wrote about trends in theater.

Editors at the *Times* were aware that Wendy had the backing of Frank Rich, but she soon made her own friends at the paper. She went to lunch with editors and charmed them. "She was a delight to be with—funny and happy and smiling and relaxed and easy to get along with and knew so much about theater," said Mervyn Rothstein, who was editing the theater section of Arts & Leisure in the Sunday *New York Times.* He assigned her stories and then provided her name to reporters looking for a quotable quip. Her glib wit soon made her a popular source.

She became a frequent contributor. For the *Times Magazine,* she wrote a romantic satire about the courtship between upwardly mobile New Yorkers, and then a piece called "Body Minimal," a whimsical diet plan. Her advice includes:

"Rest in the midmorning. This can be accomplished at home by never getting out of bed. . . ."

Wendy's career as an essayist received a significant boost when Betsy Carter, an old friend of Bruce's from the *Michigan Daily,* began a magazine called *New York Woman.* The target readership mirrored Wendy's audience—educated, ambitious, well-off Baby Boomers.

Carter came to New York after graduating from the University of Michigan and had a successful career in journalism, first at *Newsweek* and then at *Esquire.* In 1986 she left *Esquire* to begin a magazine for her contemporaries. She described the readers she imagined. "We shop, we daydream, we're neurotic, we want to do everything," she said. The cover of the first issue announced its intent: "Our Marvelous, Maddening Lives!"

Carter was a slender, attractive woman with a dazzling smile. She first met Wendy when Bruce's little sister visited him at the University of Michigan; subsequently, at Wasserstein family gatherings, Carter became as frequent a guest as André.

Shortly after she launched her new venture, Carter's handsome, charming husband of seventeen years left her, after announcing that he was gay. "Suddenly I became this person," she said. "Newly divorced, broke, dating like crazy."

Bruce Wasserstein was a true friend to Carter in that maddening, not-so-marvelous period. He began fixing her up with what seemed like every single investment banker and lawyer in New York. "If your husband leaves you because he's gay, you need that," she said. "Bruce was an excellent friend."

Carter had seen Wendy's plays and knew she was funny and smart. So even though Wendy had never written a column for magazines, Carter invited her to become a regular contributor.

She was an editor's dream—a quick study who was eager to please. "I'd read it, say this works or this doesn't, and she'd be back later in the day with a revision," said Carter. "People can give you such a hard time, fights and screaming. She was nothing like that."

The essays came easily to Wendy. Her notebooks reveal the difference in effort for her between these journalistic observations and her plays. Drafts for the plays look as though they were written under wartime conditions: scrawled, desperate missives filled with cross-outs. The essays emerge in handwriting that is comparatively neat, in sizable chunks that correspond almost verbatim with the published works.

Carter gave her a monthly column, called "The Meaning of Life." In it Wendy wrote about her childhood, her travels, boyfriends, shopping, body hair, and—more than any other topic—her family.

Insouciance was the hallmark of the Wendy character she created in her essays. But the more she began to reveal through her writing, the less her friends felt they knew her. "I felt always that she was not presenting her real self to me ninety-five percent of the time," said Rafael Yglesias. "I was only getting glimpses from time to time."

He became aware of just how intricate her attitudes toward friendship were when Frank Rich began a trial separation from his wife. Rich told Yglesias about it—in strictest confidence. By then Rich had become known as the "Butcher of Broadway"; theater people were obsessed with him, and his marital difficulties would have been a tasty morsel for the tabloids.

Wendy heard a rumor that Rich had moved out of his home and asked Yglesias if it was true. He lied. She heard the rumor a second time, and Yglesias lied again.

A month or two later, the separation was made public. Yglesias and Wendy met for one of their breakfast/lunches.

"You knew he moved out," she said to him.

He acknowledged and explained.

Her voice dropped from high nervous register to deep serious tone. "You're really a good friend of his," she said, sounding puzzled.

"We're best friends, yeah," Yglesias responded. "I thought you knew that."

She continued. "But you're really, really friends."

"Yes," he said. "But if you asked me to keep a secret like that, I would have kept it from Frank."

After that, their regular get-togethers stopped. They bumped into each other once in a while, and she was cordial, but it was clear to him that they were no longer friends.

Perhaps she was hurt that Rich trusted Yglesias more than her. Or maybe she understood, with finality, that her friendship with Rich would never develop further, even now that he was free. Like André's, for different reasons, his affection would only go so far.

Betrayal was on her mind as she began to work on the new play that André had commissioned. Much as she struggled to find her place in the world, she always seemed to come up against a barrier between her and fulfillment. Why, she wondered, did her expectations always seem out of alignment with reality?

By June 1987 she had written the first act. That summer, and for much of the autumn, she lived in London, courtesy of a four-thousand-dollar writing grant, which also included a room in the Nell Gwynn House, a serviced luxury-apartment building. Its romantic link to history would have appealed to Wendy; Nell Gwynn was a celebrated British actress from the seventeenth century, best known for being the beloved mistress of Charles II.

Away from her usual distractions, Wendy wrote in a way she never had before. *The Heidi Chronicles* flowed out of her the way the essays did, scene after scene. She fell back on some old tricks—pinning the names of friends and relatives onto characters, drawing on her memory bank for incidents and conversations. But her sociological observations and personal laments carried new weight.

Though her voice and concerns emanate from every character, for the first time a Wendy alter ego isn't visibly part of the script. Heidi Holland, the main character, is a successful art historian, in her mid-thirties. She is neither Jewish nor overweight, but still there are important similarities between author and creation. Like Wendy, Heidi feels an essential sadness about where life has taken her. The women's movement had raised consciousness and opened doors but left unanswered crucial questions about managing careers, family, relationships. Heidi laments:

"I'm sure the gray-haired fiction woman is having a bisexual relationship with a female dockworker and driving her husband crazy. I'm sure the hotshots have screwed a lot of thirty-five-year-old women, my classmates even, out of jobs, raises, and husbands. And I'm sure the mothers in the pressed blue jeans think women like me chose the wrong road. 'Oh, it's a pity they made such a mistake, that empty generation'. . ."

Heidi's peers (and Wendy's) had dropped the mantra of revolution and justice for all. During the eight-year presidency of Ronald Reagan, society had become more gentrified; the gap between rich and poor was wider than ever. In the play, Susie, the friend who takes Heidi to a woman's consciousness-raising meeting when they're in college, drops out of a Supreme Court clerkship to live in a women's health and legal collective in Montana. She winds up a Hollywood producer.

The play covers the trajectory of Wendy's generation, moving back and forth in time between 1965, when Heidi is in high school, and 1989, when she is approaching middle age, contemplating what she has become and how she should proceed.

She questions her choices and wonders if she has been misled by the promises of the feminist movement.

"I don't blame any of us," Heidi says. "We're all concerned, intelligent, good women." She pauses. "It's just that I feel stranded. And I thought the whole point was that we wouldn't feel stranded. I thought the point was that we were all in this together."

Later an old friend reminds her of the plot of her namesake *Heidi,* Johanna Spyri's classic novel about a Swiss orphan raised by her stern but loving grandfather.

"Did you know that the first section is Heidi's year of travel and learning, and the second is Heidi uses what she knows?" the friend says. "How will you use what you know, Heidi?"

Like Wendy, Heidi has a host of women friends, but her primary relationships are with men: One is Peter Patrone (carrying her old friend Mary Jane's surname), a pediatrician, who shares many characteristics with Chris Durang and André Bishop. Heidi loves him, but he is gay. The other romantic interest, also inaccessible, is Scoop Rosenbaum (who has the same name as her brother Bruce's younger son). He is a smart, competitive journalist, with traces of Frank Rich and a heavy dose of Bruce. Once idealistic, he is now a cynical publishing mogul who owns a publication called *Boomer* magazine (which resembles Betsy Carter's *New York Woman*) and assigns a grade to everything—politicians, cookies, women.

He explains to Heidi why he chose to marry his wife (whom he cheats on), rather than her. "She's the best that I can do," he says. "Is she an A-plus like you? No. But I don't want to come home to an A-plus. A-minus maybe. But not A-plus."

Just before Wendy's thirty-seventh birthday, October 18, 1987, she felt that the play was ready for André's evaluation. Back in New York from London, she gave him *The Heidi Chronicles.* He was nervous as he began reading, sitting on his sofa in the apartment on Waverly Place. The disappointment of *Miami* was still fresh, and the puncturing of their romantic bubble had put a terrible strain on their friendship.

He wanted to like the play, but what if he didn't?

Relief came quickly. He saw that something profound had been unleashed in Wendy. The wit was there, but sharpened by a new willingness to let hurt and despair stand naked, not always protected by humor. "It was a beautifully written play," he said. "Of all her plays, just in terms of grace of writing, *The Heidi Chronicles* is beyond all the others."

He saw enormous potential. "It was funny and touching and serious, it had all the elements of a sort of American Important Play, at least within the New York theater world," he said. "I just knew this was going to be her breakthrough to the really major leagues."

André couldn't—or wouldn't—marry Wendy, but he resolved to do everything in his power to make sure *Heidi* got the attention he felt it deserved. That he could, and would, do.

Lola told people Wendy won the Nobel Prize for
The Heidi Chronicles, but the Pulitzer was enough
to make Wendy very happy.

Fifteen

THE HEIDI CHRONICLES

1988–89

André quickly arranged a reading at Playwrights Horizons, with Joan Allen in the Heidi role. Allen was tall and bony, a midwestern blond beauty who had earned her acting credentials at Chicago's Steppenwolf Theatre Company, a repertory company that took a boot-camp approach, five plays per season. She had been working in New York for four years, first appearing in *And a Nightingale Sang,* winning the Clarence Derwent Award for "the most promising male and female actors on the metropolitan scene" of the 1983–84 season. Most recently she had made a splash on Broadway in *Burn This,* starring opposite John Malkovich; the play was still running when she auditioned for *Heidi.*

Wendy was six years older than Allen, but the actress connected to the play, especially the line Heidi delivers when she goes to a rap group and someone asks her, "Are you a feminist?" And she says, "No, I'm a humanist."

Allen immediately grasped the main challenge, if she decided to take the part. "Heidi was someone who watched, something I could relate to, being more of a watcher myself," she said. "With us watchers, there's a lot going on underneath that isn't shared with other people. Wendy really, really understood that."

Wendy often made this connection with actresses, who were unaccustomed to working on plays written by women. They were drawn to this friendly, empathetic playwright who came to rehearsals and showed such respect for their craft.

André wanted Jerry Zaks to direct *Heidi;* Zaks had been having success after success—Christopher Durang's *Marriage of Bette & Boo* and a revival of John Guare's *House of Blue Leaves,* for which Zaks won a Tony. After Zaks declined, André suggested they workshop the play in Seattle rather than New York. Too many opinions had gone into the making—and unmaking—of *Miami.* Just as it had been useful for Wendy to seclude herself in London to write *Heidi,* André and Wendy agreed it would be good to develop the play, with actors, out of earshot of her New York friends, whose opinions she would invariably seek.

He contacted Daniel Sullivan, who was artistic director of the Seattle Repertory Theatre. Born in Colorado, Sullivan had grown up in San Francisco but had worked as an actor and a director in New York for years before moving to Seattle. Sullivan had a reputation as a strong, intelligent director with an impressive track record. He worked on *I'm Not Rappaport* in Seattle and then moved with it to Broadway, where the play won the Tony for Best Play in 1986, under Sullivan's direction.

After they talked, André believed that Sullivan could help Wendy clarify her play's many transitions. *The Heidi Chronicles* has thirteen scenes, spread across twenty-four years, each taking place in a different location, in time periods that don't follow chronological order.

Sullivan was familiar with Wendy's work; he had seen *Isn't It Romantic* at Playwrights Horizons. He'd enjoyed the play but had felt that it was light, a boulevard comedy. He found *Heidi* to be far more ambitious. "I liked the structure of the piece, slices of someone's life, and you have to infer huge swaths of a life which are in the interstices," he said. "I liked Wendy's pugnaciousness about the women's movement at a time when it wasn't very popular to be pugnacious about it."

Sullivan noticed how invested André was in this play and this playwright.

"André had an extremely propriety relationship with Wendy, more so than I've seen with any other writer," he said. "Protective. It was an extremely brotherly relationship, I found. A tremendous amount of love

between them, I felt, and I think André felt extremely responsible to protect her. He wasn't intrusive, but more present, more watchful, more
mother-henning the thing."

By late March 1988, Wendy was in Seattle, comfortably ensconced in the
Inn at the Market, with views overlooking Elliott Bay. The hotel lay secluded
behind an ivy-covered courtyard, right next to funky, atmospheric Pike
Place Market, with its picturesque fishmongers and fruit sellers. Wendy
loved hotels, their promise of romance, the absence of demands; they became a favorite place to work.

"In order to complete my writing, I have spent weeks guzzling coffee at
Seattle's Inn at the Market or sipping tea at Manhattan's Upper East Side
Lowell Hotel," she wrote. "In other words, for me, from sea to shining sea
there was no place that didn't beat being home."

Playwrights Horizons hired four actors in New York to fly to Seattle
for the ten-day workshop; the rest of the cast came from the Seattle Rep.
Caroline Aaron was part of the New York group, cast as Susan Johnston,
Heidi's girlhood friend who becomes a high-powered television producer.

Unlike some playwrights, who abhor the tedium of rehearsals, Wendy
was there every day, eight hours a day, using the actors' performances to
inform revisions. She had a good ear for dialogue and music, often using
popular songs to signal shifts in time. But her visual imagination was weak,
so actually seeing the actors moving around the stage provided a valuable
extra dimension during rewrites.

Aaron was impressed by the collaboration between Sullivan and Wendy.
The actors would read the play, holding scripts, while Sullivan watched and
considered, then zoomed in on problems. His radar was fine-tuned for gaps
in the text, where a visual cue or additional information was needed to
ground the audience. In the original script, for example, the play began in
1965, at a high-school dance, with two sixteen-year-old girls onstage,
played by women in their thirties. One of them is Heidi, the title character.

Sullivan said to Wendy, "You can't ask the audience to believe that these
women are sixteen-year-old girls. The audience has to meet Heidi first, in
the present, so they know who she is."

Wendy went to her hotel room and emerged two days later with a scene set in 1989, the play's present. She put to use all those years of scrambling at school, the last-minute assembling of learned-sounding papers for demanding teachers. In her revision Heidi is giving a lecture, standing in front of a screen showing slides of paintings by two nineteenth-century women artists. The playwright establishes Heidi's adult voice as she laments the obscurity of women painters throughout history and then links her scholarly exegesis to the original opening scene, now believable as Heidi's implicit *memory* of a high-school dance.

In subsequent months Wendy would further improve the scene. Heidi's lecture becomes more sophisticated, and the transition to the high-school dance smoother and more poetic. Wendy's process was similar in art and in life, impulsive yet planned, notable for a willingness to keep revising.

Wendy recognized that she and Sullivan worked well together but found his matter-of-fact approach unnerving. He didn't praise, and he didn't criticize; he just pointed out what needed to be fixed. (Later, after *The Heidi Chronicles* had been pronounced a great success, André said to Sullivan, "Wendy asked me if you liked her play." Sullivan was distressed and amused. "I'm sort of a truck driver about directing," he said. "I just like to do the work. I don't get into aggrandizing anything or anybody. I just like to keep on track, keep on the work, so sometimes the obvious isn't stated.")

André saw the play onstage for the first time on April 6, 1988, having flown in from New York for the workshop production in front of Seattle Rep subscribers. The audience's enthusiasm confirmed his belief that Wendy had written something exceptional.

His feelings were shared by cast members. On the way back to New York, Caroline Aaron, the actress who'd played Susan, decided that she definitely wanted to audition again for the part, if the play moved forward. Not long after she returned to the city, however, she discovered that Playwrights Horizons was producing the play later that year and the major parts had already been cast—Joan Allen as Heidi and Ellen Parker as Susan.

Aaron was upset. She believed that she'd done a fine job. She thought

that she and Wendy had hit it off. They'd gone shopping together, discussed dating, and commiserated about dieting. Oh, well, she told herself,
that's show business.

A couple of months later, she heard from Wendy by mail. The letter,
Aaron said, "knocked me out."

> *Dearest Caroline;*
>
> *Oy Gavalt!! I've had a baguette, a Saga Blue Cheese, and a nice
> bag of Reese pieces* [sic] *before I sat down to write this note. I can't tell
> you how difficult this is, or how very fond I am of you. I almost feel
> there's no reason to really be writing this because I know I'll see you
> soon and have a chance to explain in person. However, in truth, I've
> been away writing and now I'm taking my ten year old niece the chess
> champion to Rumania, so we might not have a chance to get together
> until August.*
>
> *All right, I'm going to be very grown up and confront this all head
> on. Caroline, the part of Susan came down to be between you and
> Ellen Parker. Ellen did the reading at Playwrights previous to the
> Seattle showcase. I <u>loved</u> you in The Heidi Chronicles. You were not
> only the inspiration for my new favorite line, you became a trusted
> friend. Unlike you, I have difficulty really opening up to people and I
> consider you the new colleague and friend I made this year.*

Wendy went on to explain that she had a history with Ellen Parker, who
had played in *Uncommon Women* and had a long association with Playwrights Horizons. In fact, Wendy confessed, she'd told André that she had
written the role for Parker.

After reading Wendy's words, Caroline Aaron had no doubt that she
and Wendy would become even better friends. In all the actress's years in
show business, no one had ever acknowledged that she might have feelings
about not getting a part, much less written her a letter like that. "It was a
lesson everybody in show business could learn," she said. "Good manners
go a long way. But even people in the mafia have better manners than in
show business."

➤ ◀

In Seattle, when she was hanging around with Caroline Aaron, Wendy had made allusions to a "Mr. Right" she was seeing—though he would turn out to be yet another Mr. Wrong.

The previous October, just before her thirty-seventh birthday, about the time Wendy gave André the completed draft of *The Heidi Chronicles,* Terrence McNally—celebrated playwright, handsome chronicler of the contemporary gay experience—showed up one night at Wendy's apartment with a proposition. He wanted her to consider becoming his mate.

McNally was persuasive enough to convince Wendy to begin a romance with yet another charming man who was gay. There was one significant difference: This time the relationship was consummated, with serious thought of marriage and parenthood.

Within two months they were sharing a stateroom on the *QE2,* en route to England; McNally had a speaking gig on the ship, so the trip was free. The voyage ended dramatically. They arrived in London on January 1, 1988, to news that McNally's father had died back in Texas, where McNally had grown up. They spent the night at the Savoy, and then he flew to the States while Wendy stayed in London.

For the next three years, they continued a fraught relationship.

They shared a love of music and theater and had reciprocal wit, intellect and ambition. But they were fighting their natures. The sex didn't work.

They'd met at Yale, when McNally was teaching the playwriting seminar that Christopher Durang didn't get into, which led Chris to the class where he met Wendy. McNally and Wendy reconnected several years later, after *Uncommon Women,* when CBS gave the Dramatists Guild a grant to encourage new playwrights. The Guild appointed a committee of playwrights to choose theaters to participate. McNally was the chair; Wendy was on the committee.

For several months the group flew to different regional theaters to see plays. That's when McNally, who was a decade older than Wendy, had a chance to spend time with her and they became friends. In early 1987 they were asked by editors at the *New York Times* to explain how a play moves from a producer's office to the stage. They replied with a spoof called *The Girl from Fargo,* a one-act play overflowing with inside jokes and show-business minutiae, that was probably more fun to write than it is to read.

McNally's closest friends were not usually playwrights, but Wendy was different. "She had a very charismatic star quality," he said.

So did McNally. He'd become known as a debonair provocateur, with plays like *The Ritz,* a sex farce set in New York's gay-bathhouse scene. He was an exotic species in New York, not for being gay, or a playwright, but for being from Corpus Christi, Texas. His voice was soft and southern, his eyes a startling blue. He reminded Wendy of "a faded Gary Cooper." He'd had a fascinating life, including a long affair as protégé and lover of Edward Albee, the groundbreaking playwright.

The early phase of McNally's affair with Wendy coincided with the premiere of *Frankie and Johnny in the Clair de Lune,* his play about a one-night stand between two lonely, middle-aged people. "You just don't decide to fall in love with people out of the blue," the woman tells the man. Later Wendy would tell people that *Frankie and Johnny* reminded her of her affair with McNally, even though he'd written it before they became involved.

He was shocked to discover, years after the fact, that she'd told anyone anything about their relationship. McNally had urged Wendy to allow them to be a public couple, but she had impressed on him the need for secrecy.

He honored Wendy's request, while she assured him she never discussed their relationship with anyone. "She said, 'I'm not going to tell any of my friends, and I don't want you to,' and I said fine," he recalled.

He asked her, "What about André?"

She replied, "Oh, no, André must never know."

Yet she told André, along with many others—close confidants as well as people with whom she was merely friendly, like Honor Moore, the writer who had interviewed her at the O'Neill.

André was disturbed when Wendy gave him the news. "I wasn't frankly that interested in hearing about it," he said. "Not because of jealousy, but I couldn't quite gauge the nature of their relationship, except she indicated that it was sexual. I guess I couldn't maybe deal with that, because he was gay and I was gay and I couldn't have a sexual relationship with Wendy. It wasn't that I was jealous of him. I just didn't know what that was, she and Terrence. She certainly told a number of people."

Wendy's motives didn't seem that mysterious to Honor Moore. "She was looking for someone," she said.

That was true, but there were also larger forces at play. From Wendy's perspective (and Terrence's), the future no longer stretched out endlessly. She was repeatedly forced to contend with the prospect of mortality. Her onetime lover, the lyricist Ed Kleban, had died on December 28, 1987, from cancer of the mouth at age forty-eight. Six weeks later Wendy spoke at his memorial service, where she regaled the audience with stories of "Eddie's" eccentricities and talked about his critical aspects and his kindness. "I knew him, and I loved him," she said. "And I'll never forget him."

Far more frightening was the specter of AIDS, the plague mystifying the medical world and terrifying the gay population. For too many of Wendy's friends and acquaintances, the Peter Pan syndrome would literally mean eternal youth, because they would die too young. The theater world was hit especially hard; by 1985 casualties were widespread enough for the disease to command the attention of artists. AIDS emerged onstage that year with *As Is* by William Hoffman and *The Normal Heart* by Larry Kramer.

In 1987, 5,216 new cases were reported in New York City and 9,756 deaths, including that of Michael Bennett, creator of *A Chorus Line*. Terrence lost a lover to the disease. Peter Evans, Gerry Gutierrez's boyfriend, was sick. Harry Kondoleon, Wendy's playwright friend, specialist in elegant lunches with poached pears, would soon be infected.

Within four years the death count in New York would more than triple. Wendy's cousin Barry Kaufman, who had lived with her family when she was young, was another victim; when he died of AIDS, Morris and Lola didn't tell anyone—including Wendy—because they were ashamed.

AIDS became not just a disease but a cultural indicator. In his review of *Frankie and Johnny in the Clair de Lune*, Frank Rich observed that even though McNally's play is about a heterosexual couple and AIDS isn't the subject, "it's just possible that, in the process, he's written the most serious play yet about intimacy in the age of AIDS."

In *The Heidi Chronicles,* Wendy addresses the subject in a painful conversation between Heidi and her high-school crush, Peter Patrone, who is gay. When they are adults—she a well-known art historian, he a pediatrician—he responds to her existential angst with a bitter outburst:

"Okay, Heidi, I'd say about once a month now I gather in some church, meeting house, or concert hall with handsome men all my own age, and in the front row is usually a couple my parents' age, the father's in a suit and the mother's tasteful, a pleasant face. And we listen for half an hour to testimonials, memories, amusing anecdotes about a son, a friend, a lover, also handsome, also usually my own age, whom none of us will see again. After the first, the fifth, or the fifteenth of these gatherings, a sadness like yours seems a luxury."

These were harsh times. Maybe through Wendy, McNally was seeking an alternative that seemed less dangerous: He was approaching fifty. Wendy told friends they'd discussed the possibility of having a child. Whatever his motives, as *The Heidi Chronicles* was being prepared for production, Terrence McNally became yet another Wasserstein secret that wasn't a secret.

The frantic pace of Wendy's life accelerated. In a period of just a few months, while writing *Heidi* (in London, New York, and Seattle), she flew to Minnesota to give a speech at Carleton College, worked on *The Object of My Affection,* wrote columns for *New York Woman* as well as articles for the *New York Times* and other publications, began her romance with Terrence McNally, and zipped around the globe to fulfill work and family obligations—including chaperoning ten-year-old Pam Wasserstein (oldest of Bruce's three children) to Romania to compete in a chess tournament. Being Wendy Wasserstein looked exhausting, leading friends to speculate—in retrospect—that she was trying to outrun death, as if she knew that her time on earth was limited.

On December 12, 1988, *The Heidi Chronicles* opened at Playwrights Horizons. As always, Wendy kept cutting the play during previews; the reaction of early audiences was mixed. By opening night, however, almost all reservations appeared to have vanished. André's prediction came true: *Heidi* was received as an "American Important Play."

Writing in the *New York Times,* Mel Gussow called the play "Wendy Wasserstein's enlightening portrait of her generation."

The *New Yorker*'s Mimi Kramer was loftier still, discussing how "the Chekhovian fabric of the dialogue—the degree to which characters' ways of talking differ from one another or change over time—creates a Stanislavskian offstage life."

Howard Kissel in the *Daily News* was more down-to-earth but no less impressed. "Wasserstein reproduces the inanities and glibness of the last 20 years with a shrewd eye and a perfect ear for the self-delusional," he wrote. "This is not just a funny play, but a wise one."

With a sold-out run propelled by A-plus reviews, André was able to move the play from his 150-seat theater to the 1,102-seat Plymouth, a Broadway theater owned by the all-powerful Shubert Organization. The play cost $175,000 to produce Off-Broadway; an estimated $800,000 to $850,000 at the Plymouth. There was a bidding war, including a strong entry by Rocco Landesman, head of Jujamcyn Theaters and then-husband of Yale friend Heidi Ettinger.

Explaining why he chose the Shubert Organization, André told a *Times* reporter, "Wendy and I both felt if we could go to Broadway and go first-class, let's do it. In ten years, who knows whether or not there will even be plays on Broadway."

During Wendy's lifetime Broadway had become an anachronism for American playwrights. Because of high costs, only a handful of plays were produced there a year, while big-budget musicals—led by imports from abroad, notably *Cats, Les Misérables,* and *The Phantom of the Opera*—were thriving. Within five years after *The Heidi Chronicles* opened at the Plymouth, even Neil Simon—possibly the richest, most successful playwright in the United States—chose to open his newest play Off-Broadway, because the costs of a Broadway production had become prohibitive.

Still, the first day Wendy walked into the Plymouth—not as a spectator but as a playwright about to be produced there—she was overwhelmed.

"I stared at the delicate gray and white rococo ceiling and wondered what John Barrymore, Laurette Taylor and even William Gillette, who opened in the theater in 1917, first thought when they gazed at it," she wrote. "Bernard Jacobs of the Shubert Organization tells me the Plymouth is his shining jewel, the most beautiful theater in New York—maybe, he says, even in America. I think it is in the world."

André was determined to push *Heidi* as far as it could go. He had even moved out of his apartment for two months so Dan Sullivan could live there during the run at Playwrights Horizons.

Once the reviews were in and the deal made for Broadway, André became obsessive about a Pulitzer Prize for Wendy. He knew she could be careless about page numbers, spelling, and grammar. Before they sent the play to the Pulitzer committee, he went through the entire manuscript, page by page, line by line, correcting everything.

She always said she assumed she wouldn't win. "I'd never been someone who won prizes," she told an interviewer (even though by then Wendy had won many prizes, including the Guggenheim and the Mary Lyon Award, the highest honor bestowed by the Mount Holyoke Alumnae Association).

Maybe she understood, consciously or unconsciously, that the persona she had cultivated—shy, ingratiating, underdog Wendy—was part of her success as well as her protection from failure.

Perhaps she still felt the humiliation of her graduation from the Yale School of Drama, sitting in her chair as everyone else collected prizes. Even now Robert Brustein wasn't ready to dispense unmitigated praise, much less an A-plus. Writing in the *New Republic* on April 17, 1989, Brustein acknowledged the playwright's improvement, her "wry, self-deprecating humor," while putting down her previous work. "*The Heidi Chronicles* is not yet the work of a mature playwright," he wrote, "but it is a giant step beyond the cute dating games and Jewish mother jokes of *Isn't It Romantic.*"

However, Brustein was weak competition when it came to putting Wendy in her place.

On March 30, 1989, the day it was announced that she'd won the

Pulitzer, Wendy was home in her quilted bathrobe, surrounded by her old stuffed animals, writing a Mother's Day essay about Lola for the *New York Times*.

When the press agent for *The Heidi Chronicles* phoned and told her she'd won the Pulitzer, she said, "That's not funny."

He told her to call her mother, and she did, not because she wanted to but because she thought, "This woman's going to hear my name on the radio and think I died or something."

Lola's response: "Is that as good as a Tony?"

Wendy wasn't in the mood. So she told Lola, "Why don't you just call my brother and he'll explain it to you." Then she hung up the phone.

(After Wendy won the Tony, she confessed that she, too, felt that the theater prize was more significant, from a pragmatic point of view. "Winning the Pulitzer was never a goal of mine, but it meant a great deal to me in terms of self-esteem," she said. "Getting the Tony was quite different, because I knew that for the sake of the play and its commercial life that it was very important.")

Wendy lightened the Lola story when she wrote about winning the Pulitzer: "My sister telephones to say that not only has my mother called my aunts to inform them that I've won the Nobel Prize, but my cousins have already begun asking when I'm going to Stockholm."

Besides the Pulitzer, the Tony, and the Outer Critics Circle Award, *The Heidi Chronicles* won the Susan Smith Blackburn Prize, recognizing outstanding work by women playwrights, and the Dramatists Guild Hull-Warriner Award for "the best American play dealing with contemporary political, religious or social mores."

There was an outpouring of affirmation from friends and colleagues, none more meaningful than the letter she saved from George R. Hornig, managing director of Wasserstein, Perella & Co.

Dear Wendy:

By way of a note of congratulations on your Pulitzer prize, I thought I would share a little slice of Wasserstein Perella life. Last Friday morning I got a call from Bruce while I was working in our

London office. Nothing particularly unusual in that—Bruce calls me all the time. The typical conversation begins "Hello George, what's new?" followed by a litany of wrong decisions, problems created and otherwise substandard performance I have exhibited in my management of the Firm's administration since his last phone call the prior evening. . . .

Imagine my surprise and pleasure when the first words out of his mouth were an excited "Did you hear Wendy won the Pulitzer?" This should give you a good sense of the magnitude of your achievement. Your brother stepped out of character for a minute, and I smiled as I visualize him "kvelling" with family pride about his sister's accomplishment. What happy news for you and what a nice time for me in that he was in such a good frame of mind that Friday morning's litany was short enough to make me feel as if I did not actually miss the tour bus taking the other simians along the evolutionary trail. . . .

Wendy was happy. "The phone started ringing off the hook, it was like the phone went up and started spinning around the room," she said about winning the Pulitzer.

That day, the doorman at One Fifth asked her if she was getting married, so many flowers were delivered for her.

She went out for champagne with Bruce, Sandra, André, and Walter Shapiro, another friend of Bruce's from the *Michigan Daily* days, who was now working for *Time* and had become a friend of Wendy's. They met at The Four Seasons, the restaurant that had symbolized the apex of her city's glamour from the moment it opened in 1959, when the *New York Times* critic wrote, "There has never been a restaurant better keyed to the tempo of Manhattan. . . . It is spectacular, modern, audacious."

From there she went to the Plymouth Theatre, where Joan Allen suggested she come onstage at the end of the performance.

"No," Wendy said, "I'm much too shy."

At intermission, in the lobby, she bumped into Edward Albee, fellow Pulitzer Prize–winner. He embraced her and asked her whether she was going to take a curtain call.

When she shook her head and giggled, he said, "You never know when it is going to happen again."

Maybe she'd planned it all along, or maybe she needed Albee's encouragement. But Wendy Wasserstein did appear onstage when the play was over and began to kiss every actor who stood there with her.

The audience gave a standing ovation.

Wendy took her bow.

Part Four

DAYS OF AWE

1990–99

AFTER *HEIDI*, WENDY WAS ALWAYS OUT ON THE TOWN.
HERE SHE IS WITH CHRIS DURANG, CELEBRATING THE OPENING OF
HIS PLAY *SEX AND LONGING* IN 1996.

Sixteen

WENDY WASSERSTEIN, INC.

1990–92

Wendy's peripatetic tendencies were now jet-propelled by the force of the Pulitzer Prize—plus a Tony, a Broadway hit, (it ran there for 622 performances after ninety-nine performances at Playwrights Horizons) and a continuing stream of recognition. She was writing a *Heidi* screenplay; the show was being produced in many U.S. cities and in Australia, thanks in part to the increasing recognition of the Wasserstein brand.

"Wasserstein, a Name That Sells" was the title of the "On Stage, and Off" column in the *New York Times,* a gossipy theater column written by Alex Witchel, about to become Frank Rich's second wife.

"Any producer will tell you that the only way a show can make money is with a star," Witchel wrote. But *Heidi* had toured with lesser-known actors, she reported, and, "Much to the producers' delight the name Wendy Wasserstein sells plenty. James Walsh, a co-producer, says that . . . next to Neil Simon, Ms. Wasserstein . . . is now the only other playwright in the country who can sell tickets."

André began to refer to her as "Wendy Wasserstein, Inc."

The Guggenheim Foundation asked her to evaluate applicants. She became a regular on *The Charlie Rose Show.* Though she didn't cook, she was a "celebrity chef" for a March of Dimes gala. She became a sought-after guest at the fanciest dinner parties but also was willing to speak at the Hillel at Amherst College. She was invited to speak at the Key West Literary Seminar. The prestigious publisher Alfred A. Knopf brought out her essays in a collection called *Bachelor Girls*. (Sales were modest but respectable: 9,200 in hardcover and 11,500 in paperback.) Mount Holyoke bestowed an honorary degree, almost a decade after a smart public-relations person at the college sent a memo to the administration, with Wendy's *Isn't It Romantic* reviews attached:

> Enclosed is a batch of clippings on Wendy Wasserstein, Mount Holyoke Class of 1971, who seems to be regarded as the most promising playwright in the country.
>
> I think we ought to consider her for an honorary degree because if we don't somebody else will very quickly and it seems we should take advantage of our connection early in the game.

Wendy understood that celebrity was a commodity, and she quickly parlayed hers into a source of income. On February 1, 1990, she signed with Royce Carlton, a top-of-the-line speakers' bureau, representing literary heavyweights like Susan Sontag and Edward Albee. The Pulitzer Prize made her highly marketable; she began earning ten to twelve thousand dollars per speaking engagement.

"The fact she was a woman was very helpful," said Lucy Lepage, who founded the agency with her husband, Carlton Sedgeley. "Think about 1990, 1991. There were a handful of famous women, they were just getting their stride. A lot of colleges and universities were looking to bring women in specifically, and minorities. The fact she had won the Pulitzer and the Tony—and was a woman—put it all together. And she had the persona."

Demand for Wendy was greatest on college campuses and with Jewish groups. Lepage grew fond of her client and liked to tell a story that represented Wendy's appeal. She had returned to New York from an event for the Jewish Federation in Atlanta, Georgia, and reported in to Lepage.

After the event was over, there was time to kill, so the women organizers took Wendy to their favorite mall. They went shopping, and then she flew home.

"You know, Lucy," she said to Lepage, "I bet they would never have asked Susan Sontag to go shopping with them."

"You're right," Lepage responded. "They would never have asked Susan Sontag. These women see you as their daughter, their sister, or their personal friend."

Wendy complained about having to fly off to "speak to the Jews," but she loved it. She turned her speaking gigs into a party and invited her friends to come along.

Before Mary Jane Patrone turned forty, Wendy called her and invited her to go around the world—in seven days.

"Oh, Mary Jane, this will be so great," she said. "There will be buckets of caviar."

Wendy had been commissioned to be a speaker on a cruise ship circumnavigating the globe, with passengers who were mostly in their seventies. "The buckets of caviar were more like buckets of prunes!" recalled Mary Jane, who had long since forgiven Wendy for *Uncommon Women*.

Mary Jane was unmarried and had risen through the executive ranks at the *Boston Globe,* where she became the first woman on the masthead. (Her mother wasn't impressed. When she learned that a friend of Mary Jane's had gone to medical school ten years out of college, she sighed and told her daughter, a senior vice president by then, "I always hoped that you would have had a profession.")

The cruise lasted three months, but Wendy's gig was for a week; she was one of several speakers the company flew in and out to keep the passengers entertained. "The only thing that fit in her schedule was to fly to Singapore, and then we spent four days on the Indian Ocean, with one stop in Malaysia and one stop in Bombay. Then we got on a plane and flew back to Boston and New York. Seven days."

Mary Jane remembered the trip as a blur of laughter.

Many others had similar memories of impromptu adventures. Jane

Rosenthal—Wendy's producer friend who went on to become Robert De Niro's business partner and, eventually, cofounder of the Tribeca Film Festival—remembered picking up her telephone and hearing Wendy's voice, giggling:

"Janie, I'm going to call *Travel & Leisure* and get an assignment to go to a health spa. Wanna go?"

She began to move in the city's wealthy social strata, becoming friends with people like Mario Buatta, the designer known as the "Prince of Chintz." During this period Stephen Graham and his wife, Cathy, became an increasingly important part of Wendy's life, a bridge between her theater friends and the café society that now embraced her. Stephen and Wendy had been friends since Yale, but he never felt like a true intimate. "In the end I accepted her as this phenomenon," he said. "We spoke about a lot of things, but if conversational sharing is a bull's-eye with ten rings, probably we didn't get to the inner two rings. Because although she talked about herself, there were things she didn't reveal."

Stephen had always kept slightly aloof from Wendy, even when they were students at Yale. This reflected his natural reserve, but also his desire to make clear his lack of romantic interest. (He wasn't being self-important—she did have a crush on him.) Once he became involved with Cathy, in the mid-1980s, he felt more relaxed around Wendy. "I didn't have to think about the possibly mythical specter of getting romantically involved in some way," he said.

A few years younger than Wendy, Cathy was her physical opposite: slight, pretty, well toned. They shared a personal sweetness and an appreciation of silliness that belied their ambitions. Cathy moved to New York after graduating from the Rhode Island School of Design and worked for a while as a commercial illustrator. After her marriage she continued to draw, but her busy social life with Stephen (and later their children) became her most considered work of art. No detail in their East Side town house was left to happenstance; each flower arrangement had to have a motif, approved by Cathy. The quest for perfection was directed most stringently at herself. In the bathroom of her elegant, spacious artist's studio, a couple of doors down the street from the town house, she kept a large basket of weights of varying sizes, a yoga mat, and a huge scale.

The Grahams paid large sums to make their parties memorably insouciant. For Cathy's fortieth birthday, everyone wore long blond Barbie wigs (in honor of Cathy's infatuation with Barbie dolls) and ate at tables covered in chiffon, the whole thing arranged by Robert Isabell, deemed by Anna Wintour, editor-in-chief of *Vogue,* "the king of the event world."

The Grahams appeared to live a fabulous New York fantasy life, but they were also steadfast friends who graciously invited guests to the homes they owned or rented in Italy, Nantucket, Connecticut, or Switzerland. They were public philanthropists but also privately generous. Harry Kondoleon was another friend they had in common with Wendy. When he became so sick with AIDS that he couldn't manage the stairs to his walk-up apartment, the Grahams let him live rent-free in Cathy's SoHo loft, at Crosby and Grand, a huge, light-filled space with giant windows—and an elevator.

In February 1992 they threw a spectacular party for Kondoleon's thirty-seventh birthday, upstairs at La Grenouille, in the elegant private dining room that was once the studio of Parisian-born artist Bernard Lamotte, whose paintings were hung throughout the restaurant. The room was suffused in a pink glow. The lighting lent an exquisite theatricality to the huge bouquets of fresh flowers that filled the room, one of La Grenouille's signature touches—in retrospect a melancholy abundance of beauty. The frail guest of honor fainted from dehydration before everyone sat down to dinner and was carried out by stretcher, taken by ambulance to St. Vincent's Hospital in Greenwich Village.

The kindness of the Grahams was indisputable, and they made no pretense. They were who they were. Yet none of Wendy's friends more pointedly aroused that intrinsic conflict, her feeling of superior-inferior, than the Grahams.

They became a source of material. When Wendy began writing her novel *Elements of Style,* a decade after winning the Pulitzer, she told friends that she had loosely modeled a wealthy East Side couple on the Grahams. In the novel, Wendy describes the man as someone stuck in the shadow of a powerful father who was "both his social calling card and the source of his underlying insecurity." His wife is "stretched to the max" with "grooming, running and redecorating" her two homes, her children, and her husband. "Even with a personal assistant, a calligrapher, a dog walker, two housekeepers, a driver, and a cook, she still honestly felt she couldn't get everything done," wrote Wendy. "Or, more important, she couldn't get anything done *right*."

It was hard to gauge Wendy's feelings about the Grahams. She seemed to envy the life their wealth purchased, while disapproving of it and enjoying being part of it.

Where were the loves of her life? What had happened to Terrence and André as Wendy's orbit became more far-flung?

In September of 1990, Terrence called Wendy at her hotel in Los Angeles, where she was meeting with producers about a movie deal. The romantic part of their relationship was over, he told her.

His timing was terrible. She was turning forty. *The Heidi Chronicles* had just closed, after an eighteen-month run on Broadway,

Wendy pretended to understand. She told him she believed he loved her and she knew that his decision was meant to allow them to move on. "I wanted things, a home, children, that you could not give me," she said. "Furthermore, there is a question of sexuality, and yes, we both do deserve to have complete and fulfilling sexual lives."

But she was angry and wrote him a letter describing her feelings:

What angers me is the cruelty in the way in which you handled the situation. You told me you didn't want to sleep with me anymore while I was alone in a hotel room the day after my play closed. You then arranged not to see me the entire week I was in L.A. so that I could feel the wound and the loneliness as deeply as possible.

And now we speak everyday. "Hi, honey, how are you?" "How did your play go?" "Dominic's here for the opening." "André's coming next week." Oh, please!

You see, Terrence, what happened in the course of our time to-

gether is that I did fall in love with you. Which I can deal with, and I can recover from, and I can push down further until it hardly erupts. But you should know that you can not arrive at a person's apartment, involve them in your life, and when it is the right time for you simply turn the switch off. Well, frankly, of course you can, but there are consequences at least to that person.

Maybe in some way I am being unfair. . . . I as much as you never really tried to go "public." I don't really know what I want right now. I can tell you what you want. You want to work, and you should, and you want someone who will sort of take care of you when you desire being taken care of and will not be demanding when you don't. As for myself, I am frankly unclear about children since I don't know if I can offer them a real home life and I may, at this time in my life, be too selfish.

Actually, what I learned from my time with you is that I would like a real marriage. Not legal, perhaps, but at least to be involved in the life of a man who I respect and love and makes me laugh. . . .

I have always been someone who has trouble making decisions or moving on. But I just wanted you to know this transition is not happening easily. In fact, it remains quite painful and I am surprised. You see, Terrence, something did happen between us. And not to know that, even cherish it, is foolish and unkind.

I love you very much.

Wendy

Terrence never broke their vow of public discretion, and he did remain a loving friend. But, in addition to missing men, he was gripped by the grim reality overwhelming the gay community; his feelings were reflected in his work.

In 1990 he won an Emmy award for *André's Mother,* a drama about a mother trying to cope with her son's death from AIDS. He then returned to the stage with *Lips Together, Teeth Apart,* about two affluent couples who spend their Fourth of July weekend in the expensive beach house one of the women has just inherited from her brother, who recently died of AIDS.

Both couples are gay-friendly, enlightened types, or so they think, but none of them will enter the pool, fearing infection from its previous owner. In his review, Frank Rich said of the playwright's frame of mind, "The bright wit that has always marked Mr. McNally's writing and the wrenching sorrow that has lately invaded it are blended deftly throughout three concurrently funny and melancholy acts."

As for André, his star had also risen, as though in alignment with Wendy's.

On March 29, 1991, the board of the Lincoln Center Theater announced the appointment of a new director, forty-two-year-old André Bishop, who had been strongly supported by Bernard Gersten, executive producer, who would handle the business side of the company.

It all happened very fast.

"I disapproved of Lincoln Center and hated thrust stages and marble palaces and had nothing but disdain for Lincoln Center even though I was very impressed with what Gregory Mosher [his predecessor] and Bernie Gersten had done with relighting the theater," said André. "But I thought this would never be for me."

He didn't seek the job but quickly accepted it. "I loved Playwrights Horizons with my heart and soul and never thought I would leave it," he said. "But like Wendy I knew I couldn't make the sentimental decision. I knew I didn't want to spend the rest of my life at Playwrights Horizons. I was tormented about it, but I knew this was an opportunity for me and I had to take it. I didn't want to spend the rest of my life only working on new plays, and I wanted to work on something on a bigger scale."

That September, Joseph Papp retired from the Public Theater because of illness; two months later he died. Assessing the career of "the last of the one-man shows," Frank Rich wrote an impassioned essay about the importance of great producers, acknowledging that Papp was one of a kind.

"A producer must have the cunning of a master politician, the wiliness of a snake-oil salesman, the fanatical drive of a megalomaniac and, given the eternal precariousness of the New York theater, nerves of steel," wrote

Rich. "It doesn't hurt, either, to have some taste and a consuming passion for the stage."

Who would succeed Papp? Probably no one, Rich suggested, but there were two contenders. "While none of these producers has yet operated at Mr. Papp's epic scale, Lynne Meadow, at the burgeoning Manhattan Theatre Club, and André Bishop, soon to move from Playwrights Horizons to Lincoln Center, are poised to expand their already important roles in a brighter economy," he said.

In addition to moving uptown, to a far more political and demanding job, André fell in love.

Julia Judge, who had worked for the filmmaker Martin Scorsese for many years, was hired to be André's assistant. After helping him make the transition from Playwrights Horizons, shortly after he arrived at Lincoln Center, Judge told André she wanted to leave; her father had just died, and she thought she might want to return to the movie world. That's how Peter Manning arrived in André's life; the twenty-three-year-old theater aspirant, then working at the Manhattan Theatre Club, heard about the opening.

Manning had cute Catholic-school-boy looks, Christopher Durang minus the devilish glint and the torment. He was apprehensive about meeting his prospective boss. In the nonprofit-theater world, André Bishop was a figure of intimidating proportions. "I interviewed with André, and we had this electrifying meeting, oh, my goodness!" Manning recalled. "It was about the job, but it was clear, immediately, something else was going on."

Within a month of leaving Lincoln Center, Julia Judge returned. She had decided to remain as André's right hand. André left Peter a message, telling him the job wasn't available, and added, "Oh, let's get together sometime."

Peter was hired by the marketing department at Lincoln Center. For a year he and André pretended not to know each other at work while beginning a life together outside.

André didn't tell Wendy, though she had confided in him about Terrence.

André tried to explain why he kept quiet. "I mean, I had little affairs before I met Peter Manning, but there was no one that got in the way of Wendy."

It wasn't as though they had gone their separate ways after ending their flirtation with marriage. She'd brought him to visit the Grahams in Switzerland, where he took her on an excursion to his old boarding school. After *Heidi* they traveled to Los Angeles with Daniel Swee, the casting director at Playwrights Horizons (who followed André to Lincoln Center, along with many others). The three New Yorkers were all terrible drivers and terrified of negotiating the L.A. freeways. They stayed at a second-rate hotel in a two-room suite; Swee slept on the pullout couch in the living room, and Wendy and André shared the bed in the other room. They went together to visit Peter Evans, their actor friend (a boyfriend of Gerry Gutierrez) sick with AIDS. It was obvious to Swee that André and Wendy were not merely friends but the closest of companions.

When André began to realize that his relationship with Peter Manning was developing into something serious, he found himself in a terrible position for someone who avoided confrontation at almost any cost. "I wanted to eat my cake and have it, too," he confessed. "I was afraid it would hurt Wendy or drive her away. I was so insecure about having a relationship with someone like Peter—or anyone. I was afraid it wasn't solid yet, so in my typical way I did nothing."

Inevitably, she found out about Peter and saw how serious the relationship was, long after many others knew.

Their friendship was strong enough to take yet another hit, but André didn't forgive himself for hurting her again.

"Maybe some people say I behaved irresponsibly toward her, and I can see them saying that," he said. "It wasn't irresponsible behavior, it was a lack of taking my own contribution to her as seriously as she took it. It's my lack of acknowledgment of the importance I have in her—in anybody's—life."

For obvious reasons Wendy did not warm to Peter Manning—she called him "that bitch" when she discussed him with her girlfriends. The dislike was reciprocal. "I had no idea what I was getting into with André," he said. André had told him about his relationship with Wendy, including their discussions of marriage, but Peter hadn't understood how tightly knit the two of them remained.

"I had no idea," he said. "Wendy was mean to me from the start. She was cool and dismissive, not outwardly mean, but she was not psyched about my being there. My sense was that there were people who were not nice to me for a long time because they decided to side with Wendy in this thing."

Wendy might have been everybody else's friend, but she never became his. "I always saw the manipulative underside of Wendy," he said. "She'd be funsy Wendy, and I would be sitting there and never be that comfortable."

But he also understood that if he was to remain with André, Wendy was part of the package. So Peter tried to avoid her as much as possible, making appearances just often enough to keep things polite. "I showed up and got through it, but I was always uncomfortable," he said. "I never had Wendy love like everyone else around her."

As for Wendy, she was accustomed to realigning her relationships, and so she did—once again—with André. Their lives and careers would remain intertwined, though she was old enough to know that nothing stayed as it had been.

WENDY'S FRIENDSHIP WITH YALE PAL WILLIAM IVEY LONG DEEPENED
AND GREW MORE COMPLICATED OVER THE YEARS.

Seventeen

THICKER THAN WATER

1990-93

At the end of The Heidi Chronicles, Heidi adopts a baby and begins life as a single mother. In 1989 this was a radical decision. Single mothers still were thought of in terms of tainted clichés, either unlucky teenagers who got pregnant or divorced women whose spouses had left them to cope on their own.

The strongest critiques of the final scene came not from old-fashioned outraged moralists, however, but from feminists, disturbed by the play's possible implications: that a woman without a child was unfulfilled, that a modern woman had to choose between career and family, that babies were commodities that could be bartered to satisfy the maternal (or other) longings of affluent women.

Betty Friedan, a founding mother of the modern women's movement and a fan of Wendy's work, told reporters that the adoption ruined an otherwise satisfying theater experience. "I'm happy she won the Pulitzer Prize, but I was disturbed by the play," Friedan told reporters. "In depicting Heidi as troubled over career and family, Wendy Wasserstein inadvertently fed a media hype, a new feminine mystique about the either/or choices in a woman's life."

Helen Gurley Brown, another Wendy Wasserstein fan, also expressed dismay at the ending, which she felt ignored the hardships of being a single mother and depicted Heidi "as a victim in her personal life."

Wendy was taken aback by the criticism but defended her character's decision. "Am I saying all women should have babies?" she told a reporter. "No. I think Heidi made a choice. It is a really brave thing to do, and it is something I think about a lot. I meant it to seem powerful."

She had her mother's backing this time. Lola Wasserstein was all in favor of Heidi's decision and hoped Wendy would follow the example set by the character she'd created. Wendy saved a handwritten note Lola sent her in the early 1990s; the details are obscure, but the message is clear:

> *Hi honey!*
>
> *Thought you'd like to see this article about this girl in my dance class. She knows what she wants. I don't want to push you though. And she's not one of us anyway. Who else do we know from New Jersey?*
>
> *Morris and I are here, where are you? We're seeing Georgette now and The Doctor, but Daddy & I will be back at 11:30 to stay with you. If you spent the afternoon with people who weren't your family, you must miss us by now.*
>
> *I enjoyed our talk at lunch. Charge me a dress, honey, it never hurts to look nice. Have to go play with my wonderful grandchildren; you should try to have a baby, you might like it.*
>
> *Love, LOLA! See you at 11:30*

It was often easier for people who weren't Lola's children to appreciate her. Her niece by marriage, Freda Robbins, daughter of Morris's oldest brother, Israel, known as Herman, saw Lola's drive as admirable. In 1968, when Robbins gave birth to her first child, Lola came to the hospital and defended her decision to nurse her baby at a time when breast-feeding was not encouraged. When Robbins, a math professor, was awarded her Ph.D. at age forty, the only person in the family who acknowledged the achievement was Lola, who sent her an azalea bush.

"Lola's expectation of me was 'Why not?'" Robbins said. "Very simple.

That's the most precious gift you can give anyone. I understand she could be difficult, but she wasn't with me."

Lola was more suited to being a grandmother than a mother. Her apartment was a playland; flourishes like hanging lemons from chandeliers, embarrassing to her children, delighted her grandchildren. At Lola's it was okay to paint the brick tiles on the outdoor terrace—and cover yourself in paint, too.

She hadn't become a soft, fuzzy granny. There were no home-baked cookies at Lola's, and she could still embarrass with her shenanigans. Each grandchild had a mortifying memory: of enduring a time-share lecture in Florida just to get a free lunch; of being dragged by Lola to the front of the line at Radio City, pretending to be from Kansas, just as their parents had been; of being criticized for being too chubby.

In his sixties Morris continued to wear out ripple sole walking shoes,[*] and Lola kept dancing. The two of them traveled the world.

Age hadn't tempered her sharp tongue either. "Lola knew seismically the things you were insecure about and [would] say them to you," said Samantha, Sandra's younger daughter. "The first thing she'd say when we came home from school: 'Oh, you've blown up.'"

Melissa Levis, Georgette's younger daughter, remembered being compared to her cousin, Sandra's daughter Jenifer. "Jenifer has a boyfriend, do you have a boyfriend?" Lola would ask. "She got into an Ivy League, are you going to an Ivy League? Jenifer's engaged, are you engaged?"

"It never stopped," recalled Levis.

The grandchildren experienced the mixed message of superior-inferior. "We learned she would say these things only to us," said Samantha. "To other people she would say how fabulous you were in every way."

But they had the buffer of their own parents; their visits to Lola-land were circumscribed, placed into context. They remembered family gatherings as happy occasions.

"Really some of my fondest memories are Thanksgiving and Passover

---

[*] Wendy mentioned the shoes in *Isn't It Romantic*; Morton Hack, certified pedorthist, son of the ripple-sole inventor, Nathan Hack, wrote her a thank-you note.

and birthdays and things where we all got together," said Pamela, Bruce's eldest. "We had a lot of fun. We sang show tunes at the table and joked around a lot."

Wendy longed to be part of the generational transfer—as participant, not as observer. Privately, she had taken the first step toward fulfilling Lola's wish. After *Heidi* opened, while still involved with Terrence McNally, Wendy visited the department of reproductive medicine at Mount Sinai Hospital. Apart from a tendency to "harvest uterine polyps" and her age (thirty-nine), she was declared a viable candidate for pregnancy.

A few months later, after McNally made it clear that he would not create a family with her, Wendy decided to proceed alone, as if the ending of *Heidi* had been a blueprint for her future. She told herself she would have a baby—as soon as she finished the play that was beginning to form in her mind.

"I decided to postpone the baby until there was a tangible father and the play was well on its feet," she wrote.

In January 1991 she began sketching the scenes and characters that would become *The Sisters Rosensweig.* The idea had taken hold when she was in London, living in the Nell Gwynn apartment, working on *The Heidi Chronicles.*

In keeping with her professed desire to create more order in her life, Wendy became determined to move away from the episodic approach that characterized her work. She wanted to write a play that respected conventional dramatic unities, one with more recognizable structure. She considered Chekhov to be the standard. "Chekhov tells us a story, makes us laugh, makes us cry, changes a world, and it all happens before us, live on stage," she wrote.

She felt a personal connection to the great Russian playwright. Christopher Durang had suggested she read *Three Sisters* her first year at Yale. Wendy became obsessed with the play, seeing it as a leitmotif in her life.

She decided to write her own version of *Three Sisters,* drawing on her own sisters as a source. There would be no brothers. Wendy appeared to have taken the family vow of silence about Abner, at least for public consumption. While she had mentioned five Wasserstein siblings in early interviews, she now referred to four.

Her feelings about Bruce had become even more conflicted. His name recognition had grown with the publication in 1990 of *Barbarians at the Gate,* a bestselling account of the leveraged buyout of RJR Nabisco.

In this chronicle of breathtaking greed, Bruce was described as "arguably Wall Street's most brilliant takeover tactician." People paid him large sums of money just to keep him out of the game. "Better to hire the roly-poly deal maker and lock him in a closet than allow him to run loose and perhaps assemble a competing bidding group," the authors wrote.

Yet even his detractors acknowledged that Bruce put his family above all; he was devoted to his wife and children. Wendy had come to admire Chris Wasserstein as a mother and to adore the three children she had with Bruce. In public, brother and sister displayed their friendly, bantering attitude toward each other.

"Wendy likes to think of herself as sort of an Auntie Mame, and she's saving my children from their lives dominated by the stuffed shirts from Wall Street," Bruce told an interviewer.

To friends Wendy complained about her brother. But Michael Kinsley—editor of the *New Republic* and founding editor of the online journal *Slate*—who had become close to Wendy, recognized how much she relied on Bruce.

"To talk to her you would think she and Bruce were totally alienated, but then you would find out she had been on the phone with him three or four times in the past few days," he said. "I think they were quite close, though she would claim not. It was a shtick."

Kinsley had been invited to Passover seders at Bruce's home and saw a warmer side as Bruce played the part of paterfamilias. The baton had passed. Thanksgiving at Sandy's, Passover at Bruce's. Lola and Morris were now guests in their children's homes.

But in 1991 Bruce and Chris announced they were separating. Wendy was annoyed to see how easily her parents seemed to accept the end of

Bruce's marriage. "Don't be angry at him," Morris said. "It's an occupational hazard. It's not his fault."

Wendy wasn't as forgiving—she was bothered by the attractive women who were able to overlook Bruce's awkwardness and lack of physical beauty, and actively disliked one woman he dated, an art dealer Wendy referred to as the "Scheming Adventuress."

But the grown-up Bruce wasn't something she was prepared to deal with dramatically—not yet.

Secluding herself in a small writing room in the New York Society Library, she thought about her family and the enormous aspiration that had vaulted her and her siblings into realms Lola and Morris couldn't have imagined. She jotted notes, recalling names and incidents from the Brooklyn years.

Though Wendy had tried, after graduate school, to stop relating the plays of Chekhov to her life, feeling she was being childish, she couldn't stop noticing how his themes applied to the Wassersteins. "*The Cherry Orchard,* a play about the demise of a family, a lifestyle, a class, is hilarious, yet painfully sad," she wrote. "In Chekhov, the comic and the tragic are not separated. They are melded into one spirit."

That was the synthesis she was trying to achieve, even though the chaotic momentum of her life often left her little time to think. That's why she escaped to write, even though her apartment at One Fifth was plenty spacious for a woman and her cat.

With *The Sisters Rosensweig* she hoped to address, directly, her lifelong search for identity. In the summer of 1991, Wendy spent an extended stretch of time in Bridgehampton working on her play about three sisters. The eldest, a barely disguised Sandra Meyer, by then working at Citicorp, is Sara Goode, fifty-four, a high-powered banker and New York Jewish expatriate, divorced and living in London. Like Sandra, Sara cooks delicacies such as cassoulet. Like Sandra, Sara has recovered from "female trouble"; at age forty-seven, Sandra had been diagnosed with breast cancer, was successfully treated, and went on to become a top-ranking executive at one of the world's largest banking companies.

The youngest is Pfeni (formerly Penny) Rosensweig, forty, peripatetic world traveler and writer, never married, involved in a three-year affair with a world-renowned director and bisexual. The middle sister is Gorgeous Teitelbaum, a suburban housewife with an outsize personality. She was inspired in part by Wendy's sister Georgette—the real Gorgeous—but was more outrageous, like Lola.

The occasion for their reunion is Sara's birthday. Other guests include Pfeni's bisexual lover; Sara's hypersophisticated teenage daughter and her working-class boyfriend; and Mervyn Kant, a New York Jewish widower, who romances Sara.

The play is filled with bright chatter that covers much territory, ranging from Eastern European politics to Manolo Blahnik shoes. Sara invokes Shakespeare; Gorgeous laments her imitation Louis Vuitton. Pfeni, most often, is on the sidelines, ceding the play's strongest moments to her sisters, although Wendy used the play to describe her breakup with Terrence.

"I love you," Pfeni's boyfriend, Geoffrey, says to her. "I will always love you. But the truth is, I miss men."

The Sisters Rosensweig is Wendy's most deliberately Jewish play, beginning with the title. Daniel Sullivan, who would direct, felt the play was her way of trying to understand the path her life had taken. "The idea of coming home and a sense of rootlessness was a reason she wrote the play," he said. "Jewishness became a very important thing in it, because that was part of home to her. She had grown very far from that, and it was something she wanted to look at."

It took Wendy a long time to name the play; the title's ethnicity was deliberate. In May she typed a long list of possible titles—forty-two of them, none using the Rosensweig name. They included *Mother's Gems, Three Little Sisters, Reunion in London, Womenfolk, Sisterfolk, Tempest in a Teapot, Crumpets and Lox,* and *Thicker Than Water.*

When producers tried to discourage her from the overtly Jewish title, she stuck with *The Sisters Rosensweig.*

Chekhov was one inspiration; Flatbush was another.

Like Sandra Meyer, Sara Goode has dropped all traces of Brooklyn from her inflection and manner and is annoyed at her youngest sister for reminding her of their Jewish roots.

"Pfeni, there's something very 'New York' about your tone today," the eldest sister scolds.

Sara's daughter Tessie inquires, "What do you mean, New York?"

Pfeni explains, recalling the story of a man named Harry Rose, head salesman at their father's factory, who called their house every morning.

"Tess, Mr. Rose liked to catch Grampa to discuss the day's business just when the entire house would be waking up," Pfeni says. "So every day at seven A.M., I'd rush to pick up the phone just to hear Mr. Rose say, 'Hallo, Maury, is that you?' And then I'd answer, 'No, Mr. Rose, it's me. Maury's daughter Penny.' And he'd always say, 'Vell, excuse me for living, Penny, but how could you recognize it vas me?'"

Tess gets it. "So Mr. Harry Rose was New York?"

Her mother dismisses the story. "New York in a way that has very little to do with us. Pfeni's the one who's guilty of revisionist history, my luv. Pfeni's the one who's romanticized a world we never belonged to."

Pfeni retorts. "I was mistaken," she says sarcastically. "Mr. Rose never called our house every morning. It was Louis Auchincloss [the quintessential Wasp novelist, whose subject was New York's blueblood society]."

Sara Goode's prickly character was recognizably Sandra's. The eldest Wasserstein sibling intimidated most of Wendy's friends.

Terrence McNally found Sandra formidable. "You could sort of feel Sandy's disapproval if she didn't like something," he said. She had seen a painting in Terrence's home that she liked and asked him if she could meet the artist, a friend of Terrence's. He recalled taking her to the man's studio, and the artist began showing them his paintings. "She said the most horrible things about his work, and he was there," said Terrence.

He mimicked her.

"Look at that tree! Who would paint a tree like that? What street in New York is purple?"

Terrence was mortified. He hadn't wanted to take her, but Sandra had insisted. She'd just built a house in the Hamptons and was interested in buying some paintings. She told Terrence not to worry; she loved the man's work.

He didn't understand why she didn't just say thanks and wait until they were in the car to comment. "Wendy would be totally incapable of that kind of cruelty," he said.

If anything, Wendy used her work to cast her family in a more favorable light, sometimes sacrificing dramatic tension for wishful thinking. In real life Sandra's true love had died before they could marry. In her fictionalized version, Wendy determined to create an unlikely love affair, one that would bring her sister unexpected happiness.

She would be criticized by some for her sentimental desires.

"Wasserstein evokes Chekhov, but 'The Sisters Rosensweig' is marshmallow and adorable rather than penetrating, compassionate and great," wrote Lloyd Rose, reviewing the 1994 Kennedy Center production, in the *Washington Post.* "Obviously there's nothing wrong with Wasserstein's little lessons: Be true to your roots; face up to reality; when Mr. Right comes along, grab him. But her preachments are made in an unreal world . . . . a place without envy, maliciousness, self-destructive impulses or any problem that can't be solved with a loving face-to-face."

The draft was completed in October, just as Wendy was about to turn forty-one. The day she finished writing it, she called Chris Durang and said, "This has been a hell of a lot of effort just to find out what a good playwright Chekhov is."

She gave the play to André, who was struggling to find his footing at Lincoln Center, despite the help of Bernard Gersten, longtime producing partner of Joe Papp at the Public, who remained at Lincoln Center after André's predecessor, Gregory Mosher, left. But André felt that he had hit the ground running and hadn't landed very gracefully. He hadn't developed a strong plan for the next season and was feeling distraught.

"*Sisters Rosensweig* basically saved my ass," he said.

He and Dan Sullivan repeated *Heidi*'s path. There was a reading at Lincoln Center in February, and then a workshop at the Seattle Repertory Theatre. Like all Wendy's plays, this one was too long, but now André knew that the playwright had become expert at cutting and revising, once she saw actors in performance.

During the readings Wendy was disconcerted to discover that the play expected to be her most serious work had turned out to be a comedy. "The laughter was uncontrollable," said André. "I remember Wendy staring at me, and saying, 'I can't believe this!'"

It was a matter of casting. The part of Gorgeous had gone to Madeline Kahn, the dizzy, sexy comic genius who became well known for her roles in Mel Brooks movies. In *Young Frankenstein,* Kahn played a Transylvanian-American princess; in *Blazing Saddles* she played Lili Von Shtupp, a torch singer with a thick Teutonic accent, her costume consisting mainly of a bustier.

The minute Kahn appeared onstage in *The Sisters Rosensweig,* the audience laughed.

Kahn had natural comic instincts. During rehearsals, in a scene where Gorgeous is trying to explain to Pfeni why her romance with her bisexual boyfriend won't work, Kahn said to Wendy, "I know what I'm trying to tell her. I'm trying to tell her you can't judge a book by its cover."

Wendy went back to her hotel and wrote the line that appears in the play: "You can't judge a book by its cover, but you're in the wrong library."

As Wendy's play became funnier, her life became more sober. While she was in Seattle, she received a telephone call from Sandra. After seven years in the clear, she'd been diagnosed with a recurrence of breast cancer.

That evening Wendy sat in the audience and watched as the youngest sister, a writer, confessed to her oldest sister, a successful banker, "There is no one I rely on in life more than you. There is no one I am more grateful to than you."

The playwright began to cry and then stopped.

"In an almost Pirandellian stroke my own character version of my sister cut off my self-indulgence," Wendy wrote.

Onstage Sara Goode impatiently responds to her sister's poignant outpouring. "Pfeni, don't, and I won't," she says, picking up a newspaper to end her sister's profession of needy adoration.

When she returned to New York, Wendy accompanied Sandy to an oncologist who prescribed tamoxifen and told her, unhelpfully, that if the drug had been available after her first diagnosis, the recurrence might not have happened.

"I am to learn that breast cancer treatment is a never-ending saga of 'If only we had had this when you had that, but you never know what's coming next, so just hang in there.'" Wendy wrote.

That night Wendy slept at Sandra's and resolved to open *The Sisters Rosensweig* in New York for her sister.

The subsequent months tried her fortitude in a way in which she hadn't been tested before. In the summer of 1992, in addition to dealing with Sandy's illness, Wendy tended to two of her closest friends, both of whom were hospitalized with life-threatening conditions.

Two years earlier Bill Finn—another playwright friend from Playwrights Horizons—had been diagnosed with an arterial venous malformation of the brain; he was told at first that it was inoperable. In 1992, after winning a Tony for *Falsettos*,* he was hospitalized, facing surgery that could cure him or kill him.

Wendy came to see him every day for a month.

He was amazed she was always there. Even before *The Heidi Chronicles*, he had never known anyone who was so well connected or so busy. Afterward he couldn't imagine how she managed the demands on her life.

"When we walked down the street, all these sixty-five-year-old Jewish ladies would come up to Wendy, and she would talk to them," he said. "They'd talk about their husbands and their daughters, and when they left, I'd ask her who was that, and she'd say, 'I have no idea.' This went on constantly. People embraced her as if she were going to explain their lives to them."

The doctors told Finn they would insert a brain shunt and warned him that on the day of the procedure he couldn't eat.

On the scheduled day, the time kept moving, from 6:00 A.M. to noon to 3:00, 4:00, and 5:00. Then he learned that the procedure had been postponed.

Finn was a large man who didn't like to miss a meal, and he'd missed all of them that day. While he was prone to being overdramatic, he was being realistic when he said he believed that this meal could be his

---

* He won for Best Music and Lyrics and shared the Tony for Best Book with James Lapine.

last. He surveyed his room, full of visitors, and when his eyes landed on Wendy, he decided he wanted her to get his dinner. Wendy always knew where to go.

Wendy left and returned with roast chicken, mashed potatoes, and a vegetable from Sam's Cafe, the celebrity hangout run by Stephen Crisman, husband of Mariel (nickname "Sam") Hemingway, actress and granddaughter of the famous author.

"It was the best meal of my life," Finn said. "I felt like I was dying. Wendy knew what to get. If someone said to me, name one meal you would like to relive, that's the meal." It wasn't his last meal; he lived.

Gerry Gutierrez was also severely ill, with throat cancer.

Wendy was there for him, too, shuttling between hospitals.

A few months later, having survived his treatment, Gutierrez sent Wendy a note telling her how meaningful her help had been.

"I will NEVER be able to fully express to you how deeply grateful I am and always will be for your strength and loyalty and love during this summer 'ordeal,'" he wrote. "If I think too long about how you and André were always with me—at every step—and once in a cab going downtown you used the word 'WE' to say 'we can beat this' . . . I start to cry. I fell in love with you all over again at that moment in that cab."

When he wrote the note, he had just seen *The Sisters Rosensweig.*

Watching—and at times being part of, your life in the theatre—makes me extremely proud. For as long as I have known you, you were always witty—so were your plays. You could always move me—as did your plays. With Heidi I wept with joy at the new depth, intelligence and clear articulation of the things you HAD to say—without losing any of your wit and sensitivity. Your new play adds an even deeper understanding of the human condition with the addition of—dare I say it—melancholy—and (again) without losing your wit and sensitivity. It's like your music has suddenly added the cello section.

He concluded:

I look forward, with enormous excitement, to the miracles in our work and in our lives, that our love and friendship can accomplish together.

I love you. Gerry xxox

The Sisters Rosensweig didn't pile on prizes the way *Heidi* had, though Madeline Kahn won a Tony for Best Actress in a Drama. But the play was a crowd-pleaser and opened in theaters around the country. Its substantial run began with a ticket-selling review from long-standing supporter Mel Gussow, in the *New York Times* ("Captivating. . . . The play offers sharp truths about what can divide relatives and what can draw them together"). The play began at the Mitzi E. Newhouse Theater at Lincoln Center on October 22, 1992, and moved to the Ethel Barrymore Theatre on Broadway on March 18, 1993.

The Sunday before opening night at Lincoln Center, a feature article in the *New York Times* took note of the "tremendous amount" of publicity that surrounded Wendy Wasserstein (while contributing to it):

Part of the explanation may be that she is very much a local hero, or heroine—a New York gal. There's an Upper West Side sensibility in all her work, a sensibility shared by the traditional New York theatergoing audience—male and female alike. She's a local girl made good on the local stage, which happens to be in New York, as are many of the talk shows on which she has promoted herself and her work. Not for nothing does Ms. Wasserstein hail from a family of entrepreneurs.

As Wendy rummaged through family history to develop *The Sisters Rosensweig,* she began longing to discover the past that Lola had so firmly left behind. Therefore she was eager to accept when Sandra invited her on a Citicorp-sponsored trip to Poland, in the spring of 1993, right after *The Sisters Rosensweig* opened on Broadway.

As they followed "the Lola Schleifer Wasserstein Freedom Trail," Wendy began to understand the lives that had preceded hers. "Driving along with my big sister, who knew my grandfather Shimon, I imagine his escape through this countryside north to Gdansk, and his remaining friends and their families being herded like cattle on this road for the final solution."

For Wendy this was a rare acknowledgment of the Holocaust, and of her family's connection to the greatest of Jewish tragedies.

During the trip she was focused on a more immediate sorrow. In the preceding months, it had become evident that Sandra was growing more fragile. The week before *The Sisters Rosensweig* opened, she'd broken her arm while putting on her pantyhose.

Wendy's desire to have a child became frantic, though she didn't tell Sandra why. "My fertility had become in my mind the parallel antidote to her cancer," Wendy wrote.

She plunged into the brave new world of in vitro fertilization. Once again she was at the forefront of the zeitgeist. In 1992, three years after *The Heidi Chronicles* created a stir with Heidi's decision to become a single mother, a popular television series followed suit and set off a national debate. Dan Quayle, Republican vice-presidential candidate, was both praised and chastised for saying that Murphy Brown, the character played by Candice Bergen, undermined "the importance of fathers by birthing a child alone."

Three years after Wendy began fertility treatments, the September 4, 1995, cover of *Newsweek* blared, "Infertility: High-Tech Science Fails 3 Out of 4 Infertile Couples. Has the Hype Outweighed the Hope?"

The article was a compendium of heartbreaking stories, medical fact and fancy, filled with intimidating initialisms: IUI (intrauterine insemination), IVF (in-vitro fertilization), GIFT (gamete intrafallopian transfer), ZIFT (zygote intrafallopian transfer).

In 1993 the American Society for Reproductive Medicine reported daunting statistics. Of 41,209 assisted-reproduction procedures reported by participating clinics, 8,741 had resulted in live births, a success rate of 21.2 percent.

"There's nothing like sitting in a fertility doctor's office looking at the photos of children they've nudged into creation and knowing you're the negative statistic," Wendy wrote. "It becomes an addictive, undermining dream."

When her egg count dropped, her fertility doctor suggested she begin injecting Pergonal—a fertility drug—intramuscularly, to increase the volume.

"You know my sister has cancer," she told him.

He replied, "Yes, of course I know that."

She was blunt. "So is this Pergonal an insane thing to do?"

He said, "We have no data that proves that."

She said sarcastically, "But eventually you will."

Cancer is not among the side effects the pharmaceutical establishment associates with Pergonal. But Wendy's concern would one day seem predictive of her eventual fate, despite the absence of any proven link.

Despite being terrified of needles, she began regular visits to a Park Avenue drugstore, where the pharmacist injected her in the rump.

The doctor gave her a catalog of sperm donors. She chose number 1147, whom she described as "an English graduate student, BS in behavioral sciences and Jewish by choice."

She began taking notes for a memoir, encouraged by Sonny Mehta, editor-in-chief at Knopf, who had become a friend.

On August 14 she met Bruce for lunch at the Russian Tea Room. He was disappointed that the prestigious bar booth he wanted to sit at was occupied by Beverly Sills, the opera singer.

Wendy told him about 1147.

The lonely attempts at insemination were dispiriting. "On Thanksgiving morning I walked down Central Park West toward my sister's annual family gathering," she wrote. "Lines of fathers with children sitting on their shoulders dotted the street for the Macy's parade. I began to get anxious. I was furious at myself, the women's movement and the entire medical profession."

She and Sandra became even closer, bonded further by mutual acts of subterfuge. Sandra was hiding her illness from her employers; Wendy was hiding her attempts at having a baby from the world.

She told some people, including Cathy Graham, André, and Peter Parnell, as well as her actress friend Caroline Aaron, who had also been undergoing fertility treatments.

One day in the fall of 1993, she visited Harry Kondoleon in the loft owned by the Grahams. He was weak, and his voice had begun to sound like the evil witch's in *The Wizard of Oz.* "Everyone thought I would croak by now," he told her as they ate the salami, mozzarella, and olives that Wendy had brought in from Dean & DeLuca.

He had written a novel, *Diary of a Lost Boy,* and was determined to be at his publication party in January. Brave insouciance was his style. The first time Wendy had visited him at St. Vincent's Hospital, when she first found out he was ill, he'd asked her, "What do you think of the gown? It's Yves Saint Vincent."

He also asked her, "What's new on the baby front?"

She told him she planned to proceed, despite the pain and the frustration.

"If I were you, I'd do it," the dying man told her.

Later that day she thought, "I'm in a play costarring Harry, my sister, and 1147." Then she reprimanded herself.

"I'm making everything too neat—life and death—Harry and 1147. I need to cool it."

On October 29 she had another insemination procedure. That afternoon she attended an AIDS memorial service for Peter Schifter, who'd directed *When Dinah Shore Ruled the Earth* at Yale.

"I feel like a short story of my own generation," she wrote. "Single 43 year old woman has insemination in the morning, goes to AIDS service in the afternoon."

She wondered if it had worked. Was she pregnant?

"I have not really considered what I will tell this child about its father," she wrote. "Maybe somewhere I'm hoping this won't work. Maybe I'm hedging my bets."

The procedure failed. Wendy's doctor suggested she try a donor who could supply fresh sperm.

So began two collaborations with William Ivey Long, her old Yale friend, who had become one of the New York theater's most prominent costume designers. With his impish smile and habit of sending congratulations cards filled with sparkling confetti, Long projected an image of fey giddiness. But appearances were deceiving: Long was a serious man with strong values tied to the old-fashioned virtues of hard work, loyalty, and responsibility. However outrageous the costumes he designed, he himself always wore the uniform of his proper southern upbringing: navy blazer, white shirt, striped tie, khakis, black lace-up shoes.

Their friendship had deepened over the years. As Wendy gained prominence, dashing around to speaking engagements, William often remembered their graduate-school days, when the two of them went to see the playwright Lillian Hellman receive an honorary degree at Yale. The auditorium was packed; they sat on the floor, soaking up Hellman's words. Now Wendy was the one onstage imparting wisdom to the next generation.

He never forgot how helpful she'd been to him during his early days in New York, making him money selling his costumed dolls. His mentor, Charles James, had called him a "lost boy" in those days; Wendy's friendship offered a little oasis of security in the Neverland of Manhattan.

Now his career had taken off; he was in constant demand. He became friendly with Kevin McKenzie, the new director of the American Ballet Theatre, who was planning a fresh production of *The Nutcracker* for his debut. McKenzie asked William if he would design the sets and costumes. William agreed and suggested he hire Wendy to write the libretto, reworking the story of Clara with a feminist twist.

McKenzie met with Wendy and agreed with her point of view. "The lesson learned by the girl in the ballet," he told a reporter, "would be that beauty is on the inside." William and Wendy collaborated for a year on the project, which ended badly for William, who dropped out because of internal ABT politics. Wendy remained on board; McKenzie's *Nutcracker* made its New York premiere on May 20, 1994, with her libretto, McKenzie's choreography, and sets and costumes by somebody else.

The second, far more profound, collaboration between Wendy and

William Ivey Long would continue for years. This, too, would end badly—for him.

They were having lunch at the Colony Club, discussing *The Nutcracker.* Wendy told William she wanted a baby.

As he recalled the conversation, he replied, "I've been wanting a child *forever.*"

She said, "Do you want a child with me?"

"Yeah."

"Do you want that responsibility?"

He laughed and, with characteristic insouciance, replied, "Well, George Washington, father of the country, who doesn't want to be a father?"

They kept it light and breezy. He taped four quarters to an index card and mailed them to her, with a note: "From George Washington, father of the country, who else?"

The two of them spoke in terms that were saucy and irreverent, but they were utterly serious.

So it began.

Once again her real-life leading man—now William Ivey Long—was kept sub rosa, not even mentioned in her diary entries and given a diminished role in essays she later wrote about her procreative odyssey.

At first the methods were primitive. He became familiar with small rooms supplied with *Hustler* and *Screw* magazines, of little interest to the gay would-be father of Wendy's child. They began taking limousines to New Jersey, where Wendy's New York doctor had joined a reproductive practice. When questions were raised about the viability of William's sperm, his was added to a mix with the sperm of the anonymous donor.

"I would go to this place, and it was spun into a batter that [they] had to keep warm," Long recalled. "It was freezing cold, so I'd put it next to my heart and run down the street to the doctor's office." Wendy described receiving the mix via "a turkey baster."

Long was frustrated by the notion of the cocktail mix. Who would be the father? He was confused as to what Wendy really wanted.

"This is no good," he told Wendy. "How will we know?"

"We just want it to happen," she told him.

"Don't you want me to be part of it?" he replied.

She parried. "Do you want to be part of it?"

"Yes," he said. "Do you want me?"

She assured him.

"Yes," she said.

They tried various doctors, including the gay fertility specialist who questioned William's suitability. "How do I know this other member of the couple is safe?" he asked.

William changed his life, beginning almost seven years of celibacy, to protect his sperm from disease.

As the years went by, the technology improved, but Wendy failed to conceive. William doubted her desire to have a child. "'Why are you getting on a plane and flying to California to give a talk?'" he said he would ask her. "'You should be going home to bed. You're not giving it a real shot.' From the first time, every single time, she shot herself in the foot. She would fly off somewhere, drive to Dartmouth. She would never go home and play earth mother. She never gave it a chance to take."

Whenever he expressed his doubts—maybe she didn't want him to father her child—she reassured him. "I want your brain," she told him. "I want your DNA. I want your creativity. I want your values."

He felt honored. "It builds you up in this huge way, if this brilliant friend of yours says, 'I trust you.'"

So he resolved to stick with it, no matter how often Wendy disappeared.

Poster design by James McMullan

The Sisters Rosensweig TOOK ON FRESH
POIGNANCY AS EVENTS IN THE
WASSERSTEIN FAMILY UNFOLDED.

Eighteen

THE OBJECTS OF HER AFFECTION

1993–98

In 1993, feeling the urge to nest, Wendy began her adventures in real estate by selling her apartment at One Fifth Avenue for just under $390,000 and moving into a sublet on West Sixty-fourth Street. Thus began her search for the perfect place to raise her as-yet-imaginary child.

"She was the client from hell," said James Foreman, real-estate broker and husband of Caroline Aaron, Wendy's actress friend. "I adored her so much it didn't matter," he added.

"We would find an apartment she really liked," he said. "Then she'd say, 'I need to bring my husbands.'"

One by one they came to offer their opinions: Always André Bishop. Frequently Jane Rosenthal and Cathy Graham ("husbands" for these purposes). Occasionally William Ivey Long or Forrest Sawyer (the newsman was a favored squire for a period).

"We would always get to one friend who would say, 'Wendy, you can't live here,'" Foreman said. "And we would move on to the next apartment. After a while I started to think that was the purpose of the string of 'husbands,' to find the one who would tell her this one won't work."

He showed her at least two dozen apartments and then moved to California, after his wife joined the touring company of *The Sisters Rosensweig*.

Wendy's assistant, Ken Cassillo, took over the search; whenever Wendy received a call from her real-estate broker, she dispatched Kenny to be her scout. For two years he went to Connecticut, upstate New York, and throughout Manhattan looking at a variety of possibilities: farmhouses, East Side town houses, West Side lofts and studios. Something was always wrong.

Cassillo was bright and artistic, only in his twenties but an experienced assistant; he had worked for Jerome Robbins, the choreographer. His new job included office tasks, decorating, real-estate appraisal, and emotional support, like comforting his employer when her cat, Ginger, died.

He had helped Wendy's previous assistant, Cindy Tolan, empty Wendy's apartment at One Fifth. "When you say you were Wendy's assistant, people have no idea," Cassillo said as he described what he found on his first day of work.

"It was like a dorm room. There was just stuff everywhere," he said. "There was no filing system, just bags and bags full of papers in garbage bags. That was the filing system. We had no idea how to keep track of things, so we put things in garbage bags."

The garbage bags moved into the West Sixty-fourth sublet. While Wendy traveled, Cassillo began the daunting task of organizing Wendy's papers.

"I would go to West Sixty-fourth and open up every single crumpled piece of paper and lay it on the sink and lay it on the bed, and that's how the filing system started," he said. "I didn't know she was doing public speaking until I started going through the rubbish bags and I was finding checks for very large sums of money—ten thousand dollars. She didn't cash them if they were from schools or something. She didn't care about that. She'd speak to the school, bury the check in her purse, and then not cash the check."

Wendy liked the luxurious surroundings in her sublet at 1 West Sixty-fourth Street, located near Central Park West. One of her neighbors was Madonna; another was Arthur Sulzberger Jr., publisher of the *New York Times,* and yet another was James Lapine, who lived on the floor above her with his wife and daughter. That was the year she and "Tats" became especially close; she always told him she thought of that sublet as "our year of living well."

When the sublet ran out, she still hadn't found someplace she liked enough to buy. She took up residence at the Lowell Hotel, a small luxury hotel just across Central Park, on Sixty-third Street between Madison and Park.

"She loved the Lowell," said Judith Thurman, a writer friend. "She was so happy."

Thurman saw Wendy's relationship with the Lowell as like that of a family, without the demands. "She had these friendly relationships without conflict or tension, because she paid them," she said. "There was no reciprocity. The reciprocity was built into the bill at the end of the month. It was very freeing. It wasn't work. Relationships in the Wasserstein family were a lot of work. She would also not have been a playwright without that family. There was a lot of drama. There was no drama with the concierge at the Lowell. She loved no ties, not having to give a shit about decorating, rooms made up every day. She ordered room service or went out to the restaurant. It was freedom."

Judith Thurman felt she understood Wendy in ways other people might not. Thurman was a toothpick as an adult but she'd been a chubby child; she was also a Jewish girl from Queens who had made good in Manhattan. Now a contributor to the *New Yorker,* Thurman had won a National Book Award in 1983 for her biography of Isak Dinesen. More recently Thurman had Frenchified herself; she and Wendy met in 1993, right after Thurman had returned from Europe, where she'd spent a year researching a biography of Colette, the French novelist who became a feminist icon.

Wendy had a particular interest in Thurman, who was four years older and the single mother of a boy, then three and a half years old. They met for drinks at one of Wendy's favorite New York spots, the Café des Artistes, off Central Park West.

She inquired about Thurman's baby-making history, without revealing that she was taking fertility treatments.

Thurman told her story.

At age forty-one, the alarm went off. She realized she couldn't live with herself if she didn't at least try to have a child.

She thought, "Holy shit, I have to do this."

She went to her gynecologist, who specified, "You have to do this *right away*." The doctor explained, "Fertility declines, declines, declines, declines and at forty-one it goes like that." The doctor's hand mimicked an airplane crashing to the ground.

Thurman told Wendy she'd decided to get pregnant that year. She talked to various men friends, and some volunteered, but she worried they might want to be involved with her child, and that was not her plan. She wanted to be in charge. "I couldn't start negotiating with a man about visitation and this and that," she said.

She went to a sperm bank, so disturbing an experience that in describing it Thurman dropped her worldly veneer and reverted to being a girl from Queens.

"They're *gonifs*," she told Wendy.

A friend of Thurman's had told her that the catalogs filled with glowing descriptions of sperm donors were fiction. "C'mon," the friend said. "The guy who runs the sperm bank goes behind a screen and jerks off."

Thurman was convinced enough to agree when the friend of a former lover volunteered to father her child. They spent a week together—not a romantic affair, but sex for the purposes of conception. It worked. Now she had a son, who lived with her, though he knew his father and had a relationship with him.

Wendy told Thurman she wanted a child. But, Thurman said, "She was very secretive about how she was going to go about it."

In February 1996, Wendy purchased a 2,160-square-foot apartment that Cassillo had discovered at 75 Central Park West. The building was an elegant prewar structure. She thought the apartment, for which she paid $1.6 million, was "dingy and characterless," but it had wonderful views and a fine address. She hired Patricia Seidman, who had been Judith Thurman's architect, to renovate. As Wendy and Seidman discussed layout and design, it became clear to the architect that her forty-five-year-old client was planning a home for a family.

"She wanted a child—that was part of what she wanted her grown-up life to include—and she chose this apartment because it was a good place to raise a child," Seidman said.

Wendy instructed Seidman to turn the neglected space into an apartment that was elegant and unconventional but comfortable. Details were vague. "She was one of the least domestic people I've ever met," Seidman said. "She couldn't cook, she couldn't boil water, but she loved homey things. She was longing for a home but had no instincts on how to put it together for herself."

By then Wendy had resumed work on *The Object of My Affection*. The movie was finally about to be produced, almost a decade after Wendy had begun adapting the Stephen McCauley novel, about the romantic friendship between a gay man and his best friend, a single woman who becomes pregnant but doesn't want to marry the man she's dating.

Though *The Heidi Chronicles* had been made into a television movie starring Jamie Lee Curtis in 1995, this was Wendy's first feature film to be produced.

She was most excited about working with Nicholas Hytner, the film's director. She had met him three years earlier when, at thirty-seven, he was already a luminary of the London theater. Known for his riveting productions of Shakespeare, he had exuberant ambitions; he'd already branched out into opera and film. Wendy met him through André, who had convinced Hytner to bring his brilliantly staged *Carousel* from the National Theatre in London to Lincoln Center. Hytner came to New York to meet with André, not long after *The Sisters Rosensweig* opened at Lincoln Center.

Hytner was enchanted by Wendy.

"I don't make firm friends very easily, like a lot of Brits," said Hytner. "I'm very happy to meet people and pleased to see them, but to make firm friends doesn't happen that easy, that quickly, but we were firm friends very quickly."

In turn she was dazzled by Hytner, who was smart, charming, sophis-ticated, handsome, British—and Jewish.

"I think I want to have an affair with Nick," she wrote in her diary.

He accompanied her to the Kennedy Center Honors in Washington a few months after they met and was her date that night at the president's reception: He kept a photograph of the two of them standing with Bill and Hillary Clinton in front of the Christmas tree at the White House.

Soon they were chatting endlessly on the telephone, carrying on funny, fake conversations where each of them pretended to be the other's mother, alternately criticizing and bragging about their children.

Not long after they met, he became involved with a man in New York, whom he introduced to Wendy. It didn't occur to Hytner that Wendy's interest in him might be romantic.

"She would talk to me a huge amount on her crush—more than a crush, she was in love with André—but she was never in love with me," Hytner said, though she would refer to him as one of her "husbands."

Now that Hytner had signed on to direct *The Object of My Affection*, they had more reason to spend time with each other. Filming was set to begin in the fall of 1997.

As always, she was busy.

She continued to write essays for the *New York Times* and women's magazines, as well as for Betsy Carter, who settled at *Harper's Bazaar* after *New York Woman* ceased publication, and then moved to a maga-zine called *New Woman*. These essays became a kind of public—carefully self-censored—diary, as well as clever promotion of her work, tending to appear more frequently when she had a play opening somewhere.

In 1995 Wendy added a significant venue for her journalism, when an editor from the *New Yorker* took her to lunch at the Royalton Hotel and asked if she would like to write for the country's premier literary maga-zine. For Wendy this was the pinnacle. What was she if not the consum-mate New Yorker? The magazine became a prized venue for the personal accounts that might have been first drafts for the memoir she was planning to write.

Besides this journalistic output, in 1996 she published *Pamela's First Musical,* an illustrated children's book in which an Auntie Mame type introduces her niece to Broadway musicals. She dedicated the book to her niece Pamela, Bruce's oldest child, who was then a senior at Dalton.

That same spring Wendy also began working on *An American Daughter,* her first overtly political play.

Despite its popularity with Wendy's constituency, and commercial success as it toured the United States, *The Sisters Rosensweig* hadn't been taken as seriously as she'd hoped. Bob Brustein called the play "a step backward" from *The Heidi Chronicles.* "Wisecracks come too easily to her," he told a reporter. The play flopped in London.

Wendy had grown tired of the question that critics kept asking: "When will you show us your dark side?" She wanted to achieve the gravitas she felt continued to elude her, despite all the accolades she'd accumulated.

With the arrival of the Clintons in the White House, her generation was undeniably in charge. Her peers were no longer the up-and-comers but rather the ones who had arrived. Frank Rich left his job as the country's most powerful theater critic in 1994 to write an opinion-page column about culture and politics for the *Times.* The theater was thriving, in better shape than it had been when he began reviewing thirteen years earlier, but it seemed too narrow.

"As election year arrived, and with it the prospect of both a political and generational turnover in American life, my journalistic focus widened," he wrote in a farewell column called "Exit the Critic." "I found myself more interested in writing about the world itself rather than just the theater's version of that world." Wendy had been with him and his wife, Alex, and their friend Michiko Kakutani* as he contemplated what his debut topic should be for the new op-ed column.

Many other friends had achieved prominent positions in the establishment. André was ensconced at Lincoln Center. Peter Parnell eventually moved to Los Angeles, where in 1999 he became a coproducer on *The West*

---

* In 1998 Kakutani won the Pulitzer Prize for criticism.

Wing, a television series that mesmerized the country with its insider view of a fictional White House.

Wendy's inspiration for *An American Daughter* was "Nannygate," the political mess that followed Bill Clinton's nomination of Zoë Baird, a Washington lawyer, as attorney general. During her Senate confirmation hearings, the information emerged that she had hired illegal aliens for child care (and hadn't paid Social Security taxes for their work). Baird eventually removed her name from consideration.

Wendy felt Baird was a scapegoat, like Hillary Clinton, who had recently been lambasted for admitting on national television that she didn't want to stay home and bake cookies—and was next seen wearing a demure headband, holding her husband's hand.

She filled file folders with news reports and commentary about Zoë Baird. She debriefed her well-placed media friends, people like Donald Graham, Walter Shapiro who wrote for *Time,* Charlie Rose, Peter Schweitzer of CBS. Mike Kinsley of *Slate* and the *New Republic* threw a party, specifically to introduce her to Washington types, part of her research.

With *An American Daughter,* she hoped to expand her range, but she was also seeking refuge from the daunting realities of life. "I wanted to organize the sadness, frustration, and truth of it into play form," she wrote.

As she worked, her sister Sandra's cancer was becoming more virulent.

Sandra had left Citicorp three years earlier, after her trip with Wendy to Poland, to take a less taxing position as a management consultant. But she never quit working, not even when she was sick enough to be hospitalized. When her hair fell out, she wore wigs and an attitude that dared anyone to mention her physical changes.

"She would work from the hospital and tell the nurses to get out when she was on conference calls," said Samantha, the younger daughter. "She used to think that walking around with the wig, no one would notice. And given the guys she worked with, it's entirely possible they didn't. That's not how they looked at her."

Sandra didn't hide her illness from her daughters, nor did she dwell on it. She kept her doctors' appointments and went about her business.

"The denial was very, very strong," said Samantha. "She found the entire thing a massive inconvenience. I think the general feeling was, if you don't think about it or talk about it, everyone can get on with their lives."

Sandra made it clear that she expected her daughters to follow her example regarding her illness.

"To the extent my mother would get personal about that stuff, she would tell us we were not under any circumstances to remember her as a sick person," Samantha said. "That's what she was afraid of. . . . Her focus was to not pay attention to it."

"You absolutely can't think of me this way," Sandra instructed her daughters, and then changed the subject. "Let's go to the theater."

But there came a time when Sandra couldn't avoid paying attention. While Wendy was working on the screenplay for *The Object of My Affection* and an early draft of *An American Daughter*, she received a call from Sandra, who was crying.

"They've found cancer in my brain," she told her sister.

"When do you next see my husband?" Wendy asked. She always referred to Sandra's oncologist as her husband, because it made Sandra laugh.

It worked. Sandra laughed.

She brought Wendy with her to an appointment with her oncologist, who took his patient's sister aside. "I've never seen such a classic case of denial," he told Wendy. "I would be surprised if your sister was around in six months."

Sandra proved him wrong. In 1997, a year later, while Wendy was in Seattle, for a workshop production of *An American Daughter*, she received a call from Sandra.

"I've stumped the star," Sandra said triumphantly. To her doctor's amazement, Sandra's cancer markers had improved. She was very much alive.

Wendy was heartened by the news. The thought of losing Sandra terrified her. Her big sister remained Wendy's polestar, a valued mother figure, who balanced high standards with encouragement, ambition with realism, hauteur with discernible love.

"In many ways my mother was very much the anti-Lola and intentionally so," said Samantha Schweitzer. "She chose an opposite path. She moved to London instead of staying in New York. She often talked about how messy her parents' house was. When she got to college, she said, 'I am never living that way again.' She wanted things to be tidy and clean and efficient. She contained Lola, talking to her on Sunday mornings. It was a very tightly controlled, organized life."

Sandra's illness had an obvious effect on Wendy. Meryl Streep, playing the lead during the Seattle workshop, observed a noticeable change in the playwright's behavior. The celebrated actress had never understood why Wendy, one of the few writers to comment lucidly on the failures of the women's movement, consistently deferred in conversation to men and talked in a baby voice. Why was Wendy so often girlie and giddy, as though apologizing for her rigorous judgment? In Seattle, Streep saw a Wendy she hadn't met before.

"Her voice dropped two octaves . . . she was unequivocal in her certainty of what she wanted any given moment to convey, who spoke without all the furbelows and giggles of the social Wendy that I knew," said Streep. "And it was thrilling to be in the room with her."

Streep was even more impressed as she watched Wendy in action. She sat in the front row, next to Dan Sullivan, furiously writing and taking notes during the performances, then bringing back ruthlessly edited pages from her hotel the next day.

"It was formidable, and serious, and exacting work," the actress said, with evident admiration.

The admiration was mutual. Wendy had ranked Meryl number eight on her list of "Perfect Women Who Are Bearable."

"She'll never pass you a poison apple," Wendy wrote. "Meryl just goes about her business."

Wendy was disappointed when Streep declined to sign on for the Broadway production of *An American Daughter* the following year, even though the lead role was played by Kate Nelligan, a celebrated theater actress. Nelligan called Wendy into her dressing room on opening night.

"Did you know this play would change your life?" Nelligan asked. "Now you will be taken seriously as a playwright."

Nelligan was a far better performer than prognosticator. With few exceptions, the play was taken apart by critics.

Most crushing was the slap from the *New York Times.* "Themes (big themes), relationships (deep and confusing ones), plot complications (of the melodramatic variety) are piled to the toppling point, most of them never satisfactorily defined," wrote Ben Brantley, who had succeeded Frank Rich as chief critic. "Neither Dan Sullivan's chipper, keep-it-moving direction nor Ms. Wasserstein's justly famed ear for dialogue and bone-deep sense of craft can conceal the feeling that she doesn't know entirely where she's heading or how to get there."

Lloyd Rose of the *Washington Post,* hadn't warmed to *The Sisters Rosensweig* and liked this play less. "No doubt about it, Wendy Wasserstein is cute," was the reviewer's hope-crushing opening line. "In her latest play 'An American Daughter,' which opened last night on Broadway, she comes up with one charming witticism after another. . . . Wasserstein even comes up with a companion cliché for soccer moms: 'fast-food dads.' These are beguilingly clever remarks. If only there were a play to go with them."

Wendy had no time to absorb the resounding rejection. She felt as though she had little control over anything—neither the large questions she'd attempted to grapple with onstage nor her sister's life-and-death struggle. On April 15, 1997, two days after the play's opening, Wendy flew to Paris with Sandra and her daughters, to gather with Bruce's family and Lola and Morris for a Passover dinner at the Ritz. Sandra was frail and needed support to climb stairs.

That August, Wendy accompanied Sandra to London, to celebrate her sister's sixtieth birthday with an old friend of Sandra's from her London days.

By November the cancer had advanced to Sandra's liver. She refused to stop treatment, asking for more chemotherapy, continuing to work.

Jenifer, recently married, was torn between her job, her new husband, and her mother. Samantha took a semester away from graduate school to be home.

Nick Hytner had begun filming *The Object of My Affection,* with a cast that promised to bring the movie a lot of attention: Jennifer Aniston, who had become internationally famous as a star of *Friends,* the NBC television series, and Paul Rudd, who had become a teenage heartthrob after his performance in the 1995 film *Clueless.*

For Samantha's twenty-fifth birthday celebration, Hytner and Wendy arranged for Rudd to show up at the restaurant for dessert. The young woman had just found out that her mother's cancer had spread to her liver and pancreas. The surprise visit from Rudd gave her momentary respite from the overwhelming sadness.

Throughout all this, Wendy had been actively pursuing her quest to have a baby, confiding in very few people.

The only family member to know was Sandra, who insisted on taking Wendy to surgery for polyps, even though Sandra had pins in her hips by then and had no feeling in her hands, due to a neuropathy that developed from chemotherapy. Sandra's stoicism reinforced Wendy's feeling of helplessness, and led her to agonize over the choices she'd made.

"I thought of Sandra valiantly going to work each day in her wigs and never mentioning her ongoing struggle," she wrote. "Comparatively, I felt spoiled and ridiculous. I was convinced that every photo of a baby in the doctor's office was a plot to negate my generation's sense of worth. Every fertility failure a reminder that for every door you've opened there'll be one slammed right in your face. I was now weeping uncontrollably. I couldn't tell if it was the endless injections, the disappointments, or the fear that any buoyant hopefulness I harbored was now completely dissipated."

Ken Cassillo took care of the paperwork until he was succeeded by Angela Trento. Cathy Graham provided the names of fertility specialists and adoption lawyers. Cassillo went with Wendy to visit a lawyer who specialized in adoptions from Eastern Europe, because she thought they would share similar roots. That line of inquiry ended when news reports raised concerns about health issues suffered by Eastern European babies whose birth mothers had been exposed to nuclear fallout.

For much of her prospecting in the surreal, experimental world of fertility treatment, she had one steady, silent partner: William Ivey Long.

He experienced the humiliation of having a "lady doctor" tell him he had low-quality sperm. In layman's terms, his sperm was blunt and couldn't penetrate the egg. He and Wendy fondly referred to his sperm as "helmet heads."

They learned about intracytoplasmic sperm injection (ICSI), which isolated sperm and directly injected it into a woman's egg to create a fertilized embryo. "I paid for all these treatments to help the little losers in," said William.

They tried fertilizing Wendy's eggs and then tried with eggs they purchased through the fertility doctor. They made batches of fertilized eggs to be frozen, some with William's sperm and some from an anonymous donor. They chose him together, after reading descriptions in the catalog at the fertility doctor's office.

They visited cancer specialists together, armed with Sandra's medical history, to see if it would be safe for Wendy to become pregnant. William comforted Wendy when she became pregnant but then miscarried, several times, the fertilized eggs failing to implant.

He flew with her to Boca Raton to meet an adoption lawyer and to California to meet a possible surrogate mother. They talked about the little girl—or boy—they might create, though Wendy made it clear the baby would be hers to raise, while assuring William he would be involved. He accompanied her to the drugstore on Central Park West, where the pharmacist would give her injections meant to increase her egg production.

And then it stopped. Wendy told him she wasn't going to try anymore. "I'm sorry, William, it's not working," she told him. "I know you wanted this as much as I did."

There were no more calls for visits to doctors, no more appointments with lawyers or possible surrogate mothers, no more speculation on the men who lay behind the numbers in the fertility catalogs. When William didn't hear from Wendy for a while, he didn't think much of it. Both of them were exhausted by years of failure. They were both busy, on the road following the demands of their careers. It had always been like that. The arduous pursuit of motherhood, which for many women becomes a full-time preoccupation, was something Wendy seemed to fit into her schedule.

William didn't know that Wendy was deliberately avoiding him. He didn't realize that he had inadvertently insulted her when he'd mentioned that a Yale classmate had also asked him to donate sperm. Wendy encouraged him to try but then told another friend she was angry at him. Ultimately, he didn't even make the donation.

Later, he said, he felt that Wendy was just looking for an excuse, a way out. She wanted her baby to be hers and no one else's.

Even while William was involved, Wendy tested other options. She asked her friend Peter Schweitzer (not her former brother-in-law), a CBS news producer, if he would be a sperm donor. He had split up with Heather Watts, a ballerina with the New York City Ballet, after a long relationship and wasn't dating anyone special. "I was very touched that Wendy would ask me," he said. But after much reflection, he said no.

"I wanted to get married and have my own family, and I thought it would be a strange burden to put on a woman I would marry, to say I have this other child from another woman but it wasn't a marriage, it was a sperm donation," he said. "I remember thinking, 'I will find my mate, I will find my partner and will have that family,' and feared that Wendy would not."

As it became clear in the summer of 1997 that Sandra was reaching her final days, Wendy decided to end the fertility treatments. Her fantasy of saving Sandra by becoming pregnant was not working. There was no miracle that would save her sister.

Betsy Carter, Bruce's old Michigan friend and Wendy's longtime editor, had crossed paths with Sandra for years but had always been intimidated by her.

Their relationship changed when Carter was diagnosed with breast cancer, around the same time as Sandra's recurrence.

"That will bond you!" Carter said.

"I think to both of us it was a surprise we became such good friends," said Carter. "I'm not on anyone's A-list. I don't travel in those investment-banker circles or any of those circles. We just liked each other."

During the past year, the two of them had gone together every week to the 92nd Street Y for a Broadway musical sing-along class. Everyone sat at desks, holding song sheets, belting out the lyrics to old favorites like *Oklahoma!* and *My Fair Lady.*

"We both had an insane love of Broadway musicals," said Carter. But even in her weakened condition, Sandra maintained her strict standards. If the selection was something she didn't approve of—like a number from *The Phantom of the Opera,* Sandra would put down her music and say, "I won't sing that!"

On the morning of Christmas Eve 1997, it was Betsy Carter who telephoned Wendy and told her that Sandra's doctor wanted to have her hospitalized. Despite Sandra's worsening condition over the past months, the call came as a shock. She had always rebounded, defying doctors' predictions.

Not this time. By evening Sandra was in a coma.

Georgette had been in New York the previous day, just before Sandra went into the hospital.

The sisters were alone for a few minutes. As Georgette remembered the scene, Sandra turned to her and said, "In looking at my life, I'm happy because I was a player. I'm proud of my life. I was a player."

Georgette left as Wendy came in. Georgettte told Wendy what Sandra had said to her.

Wendy looked at Georgette strangely.

"Why did she say that to you?" Wendy asked. "I've been here all these days, and she says that to *you* to make you feel better."

Jenifer understood her Aunt Georgette's need to hear Sandra's assurance that everything was okay. She was often the odd sister out, living in Vermont, often seeming more in tune with Lola than with her high-powered siblings, who didn't always take her seriously. Though the portrayal of Gorgeous in *The Sisters Rosensweig* wasn't altogether flattering (she was ditzy; her husband wasn't able to support his family), Georgette was delighted to be part of it. She displayed a giant poster of the play in the living room at the Wilburton Inn.

Jenifer didn't believe that her mother had told Georgette the truth but rather what Sandra thought Georgette wanted to hear.

"My mother didn't have a peaceful death," Jenifer said. "She struggled against it every minute."

She and her sister had watched their mother's valiant stubbornness in horror.

"The sin of pride is a big theme," said Jenifer. "When my mother was dying, it broke my heart. She was on the phone with a colleague saying that after the Christmas break she wanted to talk to that person about corporate boards she'd been proposed for. I thought, 'This is the saddest thing I've ever heard.'" She understood her mother needed to believe she would recover and be able to return to work, but it was still excruciating.

For five nights she and Samantha slept in cots in Sandra's hospital room. Finally, when Sandra was crying out in pain, Jenifer begged the nurses to give her mother morphine.

One of the nurses told the daughters to go home and to make sure their unconscious mother knew they were leaving.

Samantha and Jenifer left at 11:00 P.M. At 1:30 A.M., December 30, 1997, they received the call that Sandra had died. She was sixty years old.

"She needed us to leave," said Jenifer. "I believe she could not have her children in the room and let go. But she was fighting. Her body was done. Her kidneys weren't functioning, her liver wasn't functioning, her body was done. It was not a graceful death."

Her daughters invited the family to a private service on Main Beach in East Hampton, on New Year's Eve 1997. Georgette wasn't there.

She had asked Sandra's daughters to postpone the ceremony a day. New Year's Eve was the inn's biggest night; they had no manager, and there was no way to make it back to Vermont in time.

The funeral took place as planned. Georgette sent one of her sons to represent her; afterward she felt guilty and wished she'd gone herself.

Wendy was angry. When she eventually wrote about Sandra's last days,* Georgette's name didn't appear.

The entire family gathered on January 19, 1998, for another memorial service for Sandra at Lincoln Center, produced by Wendy and André, directed by Gerry Gutierrez.

Lola seemed tiny, frail, cloaked in black, old, nothing like her usual self, the eighty-year-old wonder who delighted strangers with her high kicks. Morris, always quiet, seemed to be somewhere else. Later the family came to understand that he was in the early stages of dementia.

Lola's survival instincts didn't make room for death. During Sandra's last days, Lola's mean streak emerged in full force. In the hospital hallway, Wendy walked over to comfort her mother.

Lola responded bitterly. "It's a waste of a life," she said. "What a waste of a life. She never had grandchildren."

Jenifer and Samantha were standing right there.

Rhoda Brooks, a friend of Wendy's, felt compelled to say something, no matter how awkward she felt doing so. "You know your grandmother doesn't mean that."

Wendy presided over Sandra's memorial, regaling the mourners with stories of her glamorous big sister. She recalled being scandalized and enthralled, as a second-grader at Yeshivah of Flatbush, when Sandra took her into Manhattan for a risqué movie followed by spareribs and shrimp with lobster sauce at the House of Chan.

Wendy remembered Sandra advising their nephew Scoop on what books to read.

"She was the most sympathetic and sophisticated person I could even dream of," Wendy said. "There has been no major decision I made without Sandra and no major success or self-doubt and hurt without Sandra."

Jenifer was the last to speak.

---

* In "How I Spent My Forties," an essay that appears in *Shiksa Goddess.*

"Someone once told me Sam and I are very lucky and unlucky," she said, ". . . to have had such a person as a mother and to have lost her."

Jenifer told the friends and relatives who'd gathered not to worry about her and Samantha. Their mother, she said, had taught them very well.

"We tried to listen—although there was a lot of information," she said. "If each of us has half of her strength and her will and intelligence and wit, we will be fine."

Sandra's memorial took place in the Mitzi E. Newhouse Theater, the same theater where the *The Sisters Rosensweig* had premiered four years earlier. That had been a glorious night for the Family Wasserstein, as they'd been designated in *New York* magazine. Now, despite the life-affirming anecdotes and bright production numbers (a Mozart aria, a Broadway show tune), grief replaced glory.

PLAYWRIGHT TERRENCE MCNALLY BECAME ANOTHER
SECRET THAT WASN'T A SECRET.

Nineteen

FESTIVAL OF REGRETS

1998–99

Being Jewish was central to Wendy's identity, but religious belief eluded her. She rarely missed going to synagogue for the High Holidays but otherwise almost never attended services. She had internalized the mixed messages she'd received as a child, being sent to yeshiva and then hearing Lola mock Jewish ritual at home. Lola's motto was "God helps those who help themselves."

Sandra's death left a vast void. "I had come to believe not only that God didn't help those who helped themselves, but also that he couldn't care less," Wendy wrote. The emptiness she felt seemed less likely to be filled by a baby with each passing year. Wendy was now closer to fifty than to forty. When Lola had been this age, she was soon to become a grandmother.

Work offered no comfort: Wendy felt that her career as a dramatist had stalled. *The Object of My Affection* opened and closed in the spring of 1998, leaving neither shame nor acclaim in its wake. The movie generated a lot of publicity, thanks to its topical subject matter and its well-known lead actors. The *Variety* reviewer produced a fair summary: "A very vanilla romantic tale . . . , 'The Object of My Affection' tries to mix the messy realities of mismatched relationships with the structural neatness of a musical-comedy view of the world, with mild, occasionally diverting results."

Nick Hytner, the director, was disillusioned by the experience. He had been drawn to the project because he liked how the McCauley novel dealt with the love between a gay man, named George, and his roommate, Nina, the straight woman he loves. When Nina becomes pregnant (via her boyfriend), she and George, her soul mate, consider the possibility of raising the child together. The novel ends on a wistful note, acknowledging that there could be no truly happy resolution to their relationship.

Hytner wanted to remain faithful to the novel. But after testing the movie with audiences, the studio decided that the ending was too downbeat and forced an unconvincing feel-good denouement that Hytner deplored. In the version that was released, the woman has the baby alone, she and George find "suitable" partners, and they all happily participate in the child's upbringing, along with the baby's father.

For Hytner this neatly packaged resolution watered down a poignant truth about an intimate relationship between a gay man and a straight woman. In his words: "The original, melancholic ending said these two are nuts about each other, and they can't be together, and that's always going to be an unresolved pain in their lives."

For Wendy the movie was yet another sign that response to her dramatic work had noticeably cooled. She was unable to shake off the sour reaction to *An American Daughter,* which she saw as a rejection of her attempt to become a serious voice in the political arena. She directed her anger at First Lady Hillary Clinton. In an impassioned article in the *New York Times,* Wendy asked what had happened to the "idealistic, forthright Hillary" whose 1969 Wellesley College commencement address summed up the hopes of her generation in a bold declaration: "We're searching for more immediate, ecstatic, and penetrating modes of living."

Wendy wasn't a friend of the Clintons, but she'd been a guest at the White House—once escorted by Bill Finn, once by Nick Hytner, and another time by André. She had admired them. They had arrived at the White House as a revolutionary couple—the His and Hers Presidency—with revolutionary plans. No reading to kindergartners for Hillary. She was put in charge of overhauling the country's health-care system. That failed, and then her marriage floundered. The First Lady was no longer a model of the new woman, but a far more familiar species—Loyal Wife, in the kitchen baking cookies when she wasn't standing by her disgraced husband, seducer of a White House intern.

It seemed no one could talk about anything besides the Monica Lewinsky affair, which had sidelined subjects of national and international import. "Now, the impressive personal qualities—idealism, strength, and poise under pressure—that [Hillary] once directed toward influencing social policy are being used to maintain domestic tranquillity," Wendy wrote.

Wendy's outburst reflected, among other emotions, her vacillating feelings toward her brother Bruce, now married for the third time. On July 25, 1998, less than a month before the article was published, Wendy took Nick Hytner to a fund-raiser for the Clintons thrown by Bruce and his new wife, Claude; admission was twenty-five thousand dollars a couple (the fee was waived for Wendy and Nick). Claude Becker Wasserstein was tall, elegant, and impossibly good-looking, her bloodline part French, part Jewish. She was an actual raven-haired beauty, like a character from a potboiler novel. This striking combination of attributes made her an easy target for her brilliant but lumpy sister-in-law, who had spent a lifetime regarding Bruce

BRUCE WITH CLAUDE BECKER WASSERSTEIN, HIS THIRD WIFE.

variously with admiration and disappointment, adoration and anger. But Claude was also bright, gracious, and charming, making her impossible for Wendy to hate (but also difficult to fully love).

Two years earlier Wendy had hinted at her feelings about her latest sister-in-law in a diary she wrote for *Slate*, the online journal edited by her friend Mike Kinsley.

"Thinking of canceling breakfast with my mother tomorrow," Wendy had written on October 2, 1996. "She's very eager to tell me my brother's third wife is his best wife. I think I need to work."

Claude had been a producer for CBS News; she won an Emmy in 1992 for investigative journalism. With her seemingly flawless physical being, combined with a sympathetic intelligence and innate sense of style, she represented a crucial way in which Wendy and Bruce had grown apart. Claude seemed comfortable in Bruce's world in a way Wendy never believed she could be.

They eventually had homes in London, Manhattan, Paris, and East Hampton, and property in Santa Barbara. The family had celebrated Sandra's last Passover supper in Paris, because Claude and Bruce were also throwing a wedding party for themselves there.

Their showcase was Cranberry Dune, the Hamptons estate where the Democratic fund-raiser was held. The oceanfront property was located on a road called Further Lane, in an enclave of rich and famous neighbors. Nick Hytner arrived dressed to meet a president—in suit and tie—only to discover that in the Hamptons the more expensive the benefit, the more casual the clothing. All the investment bankers knew that grubby chic was the dress code. Hytner took off his necktie and declared the evening "brilliant."

Wendy was dismissive of Bruce's wealthy domain, even though she, too, had grown accustomed to slipping her feet into Manolo Blahnik shoes. Through Stephen Graham she'd become friendly with his mother, publishing mogul Katharine Graham, and developed a crush on his brother Donald, who succeeded his mother as chairman of the Washington Post Company. She became close to Clifford Ross, whose father was a Wall Street financier and philanthropist and whose aunt was Helen

Frankenthaler, a prominent artist who was married for several years to Robert Motherwell. Betsy Ross, Clifford's wife, had a Madison Avenue shop that catered to wealthy women. Wendy liked to hang out there to eavesdrop and then take Ross out for lunch, amusing her with verbatim recapitulations of overheard conversations.

In her *Slate* diary, Wendy wrote, "Sat in a friend's dress shop on Madison Avenue for an hour in the afternoon and watched women try on two-thousand-dollar dresses. I have no idea why I am so riveted by this. I tell myself it's character studies for my next play. I am fascinated by the insularity of the rich. I am appalled by their entitlement."

Appalled, perhaps, but also desirous. In late 1997 she finally moved into her new apartment on Central Park West (and wrote about the renovation for *Architectural Digest*). She had many friends in the neighborhood. James Lapine and Michiko Kakutani had moved nearby. Jane Rosenthal lived within a few blocks. André now lived and worked uptown; Lincoln Center was just blocks away.

Chris Durang continued to teach at Juilliard, a short walk from 75 Central Park West, Wendy's new address, even though he'd moved from Manhattan to Bucks County, Pennsylvania, with his partner, John Augustine. Chris longed for trees and grass—and had been worn down by a succession of ho-hum reviews in the *New York Times* from Frank Rich. Chris and John lived with their dog, Chief, in a stone farmhouse on the top of a hill, surrounded by sweeping countryside vistas. Bucks County was only a couple of hours by bus from the city, but a large psychic distance from his old life in the city.

Settled into the new apartment, Wendy shook off the bitterness that had been creeping in. After one of her expeditions to Duke University's diet center, she became thin—actually thin, not just less heavy. She began doing her hair and dressing well. She hinted that she was seeing someone but never introduced that "someone" to anyone. There were dates with a doctor from Mount Sinai, but nothing evolved.

Angela Trento had taken over from Ken Cassillo as Wendy's assistant in early 1998. "She looked great," said Trento. "She had great legs. She'd wear these short skirts and great high-heeled pumps."

PEOPLE OFTEN ASKED IF WENDY AND HER FRIEND RHODA WERE SISTERS.

Trento was much younger than Wendy, but she felt like the adult as she watched her boss going out on the town every night.

"She was out every night," Trento said. "She always had some event, being honored at, or speaking at, or at somebody's play. Her whole night was planned."

The relentless socializing wore out some of her friends, among them Rhoda Brooks, who wasn't from the theater world, even though she'd met Wendy through Bill Finn, the composer. Trained as a physician, Rhoda ran her own marketing company, and she felt she provided a respite from Wendy's high-profile existence. While they operated in completely different spheres, they found common ground as intelligent, successful Jewish women who hadn't married. People remarked that they looked as if they could have been sisters.

"At first I adored being at something where the prince of Monaco would be there, but then I preferred just being with Wendy and didn't like doing all those other things," said Rhoda. "You're at another institutional dinner with people who don't care about you."

John Lee Beatty, the set designer, could remember the moment of realization for him. He and Wendy were sharing a cab home from some event, and she said, "Oh, I'm going over to the East Side to this party with So-and-So, you want to go?'"

He started to say yes and then changed his mind. "I think I want to go home instead, you know?" he replied. "Is that okay?"

She said, "Yeah," but Beatty noticed that she had a funny look on her face, a look that told Beatty their friendship had shifted just a bit. "In your relationship with Wendy, there's a moment where you decide not to be the sidekick that goes to the party on the East Side or another restaurant for another dinner to meet yet another crowd of people," he said.

But Wendy's social schedule continued, even accelerated. There was always someone ready to venture with her into the social fray. It was as if she had decided, "This is my life." She hadn't completely given up on the idea of having a child, but at age forty-seven she was coming to terms with the idea that she might not. She kept moving at full throttle, not so different from Lola, dancing for hours on end. If she couldn't have a significant other, she could have rooms full of people who cared about her.

And if she couldn't have children, she could find other ways to be connected to the future. By then Wendy had taught at New York University and Columbia and lectured at other schools. She became mentor as well as employer to her assistants; being hired by her meant automatic enrollment in "Wendy's School for Girls." In return for deciphering her handwriting and typing scripts, and trying to bring order to her household, the young women and men who worked for her received unstinting advice and help, as well as gifts and entertainment.

At an earlier point in her life, Wendy had decided her friends were her family. Now, increasingly, her assistants filled the innermost circle. Ken Cassillo became Wendy's go-to guy for Lola and Morris, who were still living in the same apartment they'd moved into thirty-five years earlier. They refused to have help, even though Morris was becoming more and more unstable. In that way, too, Wendy had become a classic Baby Boomer, taking care of elderly parents while taking care of (or trying to have) her own children.

When Morris fell and couldn't get up, or disappeared, as he had begun to do, Wendy called Cassillo and asked him to find her father. Sometimes the assistant would simply be a companion, taking Morris to the park or to a museum. As he grew more frail, Cassillo helped him take showers and go to the bathroom.

Cassillo became fond of both Morris and Lola, though Wendy always complained about her mother. "Lola was crazy fun," he said. "She was a bundle of energy, a whirling dervish, you didn't know what was going to come your way when she started spinning. You would never think this tiny little lady would have so much energy. I'm not talking about the emotional stuff."

Wendy always said, "Oh, my poor father, how does he cope with living with my mom?" But Cassillo thought they were a great couple. "You got the sense that Morris loved Lola very much," he said. "He and Lola definitely made us assistants feel part of something."

Wendy wanted young people in her life and remained close to her nieces and nephews. In 1998, through the Theatre Development Fund,* she began to participate in a project designed to encourage love of theater in youngsters who otherwise wouldn't have access to it. Together with Roy Harris—stage manager for her last three plays, beginning with *Heidi*—Wendy took eight public-high-school students to plays over the course of a year. After the performances, over pizza, she and Harrris dissected the shows with the students, who kept journals, for which they received high-school credit.

The final play they went to that first year was *An American Daughter.* Wendy listened as the kids complained: too many characters, too many subplots, too hard to follow the story.

"Boy, have I trained you well," she said.

The program came to be known as Open Doors. Wendy encouraged her friends to become mentors. The list would include André Bishop, William Finn, Stephen Graham, James Lapine, Alex Witchel, Frank Rich.

"I am certain that I became a playwright because every Saturday my parents picked me up from the June Taylor School of Dance and brought

---

* This not-for-profit organization is aimed at making theater accessible to people who can't afford it, TDF is in charge of the city's half-price TKTS booths as well as programs to develop new audiences.

me to a Broadway matinee," she wrote in the *New York Times*, in an article about the Open Doors program. "Sadly, a New York adolescent's life as a regular theatergoer is becoming the exception to the rule."

She hoped Open Doors might change that, at least a little. Over the next dozen years, 1,220 students would spend a year going to shows with the thirty-five theater professionals who'd signed up to be mentors. It was a gift for the mentors, too. Lapine called his participation in the program "one of the great joys of my life."

Wendy had begun to reconcile herself to life without a child. "For eight years I had believed that the greatest regret of my life would be that I was childless," she wrote. "I realized now that I was finally willing to give that up."

But in early 1998, while she was having dinner with her agent, she learned a piece of news that many believed caused her to reconsider.

Arlene Donovan of ICM had heard from a fellow agent that André Bishop and Peter Manning were about to adopt a child. She mentioned it to Wendy, assuming she knew; everyone was aware of how close she and André were to each other.

"When she heard he was going to adopt that child, she paled," said Donovan. "I thought she would collapse."

Once again the person Wendy felt closest to had betrayed her. Why hadn't André told her? He knew—from experience, not telling her about Peter—that she would be furious.

Peter Manning wanted children. Unlike André, with his unhappy childhood memories, Peter remembered his suburban upbringing as a happy one. His father was a lawyer and his mother a teacher; he had four siblings. In his mind, families included children. When he and André had been together a year or two, Peter brought up the subject. The moment was so intense that he remembered exactly where the conversation took place— they were standing by the Northern Dispensary, once a clinic for the poor (Edgar Allan Poe was treated there) on Waverly Place in the Village.

Peter asked, "Do you want children?"

André didn't hesitate. "No," he said.

Then he added, "Wendy wanted to have children, and I said, 'No, it's too crazy.'"

Peter heard the finality in André's voice. "Well, I love this guy," he thought. "I'll just be a terrific uncle."

But he couldn't help himself. He raised the question again—and again.

"It took Peter Manning about three years to persuade me, at least, to come around to it," said André.

His resistance had been fortified by his fear of telling Wendy. He'd set up housekeeping with Peter, and loved him, but André and Wendy remained enmeshed with each other. On opening night of *An American Daughter,* he wrote her two notes, representing their public and private bonds, one from him and Bernie Gersten on behalf of Lincoln Center and one from just him.

André's note accompanied his customary gift, a bottle of perfume by Guerlain, because it was considered the best, choosing L'Heure Bleue, one of the romantic classics, the bottle's stopper designed by Baccarat in the shape of a hollowed-out heart.

Dear Wendy—

Some people smell nice; some write wonderful plays. You fit in both categories. Just as this may become your signature scent, so may An American Daughter become your signature play. Equal parts clove and carnation. Equal parts wit and emotion—skillfully, seamlessly blended into a perfect all enveloping whole.

So much for my writing skill . . .

A million thanks and love forever on opening night.

André

Unable to think of a way to tell her about the adoption, he simply waited.

"Wendy and I had a history of I didn't want to have children and I didn't want to have children," he said. "I should have just told her directly and suffered the consequences. I figured I'd tell her when I really decided to do it. I just kept putting it off."

Wendy wasn't the only one André kept in the dark. He hadn't told his mother that he was living with Peter, much less let her know she was about to become a grandmother. "Like everything else, I put it off, put it off, thinking, 'She's old, she won't live that long, she'll never know,'" said André. "I didn't want to tell her because I thought it would unhinge her. The baby part. The Peter part she must have suspected. She wasn't that naïve."

Finally James Lapine, whose own daughter was thirteen by then, told André he had to tell his mother, who was in poor health. "You have to settle your score with her," he said. "You'll never forgive yourself if you don't come clean in a way and have some sort of mutual understanding."

A month before Peter and André brought their newborn daughter home, André followed Lapine's instructions. He went to see his mother. "I told her that I was gay," he said, "that I had this loving relationship and we were adopting a girl—next month."

She *was* a little unhinged, as André thought she would be—and then she wasn't. "I wish you'd had your daughter ten years earlier," Felice "Fay" Harriman Francis told her fifty-year-old son.

In 1998 Wendy began working on the libretto for an opera trilogy called *Central Park,* jointly commissioned by Glimmerglass Opera, New York City Opera, and Thirteen/WNET's *Great Performances* series. Three composers and three playwrights (Terrence McNally, A. R. Gurney, and Wendy) were to provide visions of the park's meaning. When Deborah Drattell, the new composer-in-residence for the New York City Opera, heard who the playwrights were, she asked to be paired with Wendy. She had guessed, correctly, that they would like each other.

Wendy confessed to Drattell that she didn't know anything about opera, couldn't distinguish a mezzo from a soprano. The playwright offered two ideas for her part of the trilogy. One of them recalled the night in 1969 when crowds had gathered before giant screens in the park to watch Neil Armstrong step on the moon. Drattell chose the other scenario, called "Festival of Regrets," Wendy's interpretation of a Jewish ritual called *tashlich.*

The *tashlich* ceremony takes place on the first or second day of Rosh Hashanah, the beginning of the Jewish calendar year. Rosh Hashanah begins a ten-day period of repentance, known as the High Holidays or Days of Awe, which culminate on Yom Kippur, a day of fasting and atonement for sins committed the previous year. *Tashlich* is a visual representation of the casting away of sins; Jews take bread to a body of water and toss in crumbs that symbolize the misdeeds and evil thoughts being thrown away.

Wendy had been struck by the ritual's symbolic meaning one day when she was walking through Central Park during the High Holidays. She saw a group gathered at the Boat Pond by Belvedere Fountain on Seventy-second Street, not far from where she first made out with James Kaplan decades earlier. "As I watched each crumb land and be carried by the faint current," she wrote, "I thought of the generations who had come to the park to release their years of regrets."

She had written about *tashlich* before. In *An American Daughter,* a middle-aged woman who has been trying unsuccessfully to have a child watches a group of men praying by the banks of the Potomac. The woman describes watching the men tossing "their breadcrumbs of secret sorrow" into the river with her "familiar distance and disdain." Then she finds herself shredding a muffin she'd been eating, and joining the ceremony. "I wanted this God, this Yaveh, to know me," she says.

Festival of Regrets became Wendy's piece of the Central Park trilogy. The world premiere took place on July 25, 1999, at the Glimmerglass Opera, a lovely summer musical festival held in a theater situated on a former farm in central New York, eight miles from Cooperstown, about a four-hour drive northwest of New York City. Rhoda Brooks accompanied her much of the time and remembered Glimmerglass as a pleasurable experience for Wendy.

Alex Ross, music reviewer for the *New Yorker,* enjoyed the piece and described Wendy's contribution as "a lot of decent Woody Allenish jokes about plastic surgery, Starbucks, the Dalton School, and so on."

Ross liked Drattell's plaintive score and appreciated the piece's "witty, brittle look at mostly Jewish New Yorkers." The characters include a divorced couple, who independently end up at the Bethesda Fountain during the High Holidays. As the play ends, it appears the couple might reconcile—or not. "That uncertainty gives the comedy a hazy, melancholy tinge," wrote Ross.

Wendy made the trip to Cooperstown at least twice, during rehearsals and during the opera's four-week run, which ended August 21, 1999. Terrence McNally drove her back to Manhattan on a day that was boiling hot and sunny. His car was air-conditioned, but it was a long trip and the heat seeped in. Wendy seemed miserable. She had gained back all the weight she'd lost and then some.

"She had on a lot of voluminous clothes," said Terrence. "I kept thinking, 'Aren't you hot? It's summer.' She was all in black. I thought she was embarrassed by her weight. It never occurred to me that she might be pregnant."

Three weeks later, on Sunday, September 12, Terrence was scheduled to go to a party in Brooklyn, where Deborah Drattell lived with her husband and four young children. Drattell had invited everyone who worked on *Central Park* to celebrate the opera's success.

Not long before he left for Brooklyn, Terrence received a call from Wendy, who was supposed to be at the party.

She sounded exhausted. He couldn't quite grasp what she was saying.

"I don't want you to read it in the paper," she said. "I had a baby, premature, it's pretty tense, no visitors."

He was still stunned when he arrived at Drattell's home.

"I assumed Wendy called you to say she had a baby this morning," was his greeting to them.

"Deborah fainted," he said. "I never saw anyone faint in real life. That's my memory."

Drattell's memory differed.

"I did not faint," she said, but added, "Maybe I looked like I was about to!"

As she recalled, there was a story in the *New York Post* that day, on Page Six, the gossip column, saying Wendy was in the hospital, pregnant.

Terrence McNally walked in and said, "I was reading the *New York Post,* and there's a story about Wendy in the hospital, but she called and said she just had the baby!"

"I almost fainted," Drattell remembered *him* saying.

Regardless of who did or didn't faint that evening, one thing was certain: Wendy finally had her baby.

WENDY, ALREADY SHOWING SIGNS OF ILLNESS,
BRINGING LUCY JANE HOME FROM THE HOSPITAL.

Twenty

THE BIRTH OF LUCY JANE

1999

"Years rolled on again, and Wendy had a daughter," wrote J. M. Barrie, toward the end of *Peter Pan*. "This ought not to be written in ink but in a golden splash. She was called Jane, and always had an odd inquiring look, as if from the moment she arrived on the mainland she wanted to ask questions. When she was old enough to ask them, they were mostly about Peter Pan."

Lucy Jane Wasserstein's arrival seemed no less a fairy tale, albeit a very modern one. Her mother was indisputably an unusual woman, so it was fitting that the birth of her daughter was out of the ordinary.

Wendy had kept her pregnancy a mystery and was even more secretive about who Lucy Jane's father might be. There were people who knew about the pregnancy before Wendy went to the hospital, among them: Rhoda Brooks, Bruce and Claude, André, William Ivey Long, and Wendy's assistants. They understood that certain boundaries were not to be crossed. "If you knew [she was pregnant] and you told, that was the end," said Cindy Tolan, one of her assistants. "You could kiss your relationship with Wendy good-bye."

Wendy had her own definition of privacy. She treated her life as source material and—a cynic might say—as a marketing tool, a way of keeping her audience hooked as they waited for the next installment of the Wendy

Chronicles. She had learned the power of secrets from Lola and had become a master at controlling information, publicly and privately. She used self-exposure to draw people in and the illusion of secrecy to leverage relationships, to create a false sense of complicity, as she had with Terrence: demanding a vow of silence on his end but then sharing their "secret" with others.

These tactics help explain why Wendy felt compelled to make public her account of Lucy Jane's arrival, which was published in the *New Yorker* five months after the baby's birth. The aptly titled "Complications" is one of the playwright's most memorable pieces of writing—both for the intimate story it tells and for crucial details it conceals.

The *New Yorker* was the ideal venue for Wendy. With its sterling reputation and vaunted fact-checking system, the magazine was regarded as the periodical world's bastion of authenticity. The *New Yorker* had already played an important role in Wendy's ongoing self-portrait. Four years earlier, when it had become evident that Sandra's years might soon be measured in months, Wendy wrote an affectionate article about her sister in the magazine.

Published on February 26, 1996, "Don't Tell Mother" is filled with amusing childhood stories and admiring anecdotes detailing Sandra's youthful exploits in London and her subsequent climb up the corporate ladder. Her illness isn't mentioned, giving an ironic subtext to the story's cheerful tagline: "The stories my big sister would really rather I didn't repeat."

Sandra's health was likewise omitted when Wendy herself became the subject of a *New Yorker* profile the following year, April 14, 1997, eight months before Sandra died. (Abner, too, was left out; Wendy is described as "the youngest of four children.")

Now Wendy was determined to write the definitive, unassailable version of Lucy Jane's birth, in the *New Yorker*. She constructed the story to convey authenticity, providing heart-wrenching and harrowing particulars that signified utmost revelation. But she omitted as many vital facts as she included, because she was also creating a legend.

The article begins with Wendy waking up at 5:00 A.M. on August 27, 1999, to write a eulogy for Fay Francis, André Bishop's mother, dead at eighty-two. Wendy spoke at the memorial service at St. James Church. As she faced the crowd, she'd felt a tingling in her hand. "Looking out over the pews of the church," she wrote, "I recognized theatre colleagues whom I had known for a quarter of a century. Over the years, we had all become part of one another's family. Of course, as with most families, the majority of mine who had gathered at St. James that morning didn't have the slightest idea what was going on in my life. On August 27, 1999, I was forty-eight years old and six months pregnant."

Then a classic Wasserstein reversal: from dramatic revelation to wry punch line in an instant.

"It's not like I got knocked up," she wrote. "Most forty-eight-year-old women don't."

She wrote about Sandra's death—how she, Wendy, grieved and then reconciled herself to a life of childlessness, just as she became pregnant, when a last-ditch effort at in vitro fertilization took hold. Her due date was Christmas. At the end of August, she'd planned to take a trip to London but ended up going straight to Mount Sinai Hospital from Fay Francis's funeral.

Wendy was hospitalized immediately and confined to bed rest; she was at risk for preeclampsia, a dangerous condition that could lead to liver and kidney failure. Pregnancy had not diminished her power of recall: Participants confirmed that the *New Yorker* piece contained conversations they'd had with Wendy almost verbatim.

Though she distracted herself by telling jokes, she understood the gravity of her situation. "Preeclampsia, I came to learn, is better known by the name toxemia," she wrote. "It is most often diagnosed by protein in the patient's urine, swelling of extremities, and hypertension. In a pregnant woman, the condition can lead to a seizure, and possibly a coma."

Wendy wrote about calling Jane Rosenthal and telling her what was going on. Rosenthal, an experienced movie producer, knew how to get things done. She put in a call to William Ivey Long, who was in the middle of a dress rehearsal for *Contact,* about to become a hit musical. Rosenthal instructed him to "get up to Mount Sinai" and redecorate Wendy's room. She might be in the hospital for a prolonged spell.

He obeyed. "At nine in the morning, William arrived with an armful of coordinated blue floral curtains, pillows and Monet posters," Wendy wrote. "The room, formerly a beige netherworld, became the decorator showroom of the second floor."

She described William as "my fertility confidant." His more complicated relationship with her went unrecognized.

She called the Princeton theater department to say she wouldn't be able to teach her scheduled playwriting course that fall.

Gerry Gutierrez showed up. "Your ex-husband is here," a nurse informed Wendy.

At first, Wendy wrote, "I had no idea whom she could be talking about."

The complications mounted.

A week before entering the hospital, Wendy had told Lola about the pregnancy, thinking she was far enough along to bring her mother into the loop.

But now, with the changed circumstances, Wendy was loath to reveal her whereabouts. She maintained an attitude toward her mother that was both defensive and protective.

"The last time my mother, Lola Wasserstein, had been in a hospital, she had watched her oldest daughter die of cancer," she wrote. Wendy left a message on her mother's machine, pretending that she had taken the planned trip to London, to visit Flora Fraser, a friend there.

"Hello, Mother, I'm still in England with Flora," she said. "I'm having a wonderful time."

Twelve days into her stay, there was bad news. Her blood platelets had dropped, and Wendy learned that Bruce and Claude had booked the delivery room across the hall from her for the following week. Their second child was due.

Four days later, at 12:45 P.M., on September 12, 1999, Wendy was wheeled into the operating room with her two obstetricians, two nurses, an anesthesiologist—all women, she observed—and Gutierrez. Less than two hours later, she had a baby via cesarean section, weighing 790 grams, or one pound twelve ounces.

Bruce showed up at the hospital and asked to see the baby. When asked for ID, he said, "I'm Bruce Wasserstein. I'm the baby's father."

The nurse said someone else had said he was the father, referring to Gerry Gutierrez.

"Yes," said Bruce. "That's right. Well, he's the father and I'm the father."

The drama became even more convoluted. On September 19, 1999, seven days later, Bruce and Claude's second son—Dash Philippe Wasserstein—was born, in the same hospital, just before the first birthday of his brother, Jack Dumas Wasserstein. Bruce was the designated "father" of two newborns, with two separate mothers.

Wendy described the events as a Molière farce.

The "Nipple Nazis" invaded to teach her how to pump breast milk.

Lola showed up, uninvited, wearing black leather pants, a multicolored sweater, and a bright knit cap. Morris sat silently by.

"We saw the baby," Lola said. "She's very little."

Wendy ate orange Jell-O and didn't reply.

"We thought you didn't want to see us, but your father had an appointment here at Gerontology," Lola said.

"Are you O.K., Dad?" Wendy asked.

"He's fine," Lola replied.

"Lola is my father's official spokesperson," Wendy commented.

Wendy softened. "Mother, I want you to go back to see the baby and tell her you're her grandma," she said, taking Lola's hand. "I want you to pass your energy on to her. I want you to teach her how to survive!"

Lola dropped Wendy's hand. "She's my grandchild! Of course she'll survive!"

"Later," Wendy wrote, "my sister Georgette told me that when our mother first saw my baby and heard the details of my delivery she cried as inconsolably as she had when Sandra died."

Wendy described visiting her doll-size daughter in the neonatal intensive-care unit, where the tiny premature babies wait to grow in Isolettes, lined up against walls decorated with a border of rabbits and teddy bears floating in hot-air balloons.

She hesitated to hold her daughter, who was so small and attached by wires to the incubator. "Lucy Jane was almost weightless," Wendy wrote. "Her tiny legs dangled like a doll's. Her diaper was the size of a cigarette pack. I opened my sweater and put her inside. Her face was the size of a small apple. She wore a tiny pink-and-blue-striped cap that made her look like Santa's tiniest elf."

Wendy explained why she'd named her Lucy. "When she waved to me from the sonogram I thought of her as Lucy in the Sky with Diamonds, saying hello," like in the Beatles song.*

Wendy was discharged from the hospital the day before Yom Kippur, the Jewish Day of Atonement, three weeks after she had entered. James Lapine and Heidi Ettinger took her home. But Lucy would be staying in the NICU (neonatal intensive care unit) for a while, most likely until December 14, Wendy's original due date.

It would be some time before Lucy Jane was out of danger. Wendy came to the hospital twice a day, bringing "ready-to-go bottles of home-pumped milk." The baby received the milk through a tiny tube that released drops into her nose.

Lucy improved more quickly than expected, and just before Thanksgiving she was ready to go home.

The *New York Times* wrote a story.

"The Newest Wasserstein Creation Comes Home," announced the headline.

The first few paragraphs capture the essence:

Say hello to Lucy Jane Wasserstein. Mother: Pulitzer-prize winning playwright, Wendy Wasserstein. Father: not yet announced. Born: Sept. 12, 1999, in Mount Sinai Hospital, New York. Weight: 790 grams, under 2 lbs. And what a production it was!

---

* Lucy Jane was a name Wendy liked. In *The Object of My Affection*, when Nina asks George, the gay best friend she loves, who was his first sexual partner, he surprises her by saying Lucy Jane, his high-school girlfriend. Wendy told both Jane Rosenthal and Mary Jane Patrone that the Jane part was for them.

The director Gerald Gutierrez ("The Heiress," "A Delicate Balance") was in the delivery room. The costume designer William Ivey Long ("Crazy for You," "Chicago," "Guys and Dolls") decorated the hospital room. Meryl Streep, Ms. Wasserstein's friend from the Yale Drama School, sneaked in to see the baby, incognito. The writer James Lapine ("Passion," "Sunday in the Park With George") and the set designer Heidi Ettinger ("Big River," "The Secret Garden") brought mother and baby home.

"If you haven't won a Tony, can you go?" Ms. Ettinger asked as she waited outside Mount Sinai's intensive care unit for Lucy Jane to come out in her car seat for the cab ride to Ms. Wasserstein's apartment on the Upper West Side.

The father would never be announced, because Wendy couldn't decide what she was going to tell Lucy Jane about how she came into being. "I don't want Lucy to necessarily know about that," she told her assistants, referring to the in-vitro fertilization process.

The complications Wendy wrote about were minor ripples compared with the tidal waves of feeling her pregnancy (and descriptions of it) stirred up among friends and family. "The article is the truth with a nice smile on it," said Cindy Tolan, her assistant. "Without the complications of relationships, people being iced out, hurt."

William Ivey Long was particularly devastated by Wendy's decisions—personal and editorial—and with good reason. His version of Lucy Jane's birth story, while overlapping with Wendy's, provides valuable clues to her strategy for controlling her life's narrative.

Their accounts agree on this: Almost a year after Sandra's death, in the fall of 1998, Wendy was having lunch at the Café des Artistes when she ran into her first fertility doctor, who told her that technology had improved since she'd first visited him eight years earlier. The following spring Wendy watched him insert an egg-and-sperm combination into her uterus with a tube she described as "the width of a pipe cleaner."

The next night she flew to Italy, where she had won a prestigious fellowship at the American Academy in Rome, with plans of writing a new play.

When she returned home, two weeks later, she discovered she was pregnant.

Shortly thereafter she called William Ivey Long, who hadn't heard from her for several months, and gave him the news.

That's where their stories diverge, with William's account being the one verified by assistants and friends.

"Wendy told me the baby wasn't mine and then hinted that it might be," William said, though he realized there had been too much discussion of his faulty sperm for the latter to be likely. Still, he did what he thought he was supposed to do.

"We go to all the sonograms," he said. "We see the baby move. I go to all those things."

When Wendy was hospitalized right after Fay Francis's funeral, she called William, who spent the night in her room, on a reclining chair. She made sure he was there for the birth—and then left him in the waiting room, allowing the director Gerry Gutierrez, one of her other "husbands," into the delivery room. William felt relegated to the role of comic relief, the gay designer whose job was to prettify and delight. He felt betrayed by someone to whom he had revealed his most serious, adult, responsible self.

Perhaps he shouldn't have been surprised. The stakes were much higher now, but Wendy's selfishness was hardly without precedent. He had only to think of their Yale days, when Wendy sabotaged his opening-night production by leaving his costumes at the dry cleaners, to be reminded that in Wendy's world Wendy always came first.

But nothing could have prepared him for this heartbreak. Once again he felt like a Lost Boy, the nickname Charles James had given him when William had studied at the master's feet, all those years ago at the Hotel Chelsea. In his mind all his awards and accomplishments evaporated. He was nobody.

The day of Lucy Jane's birth tested his resilience in a way he'd never been tested before or since. When the nurse escorted Gerry Gutierrez into the delivery room and William was left behind, he felt himself turn beet red in front of Bruce and Claude, who were there. Claude won his eternal affection when she gave his arm a sympathetic squeeze.

"It was the worst day of my life," he said. "Even worse than when my parents died."

The *New Yorker* article accentuated his feeling of humiliation. "She only talks about me decorating the room," he said. "Boy, did I feel like a total faggot after that."

In the hospital, along with Bruce, he dutifully visited Lucy Jane, cupping the tiny infant—tubes dangling out of her—in the palm of his hand. After a week Wendy told him to stop coming. "Now, William, they're very confused about all these men visiting," she told him. "I have to limit it to Bruce." William was stunned.

After that, he didn't see Lucy Jane again until she was eighteen months old. He couldn't bear it. He sent her one of his signature cards, filled with confetti, but he needed to stay away for a while.

He wasn't imagining the distance that he felt Wendy had put between them. During the years they'd tried to have a baby together, she'd expressed concern about having William become the father for the very reason she had wanted him to try. He might be *too* responsible and want *too much* control. "She wanted him to be in Lucy's life but not tell her what to do," said Angela Trento, her assistant. "She thought it would be better to keep it clean. It would be her child; no one else would have any rights."

William never fully recovered from the blow to his ego, his feeling that Wendy had discarded him because he'd failed to help her reproduce. "I don't feel defined by being gay. Michelangelo wasn't a gay artist. I have never felt I am a gay designer," he said. "But with Wendy I felt I was part of a big group of gay men, part of the people who had disappointed her. I kept thinking, 'Why didn't you go after straight men if we were going to fail you as a group?'"

Occasionally he wondered if Lucy was his child, believing there was a million-to-one chance. Then he let it go.

He had always known he wasn't aware of everything else going on in Wendy's life. As she had become more famous, she developed a spiraling circle of acquaintances. There were circles within circles, sometimes overlapping, sometimes not. The compartmentalization bothered William, who had known Wendy before she started dividing people into boxes—and who had reason to think he did have special status, personally and professionally.

He was left with his memories and receipts for medical procedures, eventually accumulating bills well into six figures for his share of the costs, which they had agreed to split. "I had probably the most intense relationship I ever had," he said, adding wryly, "In my compartmentalized way."

He felt she hadn't taken their mutual efforts as seriously as he did. "I thought we were having a life while we were having it," he said.

Rebecca Brightman, Wendy's primary obstetrician, specialized in high-risk pregnancies, in a practice she shared with two other physicians, Laurie Goldstein and Michele K. Silverstein.

A reproductive endocrinologist referred Wendy. "When he said Wendy Wasserstein, my heart skipped a beat," said Brightman, who was in her late thirties. "I had gone with my mom to see all her plays. I was such a big fan."

Brightman enjoyed the crazy intensity of her work and often thought she should be taking notes for a sitcom or a soap opera. But as Wendy's blood pressure began to escalate that summer, Brightman was more concerned than she might normally have been. It had been a terrible year. One of her partners had gotten married and left the practice a few months earlier, so three doctors were managing the caseload of four. Brightman had two young children; the older one had broken his leg that winter and was in a body cast for two months. She'd been orchestrating two nannies, phone calls home, while dealing with more patients than usual.

That summer was the nadir of her career. One patient developed inexplicable high fevers but then delivered safely. But another woman became extremely ill after a very complicated delivery and then died.

"You never forget losing a patient," said Brightman, who never lost another. "One of the things that attracted us to this profession is that patients are healthy for the most part, for the most part it's a happy field. This was really tough."

Shortly afterward Brightman took a vacation with her family. Because of Wendy's blood pressure, Brightman called into the office just to check in.

"With any patient it would have been stressful," she said. "The fact it was Wendy made it even more stressful."

Laurie Goldstein told her, "You're not going to believe this. We have another problem. Wendy's having issues with her blood pressure, and she's now in the hospital."

Brightman remembered the old saying, "Bad luck comes in threes." She was scared.

But then, to her relief, everything turned out well for Wendy and Lucy Jane—so far as producing a healthy baby.

Brightman wasn't overly concerned that during her pregnancy Wendy developed Bell's palsy, a form of paralysis that causes one side of the face to droop. For unexplained reasons, pregnant women were more prone to Bell's palsy than the rest of the population, but the condition was almost always temporary. For Wendy, however, it became a recurrent condition. Her smile was never the same.

Yet she said she'd never been so happy. "Complications" ends as Wendy and Lucy Jane return home from the hospital. They watched an episode of *I Love Lucy* on television, right after a midnight feeding.

It happened to be the episode where Lucy gives birth to little Ricky. Her husband is doing his act at the Club Tropicana and ends up rushing to the maternity ward in his voodoo costume.

When Ricky Ricardo began to sing, Wendy wrote, Lucy Jane Wasserstein started to cry.

"She had seen a lot of things in the NICU, but she wasn't accustomed to bellowing Cuban men in feathers," wrote Wendy. "I held her close—all ten pounds of her—and told her not to be frightened. Then I looked down at her double chin and her round baby cheeks. 'I love Lucy, too,' I told her. 'And we're home.'"

Part Five

WENDY'S LAST ACT

2000–06

Ken Cassillo (holding Lucy Jane) became part of
"Wendy's School for Girls."

Twenty-one

THE NEW MILLENNIUM

2000–01

In May 1999, just after Wendy became pregnant, another monumental event occurred, another crucial plot point the writer would choose to delete from the narrative of her life. She was in Rochester, New York, as part of the Rochester Arts & Lectures series; it was an honor to be asked. Rochester might have been far from the center of Wendy's universe (Manhattan), but the series had drawn significant intellectual luminaries, including Saul Bellow, Maya Angelou, and Isabel Allende.

Shortly before Wendy's appearance, Susan Herman, one of the series' producers, received a telephone call from a social worker in a local group home for people with disabilities. "Abner Wasserstein is Wendy's brother, and he wants to come to the lecture," she said.

Herman called Wendy's booking agent to ask if he knew about this brother. "Absolutely not," he said. "She has one brother, Bruce, an investment banker."

When Wendy arrived, Herman told her about the call regarding a man who said he was her brother Abner.

"Her face was blank," Herman said. "There was nothing on her face. There was no further discussion. She wasn't inviting discussion."

The lecture was sold out to an audience of eight hundred people. That evening, standing before a podium onstage, Wendy noticed a man in a wheelchair, in the aisle, about ten feet from the stage. He was around sixty years old, accompanied by an aide. He appeared to be agitated.

The speech went well. "If she was bothered at all, she didn't show it," said Herman. "She was very composed during the entire lecture, and then the Q&A was very lively and fun."

After the lecture Abner came to the reception and approached his sister, his wheelchair pushed by his companion.

They stopped in front of Wendy, who was mingling with guests, near Susan Herman. Abner handed Wendy a copy of a book to autograph and said, haltingly, "I'm your brother Abner."

Wendy didn't know what to think or how to react. For her entire life, by then almost a half century, she believed that her brother must be unable to function, the only way she could explain his isolation from the family. She had rebelled against the family's code of silence, incurring Bruce's sharp disapproval when she included Abner's name in the dedication for *Uncommon Women and Others.* Eventually she conformed and stopped mentioning her brother, having been convinced that Abner might somehow be harmed if people knew he had a famous sister and brother.

Now the brother she didn't know was directly in front of her, clearly not in a vegetative state, upending a lifetime's worth of supposition, including her feeling that she had been Abner's champion. "Why doesn't anybody come to see me?" he asked. "Why am I stuck in this home?"

The ambush came at a vulnerable time for Wendy. She had just become pregnant, a secret she was hiding from the world. Instead of feeling compassion for her long-lost brother, she was frightened by his hostility. The thought of confronting Lola about the reality of Abner sent her into a tailspin. She just wanted to get away.

But none of that was obvious to onlookers that evening. "She shook his hand and was very kind to him," Herman said. "It was just a brief meeting."

Wendy was still shaken when she returned home and told Rhoda Brooks about the encounter. "She felt exposed and didn't know how to handle it, she didn't know what to do," said Rhoda, who had become one of Wendy's closest confidantes. "He was very angry and directed it all at her."

Abner tried to become closer, but Wendy distanced herself. She begged Rhoda to respond to his e-mails. "I pretended I was her secretary, and I wrote to him that Wendy was traveling a lot and was terribly sorry she couldn't stay in touch as frequently as she'd like," Rhoda said. "I told him I've known Wendy for years and had heard all about him. He never responded."

Now Wendy had become complicit in the family's decision to keep Abner at arm's length, but she felt she had no choice. Did she and Lola talk about the pain of separation? Was Wendy able to forgive Lola for banishing her son, now that she had experienced him firsthand? Or did Abner's fury seem a reasonable response to a sister who had felt Lola's rejection in other ways? Perhaps she decided to save the analysis for later, when she wrote the memoir she kept promising her editors at Knopf.

Bruce was not interested in discussing the matter of their missing brother. He paid for a private plane to take his parents to visit Abner, but his attention was consumed by other matters.

In September 2000 Dresdner Bank agreed to buy Wasserstein, Perella & Company for $1.56 billion—$1.37 billion in stock and an additional $190 million set aside to retain Wasserstein, Perella's top executives. Nearly half the proceeds of the sale went to Bruce.

Wendy also didn't have the time or emotional capacity for Abner. Her health hadn't rebounded from pregnancy; her once-limitless energy drained quickly, and she often felt weak and unbalanced. Despite this unfamiliar feeling of exhaustion, and the demands of an infant, she resumed work on a play she'd begun before Lucy Jane was born, returning to a subject she had tried to write about before: her brother Bruce. Her vehicle this time was *Old Money*, a commentary on the connection between the wealthy industrialists who helped create New York society in the 1890s and the mergers-and-acquisitions tycoons of the 1990s who were their descendants. Now older and far more experienced than she'd been when she wrote *Miami*, fifteen years earlier, she was no longer intent on capturing the nostalgia of her childhood but was trying to understand the excesses of the world her brother occupied—a stratosphere she claimed to disdain but couldn't resist.

The main character is a seventeen-year-old boy named Ovid Walpole Bernstein, who appears to be based on Bruce's older son (Wendy dedicated the published version of the play to her nephew, Ben Churchill Wasserstein). The play opens on the occasion of the annual summer party thrown by Ovid's father. It takes place in their Manhattan mansion, which was built almost a century earlier by a robber baron who'd made his money in coal mining.

Wendy had written most of the play at the American Academy in Rome, while she was pregnant, and then set it aside to give birth to Lucy Jane. Just as Sandra had barely skipped a beat at work when she delivered her babies, Wendy was determined not to let motherhood interfere with her writing. In the fall of 1999, while Lucy Jane was still in the hospital, Wendy gave the play to André. He wasn't sure if its complex structure could work; the drama moves back and forth in time, with the same actors playing the contemporary characters and their Victorian counterparts. But then he and Wendy talked about how it might be staged. She told him how, after Sandra died, she'd spent a great deal of time at her beloved New York City Ballet, where Sandra had first taken her as a child. After watching a performance of *Vienna Waltzes,* Wendy believed she saw a way to structure the play, as a dance, melding past and present.

André was willing to be convinced. He began to see the potential for something haunting and evocative and sent the play to Dan Sullivan, who was directing a show in San Diego.

Sullivan politely demurred. He recognized undercurrents of bitterness in the play that weren't explained by the dramatic action. "I was just a little worried," he said. "I think the entire play was an act of revenge. I think it was. When I read the play, I sort of recognized that. I wasn't sure if that kind of anger is a reason to do a play."

Undeterred, André proceeded with a New York production. The idea for *Old Money* had occurred to Wendy a few years earlier. She was at a dinner party she thought had "all the trappings of a new gilded age."

She described the table setting:

"There were a bowl of three dozen roses bunched so closely in a ponytail that each petal skimmed another; amusing jelly beans in silver thimbles; and pomegranates worthy of a Dutch still life masterfully dotting the tablecloth, as if after the meal we could all play croquet."

One of the dinner guests was Harvey Weinstein, the corpulent cofounder of Miramax Films, known as a brilliant producer and a pottymouthed bully. The subject of female playwrights came up. Weinstein mentioned a handful of those he admired, a list that didn't include Wendy, who was sitting right there.

Weinstein had become a symbol of Wendy's ongoing irritation with Hollywood. She'd had some success there: *The Heidi Chronicles* became a television movie, starring Jamie Lee Curtis, and so did *An American Daughter*, with Christine Lahti. There was *The Object of My Affection*. She earned nice money writing scripts that were never produced. But like many playwrights before her, Wendy found more frustration than satisfaction in her foray into television and movies. The money was good, but every dollar earned took a cut of one's self-worth.

Though she'd traveled to Los Angeles many times over the years, she never felt at home there. Revenge did indeed seem to be her initial inspiration for *Old Money*. Her Harvey Weinstein character is a vulgar Hollywood producer named Sid Nercessian, summed up by the way he describes the horrors of vacationing in Nantucket:

"There's no fucking food!" he says. "Every meal is corn and lobster buried in sand! Why do they do that? These people are not fucking whalers. They're Jews!"

Despite his complaints he has just bought two adjoining properties, on which he plans to build a thirty-six-room summer home, in violation of the island's more modest architectural integrity.

The Wendy character in *Old Money* is Saulina Webb, Ovid's aunt, a fifty-four-year-old noted sculptor, who is feeling that her time may be past, depressed because a recent piece in the *New Yorker* called her type of feminist art "dated and retro." In a nod to her old foe Robert Brustein, Wendy makes the author of the fictional article the dean of the Yale School of Art.

She uses the profane Weinstein-like producer to express her dismay over the crassness of Bruce's money world. But toward the Bruce stand-in—Ovid's father, Jeffrey Bernstein—her scolding is gentler, more disappointed than disgusted.

"Your father is a master at playing the world to his advantage," Saulina, the feminist sculptor, tells her nephew Ovid, and then she invokes his father's lost idealism.

"When your dad and I were in college, this house would have been the last place he'd imagine himself living in," she says. "It was his idea for us to teach together in that Head Start program. In those days your dad would have ripped this party to shreds."

Saulina expresses Wendy's disapproval, yet the playwright herself was a frequent guest at parties exactly like that. Mark Brokaw, the play's director, accompanied her to one of them, on a research trip to Cranberry Dune, where Bruce and Claude were throwing their annual summer party. When they arrived at the Hamptons estate, Brokaw was struck by the magnificent vista—the green lawn sloping downward, dune disappearing into the ocean, tables loaded with luscious delicacies, children dotting the painterly landscape as though placed by an artist's hand. Brokaw—a graduate of the Yale Drama School—had long ago left the farm where he grew up outside Aledo, Illinois, but he felt like a gangly rube who had wandered onto the set of *The Great Gatsby*.

Wendy led him inside to a wing of the house with an all-glass front, offering a window onto the scene. They sank into large, comfortable chairs and put their feet up on ottomans. Wendy began pointing out who was who, some recognizable to Brokaw—like Caroline Kennedy—most not.

In both *Old Money* and the novel she soon began working on, *Elements of Style,* the Wendy character is an idealist trying to survive in a world populated by people obsessed by money and status. Saulina is an artist; Frankie Weissman, the protagonist in *Elements of Style,* is a pediatrician, who divides her practice between the very rich and the very poor. Yet in real life, though Wendy maintained long-standing friendships, she gravitated toward the world of privilege. Lucy Jane was less than a year old when Wendy began worrying about whether she would get into Brearley or not. Even now she was haunted by the old specter of superior-inferior.

Mark Brokaw felt *Old Money* had a larger meaning for Wendy.

"She was writing a play about children," he said. "Not about having a child, but what do you pass on? What do you struggle to leave behind? What is important? She was looking at two different centuries, and what power was, moving from money and class to the culture of celebrity."

Perhaps because she didn't know exactly where she stood on these questions, *Old Money* is diffuse. Both Wendy and Brokaw recognized the problems that had to be overcome in a densely populated drama, with many shifts in time and point of view. Where was the center of the drama? They never solved these critical issues, which ended up swamping the enterprise.

Ben Brantley, the *Times* critic who had become Wendy's latest nemesis, zeroed in on the playwright's vulnerable spot. "Few things betray social insecurity as pointedly as name-dropping," he wrote after the play opened on December 7, 2000. "Certainly, it is common conversational currency among the real-life breeds of lions and climbers who inspired this latest effort from the Pulitzer Prize-winning author of 'The Heidi Chronicles.'"

He continued: "Letting the shorthand of others' celebrity do their talking for them, such souls inevitably come across as just a little desperate," the critic wrote. "So, unfortunately, does Ms. Wasserstein's play."

After deriding *Old Money* for its "slapdash" quality and sketchy characterizations, the critic praised one moment, when the female artist confesses how much she despises the Hollywood producer, even as she wants to be included on his list "of all-American greats."

Brantley finds this push-pull a redeeming moment of truth. "Yet what about the artists who find themselves drawn, despite themselves, to this shiny, hard core of people to whom they don't really belong?" he asks. "This would seem to be the territory Ms. Wasserstein is feeling out in the character of Saulina. The dizzying spirit of conflict therein has a fascination that for just a moment gives 'Old Money' an awakening sting."

Brantley identified an ongoing conflict for Wendy. She had learned all those name brands she dropped by shopping for them; despite her messy presentation, she liked designer clothes and to eat in expensive restaurants. She knew that Frédéric Fekkai was an exclusive hair salon because she'd had her hair done there. She had written essays on getting the perfect manicure.

Her household had grown, and so had her expenses. In addition to her and Lucy, and the costs associated with her fine address on Central Park West, she supported a nanny, weekend baby-sitters, and two assistants—occasionally more when she had special projects. She rented a studio apartment that didn't have a telephone, a place to write without distraction.

When she bought the apartment at 75 Central Park West, she listed her base annual income as $125,258. Certainly that amount had increased substantially by the time Lucy was born; she was earning as much as $100,000 a year just from speaking engagements. But she felt compelled to drum up more work from Hollywood, where writers could score big paychecks writing scripts that would end up on shelves.

In 2000 she made a deal to write a pilot script based on *The Sisters Rosensweig* for $60,000. She signed a deal to do two rewrites on a movie script for $450,000, also in 2000, and made deals totaling $250,000 in 2001. Every six weeks or so, she was off to a speaking engagement; her fee increased to $15,000 a gig.

But no matter how much she earned, and knowing that her share of the sizable Wasserstein Brothers fortune lay in reserve, she felt financial pressure, much of it self-induced.

"Ultimately she worried about money all the time," said Angela Trento, who managed her books. "She had enough money, she lived a good life, but nothing like her brother."

Their closeness rose and ebbed, but the sibling rivalry remained a constant. In 1998, as Wendy was feeling stung by the rejection of *An American Daughter,* Bruce was enjoying the success of his bestselling book called *Big Deal: The Battle for the Control of America's Leading Corporations,* which was reissued in 2000.

They were wary of each other's worlds, but intrigued. Bruce's peculiar bluntness could be offensive. Terrence McNally never forgot the way he expressed his brotherly support for Wendy the year *The Sisters Rosensweig* lost the Tony. The prize for Best Play went to Tony Kushner for *Angels in America: A Gay Fantasia on National Themes,* while the Best Musical award was given to *Kiss of the Spider Woman*, whose main character is a gay window dresser (Terrence collaborated on the script).

Terrence heard Bruce go up to Wendy and say, "What have they got against normal people?"

That "normal" galled Terrence, but he didn't expect Wendy to confront Bruce. She might talk angrily about her brother behind his back, but she would never fight with him. Terrence believed that no one stood up to Bruce. His wealth was intimidating, his manner perplexing. "I just found him inscrutable," said Terrence.

Still, for Wendy, the importance of family connection was even stronger, now that Lucy Jane was in the picture. Wendy wanted her daughter to be part of the Wasserstein clan, even as she was configuring a new kind of nuclear family. Motherhood was not the panacea she had anticipated, as she discovered the consuming reality of having a child. Like every mother, Wendy had to develop a different way of being, at an age where she was accustomed to charting her own course. "I had my child so late because my focus and energy was on those plays," she told an interviewer. "I couldn't do both. I would not have been able to do it until this age, and I don't even know if I can now."

Lucy Jane didn't have a father, but she was surrounded by loving adults—nannies, Wendy's assistants, family and friends, including a large contingent of people who each believed he or she was—each one—her only godfather or godmother. For her first birthday, she received many carefully chosen gifts accompanied by thoughtful notes, like the one that came with a beanbag Shakespeare doll:

Dear Goddaughter, This silly little beanbag doll represents the greatest playwright who ever lived. Your mother and I follow humbly in his footsteps. Some people would even say he was one of the greatest people who ever lived. I am one of them. I'm not sure about your mom. But Shakespeare sets an example of truth, simplicity and contributing to the general well being of our planet that we can all aspire to. Anyway, that is my wish for you today, Lucy Jane. Your loving godfather Terrence.

"My life has changed completely," Wendy told an interviewer shortly after Lucy was one year old. "I'm someone who really couldn't wait to be on an airplane."

Wendy implied that motherhood had anchored her, that she would no longer be the peripatetic traveler. But even as she gave the interview, she was preparing for the launch on May 1, 2001, of *Shiksa Goddess*, a collection of the essays she'd written over the past decade, culminating in the *New Yorker* article about the birth of Lucy Jane.

The publicity tour was packed: She had national television appearances scheduled for *The Today Show, The Rosie O'Donnell Show, Politically Incorrect*, and *Charlie Rose*; a couple of dozen newspaper and radio interviews; plus a grueling travel schedule that included bookstore signings, readings, and local media in New York, Boston, Washington, D.C., New Jersey, Chicago, Miami, Los Angeles, Seattle, San Francisco, and Vermont.

Now, instead of traveling light and alone, as she had grown accustomed to doing, she often brought an entourage—Lucy Jane, her nanny, and sometimes an assistant. Wendy, whose energy had always seemed unflagging, was often noticeably fatigued.

David Hollander, her former lawyer, had stopped practicing law a decade earlier and was living in San Francisco. Wendy called to let him know she would be in town in June to promote *Shiksa Goddess*. Her schedule was packed—arriving from Seattle at 1:00 P.M. on Thursday, June 14, for three days of readings and interviews for print, radio, and television. But she had one free evening—Saturday, June 16, her last night in San Francisco. Did he want to have dinner?

They met at a restaurant, and Hollander saw immediately that she wouldn't be able to make it through a meal. "She was just awfully sick," he said. Though Wendy was overweight and had never been the embodiment of healthful living, Hollander was shocked at her haggard appearance.

He had a drink, and she ordered a glass of seltzer. Then he said, "Let's get you back to the hotel, you're exhausted."

When they arrived, he went up to her room to say hello to Wendy's daughter. "It was the whole traveling show of Lucy Jane and nanny and assistant," he said. He stayed for a brief visit. As he left, he thought, "Wendy seemed very, very unwell."

Wendy had been experiencing a series of mysterious symptoms since giving birth. Not long before the book tour, she'd gone with Chris Durang to opening night of a revival of Stephen Sondheim's *Follies*. It was a rare night out for the old friends. Chris was worried as Wendy clutched his arm and complained of dizziness.

He was struck by how much older she seemed. Two years earlier the two of them had posed for a *New York Times* photographer in front of the Juilliard School. They both appeared round-cheeked, youthful, and gleeful, not that different from how they'd looked at Yale, twenty years earlier. He didn't know it at the time, but she had just become pregnant. He had moved far enough outside Wendy's orbit to learn about the pregnancy only when she was in the hospital and about to give birth. The last-minute notification came via a call from an assistant. Later Chris learned he wasn't alone in not knowing. Wendy told him she'd kept her pregnancy a secret because—at age forty-eight—she had valid reason to fear a miscarriage.

He first met Lucy Jane when she was in the hospital, ensconced in an incubator in the neonatal intensive-care unit. He was moved by the sight of this tiny baby, so small, comfortably fitting into a grown-up's hand. How could he not be touched? But Lucy's presence didn't fully register. He had missed the entire pregnancy, the time needed for a progression of emotion; he felt as though he'd missed the first two-thirds of a movie and arrived just in time for the end. He was still in a state of surprise and not sure what it all meant.

He didn't realize how dangerous it had been for Wendy until he learned the details—the ones Wendy chose to divulge—in the *New Yorker*. He was beginning to understand that "Complications," the title of the article, had been both descriptive and proscriptive. Within a few months of Lucy's arrival, Wendy told Chris she was having dizzy spells and didn't feel safe picking up the baby because she was afraid she would fall over. She reported other disturbing ailments: For a period of time, she had to wear sunglasses constantly, because her eyes were so sensitive to light. She became quite thin but then regained what had become her normal heft, around two hundred pounds.

After Wendy returned from the book tour, Chris stopped by to visit her and Lucy. He was shocked at the sight of his old friend. One side of her face had collapsed. She told him not to worry; it was Bell's palsy, a complication from the pregnancy. That word, with its ominous implications, kept cropping up: "complication."

She resolved to take care of her health after the book tour was over, in between looking for nursery schools for Lucy Jane.

In a ten-week period that fall Wendy—who turned fifty-one years old on October 18, 2001—went to seventeen medical examinations with at least eight different physicians, including an ear, nose, and throat specialist, two neurologists, and a naturopath. She endured a CAT scan, an MRI, spinal taps, blood workups, and a painful test that involved zapping her with electrical currents. Her niece Samantha Schweitzer accompanied her sometimes; on other occasions she took along Rhoda Brooks or her assistant, Angela Trento.

At various points she told friends she had Bell's palsy and that it might be related to Guillain-Barré syndrome, a debilitating disorder that results in a weakened nervous system and possible paralysis.* She said she had labyrinthitis and a retinal occlusion. She said no one was sure what she had. A "top" neurologist told her that her case was "very interesting," meaning he was stymied. Then he asked her if she could arrange house seats for him at a popular play.

The first of these appointments took place on September 10, 2001. The next day the World Trade Center was destroyed by a terrorist attack, leaving in its wake a changed metropolis. The brash hedonism of the late twentieth century gave way to a tentative atmosphere of deadly fear and panic. Wendy couldn't ignore the symbolic connection between the assault on the city she loved and the alarming forces wreaking havoc on her physical being.

---

* Joseph Heller, her mentor, was struck by this disease in 1981 and subsequently wrote about it in a memoir called *No Laughing Matter*.

As always, she steadied herself by transforming experience into art. She wouldn't be defeated by the unseen enemy—she would write about it. On September 16 her byline appeared in the *New York Times,* under the heading "The Fragile City." In a deft 1,100-word essay, she invokes a loss of innocence, capturing a pervasive sense of uncertainty even as she praises the heroism of her fellow New Yorkers.

The article opens with Wendy's memory of two planes colliding near the Brooklyn Ethical Culture School in 1960. She had been certain "evil Communists" must be bombing Brooklyn.

"Don't worry," her father told her when she got home. "Nothing like that can happen here. This is America."

She continued. "It wasn't just that this was America," she wrote. "This was New York. For my father, and for others, it was, and still is, a city of open opportunities. But I never imagined that the opportunities would include diabolical mass destruction."

Yet Wendy wasn't prepared to succumb to weakness. "It's very difficult to think of New York or New Yorkers as vulnerable," she wrote. "We are neurotic, oversensitive, aggressive, compassionate, ironic and tough, but not vulnerable. We can take care of ourselves, thank you very much."

Like most parents living in New York that day, she wondered what the future would hold for her child. She made it clear: She wanted her legacy to be one of hope.

Lucy Jane's second birthday was the day after the attacks. Wendy canceled her party, but she did take Lucy Jane to vote in the mayoral primary the morning of September 11, before the election was postponed. "She may not remember that day when she is older," Wendy wrote, "but if she does, I hope she recalls going to vote, not the horror in Lower Manhattan."

She wanted Lucy Jane to understand that she was a New Yorker and a Wasserstein; resilience was ingrained in her fiber.

WENDY WROTE MUCH OF *THIRD*, HER FINAL PLAY,
AT THE MACDOWELL COLONY.

Twenty-two

WELCOME TO MY RASH

2002–04

In late 2001 Wendy's friend Bill Finn felt compelled to intervene. Disturbed by her illness and concerned she wasn't dealing with it seriously enough, Finn referred her to his internist, Richard Meyer, who was also an oncologist, specializing in leukemia, lymphoma, and other blood disorders. Meyer found evidence of T-cell chronic lymphocytic leukemia (CLL), a rare form of the disease. However, Wendy's neurological symptoms—the recurrence of Bell's palsy, the problems with balance, the eye condition—were unusual.

Meyer sent Wendy to Kanti Rai, internationally renowned expert in CLL, chief of the department of hematology-oncology at Long Island Jewish Medical Center in Great Neck, New York. Wendy immediately liked this charming white-haired doctor, born in Jodhpur, India, married to a Jewish woman, of whom he would say mischievously, "If anything, I'm more Jewish than my wife."

After examining Wendy, Rai was stymied. In all his experience, he hadn't seen Wendy's kind of neurological abnormality connected to the T-cell CLL. However, because her condition was deteriorating and the neurologists she had seen couldn't explain why, he decided to treat the leukemia part of her problem. "In my mind it makes sense to treat what is treatable and see what happens," he told Wendy. "If the leukemia is successfully treated and in that course the neurological findings are improved, then it obviously is related. If it does not improve, we haven't lost anything, because at least we have the leukemia part treated."

He acknowledged that there was a chance things could get worse. "We are shooting in the dark," he told her.

In February 2002, Wendy began treatments with Campath, a monoclonal antibody, administered via an intravenous drip. She made the drive from Manhattan to Great Neck—which could be anywhere from thirty minutes to an hour and a half, depending on traffic—in a town car paid for by her brother Bruce. As with earlier medical appointments, she trusted Angela Trento to come along, and occasionally Rhoda Brooks.

During this period, while she was undergoing the Campath treatments, Wendy took two-and-a-half year-old Lucy Jane to see *Carnival*, starring Anne Hathaway, a young actress who had just finished her freshman year at Vassar and had already become a star, for her role in the Disney fantasy film *The Princess Diaries*. Wendy had adapted the musical for the Encores concert series at City Center.

Shortly after the play opened, on February 8, 2002, Wendy visited a neurologist, who told her she'd gotten a decent review from Ben Brantley in the *Times*.

"Really?" she responded.

"Now you say it," he told her. One of her symptoms was difficulty pronouncing the letter B. The name of the critic she had come to despise was a perfect test.

In her notes for a memoir, Wendy wrote, "It takes me a minute to prepare."

"Mmmmmm Ben," she said. "Mmmmmm Brantley."

"I can't believe his name has become a vocal exercise," she observed, appreciating the irony.

She likewise tried to find humor in the Campath treatments, a more challenging task. Named for the Cambridge University Department of Pathology, the treatments had a tony British pedigree that appealed to Wendy. But Campath involved a miserable process that could take several hours each visit. She experienced her share of the possible side effects listed on the Campath Web site: *fever, chills, nausea, rash, dyspnea, cytopenias (neutropenia, lymphopenia, thrombocytopenia, anemia), and infections (CMV viremia, CMV infection, other infections).* Also: *vomiting, abdominal pain, insomnia and anxiety.*

Chained to an IV drip in a well-lit cubicle in a modern cancer ward, Wendy escaped through writing. She brought along a spiral notebook and a soft-tipped pen; her grim predicament emerged as a bleak comedy. *Welcome to My Rash*—a one-act play with two characters—is essentially a long dialogue between a well-known writer, "Flora Berman," a leukemia patient, and her doctor, "Kipling Varajan." Wendy describes Kipling as "sixty-five, a demure Indian man, in a white coat. . . . Though serious, he has a bit of a twinkle."

Wendy told Kanti Rai that she had written a play with a character based on him, but he never saw it performed. Later, when he finally read *Welcome to My Rash*, he realized how extraordinary her powers of recall were. Many of their conversations were there on the page, only slightly fictionalized.

The character Flora Berman tells her doctor about a mysterious rash she had when she was in school; Wendy had experienced a similar outbreak when she was at the Yale Drama School. A physician she'd consulted there told her she might be allergic to her menstrual cycle; her condition was so rare that she became the subject of a dermatology conference at Yale–New Haven Hospital.

In the play Flora tells her doctor, "I broke out in question marks between my legs because I was so ambivalent about my entire gender. I single-handedly redefined feminine self-loathing."

Dr. Rai experienced an equally rare phenomenon with Wendy, one that occurred with perhaps a half dozen patients in more than forty years of medical practice. "The doctor-patient thing faded away, and trust and friendship developed," he said. After the treatments were over, Wendy took three-year-old Lucy Jane to Great Neck to have dinner with the doctor and his wife.

Usually he tried to avoid such relationships. "I have learned over the decades of my professional life to be on guard," he said. "I cannot afford to get personally involved, not because I don't like the person but because it will be injurious to my ability to remain objective."

Wendy told very few people—not including Lola—about the treatments. One day, however, she called Betsy Ross, her Madison Avenue fashion maven, to pick her up at the hospital in Great Neck. She knew that Ross was trustworthy. As style adviser to rich and prominent women, being circumspect was part of her business.

"Wendy knew I was a little in shock when I went in there," said Ross. "I never asked her questions and told her I wouldn't tell a soul, but I had been in enough chemo wards to know what it was."

Wendy was tired but insisted they have lunch at the Miracle Mile, a deluxe shopping center in Manhasset, near the hospital. It was Madison Avenue in the burbs, with Gucci, Hermès, Carolina Herrera, Cartier, and Tiffany among the vendors. "We went into a restaurant, and people recognized her, which happened everywhere we went in New York, especially in the theater district," said Ross, "but I was sort of surprised out there in some random restaurant."

Wendy was amused as people came over and told her, "You wrote that book for me! That's me! You and I are so much alike!"

Wendy whispered to Ross, after a blond, Waspy woman stopped by, "Don't you see the similarities? Oh, yes, we are so much alike."

In June 2002, three months after the treatments concluded, Wendy returned to Great Neck for a checkup. Her symptoms had improved. She flew to California a few days later, where Jill Eikenberry interviewed her onstage at the Jewish Community Center in Marin County. The Bell's palsy hadn't cleared up entirely; her face was still distorted. Eikenberry was impressed by Wendy's willingness to appear in public, acknowledging her imperfection in front of an audience. It reminded Eikenberry of how she felt about Wendy when the actress first read for the part of Kate in *Uncommon Women and Others* more than twenty years earlier.

"She was clearly looking kind of odd and yet was so able to be out in front of people and talking about it in a way that made people feel comfortable," said Eikenberry. "That's a big thing to offer to a room full of women who had thought a lot about what they're wearing today, how they look. It says it's okay, whoever you are, it's okay. It was a big deal for me, because that was never my way. I always had to put myself together and look fabulous, look like you're in control all the time."

At home Wendy had assembled a team to manage the somewhat-controlled chaos of her life. When Lucy Jane was a year old, Wendy hired Emmy Casamassino to be her nanny. Emmy was Italian-American, an energetic, grandmotherly type, though not much older than Wendy. Emmy ruled the household, having stepped into the void created by Wendy's meager domestic skills and insecurity as a mother. Wendy relied on Emmy, even as she complained to her friends that Emmy held too much sway over Lucy, who adored her. "I believe Lucy loves Emmy more," she jotted in a notebook.

But Emmy was reliable and honest and didn't drink like the proper English governess who had previously taken care of Lucy. Emmy was also able to tolerate Wendy's frenetic existence, which was more than other nannies who had come and gone before her managed to do. Wendy occasionally interviewed possible replacements without Emmy's knowledge but ultimately was too intimidated to get rid of her. She saw how Emmy loved Lucy.

Emmy was not stamped from the Hamptons/Upper Fifth Avenue/Central Park West nanny mold. She was not a British or an Irish governess, nor a hip young au pair; she was pure outer borough, Brooklyn bred, living on Staten Island, a family friend of Wendy's assistant, Angela Trento. Emmy generally subscribed to the same philosophy as Angela's Italian-American mother, who believed that children couldn't be overindulged or overprotected. She didn't rush toilet training and allowed Lucy Jane to drink from a baby bottle as long as she liked. She wasn't concerned that Lucy ate nothing but "white food," preferring her pasta plain with no sauce and refusing all vegetables. Emmy believed, from experience, that Lucy would eventually grow out of her baby ways—and she wasn't interested in opinions to the contrary.

Emmy was one warmhearted component of Lucy's out-of-the-ordinary childhood. Also unusual were Lucy's playmates, many of whom were Wendy's friends, including a large contingent of theater people. These adults were fanciful and perhaps childlike, though not children. Lucy didn't have a father, but she had a slew of godfathers and godmothers. "Wendy's life was like a fantasy," recalled Rhoda Brooks. "It was incredible. She and Lucy would go to Bergdorf's and get their hair cut, and they would give it to Lucy free *and* Wendy free."

Wendy believed that Lucy was happy. She rode the tricycle Rhoda bought her and went sledding in Central Park, usually with baby-sitters but at least once with her mother, who captured the moment for posterity in the pages of the *New York Times*. In the article Wendy gave Lucy Jane's sled the emblematic name of "Rosebud," after the sled in *Citizen Kane* that symbolizes childhood happiness.

"The morning was a clear winter blue," she wrote. "The skyline on 59th Street was twinkling brightly in the sun. Lucy Jane sat on her sled, ready to descend. I looked down over the park, and at my daughter, and said, 'Lucy Jane, this is a real New York childhood.'"

Jill Krementz, a well-known photographer, came to their apartment to help create more happy memories for Lucy Jane. Krementz photographed Lucy Jane in her nursery, wearing a leopard outfit, while Wendy and Lola—both barefoot—twirled around singing old show tunes.

Recalling the affecting scene, Krementz was struck by a memory of *Peter Pan*. "Wendy was the perfect name," she said. "I see her now, dancing around the nursery, . . . off to tell wonderful stories to all the lost boys."

Yet for Wendy, there was much heartache in being a mother. Her illness made it impossible for her to participate fully in parenting; she and Lucy were rarely alone together. Wendy almost never missed a speaking engagement or stopped working, but she was often too tired to play. "I should be with my child," she wrote one day when Lucy was outdoors with someone else. "I can't be with my child. I have aches in ankles and thighs."

James Lapine—"Tats"—became even closer to Wendy because of Lucy Jane. He knew from experience how exhausting young children could be and stepped in to help when Wendy wasn't feeling well.

"Sometimes the three of us would just cuddle on the bed and watch a movie, when Wendy really couldn't get out of bed, so we'd have a picnic on the bed," he said. When Lucy Jane was rambunctious, he'd find ways for her to release energy so she wouldn't wear Wendy down. "Sometimes I'd take her out and we'd go do things," he said, "or I would roughhouse with her, like I did with my own kid, run her around to get her to calm down."

Wendy's uncertainty about motherhood was reinforced when she was around her family. Just as Lola had competed with Aunt Florence, there was a natural tendency to compare and contrast Lucy with Bruce's younger children, who were close in age. Wendy herself questioned Emmy's method, which was simply to love Lucy without imposing restrictions. The impeccable Claude raised her two sons with rules and schedules, nothing like Wendy's Auntie Mame approach.

The young cousins were not that close. The families got together mainly for holiday meals, and the adults dutifully attended one another's social functions and celebrations. When it came time for Wendy to consider where Lucy should go to kindergarten, she was leaning toward Brearley, an all-girls school, rather than the coed school that Jack and Dash attended. Wendy explained to Emmy that Lucy was quieter than Bruce's rambunctious little boys. She might thrive better in an all-girls school. Then, grinning, Wendy offered another reason for not sending Lucy Jane to be with her cousins. "That would be too many Wassersteins in one school," she said.

A joke and not a joke. No doubt she didn't want to give her mother extra fodder for comparisons. When Lucy was in preschool, maybe three years old, Lola asked her if she could read.

"No," Lucy answered.

"Oh," Lola replied. "The boys can," referring to Dash and Jack.

Wendy seemed to shrug off Lola's barbs, but—following Sandra's example—she controlled her mother's visits. She would have one of the older grandchildren pick up Lola at her apartment across town—most frequently Scoop, Bruce's son, youngest of the older three children—and then meet them at the Café des Artistes. The restaurant's glory had faded by then, but its old-school elegance appealed to Lola and Wendy. Most important to Wendy was location: It was near her apartment building. She always made sure to arrive at the restaurant first, to keep Lola from coming upstairs.

Life at 75 Central Park West was unconventional, but Wendy did her best to make it warm and inviting. Sarah Saltzberg had been a struggling young actress waiting tables when she got a job as weekend baby-sitter for Lucy Jane.

"I would come on Friday at noon when Emmy left and stay until Monday morning," Saltzberg said. "I remember waking up Saturday morning, the first weekend I was there, and we were all in our pajamas, Wendy and Lucy and I. Wendy was making up a song for Lucy, and I was singing it, and I remember thinking, 'God, this is so surreal. Here I am, twenty-seven years old, with this award-winning playwright in pajamas making up a song to her two-year-old daughter. This is so weird. Keep it together, Sarah.'"

Soon, though, she felt at home. "Wendy had this incredible ability to put everybody at ease, to not make you feel you were in the presence of this very talented playwright," said Saltzberg. "She was warm and kooky and loving." Many Friday nights Wendy put together her own version of a Sabbath dinner for Lucy Jane and whichever of her assistants was around.

"We were this weird hodgepodge of a family," Saltzberg said. The meal, like the family, was nontraditional. Instead of chicken soup and matzo balls, the deliberately nonkosher menu consisted of pork strips and shrimp, ordered in from Shun Lee, the high-priced Chinese restaurant that was popular with Lincoln Center patrons and just a few blocks from Wendy's home.

"This is our family," Wendy told her assistants. "You can choose your family as well as having your family be your blood."

Wendy was faithful to that ethos. She didn't treat Saltzberg or the other assistants as if they were "the help" (though she complained to friends that she sometimes felt she was working for her assistants rather than vice versa). Wendy's innermost circle contained prominent stars of the universe that Saltzberg aspired to be part of. When people like André Bishop, Terrence

McNally, and James Lapine dropped by, Wendy introduced Saltzberg as an actress, though she was still mainly a waitress and sometimes a baby-sitter.

Saltzberg saw how differently other people treated their nannies when Wendy visited wealthy friends and brought Saltzberg along to take care of Lucy.

"We'd be in these perfect houses, and Wendy and her friends would eat at one table and the help would eat in another room or at another time," she said. "It was never like that with her, ever. It was never this class line."

Soon Saltzberg was initiated into Wendy's School for Girls. In May 2002 the young actress performed in an improvisational show about spelling bees that she and some friends were putting on in a theater on the Lower East Side. She invited Wendy to come see the show.

"I was watching her, the whole time thinking, 'Oh God, she hates it, she's not laughing,'" Saltzberg said. But after the show, Wendy said she'd loved it. She told Saltzberg the play needed original music and put her in touch with Bill Finn. That was the genesis of the 2005 Broadway hit musical called *The 25th Annual Putnam County Spelling Bee*, starring Sarah Saltzberg, directed by James Lapine, music and lyrics by William Finn.

During the show's Off-Off-Broadway beginnings, as it became apparent that the quirky little musical might be going somewhere, questions arose: How should credit be assigned? Which actors should continue? What kind of collaboration agreement, if any, should they sign? Each decision had financial implications.

That's when Sarah Saltzberg saw her boss transform from the fun-loving eccentric into a coolheaded businesswoman. "We were sitting in her office, and Lucy had gone to bed," she said. "The lawyer had sent something to me, and I was reading it. Wendy went through it step by step and literally helped me write the letter: 'Change this. Do that.' It took about an hour, and I got so worked up and started saying, 'I don't want this to fall apart! I really want it to happen!'"

Wendy cut through the escalating hysteria. "Look, in any room with two people in it, one person has to be more neurotic than the other, and that person always has to be me," she told Saltzberg, her voice deep. "Right now it's you. You have to calm down."

With that, she left the room. A few minutes later, she returned, holding a Prada handbag, which she had recently received as a gift. "If I give this to you, will that make you feel better?" she asked.

Saltzberg didn't hesitate. "I said yes!"

The Campath treatments seemed to have done the job. Wendy regained strength, though the Bell's palsy periodically recurred, twisting her features. She took Lucy to interviews for nursery schools and visited senior centers for Morris. After spending much of his life in silence, he had begun singing all the time. He usurped Lola's place as family artist. "My father likes the crafts, so does Lucy," Wendy wrote. "They both bring home their artwork."

One day she caught a glimpse of herself in the mirror and noticed, sadly, "I can't smile."

On May 2, 2003, Wendy sent the outline for a novel to Victoria Wilson, her editor at Knopf. On June 17, 2003, with the endorsement of Sonny Mehta, Knopf publisher and Wendy's friend, the playwright received an advance of half a million dollars for *Elements of Style*. Wendy had been telling her friends she wanted to write a roman à clef sending up the world of nouveau riche New York, the world she inhabited and obsessed about yet insisted wasn't hers. But the accompanying handwritten note indicated she had something more serious, more personal in mind:

> *Dear Vicky—*
>
> *Here are the two outlines I mentioned to you in December. One is for a novel, <u>Elements of Style</u>, and the other for a memoir, <u>Two</u>.*
>
> *My father is declining rapidly and my entire family has gathered for the curtain call. The one thing that has kept me sane is the thought that I will write about my dad and all of them.*

Wendy's thinking had changed in the two years since she told an interviewer about a childhood memoir she'd owed her publisher for almost a decade. "I find myself unable to touch it," she said. "Mostly because I don't even know if I could reach that kind of depth."

With the birth of her child and her father's deteriorating health, Wendy wanted to assemble the pieces of her fractured family portrait. She returned to Rochester to see Abner, accompanying Morris and Lola, in a private jet arranged by Bruce. That trip would be Morris's last visit with his stepson. Wendy watched in horror as her father urinated on the tarmac, realizing how disoriented he had become.

She didn't discuss those visits but wrote about Morris via fiction. In *Elements of Style,* the novel she was working on, there are tender moments between Frankie Weissman, a middle-aged pediatrician, and her elderly father, Abraham, who has dementia.

In one scene Frankie brings her father, a "news junkie" like Morris, the morning papers. "She knew there was no possibility of his actually reading them, but sometimes he still liked to hold the paper as if it was a distant memory, like playing with blocks," Wendy wrote. "In the past month, Abraham's disease had rapidly accelerated. Not only had he forgotten how to speak or when to pee, he had also forgotten how to eat. Now he stared at food as if he didn't know if it was a yo-yo or a turtle."

On June 3, 2003, the Wasserstein family gathered for another memorial service, for Morris, their gentle patriarch, in the building on West Eighteenth Street that had housed the Wasserstein ribbon company. The loss was enormous. Morris had been a steadfast presence, ballast in a family often rocked by Lola's whims and desires.

His elaborately staged memorial service, like Sandra's, became yet another vehicle for Wendy's construction of the Wasserstein legacy. She controlled every aspect of the production. When Melissa Levis, Georgette's younger daughter, asked to perform a song she'd written about her grandparents, Wendy said no. "We weren't allowed to speak," said Melissa. "Wendy put on a show. She had Mary Testa [a well-known stage actress] sing. Cy Coleman played the piano. That was nice, but who cares? Grandpa would have wanted family."

Wendy and her theater friends recounted Morris's extraordinary life, from his humble beginnings as an immigrant boy to successful businessman, doting husband, proud father, and beloved grandfather. Jeffrey Rosen, Bruce's business partner, read contributions from members of the family, including a touching thought from Scoop, Bruce's nineteen-year-old son, which summed up the overriding sentiment.

"I think he was the best man I ever had the pleasure to know," Rosen read on Scoop's behalf. "I guess what I'll take from him is an understanding of what really matters in life. As long as he was with his family, he was a happy man."

Wendy had already paid her respects publicly, in the May 23 *New York Times* article about Central Park where she'd discussed sledding with Lucy Jane.

"Having spent almost half a century in the Park, more than anything now, I am reminded of the people with whom I have walked there," she wrote. "I would sometimes accompany my father, Morris Wasserstein, as he walked every morning to work through the park. He entered on 76th Street and sauntered along the East Side path till he stopped at the George Delacorte Musical Clock at the entrance of the children's zoo. Before continuing to his ribbon factory downtown, he would stop and watch as the clock chimed a new hour, and a bear with a tambourine, a hippopotamus with violin, a goat with pan pipes, a kangaroo and offspring playing horns, and a penguin with a drum circled the base of the clock."

His nurse took him to the park the day before he went into a coma.

"She told me he smiled as he watched the children playing," Wendy wrote. "That would be his last outing. He passed away, four days later. I think of him, a real New Yorker in the park, happy with the life he made in the city he lived in."

Wendy flew to Rochester with Lola to tell Abner that Morris wouldn't be coming to see him anymore. "It was very hard for Abner to hear this man who had been an important part of his life had died," said Eleanor Newell, Abner's friend from the Joy Club. "He talked about how his dad dealt with Macy's and Gimbels, and how he knew all about fabric and yard goods. He had a lot of fond memories of his dad."

Abner talked with friends about seeing his mother and sister when his father died.

"I know the visit from Wendy and her mother was a very good one,"

Newell reported. "So it ended up they became a brother and sister, for a moment at least."

André Bishop knew that Wendy was ill and that she was busy with Lucy and the sadness surrounding Morris's decline and death. He was aware that she was working on a novel as well as on various screenplays and articles. She had even talked about giving up writing and going into politics. But for him the theater was what mattered. Despite their bruised history and their new, separate lives as parents, he never stopped considering himself Wendy's collaborator. He wanted to see her get back to writing plays, to recover from the *Old Money* fiasco.

André had been put on the defensive by critics like the *New Yorker*'s John Lahr, who'd questioned his judgment in producing *Old Money*. After praising André for his loyalty to authors, Lahr dryly commented that "with producing as with parenting, leniency is not always the best policy."

André understood the criticism but remained unapologetic for his decision. "People said, 'Ah, they just did it because André's friends with Wendy,' and it's true," he said. "You can't plan a season doing plays for writers just to get it out of their system, or your theater will go down the tubes. But you can do that for a few writers. She was by no means at the end of her talent."

Wendy had two one-act plays in development—*Welcome to My Rash* and *Psyche in Love,* a light romantic retelling of the myth of Cupid and Psyche. She had been invited by the Arena Stage in Washington, D.C., to participate in a festival of new plays in October 2002. Ari Roth, artistic director of Theater J in Washington, attended and offered a production at his theater. He encouraged Wendy to develop the plays further at another festival for new works, taking place at the Kennedy Center the summer of 2003. After that, in early 2004, Theater J would present them in a workshop production.

André hoped one of those one-acts could become a full-length play he could produce. In March 2003 he arranged a reading at Lincoln Center for Dan Sullivan, followed by another reading of *Pamela's First Musical,* a stage adaptation of her children's book that Wendy was working on with Cy Coleman. Dan Sullivan dismissed *Psyche* right away but thought *Welcome to My Rash* was interesting. He and André agreed to revisit the new work after the Washington workshops.

In June 2003 Wendy was a resident artist at the MacDowell Colony outside Peterborough, New Hampshire; the lovely 450-acre retreat was the oldest residency program for artists in the United States; she stayed in the studio where Thornton Wilder wrote *Our Town*. She worked on her novel and polished the one-acts but didn't get much done because she'd brought along Lucy Jane and a baby-sitter; they stayed in town while Wendy was at MacDowell. She tried to divide her time but found it hard to concentrate.

Michael Barakiva came to Peterborough as well. Barakiva, a Vassar graduate who had been Mark Brokaw's assistant during *Old Money*, had become one of Wendy's assistants. He worked with her on the libretto for *The Merry Widow*, which she adapted for a new production by the San Francisco Opera; the piece had been broadcast on PBS on Christmas Day 2002. Sometimes they would hole up together for hours in the writing studio she rented on Sixtieth Street in New York, going over edits and rewrites of whatever Wendy was writing.

"I felt I was apprenticing with a master," he said. "I was her assistant. I was her typist. I was her researcher."

He began to direct plays, and she came to see his work. One night, to celebrate a production, she took him to dinner to Lattanzi, a Theater Row restaurant known for its carciofi alla giudia, crispy fried artichokes Jewish-Italian style. He never forgot the taste of those artichokes—a treat for a struggling young director—but the evening was embedded in his memory because of the unexpected offer Wendy made that night: "I really enjoyed your work, and I'd like to work with you as a director sometime."

He thought she was being nice, but she was serious. She asked him to direct the two one-acts—*Welcome to My Rash* and *Psyche in Love*—at the Kennedy Center festival at the end of the summer.

While they were in New Hampshire, the two of them went out to dinner at the Hancock Inn, a fifteen-minute drive from MacDowell. They began talking to their waiter, a good-looking, strapping young man, who told them his story. He said he'd been a student at Wesleyan and had been accused of plagiarism three times. He was certain the accusations arose because he was a wrestler and there was an anti-jock bias. But he assured them he knew how to write a good paper; he'd gone to boarding school at Andover.

When Barakiva and Wendy left the restaurant, she told the waiter, "Next time you get accused of plagiarism, tell the professor the feminist playwright Wendy Wasserstein believes you wrote the paper."

He thanked her, but Barakiva could see that the waiter had no idea who she was. Outside, Wendy said to Barakiva, "There's a play there."

He responded, "Nah, we both just think he's attractive. I don't see it at all."

Shortly after that, Wendy began writing a one-act play she called *Third;* one character is a young man named Woodson Bull III, modeled on the waiter they'd met that night. The other is a middle-aged feminist professor, who accuses him of plagiarism.

Barakiva mentioned to Wendy a life-altering class he'd taken on *King Lear* when he was at Vassar, taught by Ann E. Imbrie, a professor about Wendy's age who had cancer. Wendy decided that the central argument between her two characters would focus on a paper the student writes about *King Lear.*

"I've never seen somebody take, like, half an idea and then make a play out of it," said Barakiva. "And now I can't imagine that play being about anything but *King Lear.* She just saw that's what it's going to be about."

When they returned home from MacDowell, they called Imbrie for thoughts on a radical feminist interpretation of *Lear.* From these discussions Wendy created an argument for her fictional professor, Laurie Jameson; shrewdly mocking academic feminism, she made Jameson the author of *Girls Will Be Boys: The Demasculinization of Tropes in Western Literature.* In the play Jameson declares that Cordelia, Lear's beloved youngest daughter, isn't the heroine of the play, but rather a victim. "What has been seen as the tragedy of Lear is actually the girlification of Cordelia," Jameson declares.

The student accused of plagiarism eventually forces Jameson to rethink her didacticism while he acknowledges she has led him to rethink the meaning of *King Lear.* Through this conceit Wendy addressed the futility of her own real-life furies.

The professor in *Third* is consumed by "free-floating anxiety." She tells her therapist, "I keep thinking about a James Taylor song I listened to when I was in college. The lyric went something like, 'Guess my feet know where they want me to go, walking down a country road.' I keep thinking about that country road, and I don't know where the hell it goes. God, I hate the times we're living in."

By August a one-act version of *Third* was ready. That fall, in preparation for the workshop at Theater J, Wendy decided to ax *Psyche in Love.* Working with Barakiva, she folded some of the play's passages into *Welcome to My Rash* and continued to develop *Third,* which was emerging as the stronger piece.

On December 15 there was another reading for Dan Sullivan at Lincoln Center of *Welcome to My Rash,* this time with *Third.* That reading clarified matters for the director. He decided that *Welcome to My Rash* didn't carry enough weight to take it further. *Third,* on the other hand, had potential but would have to be expanded. "*Third* seemed to be incomplete as an idea and too large an idea for a one-act," said Sullivan. "I suggested the idea of making it a full play."

André was heartened by Sullivan's response. He felt that Wendy, now a mature writer, was on the verge of expanding her range. "She was very involved in the world and of course her daughter's life," he said. "All of that would have renewed her. You could see her moral stature as an older person having gone through these midyears of unhappiness and anger and bitterness. Having a child, exasperating as it can be, renews you, and I feel her writing was beginning to be renewed."

But her forward momentum was given yet another massive jolt. Two weeks after the Lincoln Center reading, on December 30, 2003, Gerry Gutierrez was found dead in his apartment at age fifty-three, a decade after surviving throat cancer. Cause of death: complications from the flu. The obituary in the *Washington Post* carried biographical details Gutierrez had once listed as a joke in a theatrical Who's Who: "married Wendy J.

Wasserstein (a writer), December 3, 1983 (divorced, December, 1986); children: Ginger Joy, Phyllis Kate, Edna Elizabeth."

The "children" were Wendy's cat and Gutierrez's dogs.

At Gutierrez's memorial service the following spring, Wendy spoke about his being in the delivery room the day Lucy Jane was born. "He will always live in my heart, whenever I look at my daughter and whenever I am in a theater," she said.

The *Washington Post* obituary got it wrong, she said. "Gerry and I were never divorced. He will always be my husband."

She returned to the theme of family. "I think Gerry made me and all of us here today part of his extended family," she said. "Gerry created families in the theater."

Welcome to My Rash and *Third* were presented as a Theatre J workshop production in January 2004 and received encouraging reviews. "There is a sense of loss and a largeness of heart in these new works that show breathtaking maturity," wrote the reviewer in the *Washington Times*.

Michael Barakiva was singled out for directing "with delicacy and care." Wendy returned from Washington determined to follow Dan Sullivan's advice and expand *Third*. She had made it clear to Barakiva that if André wanted to produce the play at Lincoln Center, Dan Sullivan would replace her protégé as director.

Barakiva appreciated her directness. "I knew a twenty-seven-year old director is not going to direct Wendy Wasserstein's premiere in New York," he said. "The fact that I got to work on the plays at all—the experience and the knowledge for me—was invaluable, the defining moment of my directing career."

For most of the next year, Wendy concentrated on expanding *Third* and working on her novel, though she managed to squeeze in a book review for the *Times*, to write the introduction to the American Ballet Theatre's televised version of *A Midsummer Night's Dream,* and to testify with Stephen Sondheim and Arthur Miller before the Senate Judiciary Committee in Washington on behalf of a bill meant to give playwrights more clout in negotiating contracts with producers. She and Bruce were honored at a fund-raising dinner at the Pierre Hotel for the Bank Street College of

Education. She and Tony Kushner spoke about Jewish culture at the Jewish Community Center on the Upper West Side.

She tried to be attentive to Lucy Jane. When Lucy was four, they visited the set of *Sesame Street*, where they met the show's executive producer, Lewis Bernstein, and discovered that he was married to Wendy's old friend from yeshiva, Gaya Aranoff, now a physician. Shortly after that, they all met at a restaurant for dinner. Wendy asked Aranoff and Bernstein, who were observant Jews, if she could bring Lucy Jane to their home one Friday night for a "real" Sabbath dinner—one that wasn't ordered in from Shun Lee.

About a year later, in 2004, Wendy and Lucy visited the Aranoff-Bernsteins in Riverdale. "Wendy was funny, telling us stories," said Aranoff. "She wanted Lucy Jane to see the candles. We did kiddush, washing hands, the whole ritual with challah. I could tell that it touched her."

Despite all this activity, Wendy was growing sicker, though she refused to acknowledge it. Bill Finn confronted her one evening when they were eating out together. "Something is wrong," he told her. "We have to get you help, to take care of you." She responded by leaving the restaurant, hailing a taxi, and going home.

"Where does he get off saying this?" she asked Rhoda, their mutual friend. After that, Rhoda trod softly when talking to Wendy about medical issues. She had accompanied Wendy to doctors' appointments and listened to her friend downplay her symptoms. Wendy was an accomplished dramatist, able to convince her friends and even her doctors what she herself needed to believe: If she kept moving, she just might trick fate.

Dianne Wïest and Charles Durning starred in *Third*, Wendy's final play, which, *New York Times* critic Ben Brantley said, "exhales a gentle breath of autumn, a rueful awareness of death and of seasons past."

Twenty-three

THE FINAL PRODUCTION

2005

In January 2005 Wendy and Chris Durang agreed to be part of a
symposium on humor sponsored by the Key West Literary Seminar. The
seminar had become a popular boondoggle for writers, offering a warm
retreat in the dead of winter from colder climates and from the persistent
self-doubt and financial pressures that can overwhelm creative souls. In this
balmy, laid-back atmosphere, writers were made to feel important and comfortable. There were many opportunities to mingle with one another in a
no-compete zone, as well as to talk and perform before appreciative audiences. Key West had become more commercialized and gentrified over the
years, but this haven for gay people, literary types, and assorted dropouts
remained charming and tacky enough. Within these cozy confines, where
people typically walked or rode their bikes as a form of transportation, the
visiting writers could feel themselves to be heirs to the literary tradition of
historic locals like Ernest Hemingway and Tennessee Williams.

Chris arrived a day before Wendy, in time for the opening ceremonies
and receptions. Except for flecks of gray in his hair and a thickened middle, he still radiated a devilish sweetness, a boyish apprehension. He felt
insecure about their panel for many reasons. The lineup had changed; Terrence McNally, who had a house in Key West, was supposed to be part of
the discussion with him and Wendy, but McNally had canceled at the last

minute. Chris worried that the audience would know Wendy, from either her plays or essays or television appearances, but wouldn't know him. They were the only playwrights; this wasn't a theater crowd.

More worries: Chris had checked out talks by Billy Collins, the former poet laureate of the United States; Roy Blount Jr., the southern novelist; and Calvin Trillin, the popular *New Yorker* writer. All of them had given great performances. Chris decided he and Wendy should prepare something entertaining, so they wouldn't end up answering tedious questions like, "What's the difference between humor in theater and in books or movies?"

She was flying in late that evening with five-year-old Lucy Jane and Emmy, the nanny, so they just talked briefly, long enough to agree they shouldn't wing it. They would meet in the morning to work out the details.

Wendy was staying with Lucy Jane and Emmy at the Paradise Inn, in a snug bungalow tucked among flowering jasmine and red ginger. The next morning, while Chris waited for Wendy to get ready, he sat on a couch outside, on a screened-in porch, uncertain about what it would be like to see her. The Bell's palsy got better and worse, but it never fully disappeared.

When Wendy greeted him that morning in Key West he was relieved. Her face wasn't quite the face of Wendy the "vicious dumpling"—the smile was slightly off—but she looked good. She seemed happy as she plopped down next to him on the couch. Lucy joined them a few minutes later. The tiny baby had grown into a normal-size girl, slender and fair.

Chris didn't see Lucy that often, so she was a bit shy, sitting on the other side of Wendy. She kept peeking at Chris, and eventually they made eye contact. He waved. She waved back, and they both smiled. He was happy they'd connected and looked forward to building a real relationship with Wendy's little girl. It was a nice moment, there on the couch, and it occurred to Chris that this was the first time in years he'd seen Wendy just being relaxed. Usually she was running from thing to thing.

The entire day brought back warm memories of earlier, happier times. They left Emmy and Lucy at the bungalow and went to a nearby diner, to work on their presentation. That, too, was fun, reminding him of their earlier collaborations; the last one was in 1994, when they wrote a comedy sketch based on the Greek tragedy *Medea* for the twenty-fifth-anniversary celebration of Juilliard's drama division. While they ate eggs, Chris suggested they read from their crackpot *Medea* at the symposium.

When they went back to her bungalow so Wendy could change clothes, he noticed—with relief—that she was walking normally. They had a pleasant walk along funky, vulgar Duval Street to the San Carlos Institute, the elegant historic building where the panels took place. Only when they walked up the stairs to the stage did she need steadying. He barely noticed; she made no fuss about it.

The organizers of the literary seminar taped the sessions. Even on the recording, the connection between audience and speakers is palpable. Wendy and Chris were in top form. They read their version of *Medea*, about a scorned wife seeking to exact revenge on her philandering husband, with Wendy as Medea and Chris as everyone else. First Wendy set the stage, making the classic approachable.

"How many of you in the audience have ever acted in Greek tragedy? How many of your lives are Greek tragedy?" Her voice was deep, warm, and filled with humor.

In their slapstick version, Jason's mistress is "Dreaded Debbie, debutante from hell." Jason rebukes Medea by telling her he's keeping the children and enrolling them in the Dalton School (the Manhattan private school attended by Bruce Wasserstein's older three children). Giggling, they reached the finale, where a deus ex machina intervenes, to the tune of "Camptown Races."

As the laughter subsided, Wendy connected Medea to her own mother, Lola, about whom, she said, she was writing a play. "When Chris first met my mother, she came dressed as Patty Hearst," she said. "She had on a little beret and a little toy gun, and she said, 'Guess who I am?'" She read from an essay she'd written about her mother, and then, with a perfect comic pause, she grinned at the audience. "My mother and I go way back. . . ."

More laughter. She had worked her magic. The audience didn't seem to see a dumpy woman in her fifties with messy hair and a face that had not borne time well. They were caught up in her playfulness, her ability to turn Greek tragedy into a Jewish-mother joke, making it personal and plausible.

Chris was on another panel that evening. Afterward he went to his hotel, too tired to attend yet another champagne reception. He saw Wendy again the following morning, when she read from *Shiksa Goddess,* her collection of essays. After she was finished, he walked her outside, where a car was waiting to take her to her next appointment. She left for New York a few hours later.

Those few days in Key West were a respite from familial, social, and professional demands. Like Chris, Emmy noticed how unusually relaxed Wendy was. She strolled the quaint streets with Emmy and Lucy, all of them delighted by the chickens that ran wild everywhere. While Wendy worked at the seminar, Emmy and Lucy took an open-air bus tour of the island. Wendy brought them to see Terrence McNally's house. He wasn't there, but his housekeeper showed them around. Terrence was one of Lucy's favorite grown-up friends. Many people had wondered if he was her father, but people were always guessing who Lucy's father was, and Wendy encouraged the game.

A month later this item was reported in David Patrick Columbia's Web gossip column, "New York Social Diary":

> Feb 16, 2005. *Leaving "21," it was impossible to get a cab, so I caught a Fifth Avenue bus down to 23rd Street* where I picked up a cab who took me over to costume designer **William Ivey Long**'s newly restored and refurbished house over by Ninth Avenue in Chelsea. William was giving a book party for his close friend **Wendy Wasserstein**, the playwright who has just published a book for Oxford University Press called *Sloth.* One of the Seven Deadly Sins, if you didn't know—Oxford has published a book by different authors on each one of them. Ms. Wasserstein was assigned the subject, and, as you might imagine, she has a distinctive and get-down take on the subject. To whit [*sic*]—chapter one is called "The Sloth Plan" and begins thusly:

Everyone who holds this book in hand has at some time made a New Year's resolution to get off the couch and join a gym. People like Jack LaLanne and Arnold Schwarzenegger have made fortunes making every single reader of this book think there is something wrong with his or her horizontal instincts. Instead of eating cold pizza and beer for breakfast, we have all been led to believe we'd be better off lifting one- and two-hundred pound slabs of iron in rotation. Have you ever been to a penal colony? That's what insane criminals are forced to do.

About Long's house the gossip columnist gushed:

The top floors were recreated from scratch, including the bathrooms, although it's hard to believe because it looks and is furnished so authentically mid-Victorian you practically expect **Robert Louis Stevenson** to emerge from one of the rooms. . . . I saw Terrence McNally and Anna Sui and Betsy and Clifford Ross, Heather Watts, Caroline Kennedy and Ed Schlossberg, Paul Rudnick, Bruce and Claude Wasserstein, Susan Stroman, Frank Rich, Miko [*sic*] Kakutani, André Bishop, Jane Rosenthal and Craig Hatkoff, Sonny Mehta, Cathy and Stephen Graham, Carrie Minot, and Rafael Yglesias and dozens more just like them (William's friends are all William's fans).

It all sounds fabulous until the accompanying photographs are deconstructed. There's Wendy, standing next to Betsy Ross, her friend the fashion specialist. In the photograph Wendy's right eye is closed and her smile weirdly frozen, a frank record of the recurrence of Bell's palsy. Her sweater is askew; it might be Chanel, but brand-conscious Wendy never lost her habit of making expensive clothes look like someone else's castoffs.

Her friendship with William Ivey Long had resumed officially in 2001, when *Shiksa Goddess* was published. William threw that book party, too. Ken Cassillo remembered going to the *Shiksa Goddess* party with butterflies in his stomach, thinking, "This is going to be a toxic event." Instead it was just like old times. After all the celebrated friends left that night, Cassillo, Angela Trento, and Cindy Tolan remained with Wendy and William, drinking wine and laughing.

"It was very vivid in my mind, because after all the guests had gone, the rest of us were all flopped out casually on one of Williams's sofas/lounges, and it was one of those special and surreal events that happen only in the company of Wendy and that William could pull off with such class and style," he said. "It was truly a special evening, so I believe that whatever needed to be said was said and William and Wendy had made peace with one another."

Wendy and William revived plans to start a company that would produce everything from lingerie to plays. They had incorporated Wasserstein Ivey Long Productions, LLC in 1998—before Lucy was born—to design a line of women's evening wear and lingerie. Now they proceeded with the collection, called "Evening into Overnight." Their launch during February 2002 Fashion Week made the cover of *Women's Wear Daily;* Wendy wrote a script and lyrics for the event. That coproduction didn't bear fruit either; they hadn't worked out the details from design to manufacture.

In March, Wendy went to Dartmouth College, where she'd been chosen to be the 2005 Montgomery Fellow, part of an endowment established to bring "distinguished persons" to campus to teach, lecture, and meet with students and faculty. They came from various disciplines and had included several Nobel Prize–winners, among them the novelist Saul Bellow and Óscar Arias Sánchez, once and future president of Costa Rica.

Wendy was determined not to miss the opportunity, no matter how sick she was feeling. Dartmouth's Sanborn Library had become a favored writing refuge over the years, a throwback to her Mount Holyoke days, with its chandeliers and overstuffed armchairs, ancestral portraits hanging on wood-paneled walls, and four-o'clock teatime. At Mount Holyoke, when Wendy had felt like an outcast, a Jew among gentiles, she ridiculed exactly this kind of Anglophile gentility. Over time she had become an Anglophile herself, and the library's clubby interior appealed to that.

Peter Parnell—her playwriting buddy from the O'Neill, who became part of the Playwrights Horizons/Orphans' Christmas group—was her link to Dartmouth. He was a graduate of the school and often returned there to write. Wendy had begun joining him there in the 1980s; they would show each other drafts of works in progress. In 1989, when Peter began teaching a playwriting course at the school, Wendy began visiting Dartmouth more frequently.

She liked to stay at the Hanover Inn, a century-old piece of Americana, in a room overlooking the sprawling Dartmouth green. She and Peter would stay in their rooms and write, then meet for a walk around Occom Pond. Though Wendy was quintessentially urban, she took respite in the New England landscape. As the child of immigrants, she was particularly attracted to people and places with deep American roots.

She had practical reasons for accepting the fellowship, too. She wrote Susan Wright, director of the endowment, "I also have a play that will be at Lincoln Center the following season about a professor at a small New England College. Perhaps we could do a reading and I can talk about it afterwards."

Susan Wright was Dartmouth's first lady, not just because she was married to the president but because she had worked at the college for thirty years as a student adviser. She'd been looking forward to meeting Wendy, with whom she felt a kinship. Susan was born in 1946, just four years before Wendy, and graduated from Vassar as part of the last all-women class. She felt that *The Heidi Chronicles* was her story.

On March 29 Wendy arrived at Montgomery House on Occom Pond, where she would be staying. She brought along an animated entourage of young people: Michael Barakiva, her assistant who had directed the one-acts in Washington, was going to help with auditions and direct the student readings of *Third*; Lucy Jane; and Sarah Saltzberg, on a break from rehearsals for *Spelling Bee*, which was about to open on Broadway. Wendy remained a terrible driver, so Sarah had driven the "Ginger Mobile," the ancient Toyota Camry named in memory of Wendy's cat.

Upon seeing Wendy, Susan almost froze. The playwright's friendly e-mail notes hadn't given warning: Her physical appearance was distressing, almost freakish—puffy face, eyes unable to focus, mouth askew, the look of a stroke victim.

Wendy immediately put her hostess at ease, telling jokes, making Wright feel as though nothing could be more exciting for the playwright than to be at Dartmouth, talking to *her.* She invited Wright to sit in on auditions for the student production of *Third,* where Wendy came to life, offering adamant opinions on casting.

Wendy returned alone a month later. Her three days were packed: meetings with students who'd won a Dartmouth play competition, interviews with the student and local newspapers, rehearsals at night for *Third,* the performance, the cast party, answering questions from a classroom full of English majors. On April 27, at 5:00 p.m., she delivered the centerpiece of the Montgomery Fellow program, a public lecture open to students and the community. The five-hundred-seat Hopkins Center was full.

With her talk, titled "My Life in the Theater," and her easy informality, she sparked an immediate connection with the audience that transcended her disfigurement. She inspired the students with her own experiences and reassured them that she'd had no idea where she was going when she graduated from college. "She told them you don't open the *New York Times* with an ad saying 'Playwright wanted: fifty thousand dollars a year,'" said Peter Hackett, head of the theater department. "It was particularly pertinent to Dartmouth students."

The reading of *Third* the next day went well. "Wendy talked about what a great opportunity it was for her to hear it," Hackett remembered. "It was the first time she heard it after she made significant changes, when it changed from a one-act to full length. She took notes. She was really working on it, using this reading to make more revisions."

He looked forward to seeing her when she returned at the end of May, when she was scheduled to speak at the school's annual Arts Awards ceremony and to mentor student playwrights.

On May 2 Wendy attended the Broadway opening of *The 25th Annual Putnam County Spelling Bee.* Sarah Saltzberg's diploma from Wendy's School for Girls was a starring role in a Broadway play. The Cinderella

story behind *The 25th Annual Putnam County Spelling Bee* was incorporated into the play's public relations. Theater people love a good fairy tale,
and this one had actually happened.

Harry Haun, a columnist for *Playbill* and a fixture on the theater beat,
described how an Off-Off-Broadway play, originally called *C-R-E-P-U-S-
C-U-L-E,* about spelling-bee competitions, with audience participation,
had become a Broadway musical, directed by James Lapine, with music
composed by William Finn. Both men were Tony winners, and, more significantly, both were friends of Wendy Wasserstein. Haun wrote:

> She tends to shrug off her miracle-working. "I had a great nanny,"
> she says. [Yes, Wendy. Overtipping is one thing, but this is ridicu-
> lous.] She is obviously pleased it came to pass. Now she can get on
> with a play of her own—*Third,* which is to lead off the season at
> Lincoln Center this fall.

On Friday May 20, Wendy flew to Toronto with Lucy Jane to spend a
couple of days with Harriet Sachs and Mary Jane Patrone, two of the
Mount Holyoke friends memorialized in *Uncommon Women and Others.*
Each in her way had become emblematic of their generation. Mary Jane
was a high-ranking newspaper executive. Harriet was the founding partner of one of the first all-female law firms in Ontario and in 1998 was
appointed to the Superior Court of Justice of Ontario. Mary Jane didn't
marry until she was in her forties, to a widower with two young children.
Harriet was with the same man she began living with in 1976, a lawyer,
and they had two grown children—an old-fashioned family configuration
except that they'd never married. Their daughter, however, would rebel,
wanting a formal marriage—to a woman.

The three Mount Holyoke classmates, separated by years and geogra-
phy, lived very different lives but always stayed close, mainly by phone.

Mary Jane described her "girlfriend calls" with Wendy: "Most of the
time when she called or I called, it was, 'I have to talk to you,' me saying,
'This guy just broke my heart, I just got a promotion, my mother is sick.' I
would get similar calls: 'They are going to do my play. They are not going

to do my play. I'm thinking this way about this person. I have feelings that aren't being reciprocated. Can you believe my mother is doing this!' And sometimes she'd call and say, 'I'm going on book tour to California, you want to come?'"

They showed up for each other's events. "As you get older, that's a rarer commodity than you think," said Harriet. "If I had a big thirtieth birthday, a big fortieth-birthday party, my kid had a bat mitzvah, my kid was born, she came."

Harriet was sworn in as superior court justice in January 1998, during a serious Canadian snowstorm. "Because I didn't have a wedding, this was the most important event in my life," she recalled. "In this huge courtroom packed full of people, all I could think of was the icy weather. I just remember looking around that courtroom looking to see if Mary Jane and Wendy were there—because otherwise it would be as if my family wasn't there. When I saw them, I could relax and enjoy myself."

In the spring of 2005, Harriet really needed her friends. Clay, her lifelong partner and father of her children, was recovering from heart surgery. Her other best woman friend, the closest friendship she'd formed after Mount Holyoke, had just died.

Wendy and Lucy Jane arrived early Friday May 20 without a nanny. Both Harriet and Mary Jane were shocked at their friend's physical condition. Wendy could barely walk. Yet she had insisted on coming alone with Lucy so that Mary Jane and Harriet could get to know her. Wendy wasn't accustomed to traveling by herself with her daughter and seemed nonplussed by the enormous effort required to take care of an active five-year-old, especially from a fifty-four-year-old woman in poor health. Everything was difficult for her: bathing Lucy, reading her a story, getting her to go to bed.

But Wendy wasn't content to just hang out with her friends. She insisted on an excursion. They took a long walk to a park, then drove to an animal farm, which entailed more walking. That evening, as they cooked dinner at home, Wendy lay down on the floor of the kitchen. "I'm just really, really tired," she said.

More than once Wendy said to her friends, "You need to see Lucy more." Mary Jane felt slightly scolded but then set the feeling aside.

It was a horrible and wonderful visit. Harriet was already in rough shape when they arrived, shaken by her friend's death and worrying about Clay. Then, during the weekend, while trying to absorb the added concern of seeing Wendy so debilitated, Harriet learned that one of her daughter's best friends had died in an accident.

"There was so much pain in my house, but what I remember from all of it is that we were so happy to be together," Harriet said. "We cooked and talked and were so happy to be together even though we were in so much pain."

Wendy and Lucy Jane left Toronto early Sunday morning, May 22, so Wendy could attend the funeral of Rhoda Brooks's mother.

When they left, Harriet was struck by a terrifying thought: "Wendy is dying."

She immediately erased the thought.

"No," she said to herself. "No. You just think everyone is dying." Yet she continued to worry. Over the summer she and Mary Jane called several times, asking to visit. Wendy's response was always the same: The time wasn't right. When they insisted, she said, "Come for *Third*." They agreed they would get together in October, when the play opened.

Despite the tiring weekend in Canada, Wendy didn't slow down. When Rhoda saw Wendy at her mother's funeral, she thought Wendy didn't look well and told her not to go to the cemetery after the funeral, but she insisted.

The next evening Wendy took part in a fund-raiser for the 92nd Street Y, a tribute to Cy Coleman. The legendary Broadway composer had died the previous November, at age seventy-five, leaving behind a four year-old-child who attended the Y's nursery school with Lucy Jane. One of Coleman's last works was the music, written with lyricist David Zippel, for Wendy's play *Pamela's First Musical,* which hadn't been produced yet.

The day after the Cy Coleman tribute, Wendy returned to Dartmouth.

Susan Wright saw a noticeable change in just a month. "In May she seemed seriously ill," she said. "I was shocked at the difference. In April it was an effort, but the big difference was from April to May."

Nevertheless Wendy fulfilled her obligations, appearing at the school's Arts Awards ceremony and the student play competition and attending the dinner afterward. When Susan Wright dropped her at the airport, Wendy said, "I'll see you this summer," at which time she was to teach a course at Dartmouth's summer school, called Finding Your Voice as a Playwright.

Later her friends asked themselves and one another: Why didn't she take care of herself? Why did she take all those fertility medications? Wasn't that the reason she was sick—though not a single one of Wendy's doctors agreed there was a connection.

Why didn't she tell anyone how sick she was? Did she know she was dying? A collective sense of guilt and jealousy would set in, as friends looked back and realized that Wendy's gift had been to hold a mirror up to them, allowing them to see themselves in a flattering light, distracting them from looking too deeply at her. They wondered: Whom did she tell? Was there a more trusted group, an innermost core of the *very* best friends from which they were excluded?

Wendy tried to keep up her usual frantic pace. On June 1 she threw a book party at her apartment for Peter Parnell and his partner, Justin Richardson, a psychiatrist—the match made by Wendy and Jenny Lyn Bader, playwright and former assistant. The two men had written a children's book called *And Tango Makes Three,* about a same-sex penguin family (based on a true story). On June 2 she spoke at the graduating ceremony for Open Doors, the mentoring program for high-school students that she had started. "I can say unequivocally, this is the best thing I've ever done," she told them. This speech, too, was captured on video. Wendy's features had more or less resumed normal position; she wore an attractive black dress; her hair was "done."

It would be easy to think she was feeling better, but in fact she would soon be finding it even harder to function. The turning point came shortly after the Open Doors speech. She had taken Lucy to Chelsea Piers for a good-bye bowling date with a friend from nursery school who was moving to Connecticut. Wendy fell. After that, she used a cane.

On June 14 Heidi Ettinger, the set designer, was being honored by the League of Professional Theatre Women. Ettinger had asked Wendy to introduce her at the luncheon. "We didn't hear and didn't hear and didn't hear. She said she was in Rome, but she was not, then she said she was in Rome but too ill—a whole series of things," said Ettinger. Then, the day of the award, "Wendy sent this lovely, moving introduction which somebody read," Ettinger said.

On June 20 another cancellation: Wendy called Susan Wright at the Montgomery Endowment. "She said she hoped I and the theater department would understand, but her doctor told her she couldn't come because there was an inflammation," Wright recalled. "Then she called back and said not to tell the students this, not to tell anyone."

On June 29 Wendy met Dan Sullivan at Lincoln Center for a reading of *Third* with Dianne Wiest, Jason Ritter, and other cast members. After the reading Sullivan told Wendy there was one crucial matter that had to be dealt with before rehearsals began at the end of August. Wendy had added a character with breast cancer, who is said to be a close friend of Laurie Jameson, the feminist college professor. Sullivan didn't understand something. If the women are such good friends, why does Nancy become so furious when Laurie offers to help her?

The scene didn't make sense to Sullivan. "The anger of Nancy about the invasion of privacy when it's your best friend seemed to me sort of odd and perhaps not something an audience would understand," he said. "That ultimately began to converge with Wendy's life in some way, because it was extremely important to her. Nancy was a surrogate for Wendy. But when I was grappling with that at the beginning, I didn't know the circumstances of Wendy's illness."

Most of their subsequent discussions about the play returned to the issue of motivation. As Wendy grew noticeably sicker, Sullivan found himself talking about Nancy the character when he was trying to talk about Wendy. "It was very clear this was not something she wanted to discuss," he said. "Indirectly, as I would talk about Nancy, I would also be talking about her. I would say, 'I don't know why she is so angry when all this person is trying to do is to help.' I would have to tread very delicately, because my own feelings were wrapped up in it. She would not really respond. She would take it under advisement. Her fundamental obsession with privacy was something she was expecting an audience to simply accept."

Sullivan encouraged Wendy to make the friend's intervention very intrusive, so the audience could understand why it was so aggravating. So she wrote a scene in which Nancy's furor is triggered because Laurie, thinking her friend isn't taking care of herself, calls her doctor. "I deserve the privilege of my privacy," Nancy says angrily.

By July 29, 2005, Knopf had put in place important aspects of its marketing plan for *Elements of Style*, Wendy's novel, scheduled for release the following spring. The book was being positioned as the thinking person's *Sex and the City*.* Though the novel takes a decidedly dark turn—the glittering world of café society is struck by death and destruction—the emphasis was on the glitz; the cover was designed to resemble an Hermès shopping bag.

Wendy sent two photographs of herself for the book jacket. They would have been odd choices for any book, but particularly this one, which was being sold as a lighthearted romp. One half of her face appears to be crushed by affliction; she is staring at the camera as though daring the viewer to look at her. Was this an act of defiance? Shouting, *Take me as I am!* Was it a hint? *Can't you see I'm dying?* Or was it obliviousness? Did she see something entirely different from what everyone else saw?

Her publisher ignored her offering. The book jacket carries a photo taken a few years earlier, showing a mischievous Wendy. She is sitting with one hand hidden in her cloud of curly hair, the other cradling her chin. She is smiling, girlish, her eyes full of light, the Wendy everybody loved.

---

* Wendy's work laid the groundwork for the popular television series about four single career women living in New York, which ran between 1998 and 2004. Coincidentally, Sarah Jessica Parker, who played the main character in *Sex and the City*, had small parts in *The Heidi Chronicles*.

✦ ✦

The third week of August, Wendy and Lucy Jane visited Flora Fraser on Nantucket. Flora's life had improved considerably since she and Wendy had met a decade earlier, when Wendy considered taking up residence in London. Back then Flora was in a funk. Her mother was Lady Antonia Fraser, celebrated writer; her stepfather was Harold Pinter, renowned playwright. Flora, at the time, was the divorced mother of a four-year-old child, living in a gloomy basement apartment in an unfashionable part of town, unable to finish a biography she was working on.

As a lark the two women agreed to exchange lives and write about it. The articles weren't published, but they became friends. Subsequently Flora finished the biography and married Peter Soros, nephew of the billionaire investor and philanthropist George Soros. They had two sons.

The Nantucket get-together had become a summer tradition. Wendy and Lucy Jane planned to stay with Flora and her family and then continue their island vacation with Stephen and Cathy Graham. That year the routine seemed to be the same as always, except that Wendy couldn't decide when to make the trip. Finally she arrived at Nantucket on the ferry with Lucy and Sarah Saltzberg, who was on a short break from *Spelling Bee*.

"We did the usual things," Flora said. "We had a dinner for her at our house, and we went to the beach club in Nantucket, which she loved."

Wendy told Flora she and Lucy had spent a pleasant few days with Claude and the boys in the Hamptons earlier that summer. Wendy said she felt more comfortable with Claude than she had in the past. They'd talked about child rearing, about schools. Claude was a good mother, Flora remembered Wendy saying.

But the summer would be clouded by a rift between Wendy and the Grahams—though the Grahams wouldn't know they'd had a falling-out until later.

As Wendy got sicker, she became less able—or less willing—to mask her mixed feelings about a great many people, and she began to create quarrels out of tiny perceived slights. Resentments that had been simmering for years—fairly or unfairly—began to erupt. The Nantucket incident itself seems inconsequential, but Wendy repeated it so often to so many friends that it acquired momentum, like a factoid spinning across cable news. In the weeks before the visit to Flora and the Grahams, Wendy had been occupied with making changes to *Third*, finalizing details on *Elements of Style*, dealing with her illness, making time for Lucy. She kept changing the date for her Nantucket visit. This was of consequence in a milieu where social arrangements were handled with the kind of nervous attention usually reserved for matters involving delicate international diplomacy. Chance was not a welcome guest at the table.

And neither, for one evening, was Wendy.

The Grahams already had houseguests—parents of one of their children's school friends—the weekend Wendy finally settled on. But they urged her to come anyway.

Then came the snafu. A few weeks before Wendy changed the date, Daisy Soros, Flora's Hungarian mother-in-law, had invited the Grahams for dinner on August 23. She told them it was fine for them to bring their houseguests. But when August 23 rolled around, Wendy was also at the Grahams'.

As Stephen Graham remembered it, he called Daisy Soros and asked if he could bring Wendy, too, and Daisy said, "I can't, I don't have any room at my table."

When he told Wendy, she told him not to worry. "Oh, my God, I've seen a lot of Daisy," she said.

Stephen didn't want to "bag out" of Daisy's dinner at the last minute, since she had accommodated his other houseguests, and Wendy didn't seem to think it was a big deal. He knew she'd just spent time with the Soros family.

He arranged for their cook to make dinner for Wendy, Lucy Jane, and Sarah, and he checked with Wendy one last time. "Here's our cook, we have to go to this Daisy Soros dinner, I hope that's okay," he said.

She replied, "That's fine, it's fine, we'll be fine."

Wendy spent the next day at the library working and then excused herself from dinner with the Grahams, saying she had another obligation. The next day she left, and all was well, or so they thought.

Cathy Graham called Wendy a few weeks later, in October, asking her to write a college recommendation for their secretary's daughter.

Cathy was shocked when Wendy angrily said, "No!" She told Cathy she was quite upset about what had happened that summer. Cathy was beside herself and met with Wendy to apologize. Wendy seemed to accept Cathy's apology and then talked about her new play.

When Cathy told Stephen that Wendy had blown up at her, he thought, "Oh, shit, I must call her up."

They went for drinks at Bemelmans Bar at the Carlyle. He apologized profusely, all the while thinking, "It's a little uncharacteristic for her to take so to heart what was maybe a bit insensitive but not the sort of thing one would take to heart or Wendy would take to heart. But she did take it to heart, for whatever reason."

After they talked, he said, "I sort of felt the air had been cleared, but I don't know if it had been cleared or not."

Later people would look back and analyze events, looking for signs and portents. They saw her physical deterioration not as a final breakdown but as another relapse that would lead to another recovery. Why shouldn't they? They were taking their cues from Wendy, who staged elaborate scenarios to keep up the illusion that she could not be stopped. When she was no longer able to walk without a walker or a wheelchair, she continued to come to rehearsals for *Third* every day, even laborious tech rehearsals.

She allowed a trusted few to help her—the assistants and certain friends: Rhoda Brooks was a constant, and so were James Lapine and Jane Rosenthal. But she kept her family at bay; work was her excuse to be scarce. Rosenthal, who lived nearby, stopped by often to have a meal. Daniel Swee, the casting director at Lincoln Center, helped her get from the car that drove her the few blocks from home into the theater. Emmy brought Lucy to meet her at rehearsals and for dinner breaks. They hired a nurse to dress and bathe Wendy when Emmy could no longer hoist her from her bed.

In the theater Wendy's illness became the elephant in the room. No one commented on her early arrivals to rehearsal, so she could be seated when the cast came in. André talked to her nearly every day during rehearsal, but not about her illness. As she appeared to weaken, however, he and others began urging her to go to the Mayo Clinic for a diagnosis.

On October 18, Wendy's birthday, André stopped by the Café des Artistes, where she was having a small celebration. He'd developed an ulcer that fall and now had a cold and wasn't feeling well. "That room was a bit small and somber, and the gathering was a bit forced-jollity kind of thing," he recalled. He gave Wendy a gift but left early, afraid of passing along his germs to her, she was so frail.

Wendy was angry. "He was sitting on a stool and didn't want to kiss her because he had a cold, and he couldn't go to her rehearsal. She was so mad, she's like, 'He's got a cold, look at me!'" said Jane Rosenthal, who was there. "She wanted André's attention desperately for those rehearsals on *Third* and didn't really get what she needed. But it may have been what she needed might never have been enough from him. It would never be enough, because of their history."

The play opened the following week, on October 24, 2005. Wendy wanted the premiere party for *Third* to be splendid, which meant that no one, especially Lola, should know how sick she was.

The logistics were left to Jeremy Strong, a young actor who had worked for Wendy for two years. He had become the assistant Wendy depended on most. A month earlier he'd helped her fulfill Lucy's wish to have her sixth-birthday party at Mars 2112, a popular restaurant designed to look like outer space, where the waiters were disguised as aliens. They called ahead to make sure Wendy wouldn't have to walk far.

They arrived to find that the elevator was out of order, and they had to detour via an underground passage that was almost a block long. Strong watched Wendy trudge through that seemingly endless corridor, in obvious pain, without complaint, unwilling to miss Lucy's party.

Strong and Wendy now devised a plan to get her across Lincoln Center from the Mitzi E. Newhouse Theater to Avery Fisher Hall for the reception. Instead of a dreaded wheelchair, Wendy would sit on an office desk chair with wheels. Strong could push her through the underground passages connecting the theaters.

Jane Rosenthal was in charge of makeup and hair. She bought Wendy a long skirt by Catherine Malandrino, a stylish touch that also covered up her leg braces.

Lola made a special effort to negotiate her way through the crowd to tell Wendy how wonderful she thought the play was. But Wendy kept her distance, even when Rhoda urged her to talk to her mother. Wendy was afraid of Lola's power to detect weakness; she might see through her daughter's façade.

In Wendy's mind the evening was a success. She felt that the subterfuge had worked, and she had the chance to celebrate with the people she held dear. Even Kanti Rai, her oncologist, came to the party.

But Wendy's charade wasn't as successful as she thought. The day after the party, Lola called Georgette, who asked her mother how Wendy looked. Lola's response concerned Georgette.

"When Wendy was a child, I could tell she was sick because her eyes didn't look right," Lola said. "Her eyes didn't look right."

The reviews for *Third* the following day were mixed but overall positive, with special nods to Wendy's wit, to Dan Sullivan's thoughtful direction, to Dianne Wiest's warm performance. Even Ben Brantley was touched. "*Third* exhales a gentle breath of autumn, a rueful awareness of death and of seasons past, that makes it impossible to dismiss it as a quick-sketch comedy of political manners," he wrote. "A gracious air of both apology and forgiveness pervades its attitude to its characters." The public reaction was less equivocal: The run was sold out before previews began.

In November, Robert Brustein went to see the play. He was overcome. "I was finally willing to concede that Wendy was a major American playwright," he said. Before he began writing his review for the *New Republic*, he sent Wendy an e-mail.

Just got out of your play. Your very best—brave, complicated, clarifying, illuminating, and very very moving (Doreen cried all the way home). You alone in your generation have bitten off this very important subject, and handled it in the most balanced manner, avoiding both moral correctness and political correctness in favor of a coura-

geous capacity to live with doubts and ambiguities. Very Keatsian. Warm congratulations. You should feel very proud. Hope you are well and enjoying your grand success. Much love, Bob

He was surprised when she didn't write back promptly. She usually did. Two weeks later he received an apology. "I'm sorry it's taken me so long to respond, I have been away," she wrote. "I was so touched by your email and am very grateful for your words."

Not long after that, having heard rumors that Wendy was ill, Brustein called Chris Durang and learned the ominous meaning hidden in Wendy's words "I have been away."

LUCY JANE WITH JACK AND DASH, HER COUSINS AND HER BROTHERS.

Twenty-four

LEGACY

2005–06

Lucy Jane began kindergarten that fall of 2005, at the Brearley School, all-girl citadel of academic excellence and social privilege, fulfilling her mother's longtime dream. Wendy had been obsessed with getting Lucy Jane into the school, although she would pretend she didn't care. Heidi Ettinger remembered talking to her about it. "On one level it was really important to her that she had a place in that world," said Ettinger. "And then she would always talk horribly about the Brearley moms and their drivers, the whole scene."

For James Lapine, Brearley would forever be associated with Wendy's last days. She asked him to accompany her to the school's Open Day, on November 8, 2005. By then her fragility had become almost as breathtaking as her resolve to ignore it.

The morning of Open Day, Lapine met Wendy at her apartment and they took a town car to Brearley. Lucy had already left for school with Emmy. Wendy felt faint and insisted on stopping at a Starbucks for a Frappuccino. When they arrived at the school, Lapine helped Wendy into the wheelchair they'd brought along, and they went inside. Lucy saw them and ran over to her mother. "Lucy was starting to climb all over her, but she was in such agony she just kept trying to get Lucy off of her," Lapine recalled. That shocked him. Wendy never wanted Lucy Jane to think that anything was wrong.

"It was a hideous day," Lapine recalled. "Hideous. Awful. I remember out of that fog getting her home and into bed, she was just in such pain. We couldn't get her into bed. She had a nurse, but the nurse couldn't do it. I get chills when I think about it. It was just being with someone who was in agonizing pain trying to be there for her daughter. That was the day I realized she was dying."

He left Wendy's building in a daze. He was walking south on Central Park West when he bumped into Frank Rich at the entrance to the subway station at Seventy-second street. Lapine didn't know him very well. During the years Rich was a theater critic, he avoided getting close to many theater people. But they'd seen each other many times at social gatherings, and Lapine knew that Rich and Wendy had been close. He just blurted it.

"Wendy's dying."

He told Rich about the morning at Brearley and how Wendy wouldn't let Lucy Jane touch her. Rich couldn't fully comprehend what Lapine was saying. The newspaper columnist was on his way to a business lunch and was running late. He said he would call Lapine when he returned to the office.

"I was in a state of shock," said Rich. "As soon as I got off the subway, I called my wife and then went through the motions of having lunch with someone."

Wendy had given him *Third* to read a few months earlier and asked him for comments. The motif of death running through the play hadn't escaped him, but when he discussed it with his wife, Alex Witchel, they agreed that Wendy was writing about her father, or Sandra.

Rich had tried to get together with Wendy throughout the summer, but she'd always been busy, he assumed with rehearsals.

"Come to opening night," she'd told him.

He did. As he and Witchel walked downstairs to the Mitzi E. Newhouse Theater at Lincoln Center, André intercepted them.

"You'll be very, very shocked by Wendy's condition," he told them. "She's in a wheelchair. We're disguising it."

Rich watched Wendy at the party, holding court while seated on the rolling office chair, but looking terribly frail. He realized that her health was worse than he'd been led to believe. As he watched the play, he began to put two and two together.

He remembered wanting to call her and ask, "What the fuck is going on?"

Instead he got in touch with André, who was no help. "I don't know what the hell is going on," he told Rich.

So when Rich heard James Lapine say, "Wendy's dying," he felt shocked but not surprised.

"I couldn't believe it," he recalled, and then added, "It all made sense."

Later that day Wendy flew to Rochester, Minnesota, to the Mayo Clinic, in a private plane leased by Bruce. She was accompanied by an aide and Jeremy Strong, who brought a friend in case he needed help lifting Wendy. For the four days they were in Minnesota, the twenty-seven-year-old actor found himself in charge of his employer's medical care. Confronted with a dizzying onslaught of information, stunned by emotion, he operated by rote, taking notes, checking in by telephone with his mother, who was a nurse in Massachusetts.

On November 12 he wrote in his notebook, "Disseminated T-Cell Leukemia/Lymphoma. Neurovascular selection by Lymphoma. Blood vessels in CNS/Spinal Cord/Facial Nerve. T-Cell Clonal malignancy. Need aggressive Lymphoma treatment. Methotrexate Lymphoma therapy. Aggressive T-Cell Regimen. Says need to go to Sloan-Kettering right away. Have to tell W."

That's when the family stepped in. Bruce's wife, Claude, spoke to the Mayo Clinic physicians and arranged for Wendy to be admitted to Memorial Sloan-Kettering Cancer Center in Manhattan, one of the country's best cancer hospitals. On November 13 Wendy moved into a room in the hospital's VIP unit on the nineteenth floor, which had fourteen luxury suites, done up like an expensive hotel, marble tiles in the bathroom.

Those days became a surreal blur for Jeremy Strong, except for one moment, embedded in his memory with unyielding clarity. He recorded it in his journal:

Lucy running in through door, "Mommy!!"

In *Elements of Style,* published three months after Wendy's death, a somewhat mysterious character named Jil Taillou dies in a terrorist attack on New York. A friend of Frankie Weissman, the doctor heroine, Jil is an art dealer and a socialite who speaks with a vaguely foreign accent. Jil has left instructions with his attorney to invite friends to his apartment and to have each take a memento. At the party Frankie realizes Jil had lived a life of lies. He had no daughter, as he'd told her, but he did have a male partner of ten years' standing, whose existence he had not revealed. He was not Jil Taillou, Hungarian bon vivant, but Julius Taittenbaum, a Jew from Brooklyn, another secret.

"Frankie wasn't angry at Jil for camouflaging his life," Wendy wrote. "She just wished he'd known it was all so unnecessary."

Yet as she was reviewing the manuscript containing those words, Wendy was still trying to camouflage her own life, but with less and less success. She was losing her ability to maintain her separate spheres of friendship and confidences as illness broke down the walls of secrecy she had so carefully built. She remained determined to keep Lucy Jane from discovering her origins, even though Lucy was raised at a time, and in a social class, where it was becoming less and less unusual for children to have been conceived with help from science.

Wendy had been distraught when her daughter came home upset because someone at school had asked her who her father was.

The straightforward option—of simply telling Lucy Jane the truth, most of which had been published in the *New Yorker*—didn't seem viable to Wendy, not yet. Instead she tried to think of a plausible story and told her friend Rhoda that she might just say Lucy's father was Gerry Gutierrez. Wendy had been considering this choice for a long time. She'd invited Gutierrez into the delivery room, not William Ivey Long, to lay the groundwork. After Gutierrez died, the idea became even more appealing.

Wendy dedicated *Elements of Style* to her deceased friend, with canny wording that was a kind of subterfuge.

> For Gerald Gutierrez
> *—more than a director*

For gossips who wondered, "more than a director" could be taken as yet another clue, that Gutierrez was Lucy's father. But Wendy had begun calling her friend "more than a director" years before Lucy Jane was born. He'd been her escort at a family function where Wendy's Aunt Florence asked her, "Is he more than a director to you?" After that, Gutierrez often signed notes to Wendy, "More Than a Director" or just "MTD."

Now, without having resolved what to tell Lucy, Wendy was at Memorial Sloan-Kettering, waiting to receive a massive dose of chemotherapy, direct to her brain, where the cancer had spread. The procedure was scheduled for November 23, the day before Thanksgiving.

She had entered that hospital netherworld, where thousands of dollars are spent to prolong life yet the prospect of death must be acknowledged. A doctor told her she was "swimming between sharks," meaning that the treatment could be just as dangerous as the cancer.

The moment had arrived for her to consider subjects she'd avoided. How did she want Lucy Jane to learn the details of her birth? Who should be Wendy's health proxy—the person designated to make medical decisions—should she become unconscious? Who did she want to take care of her daughter if the treatment failed?

Wendy's behavior at this fearful juncture was not all that unusual. Like a great many intelligent, successful people—including those wealthy enough to afford the special hotel suites at the country's premier cancer hospital—she refused to believe she wouldn't outswim the sharks. She behaved as though it were predetermined that the treatment would succeed, just as Sandra had been in denial on her deathbed, making business calls until the very end. Lola's lessons had not been lost on her children.

Wendy followed her usual pattern. She tried to rewrite the scenario. Weak as she was, she proceeded as if her hospital stay were an inconvenient disruption that she could work around. She called Victoria Wilson, her editor at Knopf, to tell her she was in the hospital but assured her that an assistant was reviewing the galleys for *Elements of Style,* scheduled for publication that spring.

She called Lola to explain why she wouldn't be at Bruce's house for Thanksgiving. "I'm at Dartmouth," she lied. "I've met a man." She knew she didn't have to worry about Bruce spilling her secret; in matters of family health, he was the staunchest defender of privacy.

Wendy made it clear to the people who knew: No one was to be told that she was in the hospital unless she gave her approval.

She returned telephone messages that had piled up while she was at the Mayo Clinic.

Rafael Yglesias had called, asking why she'd missed the dinner date they'd scheduled. Wendy had gotten back in touch with him after his wife died of cancer, eighteen months earlier, and they resumed the friendship that had ended almost twenty years before. Now when he received an e-mail from her assistant, not Wendy, saying they would have to reschedule, Yglesias felt that something must be seriously wrong. A day or two later, his phone rang.

He didn't pick up on time, but when he saw the caller ID number, he felt a chill. The call had come from the room his wife had occupied at Sloan-Kettering before she died. He checked his messages and heard a familiar voice.

"Hi, Rafael," said Wendy in a cheerful tone, without revealing her whereabouts. "I've got some girls I think you should meet." She continued a stream of bright patter and then said good-bye. The message didn't click off immediately; Yglesias heard Wendy hand the telephone to someone to hang up, and then say, wearily, "That's done. I'm exhausted."

On Sunday, November 20, Gwen Feder, mother of one of Lucy Jane's nursery-school friends, left a message to ask about Thanksgiving. For the past couple of years, she and her daughters had brought croissants and doughnuts to Wendy's apartment and watched the parade with her and Lucy Jane. Wendy called back and breezily said she was in the hospital, that they'd figured out what was wrong, but she wouldn't be home by

Thanksgiving. She encouraged Feder to take her daughters, with croissants, to 75 Central Park West anyway. Lucy Jane would be expecting
them, with Rhoda and Emmy.

Wendy didn't want Lucy Jane to think that anything would change. On
Thanksgiving, Lucy Jane would watch the parade from their living-room
window, with Gwen Feder and her daughters, eating croissants and doughnuts. She would have dinner at her Uncle Bruce's house, as usual.

James Lapine saw that Wendy was ignoring the big picture and followed her lead. He simply nodded as she told him she probably wouldn't
be able to handle the tightly scheduled book tour that Knopf had planned
for *Elements of Style*. She definitely wouldn't be able to make a speaking
engagement scheduled for December.

"I figure it'll be six months," she told him. "I'll just have to get through
this, and I may not be able to walk, but I'll be back."

He couldn't see how she would survive, but he found himself becoming
convinced. "I wanted to believe that she was right," he said.

On Tuesday, November 22, the day before a chemotherapy port was
scheduled to be inserted in Wendy's head, Jane Rosenthal received a telephone call. Rosenthal was already in a lousy mood. It was pouring rain. A
movie she was producing was in a crisis. She heard Wendy shriek, "There
was an intern here, and he said I'm going to die!"

In her business, Rosenthal was accustomed to dealing with hysteria.
"The intern doesn't know what he's talking about," she said firmly. "I'll be
there in five minutes."

She and Jeremy Strong remained with Wendy until Rhoda Brooks arrived, to spend the night in the room. Rhoda didn't want to; she hadn't yet
recuperated from her mother's death a few months earlier. But she couldn't
say no to Wendy.

Both she and Jane Rosenthal broached the subject of talking to Lucy.
"I'm not like that," Wendy snapped.

But Emmy the nanny said that Wendy tried to tell Lucy something that
evening. "I need to explain a few things to you," Wendy said, but Lucy was
her mother's daughter. "I don't want to hear it," she said. Emmy believed
that even though Lucy was only six, she understood.

That night, at home, Emmy lay in bed next to Lucy as she went to sleep. "My mom is going to die," Emmy heard Lucy say.

Emmy replied carefully. "Doctors are going to give her medicine. We're going to see how it works. You don't know what's going to happen."

"I know," Lucy said. "My mom is going to die."

Emmy wanted to reassure her but didn't know how.

The following morning, November 23, Claude, Wendy's sister-in-law, came with Sandra's daughter Samantha to see Wendy before the port was put in place. Bruce wasn't there; he was sick, with bronchitis, possibly pneumonia.

Wendy told Claude that she'd been thinking about who should care for Lucy if things went badly. A few years earlier, Wendy had designated her niece Pam, Bruce and Chris's daughter, as Lucy's legal guardian and Sandra's daughter Samantha as backup, thinking of a far-off time—maybe never—not seriously considering the responsibility attached.

But now, she told Claude, she realized that her nieces were young single women, not ready to take care of someone else's child. Lucy needed a mother and father, Wendy said. She asked Claude if she and Bruce would raise Lucy if Wendy was no longer there.

Claude didn't know what to say. For years Wendy had kept the family at bay, not disclosing details of her illness. Like her friends, family members knew that if they probed too deeply, they would be shut out. With the call from the Mayo Clinic, the wall had broken. The family swooped in, trying to comprehend the situation and take control of it.

Claude's first reaction was to reassure Wendy. "It's going to be fine!" she said. "The treatment is going to work."

The previous summer, when Wendy visited Claude and Bruce in the Hamptons, Claude sensed that Wendy might be testing her, with those probing conversations about their children. "I felt she must be worried about being a mommy and how long she'll be a mommy and what will happen if she doesn't get healthier," Claude said.

Claude told a friend she believed that she and Bruce would end up with Lucy, but she didn't think it would happen this soon. Her own mother had survived cancer several times; the doctor treating Wendy at Sloan-Kettering had saved a friend of Claude's. Until now Claude hadn't imagined Wendy actually dying.

She realized what Wendy needed to hear. "Of course we'll take Lucy," she said. "Of course."

Even then she didn't believe she would be asked to fulfill her promise immediately.

"I was hoping for the best," she said, "that she would be well and the treatment would work and maybe she'll be in remission and have five years or ten years—that's a big chunk of a child's growth."

Later that morning Wendy was with Rhoda, waiting for the port to be inserted. A nurse came in and asked Wendy if she had a health-care proxy. There was a form at home that designated Bruce and Pam. But the nurse advised having another proxy available at the hospital. "You should," she said ominously, "when you are having a procedure."

Wendy looked at Rhoda, who prayed that her friend wouldn't ask her.

She didn't have to worry. Wendy told the nurse that her proxy was Bruce.

At the end it was as it had been at the beginning: family first.

Wendy didn't outswim the sharks. When the chemicals entered her brain, her vital signs began failing fast.

Bruce came to the hospital and behaved like a man accustomed to getting his way. Rhoda remembered, "He walked in that place with the loudest voice, shouting, 'I'm in charge! I don't care what it takes! I'll keep her alive!'"

Bruce brushed past Wendy's friends who were visiting. They were struck by his insensitivity.

Claude as well as Bruce's children saw a man beset by grief.

"He just couldn't stand to see her like that," said Pam, who loved her father and always defended him.

Claude felt his suffering, though she understood the harsh reactions Bruce provoked in people. She had lived with him for a long time by then.

"He suffered," she said. "Other people couldn't understand his vulnerability."

She didn't blame Lola—not entirely. "It has to be a mix of everything," she said, speaking of her husband and his siblings. "Genetics and environment and circumstances, all of it is in there. It's all a mix. They're just a little extreme in the humanity of it. We're all out there trying, and we all fall, but they're falling harder. They're trying harder and getting further, but they're also falling harder."

Bruce dreaded the hospital and kept his visits short. He visited Lucy Jane alone, in Wendy's apartment. He read her nursery stories, as he had for all his children when they were young, the way Sandra had read to him and Wendy back in Brooklyn.

Wendy's illness came close to crushing Lola. After visiting Wendy in the hospital, she told a relative, "People think I'm blessed with my kids, but I'm cursed."

For six weeks Wendy drifted between life and death, occasionally rousing to greet one of the many friends and relatives who came to see her. One day she came to consciousness and saw Jane Rosenthal and André at her bedside. To Jane she offered a shopping joke, about handbags, a familiar Wendy tactic, using wit to beat back sadness.

But she held out no false gaiety to André, her champion, who had given her so much happiness but also caused her much pain.

"Oh, André, please don't make me write any more plays," she said.

Even when desperately ill and barely conscious, Wendy knew how to reach her audience.

On January 30, 2006, she died, at age fifty-five.

The following day the news was reported on the front page of the *New York Times*. James Kaplan, her old boyfriend, was shocked but then thought of something that would amuse Wendy. "I thought, my God, when I knew her, if she'd known she would be on the front page of the *New York Times* when she died, she'd have come back to life!"

The lights of Broadway were dimmed in her honor.

A palpable sense of bereavement reverberated among the New York intelligentsia and well beyond, to the friends and strangers for whom Wendy Wasserstein had become a friendly touchstone. She didn't preach from above but invited her public to join her perplexed, witty contemplation of the rapidly changing, confusing times in which they lived. Her characters moved in tandem with Baby Boomers as they aged, helping them—women in particular—sort out the shifting definitions and demands placed on their generation.

She addressed the conflicting goals of youthful ambition in *Uncommon Women and Others* and the changing relations between men and women in *Isn't It Romantic*. With *The Heidi Chronicles,* she captured an essential dilemma: how political movements can thwart individual desire for personal fulfillment. In *Miami* and *The Sisters Rosensweig,* she grappled with the powerful pull of family, even for those children seeking a wider world. She looked to larger issues of responsibility and power in *An American Daughter* and *Old Money.* Her final plays, *Welcome to My Rash* and *Third,* dealt with aging, the breakdown of body and beliefs, questions of legacy.

Casting herself as the amiable outsider who could deliver tough messages with humor and warmth, she reinforced these dramatic themes through her essays and public appearances, her work with Open Doors, and her friendships. In doing so she became a cultural phenomenon while giving the impression that she was an unassuming part of the crowd.

In the week following her death, the *New York Times* ran five separate articles about Wendy, including an affectionate column by Gail Collins, the editorial-page editor, first woman to have held the job at the *Times.* Newspapers around the country ran articles and personal assessments, and in the *New Yorker,* Paul Rudnick remembered his Yale friend in a "Talk of the Town" piece.

Even critics who didn't like her work felt compelled to weigh in.

"I didn't think much of any of Wasserstein's plays, and I dreaded having to say so in print, since she was an exceedingly nice lady," wrote Terry Teachout, the *Wall Street Journal*'s drama critic, in his blog.

But most of the commentary carried the ache of personal loss. "She was observing life as we were living it," said Linda Winer, *Newsday*'s theater critic, on National Public Radio. "And I'm finding it just very, very difficult to process the idea that there aren't going to be any more Wendy Wasserstein plays."

Her memorial service, held at Lincoln Center on March 13, 2006, was covered as a news event in the *New York Times.* The reporter described the mourners as "scores of Broadway's biggest stars and backstage players, many of whom counted Ms. Wasserstein—whose social calendar might include everything from nights at the opera to days at the mall—as an old, and close, friend."

Many luminaries spoke or performed: playwrights Terrence McNally, William Finn, and Christopher Durang; actors Meryl Streep, Joan Allen, and Swoosie Kurtz; and directors Daniel Sullivan, André Bishop, and James Lapine. But the room was also filled with the nonfamous, old friends from every part of Wendy's life, and fans who knew her only through her writing.

In subsequent months friends from different spheres began to talk—and to discover that each of them knew a slightly different version of Wendy. They discovered how well she had deflected scrutiny with the flattering mirror she placed in front of them.

"How could the most public artist in New York keep so much locked up?" Frank Rich wrote at the end of 2006, in the *Times*'s year-end roundup of well-known people who had died that year. "I don't think I was the only friend who felt I had somehow failed to see Wendy whole. And who wondered if I had let her down in some profound way. I grieve as much for the Wendy I didn't know as the Wendy I did."

Wendy Wasserstein's plays were predictive, as though she were mapping her future. *Uncommon Women and Others* ends with large youthful dreams, of being "pretty fucking amazing." *Isn't It Romantic* concludes after Janie Blumberg, Wasserstein's heroine, decides not to conform to the conventional demands of society, represented by her boyfriend and her parents; in the final scene, Janie is dancing alone. Heidi of *The Heidi Chronicles* seeks release from her existential angst by becoming a single mother. In *Third,* the last Wasserstein play, the playwright incorporated themes from *King Lear*—Lear, who has to suffer the anguish of watching his youngest and most beloved daughter die.

Lola outlived Wendy, but not for long. Eighteen months after her youngest daughter's death, Lola attended her granddaughter Samantha's wedding, which took place in Claude and Bruce's home in the Hamptons.

Lola bought a new dress and discussed her makeup with Georgette. She had hurt her foot and couldn't dance at the party, but she stomped her cane to the beat of the music.

The following Friday, June 15, 2007, Melissa Levis, Georgette's younger daughter, took Lola to the doctor for a checkup. She received a clean bill of health.

The next day Melissa—who lived nearby—received a telephone call from Lola's doorman. Someone had reported that Lola's door was open and her mail was scattered on the floor outside her apartment. Melissa found her grandmother undressed, on the floor by her bed, curled up as though taking a nap.

Georgette felt that her mother's death began the day Wendy died. "My mother died of a broken heart," she said.

The postscript to Wendy's life contained strange twists of fate and unexpected reconciliations, the kind she might have written.

Georgette, having become Abner's guardian, reunited with her brother after more than fifty years and began to see him a few times a year. The familial embrace of the long-lost brother and uncle extended to the next generations. Three years after Wendy died, Abner came to New York with a group from Rochester to watch a Yankees game. An aide took him to a restaurant on the Upper East Side to meet members of his family who had been strangers—Bruce's daughter, Pam, and Georgette's daughters, Tajlei and Melissa, along with Tajlei's son, Theo. Within two years, Abner died at age seventy.

As for Lucy Jane, she went to live with Bruce and Claude, whom she called Mommy and Daddy. Claude oversaw the delicate transition, trying to respect Wendy's wishes while doing what she felt was best for Lucy. She fired Emmy, Lucy's nanny, and then tried to manage the many friends of Wendy who wanted to be close to her daughter.

Claude knew that some were upset by the limits she placed on visits, but she couldn't worry about the adults. "I had a house afire," she said. "I was putting out fires. You prioritize. Triage. I was doing what was best for this little girl. I'm sure they've had a big adjustment. I know they've had their issues. But at the end of the day, that's not what Wendy picked. At the end of the day, she picked me and my values. She picked me and Bruce. We were a family."

They were a family and then they weren't. In December 2008, Bruce and Claude divorced. A month later he remarried. Eight months after that, Bruce Wasserstein died at age sixty-one of heart failure; the exact cause was kept private, in keeping with his lifelong practice.

Bruce's memorial service, like Wendy's, took place at the Vivian Beaumont Theater. Thirty-one-year-old Pamela arranged for her father's favorite song to be sung—"Some Enchanted Evening," from *South Pacific*.

Two young actors, Jeremy Strong, Wendy's former assistant, and Lily Rabe, performed a scene from *Miami*.

Three of Bruce's four wives were there, along with his children, among them Lucy Jane, who stood onstage with her five siblings, who were also her cousins.

This was the family Wendy bequeathed her daughter.

Would Wendy have chosen Claude and Bruce had she known all that was going to happen to them? Claude didn't know.

"All I know is that this kid calls me Mommy now, and I'm going to do my best by her," Claude said. "We are a family. A different kind of family."

Claude kept a scrapbook containing the many letters people wrote to Lucy after Wendy died, a continuation of the writer's ongoing chronicle of her life and times. One day Lucy would want to know all about the uncommon woman who was her mother.

Until the very end, Wendy Wasserstein took comfort in being part of a larger entity, the self-defined generation that had created a unified consciousness from a mass-marketed set of cultural references. Among Wendy's last works was an essay called "Baby Boomers," published in *The World Almanac and Book of Facts 2004*, in which she addressed the hubris of the Peter Pan generation.

"The thing about being a baby boomer is, somewhere we still believe that no one is going to do it better than we did," she wrote. "No one will be better than The Beatles, no one will be more glamorous than Jack

Kennedy, no time will be as turbulent as the late 60s, no parents will be as difficult as ours were, and no psyches will be as interesting as ours."

She continued to aim for immortality, even as she mocked her own desire. "Because boomers came of age in a world fascinated by them, and partially created for them, we are often not the most cooperative when it comes to aging," she wrote. "We are, in fact, at the forefront of not just aging gracefully, but not aging at all. Against all odds, we will hold back the hands of time."

As Wendy wrote those words, she must have sensed that the clock was ticking; she was already desperately ill. She never grew old, but she lived long enough to watch her generation begin to fossilize, guarding its accumulated memories and possessions, asserting its historical preeminence as fiercely as every generation that had come before. Even as a child, it seems, she had understood that all relationships, ambitions, politics, hopes, worries, pains, ruminations, and dramatizations could command passionate attention one day and then vanish the next. Every bright, shining beacon would be extinguished and replaced, the same as tyrants and fools. But she was a gentle social critic, clarifying the pretensions of her peers and expressing frustration at their hypocrisies and self-deceptions while showing tender appreciation for their frailties and conveying genuine empathy for the desire and uncertainty that made them human. That was her gift to the world she tried to make her own.

ACKNOWLEDGMENTS

My research began less than two years after Wasserstein's death. Almost every interview—even with those who knew the playwright only professionally or casually—was punctuated by moments of intense emotion. It was evident that Wasserstein's life and death had touched something primal in a great many people. Far more complicated, but endlessly fascinating, was the journey to understanding the unusual woman who created such a strong sense of connection with friends and strangers.

Untangling Wendy Wasserstein's story required constant triangulation between her dramatic interpretations of her life and times (her plays, screenplays, unpublished stories, and novel); her "nonfiction" essays; and everything else—print and recorded interviews, reviews, and articles about her and her work, journals, letters, and my own interviews with almost three hundred people, including close family members and dozens of "best friends."

Unless otherwise indicated in the endnotes or the text, direct quotations came from these interviews, which also provided much valuable context, as did the books listed in the bibliography. Other information came from public records, video and audio recordings of speeches, and documents provided by friends and family, as well as Wasserstein's private papers, which she donated to Mount Holyoke College.

I can't overemphasize the importance of the material at Mount Holyoke, which includes not only Wasserstein's papers but all kinds of references pertaining to her career and student days. This huge trove has been beautifully organized by Jennifer Gunter King, head of Archives and Special Collections, and Patricia Albright, Archives Librarian, to whom I owe deepest gratitude and affection for their guidance and moral support throughout.

I thank everyone who helped me, with a special category of appreciation reserved for André Bishop and Christopher Durang, Wasserstein's literary executors. They were endlessly patient, sitting through hours and hours of interviews, indulging repeated follow-up questions via telephone, e-mail, lunches, and breakfasts. In addition to providing their invaluable memories and insights, their endorsement opened many crucial doors.

The Wasserstein and Schleifer families couldn't have been more gracious. Special thanks to the late Bruce Wasserstein, Pamela Wasserstein, Georgette Levis, Samantha Schweitzer, Jenifer Brooks, Claude Wasserstein, Tajlei Levis, Melissa Levis, Christine Wasserstein Rattiner, and Lynne Killin—as well as the many other relatives who spoke to me. I also want to acknowledge Ben and Scoop Wasserstein, who will become literary trustees for the Wendy Wasserstein estate as they each turn thirty years old, and Lucy Wasserstein, who will join them in that role when she turns twenty-one.

The MacDowell Colony offered me the exquisite opportunity to complete a portion of the book in the same studio where Wendy Wasserstein stayed when she was writing *Third*. It was inspiring to be among so many talented people at the Colony, including some excellent Ping-Pong players!

Julia Judge, artistic administrator at Lincoln Center Theater, fielded my barrage of requests with grace and efficiency. Sarah Geller provided much-valued research assistance, tracking down birth, death, and school records, as well as census and immigration information and other more arcane matters.

I won't list every person I talked to for the biography because some preferred to remain anonymous and because I worry about omitting someone from a list that appears all-inclusive. Likewise, apologies go to those whose insightful stories weren't included for reasons of space and narrative cohesion.

Some of Wasserstein's friends and assistants offered far more than a single interview, but also photographs, introductions, letters, helpful documents, and the willingness to be approached time and again. In this category I include: Jenny Lyn Bader, Michael Barakiva, Susan Blatt, Rhoda Brooks, Betsy Carter, Emmy Casamassino, Ken Cassillo, Anne Cattaneo, Aimee Garn, Susan Gordis, Cathy Graham, Stephen Graham, Roy Harris, Ruth Karl Julian, James Kaplan, James Lapine, William Ivey Long, Mary Jane Patrone, Ilene Rapkin, Frank Rich, Jane Rosenthal, Betsy Ross, Clifford Ross, Paul Rudnick, Harriet Sachs, Peter Schweitzer, Abigail Stewart, Jeremy Strong, Daniel Sullivan, Cindy Tolan, Angela Trento, Alex Witchel.

Special thanks to the late Adele Janovsky and to Christine Kondoleon, Stephen Soba, and Victoria Wilson.

One of Wendy Wasserstein's proudest accomplishments was establishing the Theatre Development Fund's Open Doors mentoring program with Roy Harris. Much appreciation to Marianna Houston and Patricia Bruno for their help and for the great work they do introducing high school students to the theater.

Many friends have humored my obsessions and helped me through rough patches, literary and otherwise. For various forms of sustenance throughout this project, I thank Megan Barnett, Marsha Berkowitz, Angela Botto, Delois Byrd, Bobby Cohen, Madeline DeLone, Brian De Palma, Charlie Durfee, Sally Fischer, Danny Gregory, Jack Tea Gregory, Matthew Grosek, Trish Hall, Noelle Hannon, Wayne Kabak, Barry Kramer, Sara Krulwich, Alison Lisnow, Johan Mantijano, Wendy Miller, Lynn Paltrow, Muzzy Rosenblatt, Jennifer Oddleifson, Susan Merlucci Reno, Andrew Tatarsky, Ann Temkin, Marcy Wilkov, and Zahra Zubaidi.

My agent of twenty-five years, Kathy Robbins, never fails to offer smart advice and timely encouragement, as well as providing the excellent help of Rebecca Anders, Mike Gillespie, David Halpern, and Ian King in the Robbins Office.

This is my fifth book with Ann Godoff, a brilliant contrarian who defies the much-repeated notion that great editors don't exist anymore. It's been a pleasure to work on this biography with her and with Lindsay Whalen, who has impeccable instincts. I am grateful for the top-notch professional care the book has received from Liz Calamari, Jane Cavolina, Darren Haggar, Michelle McMillian, Benjamin Platt, Maureen Sugden, Veronica Windholz, and Jaime Wolf.

Thanks to Szimi Salcman and Suzanne Salamon for everything essential, beginning with our morning chats. From Patti Gregory, Samuel Reiner, and Arthur Salcman I received gifts I can never repay, nor will I ever forget.

Above all, for editorial guidance, laughter, music, solace, perspective, and love, I always come home, to Bill, Roxie, and Eli.

ILLUSTRATION PERMISSIONS

Title page photo by Joanna Eldredge Morrissey

Chapters One and Two: Courtesy of the Wasserstein family

Chapter Three: Courtesy of The Calhoun School

Chapter Four: Courtesy of Mount Holyoke College Alumnae Association

Chapter Five: Courtesy of Mount Holyoke College Archives and
    Special Collections

Chapter Six: Courtesy of the Wasserstein family

Chapter Seven: Courtesy of the Yale Repertory Theatre, photograph by William Baker

Chapter Eight: Courtesy of Playwrights Horizons

Chapter Nine: Eugene O'Neill Theater Center, A. Vincent Scarano

Chapter Ten: Photofest, Inc.

Chapter Eleven: Courtesy of James Lapine

Chapter Twelve: Courtesy of André Bishop; *Playwrights Horizons group photo*, © Jack
    Mitchell

Chapter Thirteen: Courtesy of the Wasserstein family

Chapter Fourteen: Courtesy of André Bishop

Chapter Fifteen: Courtesy of the Wasserstein family

Chapter Sixteen: Courtesy of Christopher Durang, Photo by John Augustine

Chapter Seventeen: Courtesy of William Ivey Long

Chapter Eighteen: Poster design by James McMullan

Chapter Nineteen: *Wendy and Terrence McNally*, © Marianne Barcellona; *Bruce and
    Claude Becker Wasserstein*, Courtesy of Claude Wasserstein; *Wendy and Rhoda
    Brooks*, Courtesy of Rhoda Brooks

Chapter Twenty: Sara Krulwich/The New York Times
Chapter Twenty-One: Courtesy of Ken Cassillo
Chapter Twenty-Two: Joanna Eldredge Morrissey
Chapter Twenty-Three: © Joan Marcus
Chapter Twenty-Four: Courtesy of Claude Wasserstein

NOTES

xi. Epigraph from J. M. Barrie, *Peter Pan* (New York, Barnes & Noble, 2007).

Prologue

3. ***named for Peter's beloved friend, Wendy Darling:*** Wasserstein: "Three Sisters," in *Shiksa Goddess* (New York: Knopf, 2001), 65.

One: The Family Wasserstein

9. ***"a sisterly tour":*** Wasserstein, "Poles Apart," *Shiksa Goddess,* 159. Subsequent references to the trip by Wendy in this chapter come from this same chapter, 159–64, adapted from an article originally published in *Harper's Bazaar.*

11. Background on Wloclawek: www.jewishvirtuallibrary.org/jsource/judaica/edjud.

12. Snapshot of Ciechocinek: www.polandforvisitors.com/poland/baltic_spas_ciechocinek.

13. Picture of Jews in Poland: Lucy Davidovicz, *The War Against the Jews, 1933–1945* (New York: Holt, Rinehart and Winston, 1975), 396.

13. ***Great Migration:*** Irving Howe, *World of Our Fathers* (New York: Harcourt, Brace Jovanovich, 1976), 26.

14. ***"She had this reel of stories":*** Tajlei Levis, interview with author, May 20, 2009.

21. ***The answer was yes:*** Samantha Schweitzer, Sandra's younger daughter, interview with author, May 7, 2009.

23. ***Unable to make friends:*** Ibid.

Two: A Brooklyn Childhood, 1950-63

28. Paul Cowan, "The Merger Maestro," *Esquire,* May 1984, 58.
31. Wasserstein, "Aunt Florence's Bar Mitzvah," from *Bachelor Girls* (New York: Alfred A. Knopf, 1990), 45–46.
32. Wasserstein, "The Muse That Meowed," *Shiksa Goddess,* 123.
34. Lüchow's story, from Wasserstein, "My Mother, Then and NOW, " *Bachelor Girls,* 18.
36. Background on Yeshivah of Flatbush from *Yeshivah of Flatbush Golden Jubilee Commemorative Volume* (Brooklyn, NY: Yeshivah of Flatbush, 1977).
37. *Wendy was a smart little girl:* "The State of the Arts," *Shiksa Goddess,* 149.
38. *"running away from myself":* From undated letter (circa 1978) to Aimee Garn, a friend of Wendy's.
39. Wendy's recollections of Sandy's wedding: From "Don't Tell Mother," *Shiksa Goddess,* 79.
41. *Expresso Bongo* story: Ibid., 84.
45. Cohen bar mitzvah story: Wasserstein, "My Mother, Then and NOW," *Bachelor Girls,* 17.

Three: A Girl's Education, 1963-67

49. Ilene Goldsmith became Ilene Rapkin after marriage. These recollections came from interview with author, June 9, 2009.
50. *For Wendy's thirteenth birthday:* From "Bachelor Girl," introductory essay, *Bachelor Girls,* 3–4.
51. Wendy on Doris Day: Ibid., 7.
51. *"I never thought of myself as undesirable":* Interview with Laurie Winer, *Paris Review,* no. 14, Spring 1997, 7.
53. *"They drove an hour to Cookys":* "Ah, That First Feat in Wild Manhattan," *Shiksa Goddess,* 166.
53. *"I was on an escalator in B. Altman's":* Wendy Wasserstein, "Baby Boomers," *World Almanac and Book of Facts 2004,* Oct. 2003.
54. *"Wendy would always write her papers on time":* Ann-Ellen Lesser, telephone interview with author, Mar. 19, 2009.
55. From "Reflections of a Calhounder," a speech Wendy Wasserstein gave at the Calhoun School in Oct. 2004, at the dedication of a new arts center. The speech is posted on the school's Web site, at www.calhoun.org/page.cfm?p=888.

Four: Gracious Living, 1967-68

68. *"This is where you can take sports":* Anne Betteridge, a Mount Holyoke classmate, telephone interview with author, Feb. 21, 2010.

Five: Great Expectations, 1968-71

87. *"an incredible hottie"*: Henry Goldman, Amherst classmate, telephone interview with author, July 23, 2009.

Seven: Drama Kings and Queens, 1973-76

122. *"Albert was a close friend"*: Weaver was from a prominent show-business family. Her father, Sylvester "Pat" Weaver, was an advertising executive who became president of NBC. Weaver became known for her intelligent portrayals on the stage and screen, and her attraction to quirky roles, but she grew very famous as an unlikely action hero in science-fiction films, most notably Alien and its sequels and Avatar, which in 2010 became the highest-grossing movie in history.

122. **"The Idiots Karamazov** *hammered away at the most beloved works"*: Robert Brustein, *Making Scenes: A Personal History of the Turbulent Years at Yale 1966–1979* (New York: First Limelight Edition, New York, 1984), 188. Originally published in 1981 by Proscenium.

129. *"Streep it up"*: William Ivey Long, interview with author, Aug. 5, 2009.

129. *"The competition in the acting program"*: Andrea Stevens, "Theater: Getting Personal About Yale's Drama School," *New York Times,* Nov. 12, 2000.

134. *terror of becoming pregnant:* Ruth Karl, telephone interview with author, July 21, 2009.

134. *"a personal undertow"*: Nancy Franklin, "The Time of Her Life," the *New Yorker,* Apr. 14, 1997, 62.

Eight: A Playwright's Horizons, 1976-77

142. Theodore Gross, "Will Bob Moss Become the Next Joe Papp?" *Village Voice,* Nov. 1, 1976.

144. Edith Oliver, the *New Yorker,* May 24, 1976.

144. *"ferocious comic talent"*: Mel Gussow, "Theater: A Sea of Gags; U.S. Family Is Subject of Durang's 'Titanic,'" *New York Times,* Mar. 17, 1976, 34.

144. *"There's no ignoring the author's clownish exuberance"*: Mel Gussow, "Stage: Shorter 'Titanic'; Christopher Durang's Play, on Twin Bill With 'Lusitania,' Still Floats Poorly," *New York Times,* May 11, 1976, 26.

144. *"self-congratulatory, self-indulgent, numbingly unfunny"*: *Village Voice.*

145. *Wendy helped arrange a job . . . book about schizophrenia:* Sidney J. Blatt and Cynthia M. Wild, *Schizophrenia: A Developmental Analysis* (New York: Academic Press, 1976).

147. **"I slipped a note"**: Referring to *The Coronation of Marie de Médici in*

Saint-Denis by Peter Paul Rubens, the seventeenth-century Flemish Baroque painter.

Nine: Tryout Town, USA, Summer 1977

155. *The Eugene O'Neill Theater Center had theatrical romanticism:* The theater's history is available on its Web site, www.theoneill.org/.
155. *This beloved stretch of beach:* Tom Verde, "Eugene O'Neill Center May Get Remains of Tycoon Who Chased Him Off It," *New York Times,* Oct. 7, 1996.
159. *Until 1972, just five years before Swoosie Kurtz confronted Rita's line:* Janice Delaney, Mary Jane Lupton, Emily Toth, *The Curse: A Cultural History of Menstruation* (Champaign: University of Illinois Press edition, 1988), 134.
161. Honor Moore, "Theater Will Never Be the Same," *Ms.,* Dec. 1977.

Ten: The Emergence of Wendy Wasserstein, 1977-78

167. *"The dream kept almost materializing":* Walter Kerr, "Stage View, Farewell to a Theater, Greetings to New Talents," *New York Times,* Dec. 26, 1982.
174. *"Dramatic Wit and Wisdom Unite":* Richard Eder, "Dramatic Wit and Wisdom Unite in 'Uncommon Women and Others,'" *New York Times,* Nov. 22, 1977.
177. Anne Cattaneo, author interview, May 22, 2009.

Eleven: Orphans' Christmas, 1978-79

187. Christopher Durang, author interview, Feb. 6, 2009.
189. *"The Cheever subtlety is lost in a torrent":* John J. O'Connor, "TV: A Series of Stories by John Cheever Begins," *New York Times,* Oct. 24, 1979.
191. *He called himself a "quackster":* Wendy Wasserstein, speaking at Ed Kleban's memorial service, Feb. 11, 1988.
196. *"If I do say so myself":* Sandra's written memory of Andrew appears in Wendy's Mount Holyoke Archive as a typed document that doesn't indicate whether it was a letter, a diary entry, or a eulogy.

Twelve: Design for Living, 1980-83

205. *For years there was only one photograph:* Wendy Wasserstein, "Design for Living," *Life,* Dec. 1992.

205. *"In the theater one always forms"*: Ibid.

206. *"None of us really opposed"*: Ibid.

206. *Just twenty years earlier:* Gail Collins, *When Everything Changed* (New York: Little, Brown, 2009), 308.

209. *"I was 28 or so"*: Michiko Kakutani, "A Play and Its Author Mature," *New York Times,* Jan. 3, 1984.

210. *The New York Times ran an affectionate:* Leslie Bennetts, "An Uncommon Dramatist Prepares Her New Work," *New York Times,* May 24, 1981.

211. *Wendy never forgave the scissors:* From taped interview with Wendy and director Daniel Sullivan at Marymount Manhattan College, part of a series of lectures sponsored by the Society of Stage Directors and Choreographers and the American Theatre Wing. http://americantheatrewing. org/sdcfmasters/detail/wendy_wasserstein_and_daniel_sullivan.

212. *André liked plays that set off what he called an "unconscious click"*: Douglas C. McGill, "He Nurtures the Gifted Playwright," *New York Times,* Jan. 3, 1982.

212. *"Why am I working off Broadway?"*: John Lombardi, "Playwrights on the Horizon," *New York Times Magazine,* July 17, 1983, Section 6, 22.

212. *"Our 'social concerns'"*: Ibid.

213. *In the summer of 1983:* Ibid.

213. *A year earlier André had been:* McGill, "He Nurtures the Gifted Playwright."

216. *"At one long-forgotten fiasco"*: Frank Rich, "The Lives They Lived: Everybody's Wendy," *New York Times,* Dec. 31, 2006.

217. *"Some day, I swear"*: Frank Rich, "Comedy; Durang's 'Beyond Therapy,'" *New York Times,* May 27, 1982.

219. *"Are we eternally doomed"*: Frank Rich, "STAGE: 2 One-Act Plays by Harry Kondoleon," *New York Times,* June 20, 1984.

219. *Unlike many artists, who claim they don't read their reviews:* Claudia Barnett, "Interview with Wendy Wasserstein," in *Wendy Wasserstein: A Casebook,* Claudia Barnett, ed. (New York and London: Garland, 1999), 180.

219. *"It's the perfect time"*: Laurie Johnston, "A Director with Authenticity," *New York Times,* Feb. 21, 1984.

220. *"There's as much of me in Harriet"*: Kakutani, "A Play and Its Author Mature."

220. *Reviewers approved of the changes:* Roundup of reviews from *Wendy Wasserstein: A Casebook,* 196–208.

223. *When successful plays, like* Isn't It Romantic: Lombardi, "Playwrights on the Horizon."

Thirteen: Miami, 1984-86

228. *"If the company is run by a 65-year-old"*: Michael VerMeulen, "Yes, it's true what they say about Bruce Wasserstein," *Institutional Investor,* Apr. 1984, 140.

228. *Wider recognition, outside the business pages:* Paul Cowan, "The Merger Maestro," *Esquire,* 59.

230. *"Sometimes I wonder"*: Wasserstein, "Big Brother," *Bachelor Girls,* 82–83.

230. *"We travel in orbits"*: Ibid., 83.

230. *A reference to Bruce:* Mary Cunningham with Fran Schumer, *Powerplay, What Really Happened at Bendix.* New York: Linden Press, 1984, p. 261.

232. *"The holidays were a time"*: Wasserstein, "Christmas in Flatbush," *Bachelor Girls,* 191.

Fourteen: Rooms of Her Own, 1986-87

241. *"I was seized with panic"*: Wasserstein, "Christmas in Flatbush," *Bachelor Girls,* 191–92.

241. *In subsequent years she and Fay:* Wasserstein, "Days of Awe: The Birth of Lucy Jane," *Shiksa Goddess,* 206.

241. *He had begun wearing Brooks Brothers in prep school:* Wasserstein, "Reflections on Leather Rhinos," *Bachelor Girls.*

241. *"Seized by a moment"*: Ibid., 69.

242. *It was André who converted Wendy:* Wasserstein, "The Muse That Meowed," *Shiksa Goddess,* 124.

245. *"There isn't much to say about my relationship with Nina"*: Stephen McCauley, *The Object of My Affection* (New York: Washington Square Press, 1987), 72.

247. *The two women already knew each other:* Michiko Kakutani, "A Play and Its Author Mature," *New York Times,* Jan. 3, 1984.

247. *Wendy talked about people who had "nut-juice"*: Michiko Kakutani, "A Remembrance of Wasserstein," a booklet compiled for Wasserstein's memorial service, Mar. 13, 2006.

248. *She was married:* After having three children together, she and Landesman divorced and Ettinger dropped Landesman as her surname.

251. *For the* Times *Magazine:* Wasserstein, "Boy Meets Girl," *Bachelor Girls,* 199.

251. *"Rest in the midmorning"*: Wasserstein, "Body Minimal," *Bachelor Girls,* 24.

Fifteen: The Heidi Chronicles, 1988-89

261. *"In order to complete my writing"*: Wasserstein, "A Second Act for the Playwright's Central Park West Apartment," *Architectural Digest,* 30.

265. *They replied with a spoof:* Terrence McNally and Wendy Wasserstein, "The Girl from Fargo": A Play by Terrence McNally and Wendy Wasserstein, *New York Times,* Mar. 8, 1987.

268. *The play cost $175,000:* Laurie Winer, "In Moving Uptown, a Hopeful 'Heidi' Takes a Gamble," *New York Times,* Mar. 12, 1989.

268. *Within five years:* Donald G. McNeil Jr., "Why Neil Simon Decided to Turn His Back on Broadway," *New York Times,* Nov. 21, 1994.

269. *"I stared at the delicate":* Wasserstein, "Dear Broadway, This Isn't Really Goodbye," *Shiksa Goddess,* 156, 157.

269. *"I'd never been someone who won":* Interview with Laurie Winer, *Paris Review,* no. 14, Spring 1997, 20, 21.

270. *Wendy wasn't in the mood:* Ibid., 21.

270. *Wendy lightened the Lola story:* Wasserstein, "Winner Take All," *Bachelor Girls,* 195.

271. *"The phone started ringing off the hook":* Winer, *Paris Review,* 21.

Sixteen: Wendy Wasserstein, Inc., 1990-92

280. *"Even with a personal assistant":* Wasserstein, *Elements of Style* (New York: Vintage, 2006), 11.

282. *Both couples are gay-friendly:* Frank Rich, "Struggling to Love, but Aware of the Odds," *New York Times,* June 26, 1991.

282. *"A producer must have the cunning":* Frank Rich, "Stage View; The Last of the One-Man Shows," *New York Times,* Sept. 22, 1991.

283. *"While none of these producers":* Ibid.

Seventeen: Thicker Than Water, 1990-93

290. *"Chekhov tells us a story":* Wasserstein, "Theater Problems? Call Dr. Chekhov," *Shiksa Goddess,* 180.

292. *"The Cherry Orchard":* Ibid., 183.

296. *"In an almost Pirandellian stroke":* Wasserstein, "How I Spent My Forties," *Shiksa Goddess,* 190.

297. *"I am to learn that breast cancer treatment":* Ibid., 191.

299. *"Part of the explanation":* Judith Miller, "Theater; The Secret Wendy Wasserstein," *New York Times,* Oct. 18, 1992.

300. *As they followed "the Lola Schleifer Wasserstein Freedom Trail":* Wasserstein, "Poles Apart," *Shiksa Goddess,* 161.

300. *Wendy's desire to have a child:* Wasserstein, "How I Spent My Forties," *Shiksa Goddess,* 196.

301. *"There's nothing like sitting in a fertility doctor's office":* Ibid., 192–93.

Eighteen: The Objects of Her Affection, 1993-98

310. *She thought the apartment:* Wasserstein, "A Second Act for the Playwright's Central Park West Apartment," *Architectural Digest,* 40.
313. *"As election year arrived":* Frank Rich, "Exit the Critic," *New York Times,* Feb. 13, 1994.
314. *Wendy felt Baird was a scapegoat:* Wasserstein, "Hillary Clinton's Muddled Legacy," *Shiksa Goddess,* 19.
315. *She brought Wendy with her:* Wasserstein, "How I Spent My Forties," *Shiksa Goddess,* 196.
315. *"I've stumped the star":* Ibid.
316. *The admiration was mutual:* Wasserstein, "Perfect Women Who Are Bearable," *Bachelor Girls,* 78.
317. *Most crushing was the slap:* Ben Brantley, "In the Hostile Glare of Washington, the Media Define and Defy," *New York Times,* Apr. 14, 1997.
317. *Lloyd Rose of the* **Washington Post***:* Lloyd Rose, "Wasserstein's Daughter: Thin and Flighty," *Washington Post,* Apr. 14, 1997.
318. *The only family member to know was Sandra:* Wasserstein, "How I Spent My Forties," *Shiksa Goddess,* 194–95.
318. *"I thought of Sandra valiantly":* Ibid., 194.

Nineteen: Festival of Regrets, 1998-99

328. *In an impassioned article:* Wasserstein, "Hillary Clinton's Muddled Legacy," *New York Times,* Aug. 25, 1998.
329. *"Now, the impressive personal qualities":* Ibid.
333. Beatty designed the sets for *The Sisters Rosensweig* and *An American Daughter.*
335. *"I am certain that I became a playwright":* Wasserstein, "A Place They'd Never Seen: The Theater," *Shiksa Goddess,* 7.
335. *Wendy had begun to reconcile herself:* Wasserstein, "Days of Awe: The Birth of Lucy Jane," *Shiksa Goddess,* 209.
336. *Wendy had been struck:* Wasserstein, "My Manhattan; A Lifetime of Memories and Magic," *New York Times,* May 23, 2003.

Twenty: The Birth of Lucy Jane, 1999

344. *These tactics help explain:* Wasserstein, "Complications," the *New Yorker,* Feb. 21, 2000, 87.

Twenty-One: The New Millennium, 2000-01

360. *After watching a performance of* Vienna Waltzes: Wasserstein, *Old Money* (New York: Harcourt), x.
360. *"There were a bowl of three dozen roses":* Ibid., vii, viii.
365. *"I had my child so late":* Interview with A. M. Homes, *Bomb* magazine, Spring 2001.
365. *"My life has changed completely":* Ibid.

Twenty-Two: Welcome to My Rash, 2002-04

373. *She experienced her share of the side effects:* www.compath.com.
376. *"The morning was a clear winter blue":* Wasserstein, "My Manhattan; A Lifetime of Memories and Magic," *New York Times,* May 23, 2003.
376. *Recalling the affecting scene:* Jill Krementz in "A Remembrance of Wendy Wasserstein," booklet compiled for her memorial service at Lincoln Center Theater, Mar. 13, 2006.
381. *"I find myself unable to touch it":* A. M. Homes, *Bomb,* Spring 2001.
383. *André had been put on the defensive:* John Lahr, "Deep Pockets Run Shallow," the *New Yorker,* Dec. 25, 2000 & Jan. 1, 2001, 167.

Twenty-Four: Legacy, 2005-06

416. *"Frankie wasn't angry":* Wasserstein, *Elements of Style,* 281.
424. *Her memorial service:* Jesse McKinley, "An Overflow Crowd Attends a Wendy Wasserstein Tribute," *New York Times,* Mar. 14, 2006.
424. *"How could the most public artist":* Frank Rich, "Everybody's Wendy," *New York Times,* Dec. 31, 2006.

BIBLIOGRAPHY

Balakian, Jan. *Reading the Plays of Wendy Wasserstein*. New York: Applause Theatre & Cinema Books, 2010.

Barnett, Claudia, ed. *Wendy Wasserstein: A Casebook*. New York and London: Garland, 1999.

Barrie, J. M., *Peter Pan*. New York: Barnes & Noble Classics, 2007. (First published as *Peter and Wendy* in 1911.)

Bianco, Anthony. *Ghosts of 42nd Street: A History of America's Most Infamous Block*. New York: HarperCollins, 2004.

Brustein, Robert. *Making Scenes: A Personal History of the Turbulent Years at Yale 1966–1979*. New York: First Limelight Edition, 1984.

Burrough, Bryan and John Helyar. *Barbarians at the Gate: The Fall of RJR Nabisco*. 20th Anniversary Edition. New York: HarperCollins, 2008.

Ciociola, Gail. *Wendy Wasserstein: Dramatizing Women, Their Choices and Their Boundaries*. Jefferson, NC: McFarland, 1998.

Cohan, William D. *The Last Tycoons: The Secret History of Lazard Frères & Co*. New York: Doubleday, 2007.

Collins, Gail. *When Everything Changed: The Amazing Journey of American Women From 1960 to the Present*. New York: Little, Brown, 2009.

Collins, Ken (photographer) and Wishna, Victor (interviewer). *In Their Company: Portraits of American Playwrights*. New York: Umbrage Editions, 2006.

Cunningham, Mary, with Fran Schumer. *Powerplay: What Really Happened at Bendix*. New York: Linden Press, 1984.

DeMott, Benjamin. *Surviving the 70's*. New York: Dutton, 1971.

Epstein, Helen. *Joe Papp: An American Life*. Boston: Little, Brown, 1994.

Friedman, Martha. *Overcoming the Fear of Success*. New York: Warner Books, 1980.

Harris, Roy. *Conversations in the Wings*. Portsmouth, NH: Heinemann, 1994.

———. *Eight Women of the American Stage: Talking about Acting*. Portsmouth, NH: Heinemann, 1997.

Heilbrun, Carolyn G. *Writing a Woman's Life*. New York: Ballantine Books, 1988.

Kondoleon, Harry. *Diary of a Lost Boy*. New York: Knopf, 1994.

Lecomte du Noüy, Mary. *The Road to Human Destiny: A Life of Pierre Lecomte du Noüy*. New York: Longmans, Green, 1955.

McCauley, Stephen. *The Object of My Affection*. New York: Washington Square Press, 1988.

Nisbett, Richard E. *Intelligence and How to Get It*. New York: Norton, 2009.

Rich, Frank. *Hot Seat: Theater Criticism for "The New York Times," 1980–1993*. New York: Random House, 1998.

Salinger, J. D. *Franny and Zooey*. New York: Little, Brown, 1961.

Vilga, Edward. *Acting Now: Conversations on Craft and Career*. New Brunswick, NJ: Rutgers University Press, 1997.

Wasserstein, Bruce. *Big Deal: Mergers and Acquisitions in the Digital Age*. New York, Warner Business, 1998.

Wasserstein, Bruce, and Mark J. Green, eds. *With Justice for Some: An Indictment of the Law by Young Advocates*. Boston: Beacon Press, 1972.

Wasserstein, Wendy. *An American Daughter*. New York: Harcourt Brace, 1998.

———. *Bachelor Girls*. New York: Knopf, 1990.

———. *Elements of Style*. New York: Knopf, 2006.

———. *The Heidi Chronicles & Other Plays*. New York: Harcourt Brace Jovanovich, 1990.

———. *Seven One-Act Plays*. New York: Dramatists Play Service, 2000.

———. *Shiksa Goddess: Or, How I Spent My Forties*. New York: Knopf, 2001.

———. *The Sisters Rosensweig*. New York: Dramatists Play Service, 1993, 1997.

———. *Sloth*. New York: Oxford University Press, 2005.

———. *Third*. New York: Dramatists Play Service, 2008.

———. *Old Money*. New York: Harcourt, 2002.

Wasserstein, Wendy, and Andrew Jackness, illus. *Pamela's First Musical*. New York: Hyperion Books for Children, 1996.

Wouk, Herman. *Marjorie Morningstar*. New York: Back Bay Books, 1955, renewed 1983.

Yeshivah of Flatbush Editorial Board. *Yeshivah of Flatbush Golden Jubilee Commemorative Volume: 1927–1977*. Brooklyn, NY: Yeshivah of Flatbush, 1977.

Yglesias, Rafael. *A Happy Marriage*. New York: Scribner, 2009.

INDEX

ABOUT THE AUTHOR

Julie Salamon is the author of *Hospital*, about the inner workings of a big city hospital, as well as the *New York Times* bestseller *The Christmas Tree*; the true-crime narrative *Facing the Wind*; the novel *White Lies*; the film classic *The Devil's Candy*; a family memoir, *The Net of Dreams*; and *Rambam's Ladder*. Previously a reporter and critic with the *Wall Street Journal*, and the *New York Times*, she has also written for the *New Yorker, Vanity Fair, Vogue,* and the *New Republic.*